Penguin Education

Penguin Critical Anthologies

General Editor: Christopher Ricks

Walt Whitman

Edited by Francis Murphy

D0451273

Walt Whitman

A critical anthology

edited by Francis Murphy

Penguin Books

Contents

6   Contents

Part Two The Developing Debate

7 Contents

8 Contents

Part Three Modern Views

9 Contents

Preface

This collection does not purport to include everything of historical or critical interest on Whitman. Instead, I have chosen essays – whether favourable or not – which raise essential questions in the evaluation of his work. Even in a selection as generous as this, however, it was still not possible to include some things which I very much admire. The bibliography appended is not short, but I hope the interested reader will not be deterred by this and will pursue many of the books and articles listed there. All quotations from Whitman appearing in the various passages and essays have been identified, and a table of dates has been provided to help in sorting out the many editions of *Leaves of Grass* (p. 18). Footnotes are the work of individual authors unless noted as by the present editor.

Daniel Aaron and David Cavitch of Smith College and Leo Marx of Amherst kindly made suggestions which they will recognize as contributions to this volume. The staff of the Nielson Library at Smith College, and in particular Miss Dorothy King, Curator of Rare Books, extended a number of courtesies which I would like to acknowledge. My greatest debt is to Christopher Ricks, the general editor, and to Martin Lightfoot, Susan Hogg and Elizabeth Excell of Penguin Education for generous advice and assistance in the preparation of the manuscript.

Smith College, Massachusetts   F.M.

Table of Dates

1856   In the summer Whitman publishes the second edition of
        Leaves of Grass. Fowler and Wells served as agents for the
        book but soon renounced all responsibility for it. The
        author's name is acknowledged on the cover. On the
        back Whitman printed a statement from Emerson's
        letter: 'I greet you at the beginning of a great career.'
        Whitman included the letter and a reply as an
        appendix. There are thirty-two poems, titled and
        numbered. The poem which was eventually to be called
        Song of Myself (1881) appears here as *Poem of Walt
        Whitman, an American*. In a section entitled 'Leaves-
        Droppings' Whitman appended a selection of reviews of
        the 1855 edition.

1857–9 From the spring of 1857 to the summer of 1859
        Whitman edited the Brooklyn *Times*. Enters what he
        liked to think of as his Bohemian period.

1860   Whitman goes to Boston in March to see the third
        edition of *Leaves of Grass*, published by Thayer and
        Eldridge, through the press. This is the first edition
        which Whitman did not publish himself. The firm went
        bankrupt in 1861 and the edition was pirated. This
        volume contained 154 poems. As in 1855, Whitman
        identified himself by including a portrait. Most of the
        new poems are to be found in *Chants Democratic*,
        Enfans d'Adam (later called *Children of Adam*), *Calamus*,
        Messenger Leaves, and *Thoughts*. This volume prints for
        the first time *A Word Out of the Sea* (later called *Out
        of the Cradle Endlessly Rocking*) and *As I Ebb'd with the
        Ocean of Life*.

1861   The Civil War begins; Whitman's brother George
        enlists.

1862   Goes to Fredericksburg, Virginia, to see his wounded
        brother.

1863–4 Whitman remains in Washington, D.C., and works
        part-time in the Army Paymaster's office; he serves as a
        volunteer nurse in army hospitals, returning to Brooklyn
        ill.

1865   Employed as a clerk in the Department of the Interior;
        meets Peter Doyle; witnesses Lincoln's second
        inauguration. In April, Lincoln is assassinated. In May,
        Drum-Taps is published. Fired by Secretary James
        Harlan who thought *Leaves of Grass* indecent;
        re-employed in the Attorney General's office. In the
        autumn *Sequel to Drum-Taps* is published, including
        When Lilacs Last in the Dooryard Bloom'd. These were
        added to the 1867 edition as annexes but in 1870–71 were
        incorporated in the main body of *Leaves of Grass.*
        Drum-Taps contains fifty-three new poems, dealing with
        the outbreak of the Civil War and Whitman's
        experiences in the army hospitals.

1866   William D. O'Connor's *The Good Gray Poet* appears.

1867   The fourth edition of *Leaves of Grass* is published.
        Exclusive of the annexes described above, this edition
        contains eight new poems. The edition is important
        primarily for its extensive revisions, deletions and
        rearrangements.

1868   William Michael Rossetti's selection of *Poems by Walt
        Whitman* is published in London.

1871   The fifth edition of *Leaves of Grass* appears. A second
        issue including *Passage to India* and seventy-one other
        poems, some new. *Democratic Vistas* published.

1872   Travels to Hanover, New Hampshire, for the Dartmouth
        commencement. Reads *As a Strong Bird on Pinions Free*,
        later published with a Preface.

1873   Partially paralysed on 23 January; Whitman's mother
        dies on 23 May; stays with his brother George in
        Camden, New Jersey.

1876   The sixth edition of *Leaves of Grass* appears, a two-
        volume centennial edition, one volume a reprint of the
        fifth edition, the other a collection (entitled *Two
        Rivulets*) of prose and poetry. *Two Rivulets* contains a
        Preface Whitman said was for 'all my writings'.

1879   Gives the first of his annual Lincoln lectures. In

will do as it pleases with the book. I am determined to have the world know what I was pleased to do.' Whitman dies on 26 March and is buried in Harleigh Cemetery, Camden, New Jersey. *Complete Prose Works* published.

1897   The tenth edition of *Leaves of Grass* is published in Boston with the addition of *Old Age Echoes*, posthumous poems.

Note on **Quotations**

All quotations of Whitman's verse are from the 1892 'Deathbed Edition' unless otherwise stated. The following dates have been used to identify earlier editions:

1855	*Leaves of Grass*, first edition
1856	*Leaves of Grass*, second edition, containing 'Leaves-Droppings'
1860	*Leaves of Grass*, third edition
1865	*Drum-Taps*
1865 Sequel	*Sequel to Drum-Taps*
1867	*Leaves of Grass*, fourth edition
1868	*Poems by Walt Whitman* (Rossetti)
1871	*Leaves of Grass*, fifth edition
1871 Second Issue	*Leaves of Grass* (fifth edition, second issue), including *Passage to India*
1876	*Leaves of Grass*, sixth edition (two volumes)
1881–2	*Leaves of Grass*, seventh edition
1888	*November Boughs*
1888 Complete	*Complete Poems and Prose of Walt Whitman*
1889	*Leaves of Grass*, eighth edition
1897	*Leaves of Grass*, tenth edition

For the 1855 and 1856 editions references are to page numbers; in subsequent editions references are to verse paragraph numbers.

Part One Contemporaneous Criticism

Introduction

In September of 1855, Charles Eliot Norton reported to James Russell Lowell on his summer reading. The highlights consisted of Longfellow's *Hiawatha*, just about to appear, and Walt Whitman's *Leaves of Grass*. Since Norton's letter expresses his response in a more unbuttoned way than his anonymous review in *Putnam's Monthly*, it is worth quoting entire:

A new book called *Leaves of Grass* has just come out which is worth knowing about. It is a quarto volume of unmetrical poetry, and its author is 'Walt Whitman, one of the roughs, a kosmos'. It is a book which has excited Emerson's enthusiasm. He has written a letter to this 'one of the roughs' which I have seen, expressing the warmest admiration and encouragement. It is no wonder that he likes it, for Walt Whitman has read the *Dial* and *Nature*, and combines the characteristics of a Concord philosopher with a New York fireman. There is little original thought but much original expression in it. There are some superbly graphic descriptions, great stretches of imagination – and then passages of intolerable coarseness, – not gross and licentious, but simply disgustingly coarse. The book is such, indeed, that one cannot leave it about for chance readers, and would be sorry to know that any woman had looked into it past the title-page. I have got a copy for you, for there are things in it that you will admire, and it is worth having merely as a literary curiosity, for the external appearance of it, the covers, the portrait, the print, are as odd as the inside. . . .

Norton erred in thinking that Lowell would find in Whitman's work anything to admire. Although Lowell's response was not as horrified as Whittier's (who threw his copy into the fire), the critic who had written seven years before that 'true vigor and heartiness of phrase do not pass from page to page, but from man to man', was not ready to hear a man talking. In a tone which Lowell acknowledged as professorial, he lectured to Norton on the upstart

poet. There is little evidence that Lowell actually read Whitman.
He was one of the first American men of letters to be less offended
by the book than by Whitman's advertisements for himself.

Given the extraordinary circumstances surrounding its
publication – the fact that it bore no author's name, nor publisher's
imprint, and that it was distributed by a firm primarily interested
in phrenology – it is remarkable that Whitman's book was
noticed at all. The sale of the first edition still remains a mystery.
Whitman later contradicted his claim that the book's 'one thousand
copies readily sold' and said that not a single copy was bought.
It is clear that more copies were given away than sold (Gay
Wilson Allen, Whitman's biographer, suggests that the sale of
three dozen copies is a likely figure). The decision to send a copy
to Emerson was fortuitous. Emerson's letter of 21 July (p. 29),
written two weeks after the book was published, set Whitman
crowing. No writer in America could have asked for a more
heartening response. Emerson's letter assured Whitman of his
vocation and confirmed his daring treatment of sex. Emerson was
taken aback when he learned that Whitman printed his letter in
the New York *Tribune* (he is supposed to have remarked 'I
should have enlarged the "but" very much') but he forgave
Whitman and made his enthusiasm known in Boston. Without
Emerson's endorsement it is doubtful that Whitman's book would
have been reviewed. In the immediate silence that followed
publication Whitman set about writing three 'anonymous'
reviews himself. He must have known that his book would
offend many readers, and it did. As one indignant reviewer put
it, 'Walt Whitman is as unacquainted with art as a hog with
mathematics.' But the reviews were actually more favourable than
not – in general the book was better received in Boston than
New York – and no self-educated printer who found himself
the friend of Emerson, Thoreau and Alcott, praised by the
North American Review (in the essay reprinted here by Edward

Everett Hale (p. 42)), *Putnam's Monthly* and the *London Weekly Dispatch* (p. 57) could consider his book a failure. Whitman's family was as much surprised as anyone to discover what he had been up to during those notebook-making years when Emerson 'brought him to a boil'; but Walt's mother had enough literary sense to know that if '*Hiawatha* was poetry, Walt's was too'.

With the publication of *Drum-Taps* in 1865, Whitman had every reason to suppose that he would be acknowledged as the representative American poet. The sales of the third edition of *Leaves of Grass* in 1860 approached five thousand copies, and if the book was often parodied, it was widely reviewed and more favourably than not. Henry James's suggestion that Whitman would capitalize on his role during the Civil War seems callous, but it is true that Whitman could not help but profit from the notoriety he achieved. In the light of reviews that followed, Whitman's letter to William O'Connor, dated 6 January 1865, is a useful illustration of the discrepancy between Whitman's intentions and the critical evaluation which followed:

[*Drum-Taps*] is in my opinion superior to *Leaves of Grass* – certainly more perfect as a work of art, being adjusted in all its proportions, and its passion having the indispensable merit that though to the ordinary reader let loose with wildest abandon, the true artist can see it as yet under control. . . . I probably mean [superior] as a piece of art, and from the more simple and winning nature of the subject, and also because I have in it only succeeded to my satisfaction in removing all superfluity from it, verbal superfluity, I mean. I delight to make a poem where I feel clear that not a word but is indispensable part thereof and of my meaning.

No volume of Whitman's was more ignored. His literary reputation in the sixties was so low that, as Gay Wilson Allen put it, 'nothing could have reconciled the countless admirers of Longfellow and

Lowell to anything published' under Whitman's name. Both
Henry James (p. 80) and William Dean Howells (p. 85),
representing the voice of the younger generation, treated
Whitman as a man who had acquired a largely undeserved
reputation. Although Howells never seemed to have recovered
from the revulsion he felt upon reading *Leaves of Grass*, he did
grant Whitman a few poetic moments. James, however, granted
Whitman nothing, and attacked him not because of his
improprieties, but because of his insensitiveness to language. It is
the work of a man, James said, who has an ear for neither music
nor words: it 'begins like verse and turns out to be prose', but
'prose, in order to be good poetry, must first be good prose'.
Like Howells, James felt that Whitman's work was 'no more put
up than the atmosphere'. James's attack must have hurt the most;
for in spite of Whitman's public role as the spokesman for the
spontaneous in art, his letter to O'Connor proves that he
respected the literary criteria that James had accused him of
disregarding. To be an artist, James remarked, it is not enough to
be 'rude, lugubrious, and grim'; you must eliminate 'personality'
and detach yourself from the subject of your art; 'you must be
possessed, and you must strive to possess your possession. If in
your striving you break into divine eloquence, then you are a poet.
If the idea which possesses you is the idea of your country's
greatness, then you are a national poet; and not otherwise.'
   In concluding that 'Fine writing with Whitman goes for
nought', and that Whitman's readers will find no pleasure in any
particular 'word' or 'metaphor', but rather in the 'atmosphere'
of his poems, the most judicious member of Whitman's circle,
John Burroughs (p. 89), might seem to provide only more
ammunition for the enemy. In suggesting, however, that in
reading Whitman we take our pleasure from forms which are closer
to the repetitive and associative forms of music, Burroughs offered an
alternative to the criticism of James and Howells, and anticipated

a much later response by reminding his readers that Whitman is often closer to the psalmist than the conventional lyric poet.

To counteract the disenchantment of the literary establishment, Whitman needed a criticism which would be susceptible to his virtues without excusing his faults. Ardent admirers like William O'Connor, who saw Whitman as a Christ-figure suffering from Romans in places of high office, and Whitman's Canadian friend, Dr R. M. Bucke, who proposed Whitman as an example of 'cosmic consciousness' and thought Whitman 'either actually a god or in some sense preterhuman', did Whitman more harm than good. William Michael Rossetti's selection of *The Poems of Walt Whitman* (an edition which was not expurgated, but consciously omitted *Song of Myself*), published in London in 1868, brought Whitman an honest fame. Although it has been observed that Whitman's English enthusiasts were primarily those men who admired his sexual boldness, readers like John Addington Symonds, Swinburne, Rossetti, Robert Louis Stevenson and Gerard Manley Hopkins were perfectly capable of recognizing a good poem when they saw one. Swinburne's admiration in his letters for *Song of Myself* and *The Sleepers* suggests that from the beginning he was alert to both the best and the worst in Walt Whitman. The extraordinary outpouring of invective he directed at Whitman in his later years (I am thinking of his essay 'Whitmania', 1887) can only be explained by the personal animosity Swinburne felt toward some of Whitman's friends. In his earlier writings on Whitman, and in the passage quoted here from *Under the Microscope* (p. 91), Swinburne could balance his hatred for Whitman the rhetorician with his admiration of Whitman the poet. Edward Dowden (p. 136), the best of Whitman's English critics, is one of the first to acknowledge a shifting, dilating Whitman, one who, to anticipate Yeats's criticism, is not ignorant of the darker side of democratic life.

Whitman died an international celebrity, more honoured abroad than at home. 'How good that English crowd has always been to me,' he told Horace Traubel. In America some of his earliest detractors now spoke more favourably of him. Edith Wharton recalled how James took pleasure in reading Whitman aloud, and James, in his review of *Calamus* (p. 151), spoke of the joy he found in hearing 'an audible New Jersey voice': 'Whitman wrote to his friend of what they both saw, and touched, enormities of the common, sordid occupations, dreary amusements, undesirable food; and the record remains, by a mysterious marvel, a thing positively delightful.' Howell's review of *November Boughs* (*Harper's*, 1882) is sometimes cited as another instance of reconciliation with Whitman. But if Howells conceded that Whitman enlarged the range of literary experience and 'emancipated' poetry from the conventions of the day, he took with one hand what he gave with the other. In making literature 'more direct and natural', Howells declared that Whitman was celebrating 'that which does not need celebration'. He hoped that one day an editor would 'clean-up' Walt Whitman, but in the meantime no reader would be offended by *November Boughs*; the poems here are 'as innocent as so many sprays of apple blossom'. Whitman would have had every right to complain of the patronizing manner of his contemporaries. In 1873, when Emerson published an anthology, *Parnassus*, he omitted Walt Whitman entirely.

The reception of *Leaves of Grass* in 1855 is a subject worth its own study. Whitman appended a selection of reviews ('Leaves-Droppings') to the edition of 1856 and prepared a collection of reviews (*Leaves of Grass Imprints*) to promote the edition of 1860. Because early reviews of Whitman are difficult to come by, I have included a brief selection from 'Leaves-Droppings', recognizing that these essays are sometimes more interesting as indicators of the moral climate than criticism. The best critic of

the edition of 1855 is Whitman himself. Readers of the 'Preface'
of 1855 should have recognized Whitman's voice in the essay
which appeared in the *United States Review*; the more daring
essay is Whitman's review of his own work and that of
Tennyson's, an essay in which he adopts the pose of the shocked
first reader of *Leaves of Grass*. Whitman provided essays for the
editions of 1855, 1856, 1872, 1876 and 1888. I have included his
'A Letter to Ralph Waldo Emerson' (1856) and 'A Backward
Glance O'er Travel'd Roads' (1888). The essay of 1856 is the
least frequently reprinted of Whitman's 'prefaces' and his edition
of 1856 the most underestimated of his volumes. The note of
assurance expressed here is in sharp contrast to Whitman's
deeply moving retrospective essay: 'A Backward Glance' is an
essay which, as Whitman tells us, blends the 'weft of first purpose
and speculations, with the warp of that experience afterwards,
always bringing strange developments'.

   Most of the writing about Whitman during his lifetime was
biographical rather than critical. Whitman encouraged his friends
to describe him as the figure he wished to become, and Whitman
himself was responsible for much that was factually untrue in the
work of William O'Connor (*The Good Gray Poet*, 1867), John
Burroughs (*Notes on Walt Whitman as Poet and Person*, 1867), and
R. M. Bucke (*Walt Whitman*, 1883). In England, William Rossetti,
Anne Gilchrist and J. A. Symonds did much, as I have suggested,
to make Whitman famous. While Symonds's book, published the
year after Whitman's death, is still readable and raised a plea for
the objective study of Whitman, I have not included anything
from it here because it is, in essence, a summary of Whitman's
views. In the essays by Dowden, Swinburne, Burroughs and
Santayana, Whitman's work received that kind of balanced
critical appraisal which, to the despair of his friends, has proved
the only adequate assessment of his worth.

Ralph Waldo Emerson

Letter to Walt Whitman 21 July 1855

Concord
Masstts

Dear Sir,

I am not blind to the worth of the wonderful gift of *Leaves of Grass*. I find it the most extraordinary piece of wit and wisdom that America has yet contributed. I am very happy in reading it, as great power makes us happy. It meets the demand I am always making of what seemed the sterile and stingy Nature, as if too much handiwork or too much lymph in the temperament were making our western wits fat and mean. I give you joy of your free and brave thought. I have great joy in it. I find incomparable things said incomparably well, as they must be. I find the courage of treatment, which so delights us, and which large perception only can inspire. I greet you at the beginning of a great career, which yet must have had a long foreground somewhere, for such a start. I rubbed my eyes a little to see if this sunbeam were no illusion; but the solid sense of the book is a sober certainty. It has the best merits, namely, of fortifying and encouraging.

I did not know until I, last night, saw the book advertised in a newspaper, that I could trust the name as real and available for a post-office. I wish to see my benefactor, and have felt much like striking my tasks, and visiting New York to pay you my respects.

R. W. Emerson

Mr Walter Whitman

Walt Whitman (anonymously)

'Walt Whitman and his Poems', *United States Review* September 1855 (reprinted in *In Re Walt Whitman*, ed. Horace Traubel, 1893)

An American bard at last! One of the roughs, large, proud, affectionate, eating, drinking, and breeding, his costume manly and free, his face sunburnt and bearded, his postures strong and erect, his voice bringing hope and prophecy to the generous races of young and old. We shall cease shamming and be what we really are. We shall start an athletic and defiant literature. We realize now how it is, and what was most lacking. The interior American republic shall also be declared free and independent.

For all our intellectual people, followed by their books, poems, novels, essays, editorials, lectures, tuitions and criticisms, dress by London and Paris modes, receive what is received there, obey the authorities, settle disputes by the old tests, keep out of rain and sun, retreat to the shelter of houses and schools, trim their hair, shave, touch not the earth barefoot, and enter not the sea except in a complete bathing dress. One sees unmistakably genteel persons, travelled, college-learned, used to be served by servants, conversing without heat or vulgarity, supported on chairs, or walking through handsomely carpeted parlours, or along shelves bearing well-bound volumes, and walls adorned with curtained and collared portraits, and china things, and nick-nacks. But where in American literature is the first show of America? Where are the gristle and beards, and broad breasts, and space, and ruggedness, and nonchalance, that the souls of the people love? Where is the tremendous outdoors of these states? Where is the majesty of the federal mother, seated with more than antique grace, calm, just, indulgent to her brood of children, calling them around her, regarding the little and the large, and the younger and the older, with perfect impartiality? Where is the vehement growth of our cities? Where is the spirit of the strong rich life of the American mechanic, farmer, sailor, hunter, and miner? Where is the huge composite of all other nations, cast in a fresher and brawnier matrix, passing adolescence, and needed this day, live and arrogant, to lead the marches of the world?

Self-reliant, with haughty eyes, assuming to himself all the attributes of his country, steps Walt Whitman into literature, talking like a man unaware that there was ever hitherto such a production as a book, or such a being as a writer. Every move of him has the free play of the muscle of one who never knew what it was to feel that he stood in the presence of a superior. Every word that falls from his mouth shows silent disdain and defiance of the old theories and forms. Every phrase announces new laws; not once do his lips unclose except in conformity with them. With light and rapid touch he first indicates in prose the principles of the foundation of a race of poets so deeply to spring from the American people, and become ingrained through them, that their Presidents shall not be the common referees so much as that great race of poets shall. He proceeds himself to exemplify this new school, and sets models for their expression and range of subjects. He makes audacious and native use of his own body and soul. He must recreate poetry with the elements always at hand. He must imbue it with himself as he is, disorderly, fleshy, and sensual, a lover of things, yet a lover of men and women above the whole of the other objects of the universe. His work is to be achieved by unusual methods. Neither classic nor romantic is he, nor a materialist any more than a spiritualist. Not a whisper comes out of him of the old stock talk and rhyme of poetry – not the first recognition of gods or goddesses, or Greece or Rome. No breath of Europe, or her monarchies or priestly conventions, or her notions of gentlemen and ladies, founded on the idea of caste, seems ever to have fanned his face or been inhaled into his lungs.

The movement of his verses is the sweeping movement of great currents of living people, with a general government and state and municipal governments, courts, commerce, manufactures, arsenals, steamships, railroads, telegraphs, cities with paved streets, and aqueducts, and police, and gas – myriads of travellers arriving and departing – newspapers, music, elections, and all the features and processes of the nineteenth century, in the wholesomest race and the only stable forms of politics at present upon the earth. Along his words spread the broad impartialities of the United States. No innovations must be permitted on the stern severities of our liberty and equality. Undecked also is this poet with sentimentalism, or jingle, or nice conceits, or flowery similes. He appears in his poems surrounded by women and children, and by young men, and by common objects and qualities. He gives to each just what belongs to it, neither more nor less. That person nearest him, that person he ushers hand in hand with himself. Duly take places in his flowing procession, and step to the sounds of the jubilant music, the essences of American things, and past and present events – the enormous diversity of temperature, and agriculture, and mines – the tribes of red aborigines – the weather-beaten vessels entering new ports, or making landings on rocky coasts – the first settlements north and south – the rapid stature and impatience of outside control – the sturdy defiance of '76, and the war and peace, and the leadership of Washington, and the formation of the constitution – the union always surrounded by blatherers and always calm and impregnable – the perpetual coming of immigrants – the wharf-hemmed cities and superior marine – the unsurveyed interior – the log-houses and clearings, and wild animals and hunters and trappers – the fisheries, and whaling, and gold-digging – the endless gestation of new States – the convening of Congress every December, the members coming up from all climates, and from the uttermost parts – the noble character of the free American workman and workwoman – the fierceness of the people when well roused – the ardor of their friendships – the large amativeness – the equality of the female with the male – the Yankee swap – the New York firemen and the target excursion – the southern plantation life – the character of the northeast and of the northwest and southwest – and the character of America and the American people everywhere. For these the old usages of poets afford Walt Whitman no means sufficiently fit and free, and he rejects the old usages. The style of the bard that is waited for, is to be transcendent and new. It is to be indirect, and not direct or descriptive or epic. Its quality is to go through these to much more. Let the age and wars (he says) of other nations be chanted, and their eras and characters be illustrated, and that finish the verse. Not so (he continues) the great psalm of the republic. Here the theme is creative and has vista. Here comes one among the well-beloved stone cutters, and announces himself, and plans with decision and science, and sees the solid and beautiful forms of the future where there are now no solid forms.

The style of these poems, therefore, is simply their own style, just born and red. Nature may have given the hint to the author of the *Leaves of Grass*, but there exists no book or fragment of a book which can have given the hint to them. All beauty, he says, comes from beautiful blood and a beautiful brain. His rhythm and uniformity he will conceal in the roots of his verses, not to be seen of themselves, but to break forth loosely as lilacs on a bush, and take shapes compact, as the shapes of melons, or chestnuts, or pears.

The poems of the *Leaves of Grass* are twelve in number. Walt Whitman at first proceeds to put his own body and soul into the new versification:

I celebrate myself,
And what I assume you shall assume,
For every atom belonging to me as good belongs to you.

(1855, 'I celebrate myself', p. 13)

He leaves houses and their shuttered rooms, for the open air. He drops disguise and ceremony, and walks forth with the confidence and gayety of a child. For the old decorums of writing he substitutes his own decorums. The first glance out of his eyes electrifies him with love and delight. He will have the earth receive and return his affection; he will stay with it as the bridegroom stays with the bride. The cool-breath'd ground, the slumbering and liquid trees, the just-gone sunset, the vitreous pour of the full moon, the tender and growing night, he salutes and touches, and they touch him. The sea supports him, and hurries him off with its powerful and crooked fingers. Dash me with amorous wet! then, he says; I can repay you.

The rules of polite circles are dismissed with scorn. Your stale modesties, he seems to say, are filthy to such a man as I.

I believe in the flesh and the appetites,
Seeing hearing and feeling are miracles, and each part and tag of
  me is a miracle.

I do not press my finger across my mouth,
I keep as delicate around the bowels as around the head and heart,
Copulation is no more rank to me than death is.

(1855, 'I celebrate myself', p. 29)

No skulker or tea-drinking poet is Walt Whitman. He will bring poems to fill the days and nights – fit for men and women with the attributes of throbbing blood and flesh. The body, he teaches, is beautiful. Sex is also beautiful. Are you to be put down, he seems to ask, to that shallow level of literature and conversation that stops a man's recognizing the delicious pleasure of his sex, or a woman hers? Nature he proclaims inherently clean. Sex will not be put aside; it is a great ordination of the universe. He works the muscle of the male and the teeming fibre of the female throughout his writings, as wholesome realities, impure only by deliberate intention and effort. To men and women he says, You can have healthy and powerful breeds of children on no less terms than these of mine. Follow me, and there shall be taller and richer crops of humanity on the earth.

Especially in the *Leaves of Grass* are the facts of eternity and immortality largely treated. Happiness is no dream, and perfection is no dream. Amelioration is my lesson, he says with calm voice, and progress is my lesson and the lesson of all things. Then his persuasion becomes a taunt, and his love bitter and compulsory. With strong and steady call he addresses men. Come, he seems to say, from the midst of all that you have been your whole life surrounding yourself with. Leave all the preaching and teaching of others, and mind only these words of mine.

Long enough have you dreamed contemptible dreams,
Now I wash the gum from your eyes,
You must habit yourself to the dazzle of the light and of every
    moment of your life.

Long have you timidly waded, holding a plank by the shore,
Now I will you to be a bold swimmer,
To jump off into the midst of the sea, and rise again and nod to
    me and shout, and laughingly dash with your hair.

I am the teacher of athletes,
He that by me spreads a wider breast than my own proves the
    width of my own,
He most honors my style who learns under it to destroy the teacher.

The boy I love, the same becomes a man not through derived
    power but in his own right,
Wicked, rather than virtuous out of conformity or fear,
Fond of his sweetheart, relishing well his steak,
Unrequited love or a slight cutting him worse than a wound cuts,
First rate to ride, to fight, to hit the bull's eye, to sail a skiff, to
    sing a song or play on the banjo,
Preferring scars and faces pitted with smallpox over all latherers
    and those that keep out of the sun.

I teach straying from me, yet who can stray from me?
I follow you whoever you are from the present hour;
My words itch at your ears till you understand them.

I do not say these things for a dollar, or to fill up the time while I
    wait for a boat;

It is you talking just as much as myself . . . I act as the tongue of
    you,
It was tied in your mouth . . . in mine it begins to be loosened.

I swear I will never mention love or death inside a house,
And I swear I never will translate myself at all, only to him or
    her who privately stays with me in the open air.

(1855, 'I celebrate myself', p. 52)

The eleven other poems have each distinct purposes, curiously
veiled. Theirs is no writer to be gone through with in a day or a
month. Rather it is his pleasure to elude you and provoke you for
deliberate purposes of his own.

Doubtless in the scheme this man has built for himself, the writing
of poems is but a proportionate part of the whole. It is plain that public
and private performance, politics, love, friendship, behavior, the
art of conversation, science, society, the American people, the
reception of the great novelties of city and country, all have their
equal call upon him, and receive equal attention. In politics he could
enter with the freedom and reality he shows in poetry. His scope of
life is the amplest of any yet in philosophy. He is the true spiritualist.
He recognizes no annihilation, or death, or loss of identity. He is the
largest lover and sympathizer that has appeared in literature. He loves
the earth and sun and the animals. He does not separate the learned
from the unlearned, the northerner from the southerner, the white
from the black, or the native from the immigrant just landed at the
wharf. Every one, he seems to say, appears excellent to me; every
employment is adorned, and every male and female glorious.

The press of my foot to the earth springs a hundred affections,
They scorn the best I can do to relate them.

I am enamored of growing outdoors,
Of men that live among cattle or taste of the ocean or woods,
Of the builders and steerers of ships, of the wielders of axes and
    mauls, of the drivers of horses,
I can eat and sleep with them week in and week out.

What is commonest and cheapest and nearest and easiest is Me,
Me going in for my chances, spending for vast returns,

Adorning myself to bestow myself on the first that will take me,
Not asking the sky to come down to my goodwill,
Scattering it freely forever.

(1855, 'I celebrate myself', p. 21)

If health were not his distinguishing attribute, this poet would be
the very harlot of persons. Right and left he flings his arms, drawing
men and women with undeniable love to his close embrace, loving
the clasp of their hands, the touch of their necks and breasts, and the
sound of their voices. All else seems to burn up under his fierce
affection for persons. Politics, religions, institutions, art, quickly fall
aside before them. In the whole universe, he says, I see nothing more
divine than human souls.

When the psalm sings instead of the singer,
When the script preaches instead of the preacher,
When the pulpit descends and goes instead of the carver that
    carved the supporting desk,
When the sacred vessels or the bits of the eucharist, or the lath and
    plast, procreate as effectually as the young silversmiths or bakers,
    or the masons in their overalls,
When a university course convinces like a slumbering woman and
    child convince,
When the minted gold in the vault smiles like the night-
    watchman's daughter,
When warrantee deeds loafe in chairs opposite and are my
    friendly companions,
I intend to reach them my hand and make as much of them as I
    make of men and women.

(1855, 'Come closer to me'[1])

Who then is that insolent unknown? Who is it, praising himself as
if others were not fit to do it, and coming rough and unbidden among
writers, to unsettle what was settled, and to revolutionize in fact our
modern civilization? Walt Whitman was born on Long Island, on
the hills about thirty miles from the greatest American city, on the
last day of May 1819, and has grown up in Brooklyn and New York
to be thirty-six years old, to enjoy perfect health, and to understand
his country and its spirit.

1 This was later called *A Song for Occupations*. [Ed.]

Interrogations more than this, and that will not be put off un-answered, spring continually through the perusal of *Leaves of Grass:*

Must not the true American poet indeed absorb all others, and present a new and far more ample and vigorous type?

Has not the time arrived for a school of life writing and tuition consistent with the principles of these poems? consistent with the free spirit of this age, and with the American truths of politics? consistent with geology, and astronomy, and phrenology, and human physiology? consistent with the sublimity of immortality and the directness of common sense?

If in this poem the United States have found their poetic voice and taken measure and form, is it any more than a beginning? Walt Whitman himself disclaims singularity in his work, and announces the coming after him of great successions of poets, and that he but lifts his finger to give the signal.

Was he not needed? Has not literature been bred in-and-in long enough? Has it not become unbearably artificial?

Shall a man of faith and practice in the simplicity of real things be called eccentric, while every disciple of the fictitious school writes without question?

Shall it still be the amazement of the light and dark that freshness of expression is the rarest quality of all?

You have come in good time, Walt Whitman! In opinions, in manners, in costumes, in books, in the aims and occupancy of life, in associates, in poems, conformity to all unnatural and tainted customs passes without remark, while perfect naturalness, health, faith, self-reliance, and all primal expressions of the manliest love and friendship, subject one to the stare and controversy of the world.

(13–21)

Walt Whitman (anonymously)

'An English and an American Poet', *American Phrenological Journal* October 1855 (reprinted in *In Re Walt Whitman*, ed. Horace Traubel, 1893)

It is always reserved for second-rate poems immediately to gratify. As first-rate or natural objects, in their perfect simplicity and proportion, do not startle or strike, but appear no more than matters of course, so probably natural poetry does not, for all its being the rarest, and telling of the longest and largest work. The artist or writer whose talent is to please the connoisseurs of his time, may obey the laws of his time, and achieve the intense and elaborated beauty of parts. The perfect poet cannot afford any special beauty of parts, or to limit himself by any laws less than those universal ones of the great masters, which include all times, and all men and women, and the living and the dead. For from the study of the universe is drawn this irrefragable truth, that the law of the requisites of a grand poem, or any other complete workmanship, is originality, and the average and superb beauty of the ensemble. Possessed with this law, the fitness of aim, time, persons, places, surely follows. Possessed with this law, and doing justice to it, no poet or any one else will make anything ungraceful or mean, any more than any emanation of nature is.

The poetry of England, by the many rich geniuses of that wonderful little island, has grown out of the facts of the English race, the monarchy and aristocracy prominent over the rest, and conforms to the spirit of them. No nation ever did or ever will receive with national affection any poets except those born of its national blood. Of these, the writings express the finest infusions of government, traditions, faith, and the dependence or independence of a people, and even the good or bad physiognomy, and the ample or small geography. Thus what very properly fits a subject of the British crown may fit very ill an American freeman. No fine romance, no inimitable delineation of character, no grace of delicate illustrations, no rare picture of shore or mountain or sky, no deep thought of the intellect, is so important to a man as his opinion of himself is; everything receives its tinge from that. In the verse of all those undoubtedly great writers, Shakespeare just as much as the rest, there is the air which to America is the air of death. The mass of the people, the laborers and all who serve, are slag, refuse. The countenances of kings and great lords are beautiful; the countenances of mechanics are ridiculous and deformed. What play of Shakespeare, represented in America, is not an insult to America, to the marrow in its bones? How can the tone never silent in their plots and characters be applauded, unless Washington should have been caught and hung, and Jefferson was the most enormous of liars, and common persons, north and south, should bow low to their betters, and to organic superiority of blood? Sure as the heavens envelop the earth, if the Americans want a race of bards worthy of 1855, and of the stern reality of this republic, they must cast around for men essentially different from the old poets, and from the modern successions of jinglers and snivellers and fops.

English versification is full of these danglers, and America follows after them. Everybody writes poetry, and yet there is not a single poet. An age greater than the proudest of the past is swiftly slipping away, without one lyric voice to seize its greatness, and speak it as an encouragement and onward lesson. We have heard, by many grand announcements, that he was to come, but will he come?

A mighty Poet whom this age shall choose
To be its spokesman to all coming times.
In the ripe full-blown season of his soul,
He shall go forward in his spirit's strength,
And grapple with the questions of all time,
And wring from them their meanings. As King Saul
Called up the buried prophet from his grave
To speak his doom, so shall this Poet-king
Call up the dread past from its awful grave
To tell him of our future. As the air
Doth sphere the world, so shall his heart of love –
Loving mankind, not peoples. As the lake
Reflects the flower, tree, rock, and bending heaven,
Shall he reflect our great humanity;
And as the young Spring breathes with living breath
On a dead branch, till it sprouts fragrantly
Green leaves and sunny flowers, shall he breathe life
Through every theme he touch, making all Beauty
And Poetry forever like the stars.

                              (Alexander Smith)

The best of the school of poets at present received in Great Britain and America is Alfred Tennyson. He is the bard of ennui and of the aristocracy, and their combination into love. This love is the old stock love of playwrights and romancers, Shakespeare the same as the rest. It is possessed of the same unnatural and shocking passion for some girl or woman, that wrenches it from its manhood, emasculated and impotent, without strength to hold the rest of the objects and goods of life in their proper positions. It seeks nature for sickly uses. It goes screaming and weeping after the facts of the universe, in their calm beauty and equanimity, to note the occurrence of itself, and to sound the news, in connexion with the charms of the neck, hair, or complexion of a particular female.

Poetry, to Tennyson and his British and American eleves, is a gentleman of the first degree, boating, fishing, and shooting genteelly through nature, admiring the ladies, and talking to them, in company, with that elaborate half-choked deference that is to be made up by the terrible license of men among themselves. The spirit of the burnished society of upper-class England fills this writer and his effusions from top to toe. Like that, he does not ignore courage and the superior qualities of men, but all is to show forth through dandified forms. He meets the nobility and gentry half-way. The models are the same both to the poet and the parlors. Both have the same supercilious elegance, both love the reminiscences which extol caste, both agree on the topics proper for mention and discussion, both hold the same undertone of church and state, both have the same languishing melancholy and irony, both indulge largely in persiflage, both are marked by the contour of high blood and a constitutional aversion to anything cowardly and mean, both accept the love depicted in romances as the great business of a life or a poem, both seem unconscious of the mighty truths of eternity and immortality, both are silent on the presumptions of liberty and equality, and both devour themselves in solitary lassitude. Whatever may be said of all this, it harmonizes and represents facts. The present phases of high-life in Great Britain are as natural a growth there, as Tennyson and his poems are a natural growth of those phases. It remains to be distinctly admitted that this man is a real first-class poet, infused amid all that ennui and aristocracy.

Meanwhile a strange voice parts others aside and demands for its owner that position that is only allowed after the seal of many returning years has stamped with approving stamp the claims of the loftiest leading genius. Do you think the best honors of the earth are won so easily, Walt Whitman? Do you think city and country are to fall before the vehement egotism of your recitative of yourself?

I am the poet of the body,
And I am the poet of the soul.

The pleasures of heaven are with me, and the pains of hell are
    with me,
The first I graft and increase upon myself . . . the latter I translate
    into a new tongue.

I am the poet of the woman the same as the man,
And I say it is as great to be a woman as to be a man,
And I say there is nothing greater than the mother of men.

I chant a new chant of dilation or pride,
We have had ducking and deprecating about enough,
I show that size is only development.

(1855, 'I celebrate myself', p. 26)

It is indeed a strange voice! Critics and lovers and readers of poetry
as hitherto written, may well be excused the chilly and unpleasant
shudders which will assuredly run through them, to their very blood
and bones, when they first read Walt Whitman's poems. If this is
poetry, where must its foregoers stand? And what is at once to become
of the ranks of rhymesters, melancholy and swallow-tailed, and of all
the confectioners and upholsterers of verse, if the tan-faced man
here advancing and claiming to speak for America and the nineteenth
hundred of the Christian list of years, typifies indeed the natural and
proper bard?

The theory and practice of poets have hitherto been to select certain
ideas or events or personages, and then describe them in the best
manner they could, always with as much ornament as the case allowed.
Such are not the theory and practice of the new poet. He never presents for perusal a poem ready-made on the old models, and ending
when you come to the end of it; but every sentence and every passage
tells of an interior not always seen, and exudes an impalpable something which sticks to him that reads, and pervades and provokes him
to tread the half-invisible road where the poet, like an apparition, is
striding fearlessly before. If Walt Whitman's premises are true, then
there is a subtler range of poetry than that of the grandeur of acts and
events, as in Homer, or of characters, as in Shakespeare – poetry to
which all other writing is subservient, and which confronts the very

meanings of the works of nature and competes with them. It is the direct bringing of occurrences and persons and things to bear on the listener or beholder, to reappear through him or her; and it offers the best way of making them a part of him and her as the right aim of the greatest poet.

Of the spirit of life in visible forms – of the spirit of the seed growing out of the ground – of the spirit of the resistless motion of the globe passing unsuspected but quick as lightning along its orbit – of them is the spirit of this man's poetry. Like them it eludes and mocks criticism, and appears unerringly in results. Things, facts, events, persons, days, ages, qualities, tumble pellmell, exhaustless and copious, with what appear to be the same disregard of parts, and the same absence of special purpose, as in nature. But the voice of the few rare and controlling critics, and the voice of more than one generation of men, or two generations of men, must speak for the inexpressible purposes of nature, and for this haughtiest of writers that has ever yet written and printed a book. He is to prove either the most lamentable of failures or the most glorious of triumphs, in the known history of literature. And after all we have written we confess our brain-felt and heart-felt inability to decide which we think it is likely to be.

(29–32)

Edward Everett Hale (anonymously)

Review of *Leaves of Grass, North American Review* January 1856

Everything about the external arrangement of this book was odd and out of the way. The author printed it himself, and it seems to have been left to the winds of heaven to publish it. So it happened that we had not discovered it before our last number, although we believe the sheets had then passed the press. It bears no publisher's name, and, if the reader goes to a bookstore for it, he may expect to be told at first, as we were, that there is no such book and has not been. Nevertheless, there is such a book, and it is well worth going twice to the bookstore to buy it. Walter Whitman, an American, – one of the roughs, – no sentimentalist, – no stander above men and women, or apart from them, – no more modest than immodest, – has tried to write down here, in a sort of prose poetry, a good deal of what he has seen, felt, and guessed at in a pilgrimage of some thirty-five years. He has a horror of conventional language of any kind. His theory of expression is, that, 'to speak in literature with the perfect rectitude and insouciance of the movements of animals, is the flawless triumph of art.' Now a great many men have said this before. But generally it is the introduction to something more artistic than ever, – more conventional and strained. Antony began by saying he was no orator, but none the less did an oration follow. In this book, however, the prophecy is fairly fulfilled in the accomplishment. 'What I experience or portray shall go from my composition without a shred of my composition. You shall stand by my side and look in the mirror with me.'

So truly accomplished is this promise, – which anywhere else would be a flourish of trumpets, – that this thin quarto deserves its name. That is to say, one reads and enjoys the freshness, simplicity, and reality of what he reads, just as the tired man, lying on the hill-side in summer, enjoys the leaves of grass around him, – enjoys the shadow, – enjoys the flecks of sunshine, – not for what they 'suggest to him', but for what they are.

So completely does the author's remarkable power rest in his simplicity, that the preface to the book – which does not even have large letters at the beginning of the lines, as the rest has – is perhaps the very best thing in it. We find more to the point in the following analysis of the 'genius of the United States', than we have found in many more pretentious studies of it.

Other states indicate themselves in their deputies, but the genius of the United States is not best or most in its executives or legislatures, nor in its ambassadors or authors, or colleges or churches or parlors, nor even in its newspapers or inventors; – but always most in the common people. Their manners, speech, dress, friendships; – the freshness and candor of their physiognomy, the picturesque looseness of their carriage, their deathless attachment to freedom, their aversion to everything indecorous or soft or mean, the practical acknowledgment of the citizens of one State by the citizens of all other States, the fierceness of their roused resentment, their curiosity and welcome of novelty, their self-esteem and wonderful sympathy, their susceptibility to a slight, the air they have of persons who never knew how it felt to stand in the presence of superiors, the fluency of their speech, their delight in music (the sure symptom of manly tenderness and native elegance of soul), their good temper and open-handedness, the terrible significance of their elections, the President's taking off his hat to them, not they to him, – these too are unrhymed poetry. It awaits the gigantic and generous treatment worthy of it.

The book is divided into a dozen or more sections, and in each one of these some thread of connexion may be traced, now with ease, now with difficulty, – each being a string of verses, which claim to be written without effort and with entire *abandon*. So the book is a collection of observations, speculations, memories, and prophecies, clad in the simplest, truest, and often the most nervous English, – in the midst of which the reader comes upon something as much out of place as a piece of rotten wood would be among leaves of grass in the meadow, if the meadow had no object but to furnish a child's couch. So slender is the connexion, that we hardly injure the following scraps by extracting them.

I am the teacher of athletes,
He that by me spreads a wider breast than my own, proves the
    width of my own,
He most honors my style who learns under it to destroy the
    teacher.
The boy I love, the same becomes a man not through derived
    power but in his own right,
Wicked, rather than virtuous out of conformity or fear,
Fond of his sweetheart, relishing well his steak,
Unrequited love or a slight cutting him worse than a wound cuts,
First-rate to ride, to fight, to hit the bull's-eye, to sail a skiff, to
    sing a song or to play on the banjo,
Preferring scars and faces pitted with smallpox over all latherers
    and those that keep out of the sun.

                              (1855, 'I celebrate myself', p. 52)

Here is the story of the gallant seaman who rescued the passengers on the San Francisco:

I understand the large heart of heroes,
The courage of present times and all times;
How the skipper saw the crowded and rudderless wreck of the
    steamship, and death chasing it up and down the storm,
How he knuckled tight and gave not back one inch, and was
    faithful of days and faithful of nights,
And chalked in large letters on a board, Be of good cheer, We
    will not desert you;
How he saved the drifting company at last,
How the lank loose-gowned women looked when boated from
    the side of their prepared graves,
How the silent old-faced infants, and the lifted sick, and the sharp-
    lipped unshaven men;
All this I swallow, and it tastes good ... I like it well, and it becomes
    mine,
I am the man ... I suffered ... I was there.

(1855, 'I celebrate myself', p. 38)

Claiming in this way a personal interest in every thing that has
ever happened in the world, and, by the wonderful sharpness and
distinctness of his imagination, making the claim effective and reasonable, Mr 'Walt Whitman' leaves it a matter of doubt where he has
been in this world, and where not. It is very clear, that with him, as
with most other effective writers, a keen, absolute memory, which
takes in and holds every detail of the past, – as they say the exaggerated
power of the memory does when a man is drowning, – is a gift of his
organization as remarkable as his vivid imagination. What he has
seen once, he has seen for ever. And thus there are in this curious
book little thumb-nail sketches of life in the prairie, life in California,
life at school, life in the nursery, – life, indeed, we know not where
not, – which, as they are unfolded one after another, strike us as real,
– so real that we wonder how they came on paper.

For the purpose of showing that he is above every conventionalism,
Mr Whitman puts into the book one or two lines which he would not
address to a woman nor to a company of men. There is not anything,
perhaps, which modern usage would stamp as more indelicate than are
some passages in Homer. There is not a word in it meant to attract
readers by its grossness, as there is in half the literature of the last

century, which holds its place unchallenged on the tables of our drawing-rooms. For all that, it is a pity that a book where everything else is natural should go out of the way to avoid the suspicion of being prudish.

(275–7)

Walt Whitman

'A Letter to Ralph Waldo Emerson', *Leaves of Grass* 1856

Brooklyn, August 1856

Here are thirty-two Poems, which I send you, dear Friend and Master, not having found how I could satisfy myself with sending any usual acknowledgment of your letter. The first edition, on which you mailed me that till now unanswered letter, was twelve poems – I printed a thousand copies, and they readily sold; these thirty-two Poems I stereotype, to print several thousand copies of. I much enjoy making poems. Other work I have set for myself to do, to meet people and The States face to face, to confront them with an American rude tongue; but the work of my life is making poems. I keep on till I make a hundred, and then several hundred – perhaps a thousand. The way is clear to me. A few years, and the average annual call for my Poems is ten or twenty thousand copies – more, quite likely. Why should I hurry or compromise? In poems or in speeches I say the word or two that has got to be said, adhere to the body, step with the countless common footsteps, and remind every man and woman of something.

Master, I am a man who has perfect faith. Master, we have not come through centuries, caste, heroisms, fables, to halt in this land today. Or I think it is to collect a ten-fold impetus that any halt is made. As nature, inexorable, onward, resistless, impassive amid the threats and screams of disputants, so America. Let all defer. Let all attend respectfully the leisure of These States, their politics, poems, literature, manners, and their free-handed modes of training their own offspring. Their own comes, just matured, certain, numerous and capable enough, with egotistical tongues, with sinewed wrists, seizing openly what belongs to them. They resume Personality, too long left out of mind. Their shadows are projected in employments, in books, in the cities, in trade; their feet are on the flights of the steps of the Capitol; they dilate, a larger, brawnier, more candid, more democratic, lawless, positive native to The States, sweet-bodied, completer, dauntless, flowing, masterful, beard-faced, new race of men.

Swiftly, on limitless foundations, the United States too are founding a literature. It is all as well done, in my opinion, as could be practicable. Each element here is in condition. Every day I go among the people of Manhattan Island, Brooklyn, and other cities, and among the young men, to discover the spirit of them, and to refresh myself. These are to be attended to; I am myself more drawn here than to those authors, publishers, importations, reprints, and so forth. I pass coolly through those, understanding them perfectly well, and that they do the indispensable service, outside of men like me, which nothing else could do. In poems, the young men of The States shall be represented, for they out-rival the best of the rest of the earth.

The lists of ready-made literature which America inherits by the mighty inheritance of the English language – all the rich repertoire of traditions, poems, histories, metaphysics, plays, classics, translations, have made, and still continue, magnificent preparations for that other plainly signified literature, to be our own, to be electric, fresh, lusty, to express the full-sized body, male and female – to give the modern meanings of things, to grow up beautiful, lasting, commensurate with America, with all the passions of home, with the inimitable sympathies of having been boys and girls together, and of parents who were with our parents.

What else can happen [to] The States, even in their own despite? That huge English flow, so sweet, so undeniable, has done incalculable good here, and is to be spoken of for its own sake with generous praise and with gratitude. Yet the price The States have had to lie under for the same has not been a small price. Payment prevails; a nation can never take the issues of the needs of other nations for nothing. America, grandest of lands in the theory of its politics, in popular reading, in hospitality, breadth, animal beauty, cities, ships, machines, money, credit, collapses quick as lightning at the repeated, admonishing, stern words, Where are any mental expressions from you, beyond what you have copied or stolen? Where the born throngs of poets, literats, orators, you promised? Will you but tag after other nations? They struggled long for their literature, painfully working their way, some with deficient languages, some with priest-craft, some in the endeavor just to live – yet achieved for their times, works, poems, perhaps the only solid consolation left to them through ages afterward of shame and decay. You are young, have the perfectest of dialects, a free press, a free government, the world forwarding its best to be with you. As justice has been strictly done to you, from this hour do strict justice to yourself. Strangle the singers who will not sing you loud and strong. Open the doors of The West. Call for new great masters to comprehend new arts, new perfections, new wants. Submit to the most robust bard till he remedy your barrenness. Then you will not need to adopt the heirs of others; you will have true heirs, begotten of yourself, blooded with your own blood.

With composure I see such propositions, seeing more and more every day of the answers that serve. Expressions do not yet serve, for sufficient reasons; but that is getting ready, beyond what the earth has hitherto known, to take home the expressions when they come, and to identify them with the populace of The States, which is the schooling cheaply procured by any outlay any number of years. Such schooling The States extract from the swarms of reprints, and from the current authors and editors. Such service and extract are done after enormous, reckless, free modes, characteristic of The States. Here are to be attained results never elsewhere thought possible; the modes are very grand too. The instincts of the American people are all perfect, and tend to make heroes. It is a rare thing in a man here to understand The States.

All current nourishments to literature serve. Of authors and editors I do not know how many there are in The States, but there are thousands, each one building his or her step to the stairs by which giants shall mount. Of the twenty-four modern mammoth two-double, three-double, and four-double cylinder presses now in the world, printing by steam, twenty-one of them are in These States. The twelve thousand large and small shops for dispensing books and newspapers – the same number of public libraries, any one of which has all the reading wanted to equip a man or woman for American reading – the three thousand different newspapers, the nutriment of the imperfect ones coming in just as usefully as any – the story papers, various, full of strong-flavored romances, widely circulated – the one-cent and two-cent journals – the political ones, no matter what side – the weeklies in the country – the sporting and pictorial papers – the monthly magazines, with plentiful imported feed – the sentimental novels, numberless copies of them – the low-priced flaring tales, adventures, biographies – all are prophetic; all waft rapidly on. I see that they swell wide, for reasons. I am not troubled at the movement of them, but greatly pleased. I see plying shuttles, the active ephemeral myriads of books also, faithfully weaving the garments of a genera-tion of men, and a generation of women, they do not perceive or know. What a progress popular reading and writing has made in fifty years! What a progress fifty years hence! The time is at hand when inherent literature will be a main part of These States, as general and real as steam-power, iron, corn, beef, fish. First-rate American persons are to be supplied. Our perennial materials for fresh thoughts, histories, poems, music, orations, religious, recitations, amusements, will then not be disregarded, any more than our perennial fields, mines, rivers, seas. Certain things are established, and are immovable; in those things millions of years stand justified. The mothers and fathers of whom modern centuries have come, have not existed for nothing; they too had brains and hearts. Of course all literature, in all nations and years, will share marked attributes in common, as we all, of all ages, share the common human attributes. America is to be kept coarse and broad. What is to be done is to withdraw from precedents, and be directed to men and women – also to The States in their federalness; for the union of the parts of the body is not more necessary to their life than the union of These States is to their life.

A profound person can easily know more of the people than they know of themselves. Always waiting untold in the souls of the armies of common people, is stuff better than anything that can possibly appear in the leadership of the same. That gives final verdicts. In every department of These States, he who travels with a coterie, or with selected persons, or with imitators, or with infidels, or with the owners of slaves, or with that which is ashamed of the body of a man, or with that which is ashamed of the body of a woman, or with any thing less than the bravest and the openest, travels straight for the slopes of dissolution. The genius of all foreign literature is clipped and cut small, compared to our genius, and is essentially insulting to our usages, and to the organic compacts of These States. Old forms, old poems, majestic and proper in their own lands here in this land are exiles; the air here is very strong. Much that stands well and has a little enough place provided for it in the small scales of European kingdoms, empires, and the like, here stands haggard, dwarfed, ludicrous, or has no place little enough provided for it. Authorities, poems, models, laws, names, imported into America, are useful to America today to destroy them, and so move disencumbered to great works, great days.

Just so long, in our country or any country, as no revolutionists advance, and are backed by the people, sweeping off the swarms of routine representatives, officers in power, book-makers, teachers, ecclesiastics, politicians, just so long, I perceive, do they who are in power fairly represent that country, and remain of use, probably of very great use. To supersede them, when it is the pleasure of These States, full provision is made; and I say the time has arrived to use it with a strong hand. Here also the souls of the armies have not only overtaken the souls of the officers, but passed on, and left the souls of the officers behind out of sight many weeks' journey; and the souls of the armies now go *en masse* without officers. Here also formulas, glosses, blanks, minutiae, are choking the throats of the spokesmen to death. Those things most listened for, certainly those are the things least said. There is not a single History of the World. There is not one of America, or of the organic compacts of These States, or of Washington, or of Jefferson, nor of Language, nor any Dictionary of the English Language. There is no great author; every one has demeaned himself to some etiquette or some impotence. There is no manhood or life-power in poems; there are shoats and geldings more like. Or literature will be dressed up, a fine gentleman, distasteful to our instincts, foreign to our soil. Its neck bends right and left wherever it goes. Its costumes and jewelry prove how little it knows Nature. Its flesh is soft; it shows less and less of the indefinable hard something that is Nature. Where is any thing but the shaved Nature of synods and schools? Where is a savage and luxuriant man? Where is an overseer? In lives, in poems, in codes of law, in Congress, in tuitions, theatres, conversations, argumentations, not a single head lifts itself clean out, with proof that it is their master, and has subordinated them to itself, and is ready to try their superiors. None believes in These States, boldly illustrating them in himself. Not a man faces round at the rest with terrible negative voice, refusing all terms to be bought off from his own eye-sight, or from the soul that he is, or from friendship, or from the body that he is, or from the soil and sea. To creeds, literature, art, the army, the navy, the executive, life is hardly proposed, but the sick and dying are proposed to cure the sick and dying. The churches are one vast lie; the people do not believe them, and they do not believe themselves; the priests are continually telling what they know well enough is not so, and keeping back what they know is so. The spectacle is a pitiful one. I think there can never be again upon the festive earth more bad-disordered persons deliberately taking seats, as of late in These States, at the heads of the public tables – such corpses' eyes for judges – such a rascal and thief in the Presidency.

Up to the present, as helps best, the people, like a lot of large boys, have no determined tastes, are quite unaware of the grandeur of themselves, and of their destiny, and of their immense strides – accept with voracity whatever is presented them in novels, histories, newspapers, poems, schools, lectures, every thing. Pretty soon, through these and other means, their development makes the fibre that is capable of itself, and will assume determined tastes. The young men will be clear what they want, and will have it. They will follow none except him whose spirit leads them in the like spirit with themselves. Any such man will be welcome as the flowers of May. Others will be put out without ceremony. How much is there anyhow, to the young men of These States, in a parcel of helpless dandies, who can neither fight, work, shoot, ride, run, command – some of them devout, some quite insane, some castrated – all second-hand, or third, fourth, or fifth-hand – waited upon by waiters, putting not this land first, but always other lands first, talking of art, doing the most ridiculous things for fear of being called ridiculous, smirking and skipping along, continually taking off their hats   no one behaving, dressing, writing, talking, loving, out of any natural and manly tastes of his own, but each one looking cautiously to see how the rest behave, dress, write, talk, love – pressing the noses of dead books upon themselves and upon their country – favoring no poets, philosophs, literats here, but dog-like danglers at the heels of the poets, philosophs, literats, of enemies' lands – favoring mental expressions, models of gentlemen and ladies, social habitudes in These States, to grow up in sneaking defiance of the popular substratums of The States? Of course they and the likes of them can never justify the strong poems of America. Of course no feed of theirs is to stop and be made welcome to muscle the bodies, male and female, for Manhattan Island, Brooklyn, Boston, Worcester, Hartford, Portland, Montreal, Detroit, Buffalo, Cleaveland, Milwaukee, St Louis, Indianapolis, Chicago, Cincinnati, Iowa City, Philadelphia, Baltimore, Raleigh, Savannah, Charleston, Mobile, New Orleans, Galveston, Brownsville, San Francisco, Havana, and a thousand equal cities, present and to come. Of course what they and the likes of them have been used for, draws toward its close, after which they will be discharged, and not one of them will ever be heard of any more.

America, having duly conceived, bears out of herself offspring of her own to do the workmanship wanted. To freedom, to strength, to poems, to personal greatness, it is never permitted to rest, not a generation or part of a generation. To be ripe beyond further increase is to prepare to die. The architects of These States laid their foundations, and passed to further spheres. What they laid is a work done; as much more remains. Now are needed other architects, whose duty is not less difficult, but perhaps more difficult. Each age forever needs architects. America is not finished, perhaps never will be; now America is a divine true sketch. There are Thirty-Two States sketched – the population thirty millions. In a few years there will be Fifty States. Again in a few years there will be A Hundred States, the population hundreds of millions, the freshest and freest of men. Of course such men stand to nothing less than the freshest and freest expression.

Poets here, literats here, are to rest on organic different bases from other countries; not a class set apart, circling only in the circle of themselves, modest and pretty, desperately scratching for rhymes, pallid with white paper, shut off, aware of the old pictures and traditions of the race, but unaware of the actual race around them – not breeding in and in among each other till they all have the scrofula. Lands of ensemble, bards of ensemble! Walking freely out from the old traditions, as our politics has walked out, American poets and literats recognize nothing behind them superior to what is present with them – recognize with joy the sturdy living forms of the men and women of These States, the divinity of sex, the perfect eligibility of the female with the male, all The States, liberty and equality, real articles, the different trades, mechanics, the young fellows of Manhattan Island, customs, instincts, slang, Wisconsin, Georgia, the noble Southern heart, the hot blood, the spirit that will be nothing less than master, the filibuster spirit, the Western man, native-born perceptions, the eye for forms, the perfect models of made things, the wild smack of freedom, California, money, electric-telegraphs, free-trade, iron and the iron mines – recognize without demur those splendid resistless black poems, the steam-ships of the sea-board states, and those other resistless splendid poems, the locomotives, followed through the interior states by trains of rail-road cars.

A word remains to be said, as of one ever present, not yet permitted to be acknowledged, discarded or made dumb by literature, and the results apparent. To the lack of an avowed, empowered, unabashed development of sex, (the only salvation for the same,) and to the fact of speakers and writers fraudently assuming as always dead what every one knows to be always alive, is attributable the remarkable non-personality and indistinctness of modern productions in books, art, talk; also that in the scanned lives of men and women most of them appear to have been for some time past of the neuter gender; and also the stinging fact that in orthodox society today, if the dresses were changed, the men might easily pass for women and the women for men.

Infidelism usurps most with foetid polite face; among the rest infidelism about sex. By silence or obedience the pens of savans, poets, historians, biographers, and the rest, have long connived at the filthy law, and books enslaved to it, that what makes the manhood of a man, that sex, womanhood, maternity, desires, lusty animations, organs, acts, are unmentionable and to be ashamed of, to be driven to skulk out of literature with whatever belongs to them. This filthy law has to be repealed – it stands in the way of great reforms. Of women just as much as men, it is the interest that there should not be infidelism about sex, but perfect faith. Women in These States approach the day of that organic equality with men, without which, I see, men cannot have organic equality among themselves. This empty dish, gallantry, will then be filled with something. This tepid wash, this diluted deferential love, as in songs, fictions, and so forth, is enough to make a man vomit; as to manly friendship, everywhere observed in The States, there is not the first breath of it to be observed in print. I say that the body of a man or woman, the main matter, is so far quite unexpressed in poems; but that the body is to be expressed, and sex is. Of bards for These States, if it come to a question, it is whether they shall celebrate in poems the eternal decency of the amativeness of Nature, the motherhood of all, or whether they shall be the bards of the fashionable delusion of the inherent nastiness of sex, and of the feeble and querulous modesty of deprivation. This is important in poems, because the whole of the other expressions of a nation are but flanges out of its great poems. To me, henceforth, that theory of any thing, no matter what, stagnates in its vitals, cowardly and rotten, while it cannot publicly accept, and publicly name, with specific words, the things on which all existence, all souls, all realization, all decency, all health, all that is worth being here for, all of woman and of man, all beauty, all purity, all sweetness, all friendship, all strength, all life, all immortality depend. The courageous soul, for a year or two to come, may be proved by faith in sex, and by disdaining concessions.

To poets and literats – to every woman and man, today or any day, the conditions of the present, needs, dangers, prejudices, and the like, are the perfect conditions on which we are here, and the conditions for wording the future with undissuadable words. These States, receivers of the stamina of past ages and lands, initiate the outlines of repayment a thousand fold. They fetch the American great masters, waited for by old worlds and new, who accept evil as well as good, ignorance as well as erudition, black as soon as white, foreign-born materials as well as home-born, reject none, force discrepancies into range, surround the whole, concentrate them on present periods and places, show the application to each and any one's body and soul, and show the true use of precedents. Always America will be agitated and turbulent. This day it is taking shape, not to be less so, but to be more so, stormily, capriciously, on native principles, with such vast proportions of parts! As for me, I love screaming, wrestling, boiling-hot days.

Of course, we shall have a national character, an identity. As it ought to be, and as soon as it ought to be, it will be. That, with much else, takes care of itself, is a result, and the cause of greater results.

With Ohio, Illinois, Missouri, Oregon – with the states around the Mexican sea – with cheerfully welcomed immigrants from Europe, Asia, Africa – with Connecticut, Vermont, New Hampshire, Rhode Island – with all varied interests, facts, beliefs, parties, genesis – there is being fused a determined character, fit for the broadest use for the freewomen and freemen of The States, accomplished and to be accomplished, without any exception whatever – each indeed free, each idiomatic, as becomes live states and men, but each adhering to one enclosing general form of politics, manners, talk, personal style, as the plenteous varieties of the race adhere to one physical form. Such character is the brain and spine to all, including literature, including poems. Such character, strong, limber, just, open-mouthed, American-blooded, full of pride, full of ease, of passionate friendliness, is to stand compact upon that vast basis of the supremacy of Individuality – that new moral American continent without which, I see, the physical continent remained incomplete, may be a carcass, a bloat – that newer America, answering face to face with The States, with ever-satisfying and ever-unsurveyable seas and shores.

Those shores you found. I say you have led The States there – have led Me there. I say that none has ever done, or ever can do, a greater deed for The States, than your deed. Others may line out the lines, build cities, work mines, break up farms; it is yours to have been the original true Captain who put to sea, intuitive, positive, rendering the first report, to be told less by any report, and more by the mariners of a thousand bays, in each tack of their arriving and departing, many years after you.

Receive, dear Master, these statements and assurances through me, for all the young men, and for an earnest that we know none before you, but the best following you; and that we demand to take your name into our keeping, and that we understand what you have indicated, and find the same indicated in ourselves, and that we will stick to it and enlarge upon it through These States.

(346–58)

Henry David Thoreau

Letter to Harrison Blake 7 December 1856

That Walt Whitman of whom I wrote to you, is the most interesting
fact to me at present. I have just read his second edition (which he
gave me), and it has done me more good than any reading for a long
time. Perhaps I remember best the poem of Walt Whitman, an
American, and the Sun-Down Poem. There are two or three pieces
in the book which are disagreeable, to say the least; simply sensual.
He does not celebrate love at all. It is as if the beasts spoke. I think that
men have not been ashamed of themselves without reason. No doubt
there have always been dens where such deeds were unblushingly
recited, and it is no merit to compete with their inhabitants. But even
on this side he has spoken more truth than any American or modern
that I know. I have found his poem exhilarating, encouraging. As
for its sensuality, – and it may turn out to be less sensual than it
appears, – I do not so much wish that those parts were not written,
as that men and women were so pure that they could read them without harm, that is, without understanding them. One woman told me
that no woman could read it, – as if a man could read what a woman
could not. Of course Walt Whitman can communicate to us no
experience, and if we are shocked, whose experience is it that we are
reminded of?

On the whole, it sounds to me very brave and American, after
whatever deductions. I do not believe that all the sermons, so called,
that have been preached in this land put together are equal to it for
preaching.

We ought to rejoice greatly in him. He occasionally suggests something a little more than human. You can't confound him with the
other inhabitants of Brooklyn or New York. How they must shudder
when they read him! He is awfully good.

To be sure I sometimes feel a little imposed on. By his heartiness
and broad generalities he puts me into a liberal frame of mind prepared to see wonders – as it were, sets me upon a hill or in the midst
of a plain, – stirs me well up, and then – throws in a thousand of
brick. Though rude, and sometimes ineffectual, it is a great primitive
poem, – an alarum or trumpet-note ringing through the American

camp. Wonderfully like the Orientals, too, considering that when I asked him if he had read them, he answered, 'No; tell me about them.'

I did not get far in conversation with him, – two more being present, – and among the few things which I chanced to say, I remember that one was, in answer to him as representing America, that I did not think much of America or of politics, and so on, which may have been somewhat of a damper to him.

Since I have seen him, I find that I am not disturbed by any brag or egoism in his book. He may turn out the least of a braggart of all, having a better right to be confident.

He is a great fellow.

Henry Thoreau

William Howitt and others (anonymously)

from 'Leaves-Droppings', a selection of reviews appended by Whitman to the 1856 edition of Leaves of Grass

From the London Weekly Dispatch (London, England)

Leaves of Grass, by Walt Whitman, Horsell, Oxford Street

We have before us one of the most extraordinary specimens of Yankee intelligence and American eccentricity in authorship, it is possible to conceive. It is of a genus so peculiar as to embarrass us, and has an air at once so novel, so audacious, and so strange as to verge upon absurdity, and yet it would be an injustice to pronounce it so, as the work is saved from this extreme by a certain mastery over diction not very easy of definition. What Emerson has pronounced to be good must not be lightly treated, and before we pronounce upon the merits of this performance it is but right to examine them. We have, then, a series of pithy prose sentences strung together – forming twelve grand divisions in all, but which, having a rude rhymical cadence about then, admit of the designation poetical being applied. They are destitute of rhyme, measure of feet, and the like, every condition under which poetry is generally understood to exist being absent; but in their strength of expression, their fervour, hearty wholesomeness, their originality, mannerism, and freshness, one finds in them a singular harmony and flow, as if by reading, they gradually formed themselves into melody, and adopted characteristics peculiar and appropriate to themselves alone. If, however, some sentences be fine, there are others altogether laughable; nevertheless, in the bare strength, the unhesitating frankness of a man who 'believes in the flesh and the appetites', and who dares to call simplest things by their plainest names, conveying also a large sense of the beautiful, and with an emphasis which gives a clearer conception of what manly modesty really is than any thing we have, in all conventional forms of word, deed, or act so far known of, that we rid ourselves, little by little, of the strangeness with which we greet this bluff newcomer, and, beginning to understand him better, appreciate him in proportion as he becomes more known. He will soon make his way into the confidence of his readers, and his poems in time will become a pregnant text-book, out of which quotation as sterling as the minted gold will be taken and applied to every form and phase of the 'inner' or the 'outer' life; and we express our pleasure in making the acquaintance of Walt Whitman, hoping to know more of him in time to come.   [William Howitt]

From the *Critic* (London, England)

Leaves of Grass, New York, 1855, London: Horsell

We had ceased, we imagined, to be surprised at anything that America could produce. We had become stoically indifferent to her Woolly Horses, her Mermaids, her Sea Serpents, her Barnums, and her Fanny Ferns; but the last monstrous importation from Brooklyn, New York, has scattered our indifference to the winds. Here is a thin quarto volume without an author's name on the title-page; but to atone for which we have a portrait engraved on steel of the notorious individual who is the poet presumptive. This portrait expresses all the features of the hard democrat, and none of the flexile delicacy of the civilized poet. The damaged hat, the rough beard, the naked throat, the shirt exposed to the waist, are each and all presented to show that the man to whom these articles belong scorns the delicate arts of civilization. The man is the true impersonation of his book – rough, uncouth, vulgar. It was by the merest accident that we discovered the name of this erratic and newest wonder; but at page 29 we find that he is

Walt Whitman, an American, one of the roughs, a kosmos, Disorderly, fleshly, and sensual.

(1855, 'I celebrate myself', p. 29)

The words 'an American' are a surplusage, 'one of the roughs' too painfully apparent; but what is intended to conveyed by 'a kosmos' we cannot tell, unless it means a man who thinks that the fine essence of poetry consists in writing a book which an American reviewer is compelled to declare is 'not to be read aloud to a mixed audience'. We should have passed over this book, *Leaves of Grass*, with indignant contempt, had not some few Transatlantic critics attempted to 'fix' this Walt Whitman as the poet who shall give a new and independent literature to America – who shall form a race of poets as Banquo's issue formed a line of kings. Is it possible that the most prudish nation in the world will adopt a poet whose indecencies stink in the nostrils? We hope not; and yet there is a probability, and we will show why, that this Walt Whitman will not meet with the stern rebuke which he so richly deserves. America has felt, oftener perhaps than we have declared, that she has no national poet – that each one of her children of song has relied too much on European inspiration, and clung too fervently to the old conventionalities. It is therefore not unlikely that she may believe in the dawn of a thoroughly original literature, now there has arisen a man who scorns the Hellenic deities, who has no belief in, perhaps because he has no knowledge of, Homer and Shakespeare; who relies on his own rugged nature, and trusts to his own rugged language, being himself what he shows in his poems. Once transfix him as the genesis of a new era, and the manner of the man may be forgiven or forgotten. But what claim has this Walt Whitman to be thus considered, or to be considered a poet at all? We grant freely enough that he has a strong relish for nature and freedom, just as an animal has; nay, further, that his crude mind is capable of appreciating some of nature's beauties; but it by no means follows that, because nature is excellent, therefore art is contemptible. Walt Whitman is as unacquainted with art, as a hog is with mathematics. His poems – we must call them so for convenience – twelve in number, are innocent of rhythm, and resemble nothing so much as the war-cry of the Red Indians. Indeed, Walt Whitman has had near and ample opportunities of studying the vociferations of a few amiable savages. Or rather, perhaps, this Walt Whitman reminds us of Caliban flinging down his logs, and setting himself to write a poem. In fact, Caliban, and not Walt Whitman, might have written this:

I too am not a bit tamed . . . I too am untranslatable,
I sound my *barbaric yawp* over the roofs of the world.[1]

(1855, 'I celebrate myself', p. 55)

Is this man with the 'barbaric yawp' to push Longfellow into the shade, and he meanwhile to stand and 'make mouths' at the sun? The chance of this might be formidable were it not ridiculous. That object or that act which most develops the ridiculous element carries in its bosom the seeds of decay, and is wholly powerless to trample out of God's universe one spark of the beautiful. We do not, then, fear this Walt Whitman, who gives us slang in the place of melody, and rowdyism in the place of regularity. The depth of his indecencies will be the grave of his fame, or ought to be if all proper feeling is not extinct. The very nature of this man's compositions excludes us from proving by extracts the truth of our remarks; but we, who are not prudish, emphatically declare that the man who wrote page 79 of the *Leaves of Grass* deserves nothing so richly as the public executioner's whip. Walt Whitman libels the highest type of humanity, and calls his free speech the true utterance of *a man*: we, who may have been misdirected by civilization, call it the expression of *a beast*. . . .

We will neither weary nor insult our readers with more extracts from this notable book. Emerson *has praised it*, and called it the 'most extraordinary piece of wit and wisdom America has yet contributed'. Because Emerson has grasped substantial fame, he can afford to be generous; but Emerson's generosity must not be mistaken for justice. If this work is really a work of genius – if the principles of those poems, their free language, their amazing and audacious egotism, their animal vigour, be real poetry and the divinest evidence of the true poet – then our studies have been in vain, and vainer still the homage which we have paid the monarchs of Saxon intellect, Shakespeare, and Milton and Byron. This Walt Whitman holds that his claim to be a poet lies in his robust and rude health. He is, in fact, as

1 The italics are not Whitman's. [Ed.]

he declares, 'the poet of the body'. Adopt this theory, and Walt Whitman is a Titan; Shelley and Keats the merest pigmies. If we had commenced a notice of *Leaves of Grass* in anger, we could not but dismiss it in grief, for its author, we have just discovered, is conscious of his affliction. He says, at page 33,

I am given up by traitors;
I talk wildly, I am mad.[1]

(1855, 'I celebrate myself')

From the *London Leader*, 'Transatlantic Latter-day Poetry'

Leaves of Grass, Brooklyn, New York, 1855, London: Horsell

'Latter-day poetry' in America is of a very different character from the same manifestation in the old country. Here, it is occupied for the most part with dreams of the middle ages, of the old knightly and religious times; in America it is employed chiefly with the present, except when it travels out into the undiscovered future. Here our latter-day poets are apt to whine over the times, as if heaven were perpetually betraying the earth with a show of progress that is in fact retrogression, like the backward advance of crabs; there, the minstrels of the stars and stripes blow a loud note of exultation before the grand new epoch, and think the Greeks and Romans, the early Oriental races, and the later men of the middle centuries, of small account before the onward tramping of these present generations. Of this latter sect is a certain phenomenon who has recently started up in Brooklyn, New York – one Walt Whitman, author of *Leaves of Grass*, who has been received by a section of his countrymen as a sort of prophet, and by Englishmen as a kind of fool. For ourselves, we are not disposed to accept him as the one, having less faith in latter-day prophets than in latter-day poets; but assuredly we cannot regard him as the other. Walt is one of the most amazing, one of the most startling, one of the most perplexing creations of the modern American mind; but he is no fool, though abundantly eccentric, nor is his book mere food for laughter, though undoubtedly containing much that may easily and fairly be turned into ridicule.

The singularity of the author's mind – his utter disregard of ordinary forms and modes – appears in the very title-page and frontis-

1 Whitman's line is 'I talk wildly . . . I have lost my wits . . .' [Ed.]

piece of his work. Not only is there no author's name, (which in itself would not be singular) but there is no publisher's name – that of the English bookseller being a London addition. Fronting the title is the portrait of a bearded gentleman in his shirt-sleeves and a Spanish hat, with an all-pervading atmosphere of Yankee-doodle about him; but again there is no patronymic, and we can only infer that this roystering blade is the author of the book. Then follows a long prose treatise by way of preface (and here once more the anonymous system is carried out, the treatise having no heading whatever); and after that we have the poem, in the course of which a short autobiographical discourse reveals to us the name of the author.

A passage from the Preface, if it may be so called, will give some insight into the character and objects of the work.

Other states indicate themselves in their deputies . . . but the genius of the United States is not best or most in its executives or legislatures, nor in its ambassadors, or authors, or colleges, or churches, or parlors, nor even in its newspapers or inventors . . . but always most in the common people. Their manners, speech, dress, friendships – the freshness and candor of their physiognomy – the picturesque looseness of their carriage . . . their deathless attachment to freedom – their aversion to any thing indecorous – or soft or mean – the practical acknowledgment of the citizens of one state by the citizens of all other states – the fierceness of their roused resentment – their curiosity and welcome of novelty – their self-esteem and wonderful sympathy – their susceptibility to a slight – the air they have of persons who never knew how it felt to stand in the presence of superiors – the fluency of their speech – their delight in music, the sure symptom of manly tenderness and native elegance of soul . . . their good temper and open-handedness – the terrible significance of their elections – the President's taking off his hat to them, not they to him – these too are unrhymed poetry. It awaits the gigantic and generous treatment worthy of it.

This 'gigantic and generous treatment', we presume, is offered in the pages which ensue. The poem is written in wild, irregular, un-rhymed, almost unmetrical 'lengths', like the measured prose of Mr Martin Farquhar Tupper's *Proverbial Philosophy*, or some of the

Oriental writings. The external form, therefore, is startling, and by no means seductive, to English ears, accustomed to the sumptuous music of ordinary metre; and the central principle of the poem is equally staggering. It seems to resolve itself into an all-attracting egotism – an eternal presence of the individual soul of Walt Whitman in all things, yet in such wise that this one soul shall be presented as a type of all human souls whatsoever. He goes forth into the world, this rough, devil-may-care Yankee; passionately identifies himself with all forms of being, sentient, or inanimate; sympathizes deeply with humanity; riots with a kind of Bacchanal fury in the force and fervour of his own sensations; will not have the most vicious or abandoned shut out from final comfort and reconciliation; is delighted with Broadway, New York, and equally in love with the desolate back-woods, and the long stretch of the uninhabited prairie, where the wild beasts wallow in the reeds, and the wilder birds start upward from their nests among the grass; perceives a divine mystery wherever his feet conduct or his thoughts transport him; and beholds all things tending toward the central and sovereign Me. Such, as we conceive, is the key to this strange, grotesque, and bewildering book; yet we are far from saying that the key will unlock all the quirks and oddities of the volume. Much remains of which we confess we can make nothing; much that seems to us purely fantastical and pre-posterous; much that appears to our muddy vision gratuitously prosaic, needlessly plain-speaking, disgusting without purpose, and singular without result. There are so many evidences of a noble soul in Whitman's pages that we regret these aberrations, which only have the effect of discrediting what is genuine by the show of something false; and especially do we deplore the unnecessary openness with which Walt reveals to us matters which ought rather to remain in sacred silence. It is good not to be ashamed of Nature; it is good to have an all-inclusive charity; but it is also good, sometimes, to leave the veil across the Temple.

From the *Boston Intelligencer*, 3 May 1856

Leaves of Grass, Brooklyn, New York, 1855

We were attracted by the very singular title of the work, to seek the work itself, and what we thought ridiculous in the title is eclipsed in the pages of this heterogeneous mass of bombast, egotism, vulgarity, and nonsense. The beastliness of the author is set forth in his own description of himself, and we can conceive no better reward than the lash for such a violation of decency as we have before us. Speaking of 'this mass of stupid filth', the *Criterion* says: 'It is impossible to imagine how any man's fancy could have conceived it, unless he were possessed of the soul of a sentimental donkey that had died of disappointed love.'

This book should find no place where humanity urges any claim to respect, and the author should be kicked from all decent society as below the level of the brute. There is neither wit nor method in his disjointed babbling, and it seems to us he must be some escaped lunatic, raving in pitiable delirium.

Walt Whitman

An American Primer between 1855 and 1860 (first published in the *Atlantic Monthly*, vol. 93, 1904; edited by Horace Traubel)

Much is said of what is spiritual, and spirituality, in this, that, or the other, – in objects, expressions. For me, I see no object, no expression, no animal, no tree, no art, no book, but I see, from morning to night, and from night to morning, the spiritual. Bodies are all spiritual. All words are spiritual – nothing is more spiritual than words. Whence are they? Along how many thousands and tens of thousands of years have they come? – those eluding, fluid, beautiful, fleshness realities, Mother, Father, Water, Earth, Me, This, Soul, Tongue, House, Fire.

A great observation will detect sameness through all languages, however old, however new, however polished, however rude. As humanity is one under its amazing diversities, language is one under its. The flippant read on some long past age, wonder at its dead costumes [customs?], its amusements, etc.; but the master understands well the old, ever-new, ever-common grounds, below those animal growths, and, between any two ages, any two languages and two humanities, however wide apart in time and space, marks well not the superficial shades of difference, but the mass shades of a joint nature.

In a little while, in the United States, the English language, enriched with contributions from all languages, old and new, will be spoken by a hundred millions of people: perhaps a hundred thousand words ('seventy or eighty thousand words' – Noah Webster).

The Americans are going to be the most fluent and melodious voiced people in the world – and the most perfect users of words. Words follow character, – nativity, independence, individuality.

I see that the time is nigh when the etiquette of salons is to be discharged from that great thing, the renovated English speech in America. The occasions of the English speech in America are immense, profound – stretch over ten thousand vast cities, over through thousands of years, millions of miles of meadows, farms, mountains, men. The occasions of salons are for a coterie, a bon soir or two – involve waiters standing behind chairs, silent, obedient, with backs that can bend and must often bend.

What beauty there is in words. What a lurking curious charm in the sound of some words! Then voices! Five or six times in a lifetime (perhaps not so often) you have heard from men and women such voices, as they spoke the most common word! What can it be that from those few men and women made so much out of the most common word! Geography, shipping, steam, the mint, the electric telegraph, railroads, and so forth, have many strong and beautiful words. Mines – iron works – the sugar plantations of Louisiana – the cotton crop and the rice crop – Illinois wheat – Ohio corn and pork – Maine lumber – all these sprout in hundreds and hundreds of words, all tangible and clean-lived, all having texture and beauty.

To all thoughts of your or any one's mind, – to all yearnings, passions, love, hate, ennui, madness, desperation of men for women, and of women for men, – to all charging and surcharging, – that head which poises itself on your neck and is electric in the body beneath your head, or runs with the blood through your veins, or in those curious incredible miracles you call eyesight or hearing, – to all these, and the like of these, have been made words. Such are the words that are never new and never old.

What a history is folded, folded inward and inward again, in the single word I.

The words of the Body! The words of Parentage! The words of Husband and Wife! The words of Offspring! The word Mother! The word Father!

The words of Behavior are quite numerous. They follow the law; they are courteous, grave, have polish, have a sound of presence, and abash all furniture and shallowness out of their sight.

The words of maternity are all the words that were ever spoken by the mouth of man, the child of woman, – but they are reborn words, and the mouth of the full-sized mother, daughter, wife, amie, does not offend by using any one of them.

Medicine has hundreds of useful and characteristic words – new means of cure – new schools of doctors – the wonderful anatomy of the body – the names of a thousand diseases – surgeon's terms – hydropathy – all that relates to the great organs of the body. The medical art is always grand – nothing affords a nobler scope for superior men and women. It, of course, will never cease to be near man, and add new terms.

Law, Medicine, Religion, the Army, the personnel of the Army and Navy, the Arts, stand on their old stock of words, without increase. In the law is to be noticed a growing impatience with formulas, and with diffuseness, and venerable slang. The personnel of the Army and the Navy exists in America, apart from the throbbing life of America, – an exile in the land, foreign to the instincts and tastes of the people, and, of course, soon in due time to give place to something native, something warmed with throbs of our own life.

These States are rapidly supplying themselves with new words, called for by new occasions, new facts, new politics, new combinations. Far plentier additions will be needed, and, of course, will be supplied.

Because it is a truth that the words continually used among the people are, in numberless cases, not the words used in writing, or recorded in the dictionaries by authority, there are just as many words in daily use, not inscribed in the dictionary, and seldom or never in any print. Also, the forms of grammar are never persistently obeyed, and cannot be.

The Real Dictionary will give all the words that exist in use, the bad words as well as any. The Real Grammar will be that which declares itself a nucleus of the spirit of the laws, with liberty to all to carry out the spirit of the laws, even by violating them, if necessary. The English Language is grandly lawless like the race who use it, – or, rather, breaks out of the little laws to enter truly the higher ones.

It is so instinct with that which underlies laws and the purports of laws it refuses all petty interruptions in its way.

Books themselves have their peculiar words, – namely, those that are never used in living speech in the real world, but only used in the world of books. Nobody ever actually talks as books and plays talk.

The Morning has its words and the Evening has its words. How much there is in the word Light! How vast, surrounding, falling, sleepy, noiseless, is the word Night! It hugs with unfelt yet living arms.

Character makes words. The English stock, full enough of faults, but averse to all foldcrol, equable, instinctively just, latent with pride and melancholy, ready with brawned arms, with free speech, with the knife-blade for tyrants and the reached hand for slaves – have put all these in words. We have them in America, – they are the body of the whole of the past. We are to justify our inheritance, – we are to pass it on to those who are to come after us, a thousand years hence, as we have grown out of the English of a thousand years ago: American geography – the plenteousness and variety of the great nations of the Union – the thousands of settlements – the seacoast – the Canadian North – the Mexican South – California and Oregon – the inland seas – the mountains – Arizona – the prairies – the immense rivers.

Many of the slang words among fighting men, gamblers, thieves, prostitutes, are powerful words. These words ought to be collected, – the bad words as well as the good. Many of these bad words are fine.

Music has many good words, now technical, but of such rich and juicy character that they ought to be taken for common use in writing and speaking.

New forms of science, newer, freer characters, may have something in them to need new words. One beauty of words is exactitude. To me each word out of the — that now compose the English language, has its own meaning, and does not stand for anything but itself – and there are no two words the same any more than there are two persons the same.

Much of America is shown in its newspaper names, and in the names of its steamboats, ships, – names of characteristic amusements and games.

What do you think words are? Do you think words are positive and original things in themselves? No. Words are not original and arbitrary in themselves. Words are a result – they are the progeny of what has been or is in vogue. If iron architecture comes in vogue, as it seems to be coming, words are wanted to stand for all about iron architecture, for the work it causes, for the different branches of work and of the workman – those blocks of buildings, seven stories high, with light, strong façades, and girders that will not crumble a mite in a thousand years.

Also words to describe all American peculiarities, – the splendid and rugged characters that are forming among these states, or are already formed – in the cities, the firemen of Mannahatta, and the target excursionist and Bowery boy – the Boston truckman – the Philadelphian.

In America an immense number of new words are needed to embody the new political facts, the compact of the Declaration of Independence, and of the Constitution – the union of the States – the new States – the Congress – the modes of election – the stump speech – the ways of electioneering – addressing the people – stating all that is to be said in modes that fit the life and experience of the Indianian, the Michiganian, the Vermonter, the men of Maine. Also words to answer the modern, rapidly spreading faith of the vital equality of women with men, and that they are to be placed on an exact plane, politically, socially, and in business, with men. Words are wanted to supply the copious trains of facts, and flanges of facts, arguments, and adjectival facts, growing out of all new knowledges. (Phrenology.)

Drinking brandy, gin, beer, is generally fatal to the perfection of the voice; meanness of mind the same; gluttony in eating of course the same; a thinned habit of body, or a rank habit of body rots the voice. . . . The great Italian singers are above all others in the world from causes quite the same as those that make the voices of native healthy substrata of Mannahatta young men, especially the drivers of horses, and all whose work leads to free loud calling and commanding, have such a ring and freshness.

Pronunciation of Yankees is nasal and offensive – it has the flat tones. It could probably be changed by placing only those teachers in schools who have rich ripe voices – and by the children practicing to speak from the chest and in the guttural and baritone methods. All sorts of physical, moral, and mental deformities are inevitably returned in the voice.

The races that in their realities are supple, obedient, cringing, have hundreds of words to express hundreds of forms of acts, thoughts, flanges, of those realities, which the English language knows nothing of.

The English tongue is full of strong words native or adopted to express the blood-born passion of the race for rudeness and resistance, as against polish and all acts to give in: Robust, brawny, athletic, muscular, acrid, harsh, rugged, severe, pluck, grit, effrontery, stern, resistance, bracing, rude, rugged, rough, shaggy, bearded, arrogant, haughty. These words are alive and sinewy, – they walk, look, step, with an air of command. They will often lead the rest, – they will not follow. How can they follow? They will appear strange in company unlike themselves.

English words. Even people's names were spelt by themselves, sometimes one way, sometimes another. Public necessity remedies all troubles. Now, in the eightieth year of these States, there is a little diversity in the ways of spelling words, and much diversity in the ways of pronouncing them. Steamships, railroads, newspapers, submarine telegraphs, will probably bring them in. If not, it is not important.

So in the accents and inflections of words. Language must cohere – it cannot be left loosely to float or to fly away. Yet all the rules of the accents of and inflections of words drop before a perfect voice – that may follow the rules or be ignorant of them – it is indifferent which. Pronunciation is the stamina of language, – it is language. The noblest pronunciation, in a city or race, marks the noblest city or race, or descendants thereof.

Why are names (words) so mighty? Because facts, ancestry, maternity, faiths, are. Slowly, eternally, inevitably, move the souls of the earth, and names (words) are its (their) signs.

Kosmos words, words of the free expansion of thought, history, chronology, literature, are showing themselves, with foreheads, muscular necks and breasts. These gladden me. I put my arms around them – touch my lips to theirs. The past hundred centuries have confided much to me, yet they mock me, frowning. I think I am done with many of the words of the past hundred centuries. I am mad that their poems, bibles, words, still rule and represent the earth, and are not yet superseded. But why do I say so? I must not, will not, be impatient.

The American city excursions, for military practice, for firing at the target, for all the exercises of health and manhood, – why should not women accompany them? I expect to see the time in Politics, Business, Public Gatherings, Processions, Excitements, when women shall not be divided from men, but shall take their part on the same terms as men. What sort of women have Massachusetts, Ohio, Virginia, Pennsylvania, and the rest, correspondent with what they continually want. Sometimes I have fancied that only from superior, hardy women can rise the future superiorities of these States.

Man's words, for the young men of these States, are all words that have arisen out of the qualities of mastership, going first, brunting danger first, – words to identify a hardy boyhood – knowledge – an erect, sweet, lusty body, without taint – choice and chary of its love-power.

The spelling of words is subordinate. Morbidness for nice spelling and tenacity for or against some one letter or so means dandyism and impotence in literature. Of course the great writers must have digested all these things, – passed lexicons, etymologies, orthographies, through them and extracted the nutriment. Modern taste is for brevity and for ranging words in spelling classes. Probably the words of the English tongue can never be ranged in spelling classes. The phonetic (?) spelling is on natural principles – it has arbitrary forms of letters and combinations of letters for all sounds. It may in time prevail, – it surely will prevail if it is best it should. For many hundred years there was nothing like settled spelling.

A perfect user of words uses things – they exude in power and beauty from him – miracles from his hands – miracles from his mouth – lilies, clouds, sunshine, woman, poured copiously – things whirled like chain-shot rocks, defiance, compulsion, horses, iron, locomotives, the oak, the pine, the keen eye, the hairy breast, the Texan ranger, the Boston truckman, the woman that arouses a man, the man that arouses a woman.

Tavern words, such as have reference to drinking, or the compliments of those who drink, – the names of some three hundred different tavern drinks in one part or another of these States.

Words of all degrees of dislike, from just a tinge, onward or deepward.

Words of approval, admiration, friendship. This is to be said among the young men of these States, that with a wonderful tenacity of friendship, and passionate fondness for their friends, and always a manly readiness to make friends, they yet have remarkably few words of names for the friendly sentiments. They seem to be words that do not thrive here among the muscular classes, where the real quality of friendship is always truly to be found. Also, they are words which the muscular classes, the young men of these States, rarely use and have an aversion for; they never give words to their most ardent friendships.

Words of politics are numerous in these States, and many of them peculiar. The Western States have terms of their own: the President's message – the political meeting – the committees – the resolutions: new vegetables – new trees – new animals.

If success and breed follow camels and dromedaries, that are now just introduced into Texas, to be used for travel and traffic over the vast wilds between the lower Mississippi and the Pacific, a number of new words will also have to be tried after them.

The appetite of the people of these States, in popular speeches and writings, is for unhemmed latitude, coarseness, directness, live epithets, expletives, words of opprobrium, resistance. This I understand because I have the taste myself as large, as largely, as any one. I have pleasure in the use, on fit occasions, of – traitor, coward, liar, shyster, skulk, doughface, trickster, mean cuss, backslider, thief, impotent, lickspittle.

The great writers are often select of their audiences. The greatest writers only are well pleased and at their ease among the unlearned, – are received by common men and women familiarly, do not hold out obscure, but come welcome to table, bed, leisure, by day and night.

A perfect writer would make words sing, dance, kiss, bear children, weep, bleed, rage, stab, steal, fire cannon, steer ships, sack cities, charge with cavalry or infantry, or do anything that man or woman or the natural powers can do.

Latent, in a great user of words, must actually be all passions, crimes, trades, animals, stars, God, sex, the past, might, space, metals, and the like – because these are the words, and he who is not these plays with a foreign tongue, turning helplessly to dictionaries and authorities. How can I tell you? I put many things on record that you will not understand at first, – perhaps not in a year, – but they must be (are to be) understood. The earth, I see, writes with prodigal clear hands all summer, forever, and all winter also, content, and certain to be understood in time. Doubtless, only the greatest user of words himself fully enjoys and understands himself.

Words of names of places are strong, copious, unruly, in the repertoire for the American pens and tongues. The names of these States – the names of Countries, Cities, Rivers, Mountains, Villages, Neighborhoods – borrowed plentifully from each of the languages that graft the English language – or named from some natural peculiarity of water or earth, or some event that happened there – often named from death, from some animal, from some of those subtle analogies that the common people are so quick to perceive. The names in the list of the Post Offices of these States are studies.

What name a city has – what name a State, river, sea, mountain, wood, prairie, has – is no indifferent matter. All aboriginal names sound good. I was asking for something savage and luxuriant, and behold here are the aboriginal names. I see how they are being preserved. They are honest words, – they give the true length, breadth, depth. They all fit. Mississippi! – the word winds with chutes – it rolls a stream three thousand miles long. Ohio, Connecticut, Ottawa, Monongahela, all fit.

Names are magic. One word can pour such a flood through the soul. Today I will mention Christ's before all other names. Grand words of names are still left. What is it that flows through me at the sight of the word Socrates, or Cincinnatus, or Alfred of the olden time – or at the sight of the word Columbus, or Shakespeare, or Rousseau, or Mirabeau – or at the sight of the word Washington, or Jefferson, or Emerson?

Out of Christ are divine words – out of this savior. Some words are fresh smelling, like lilies, roses, to the soul, blooming without failure. The name of Christ – all words that have arisen from the life and death of Christ, the divine son, who went about speaking perfect words, no patois – whose life was perfect, – the touch of whose hands and feet was miracles, – who was crucified, – his flesh laid in a shroud, in the grave.

Words of names of persons, thus far, still return the old continents and races – return the past three thousand years – perhaps twenty thousand – return the Hebrew Bible, Greece, Rome, France, the Goths, the Celts, Scandinavia, Germany, England. Still questions come: what flanges are practicable for names of persons that mean these States? What is there in the best aboriginal names? What is there in strong words of qualities, bodily, mental, – a name given to the cleanest and most beautiful body, or to the offspring of the same? What is there that will conform to the genius of these States, and to all the facts? What escape with perfect freedom, without affectation, from the shoals of Johns, Peters, Davids, Marys? Or on what happy principle, popular and fluent, could other words be prefixed or suffixed to these, to make them show who they are, what land they were born in, what government, which of the States, what genius, mark, blood, times, have coined them with strong-cut coinage?

The subtle charm of beautiful pronunciation is not in dictionaries, grammars, marks of accent, formulas of a language, or in any laws or rules. The charm of the beautiful pronunciation of all words, of all tongues, is in perfect flexible vocal organs, and in a developed harmonious soul. All words, spoken from these, have deeper, sweeter sounds, new meanings, impossible on any less terms. Such meanings, such sounds, continually wait in every word that exists – in these words – perhaps slumbering through years, closed from all tympans of temples, lips, brains, until that comes which has the quality patiently waiting in the words. . . . Likely there are other words wanted. Of words wanted, the matter is summed up in this: When the time comes for them to represent anything or any state of things, the words will surely follow. The lack of any words, I say again, is as historical as the existence of words. As for me, I feel a hundred realities, clearly determined in me, that words are not yet formed to represent. Men like me – also women, our counterparts – perfectly equal – will gradually get to be more and more numerous, – perhaps swiftly, in shoals; then the words will also follow, in shoals. It is the glory and superb rose-hue of the English language, anywhere, that it favors growth as the skin does, that it can soon become, whenever that is needed, the tough skin of a superior man or woman.

The art of the use of words would be a stain, a smutch, but for the stamina of things. For in manners, poems, orations, music, friendship, authorship, what is not said is just as important as what is said, and holds just as much meaning. Fond of men, as a living woman is – fond of women, as a living man is.

I like limber, lasting, fierce words. I like them applied to myself, – and I like them in newspapers, courts, debates, congress. Do you suppose the liberties and the brawn of these States have to do only with delicate lady-words? with gloved gentlemen words? Bad Presidents, bad judges, bad clients, bad editors, owners of slaves, and the long ranks of Northern political suckers (robbers, traitors, suborned), monopolists, infidels, ... shaved persons, supplejacks, ecclesiastics, men not fond of women, women not fond of men, cry down the use of strong, cutting, beautiful, rude words. To the manly instincts of the People they will forever be welcome.

In words of names, the mouth and ear of the people show an antipathy to titles, misters, handles. They love short first names abbreviated to their lips: Tom, Bill, Jack. These are to enter into literature, and be voted for on political tickets for the great offices: Expletives, ... curious words and phrases of assent or inquiry, nicknames either to persons or customs. Many actions, many kinds of character, and many of the fashions of dress have names among two thirds of the people, that would never be understood among the remaining third, and never appear in print.

Factories, mills, and all the processes of hundreds of different manufacturers grow thousands of words. Cotton, woollen, and silk goods, – hemp, rope, carpets, paper-hangings, paints, roofing preparations, hardware, furniture, paper mills, the printing offices with their wonderful improvements, engraving, daguerreotyping.

This is the age of the metal iron. Iron, with all that it does, or that belongs to iron, or flanges from it, results in words: from the mines they have been drawn, as the ore has been drawn. Following the universal laws of words, these are welded together in hardy forms and characters. They are ponderous, strong, definite, not indebted to the antique, – they are iron words, wrought and cast. I see them all good, faithful, massive, permanent words, – I love well these iron words of 1856. Coal has its words also, that assimilate very much with those of iron.

Gold, of course, has always its words. The mint, the American coinage, the dollar piece, the fifty dollar or one hundred dollar piece.

California, the metallic basis of banking, chemical tests of gold, – all these have their words: Canada words, Yankee words, Mannahatta words, Virginia words, Florida and Alabama words, Texas words, Mexican and Nicaraguan words, Ohio, Illinois, and Indiana words.

The different mechanics have different words, – all, however, under a few great over-arching laws. These are carpenter's words, mason's words, blacksmith's words, shoemaker's words, tailor's words, hatter's words, weaver's words, painter's words.

The farmer's words are immense. They are mostly old, partake of ripeness, home, the ground, – have nutriment, like wheat and milk. Farm words are added to, now, by a new class of words, from the introduction of chemistry into farming, and from the introduction of numerous machines into the barn and field.

The nigger dialect furnishes hundreds of *outré* words, many of them adopted into the common speech of the masses of the people. Curiously, these words show the old English instinct for wide open pronunciations, as *yallah* for yellow, – *massah* for master, – and for rounding of all the corners of words. The nigger dialect has hints of the future theory of the modification of all the words of the English language, for musical purposes, for a native grand opera in America, leaving the words just as they are for writing and speaking, but the same words so modified as to answer perfectly for musical purposes, on grand and simple principles. Then we should have two sets of words, male and female as they should be, in these States, both equally understood by the people, giving a fit, much-needed medium to that passion for music which is deeper and purer in America than in any other land in the world. The music of America is to adopt the Italian method, and expand it to vaster, simpler, far superber effects. It is not to be satisfied till it comprehends the people and is comprehended by them.

Sea words, coast words, sloop words, sailor's and boatman's words, words of ships, are numerous in America. One fourth of the people of these States are aquatic, – love the water, love to be near it, smell it, sail on it, swim in it, fish, clam, trade to and fro upon it. To be much on the water, or in constant sight of it, affects words, the voice, the passions. Around the markets, among the fish-smacks, along the wharves, you hear a thousand words, never yet printed in the repertoire of any lexicon, – words, strong words solid as logs, and more beauty to me than any of the antique. . . .

In most instances a characteristic word once used in a poem, speech, or what not, is then exhausted; he who thinks he is going to produce effects by freely using strong words is ignorant of words. One single name belongs to one single place only, – as a keyword of a book may be best used only once in the book. A true composition in words returns the human body, male or female, – that is the most perfect composition, and shall be best beloved by men and women, and shall last the longest, which slights no part of the body, and repeats no part of the body. To make a perfect composition in words is more than to make the best building or machine, or the best statue or picture. It shall be the glory of the greatest masters to make perfect compositions in words.

The plays of Shakespeare and the rest are grand. Our obligations to them are incalculable. Other facts remain to be considered: their foreignness to us in much of their spirit – the sentiment under which they were written, that caste is not to be questioned – that the nobleman is of one blood and the people of another.

Costumes are retrospective – they rise out of the sub-strata of education, equality, ignorance, caste, and the like. A nation that imports its costumes imports deformity. Shall one man be afraid, or one woman be afraid, to dress in a beautiful, decorous, natural, wholesome, inexpensive manner, because many thousands dress in the reverse manner? There is this, also, about costumes, – many save themselves from being exiled, and keep each other in countenance, by being alike foolish, dapper, extravagant. I see that the day is to come very soon in America when there will not be a flat level of costumes.

Probably there is this to be said about the Anglo–Saxon breed, – that in real vocal use it has less of the words of the various phases of friendship and love than any other race, and more friendship and love. The literature, so full of love, is begotten of the old Celtic metrical romances, and of the extravagant lays of those who sang and narrated, in France, and thence in England, – and of Italian extravaganzas, – and all that sighing, vowing, kissing, dying, that was in songs in European literature in the sixteenth century. Still, it seems as if this love sickness engrafted on our literature were only a fair response and enjoyment that people nourish themselves with, after repressing their words. The Americans, like the English, probably make love worse than any other race. Voices follow character, and nothing is better than a superb vocalism. I think this land is covered with the weeds and chaff of literature.

California is sown thick with the names of all the little and big saints. Chase them away and substitute aboriginal names. What is the fitness – what the strange charm – of aboriginal names? Mononga-hela: it rolls with venison richness upon the palate. Among names to be revolutionized: that of the city of 'Baltimore'.

Never will I allude to the English Language or tongue without exultation. This is the tongue that spurns laws, as the greatest tongue must. It is the most capacious vital tongue of all, – full of ease, definiteness, and power, – full of sustenance, – an enormous treasure house, or ranges of treasure houses, arsenals, granary, chock full of so many contributions from the north and from the south, from Scandi-navia, from Greece and Rome – from Spaniards, Italians, and the French – that its own sturdy home-dated Angles-bred words have long been outnumbered by the foreigners whom they lead – which is all good enough, and indeed must be. America owes immeasurable respect and love to the past, and to many ancestries, for many inheritances, – but of all that America has received from the past, from the mothers and fathers of laws, arts, letters, etc., by far the greatest inheritance is the English Language – so long in growing – so fitted.

All the greatness of any land, at any time, lies folded in its names. Would I recall some particular country or age? the most ancient? the greatest? I recall a few names – a mountain or sierra of mountains – a sea or bay – a river – some mighty city – some deed of persons, friends or enemies, – some event, perhaps a great war, perhaps a greater peace – some time-marking and place-marking philosoph, divine person, king, bard, goddess, captain, discoverer, or the like. Thus does history in all things hang around a few names. Thus does all human interest hang around names. All men experience it, but no man ciphers it out.

What is the curious rapport of names? I have been informed that there are people who say it is not important about names, – one word is as good as another if the designation be understood. I say that nothing is more important than names. Is art important? Are forms? Great clusters of nomenclature in a land (needed in American nomenclature) include appropriate names for the months (those now used perpetuate old myths); appropriate names for the days of the week (those now used perpetuate Teutonic and Greek divinities); appropriate names for persons American – men, women, and children; appropriate names for American places, cities, rivers, counties, etc. The word 'country' itself should be changed. Numbering the streets, as a general thing, with a few irresistible exceptions, is very good. No country can have its own poems without it have its own names. The name of Niagara should be substituted for the St Lawrence. Among the places that stand in need of fresh appropriate names are the great cities of St Louis, New Orleans, St Paul.

The whole theory and practice of the naming of college societies must be remade on superior American principles. The old theory and practice of classical education is to give way, and a new race of teachers is to appear. I say we have here, now, a greater age to celebrate, greater ideas to embody, than anything even in Greece or Rome, or in the names of Jupiters, Jehovahs, Apollos, and their myths. The great proper names used in America must commemorate things belonging to America and dating thence. Because, what is America for? To commemorate the old myths and the gods? To repeat the Mediterranean here? Or the uses and growths of Europe here? No (nä-o-o), but to destroy all those from the purposes of the earth, and to erect a new earth in their place.

All lies folded in names. I have heard it said that when the spirit arises that does not brook submission and imitation, it will throw off the ultramarine names. That Spirit already walks the streets of the cities of these States. I, and others, illustrate it. I say that America, too, shall be commemorated, – shall stand rooted in the ground in names, – and shall flow in the water in names, and be diffused in time, in days, in months, in their names. Now the days signify extinct gods and goddesses, – the months half-unknown rites and emperors, – and chronology with the rest is all foreign to America, – all exiles and insults here.

But it is no small thing, – no quick growth; not a matter of ruling out one word and of writing another. Real names never come so easily. The greatest cities, the greatest politics, the greatest physiology and soul, the greatest orators, poets, and literati, – the best women, the freest leading men, the proudest national character, – such, and the like, are indispensable beforehand. Then the greatest names will follow, for they are results, – and there are no greater results in the world.

Names are the turning point of who shall be master. There is so much virtue in names that a nation which produces its own names, haughtily adheres to them, and subordinates others to them, leads all the rest of the nations of the earth. I also promulge that a nation which has not its own names, but begs them of other nations, has no identity, marches not in front, but behind.

Names are a test of the aesthetic and of spirituality. A delicate subtle something there is in the right name – an undemonstrable nourishment – that exhilarates the soul. Masses of men, unaware what they like, lazily inquire what difference there is between one name and another. But the few fine ears of the world decide for them, – the masses being always as eligible as any whether they know it or not. All that immense volumes, and more than volumes, can tell, is conveyed in the right name. The right name of a city, State, town, man, or woman, is a perpetual feast to the aesthetic and musical nature. Take the names of newspapers. What has such a name as the *Ægis*, the *Mercury*, the *Herald*, to do in America?

Californian, Texan, New Mexican, and Arizonian names have the sense of the ecstatic monk, the cloister, the idea of miracles, and of devotees canonized after death. They are the results of the early missionaries and the element of piety in the old Spanish character. They have, in the same connexion, a tinge of melancholy and of a curious freedom from roughness and money-making. Such names stand strangely in California. What do such names know of democracy, – of the hunt for the gold leads and the nugget, or of the religion that is scorn and negation?

American writers are to show far more freedom in the use of words. Ten thousand native idiomatic words are growing, or are to-day already grown, out of which vast numbers could be used by American writers, with meaning and effect, – words that would be welcomed by the nation, being of the national blood, – words that would give that taste of identity and locality which is so dear in literature.

(1160–70)

Henry James

'Mr Walt Whitman', a review of *Drum-Taps*, *The Nation* November
1865

It has been a melancholy task to read this book; and it is a still more
melancholy one to write about it. Perhaps since the day of Mr
Tupper's 'Philosophy' there has been no more difficult reading of the
poetic sort. It exhibits the effort of an essentially prosaic mind to lift
itself, by a prolonged muscular strain, into poetry. Like hundreds of
other good patriots, during the last four years, Mr Walt Whitman has
imagined that a certain amount of violent sympathy with the great
deeds and sufferings of our soldiers, and of admiration for our national
energy, together with a ready command of picturesque language, are
sufficient inspiration for a poet. If this were the case, we had been a
nation of poets. The constant developments of the war moved us
continually to strong feeling and to strong expression of it. But in
those cases in which these expressions were written out and printed
with all due regard to prosody, they failed to make poetry, as any one
may see by consulting now in cold blood the back volumes of the
Rebellion Record. *Of course* the city of Manhattan, as Mr Whitman
delights to call it, when regiments poured through it in the first
months of the war, and its own sole god, to borrow the words of a
real poet, ceased for a while to be the millionaire, was a noble spectacle, and a poetical statement to this effect is possible. *Of course* the
tumult of a battle is grand, the results of a battle tragic, and the
untimely deaths of young men a theme for elegies. But he is not a
poet who merely reiterates these plain facts *ore rotundo*. He only
sings them worthily who views them from a height. Every tragic event
collects about it a number of persons who delight to dwell upon its
superficial points – of minds which are bullied by the *accidents* of the
affair. The temper of such minds seems to us to be the reverse of the
poetic temper; for the poet, although he incidentally masters, grasps,
and uses the superficial traits of his theme, is really a poet only in so
far as he extracts its latent meaning and holds it up to common
eyes. And yet from such minds most of our war-verses have come,
and Mr Whitman's utterances, much as the assertion may surprise his
friends, are in this respect no exception to general fashion. They are

an exception, however, in that they openly pretend to be something better; and this it is that makes them melancholy reading. Mr Whitman is very fond of blowing his own trumpet, and he has made very explicit claims for his book. 'Shut not your doors', he exclaims at the outset –

Shut not your doors to me, proud libraries,
For that which was lacking among you all, yet needed most, I
   bring;
A book I have made for your dear sake, O soldiers,
And for you, O soul of man, and you, love of comrades;
The words of my book nothing, the life of it everything;
A book separate, not link'd with the rest, nor felt by the intellect;
But you will feel every word, O Libertad! arm'd Libertad!
It shall pass by the intellect to swim the sea, the air,
With joy with you, O soul of man.

                  (1865, *Shut Not Your Doors*)

These are great pretensions, but it seems to us that the following are even greater:

From Paumanok starting, I fly like a bird,
Around and around to soar, to sing the idea of all;
To the north betaking myself, to sing there arctic songs,
To Kanada, 'till I absorb Kanada in myself – to Michigan then,
To Wisconsin, Iowa, Minnesota, to sing their songs (they are
   inimitable);
Then to Ohio and Indiana, to sing theirs – to Missouri and Kansas
   and Arkansas to sing theirs,
To Tennessee and Kentucky – to the Carolinas and Georgia, to
   sing theirs,
To Texas, and so along up toward California, to roam accepted
   everywhere;
To sing first (to the tap of the war-drum, if need be)
The idea of all – of the western world, one and inseparable,
And then the song of each member of These states.

                (1865, *From Paumanok Starting I
                Fly Like a Bird*)

Mr Whitman's primary purpose is to celebrate the greatness of our armies; his secondary purpose is to celebrate the greatness of the city of New York. He pursues these objects through a hundred pages of matter which remind us irresistibly of the story of the college professor who, on a venturesome youth's bringing him a theme done in blank verse, reminded him that it was not customary in writing prose to begin each line with a capital. The frequent capitals are the only marks of verse in Mr Whitman's writing. There is, fortunately, but one attempt at rhyme. We say fortunately, for if the inequality of Mr Whitman's lines were self-registering, as it would be in the case of an anticipated syllable at their close, the effect would be painful in the extreme. As the case stands, each line starts off by itself, in resolute independence of its companions, without a visible goal. But if Mr Whitman does not write verse, he does not write ordinary prose. The reader has seen that liberty is 'libertad'. In like manner, comrade is 'camerado', Americans are 'Americanos', a pavement is a 'trottoir', and Mr Whitman himself is a 'chansonnier'. If there is one thing that Mr Whitman is not, it is this, for Béranger was a *chansonnier*. To appreciate the force of our conjunction, the reader should compare his military lyrics with Mr Whitman's declamations. Our author's novelty, however, is not in his words, but in the form of his writing. As we have said, it begins for all the world like verse and turns out to be arrant prose. It is more like Mr Tupper's proverbs than anything we have met. But what if, in form, it *is* prose? it may be asked. Very good poetry has come out of prose before this. To this we would reply that it must first have gone into it. Prose, in order to be good poetry, must first be good prose. As a general principle, we know of no circumstance more likely to impugn a writer's earnestness than the adoption of an anomalous style. He must have something very original to say if none of the old vehicles will carry his thoughts. Of course he *may* be surprisingly original. Still, presumption is against him. If on examination the matter of his discourse proves very valuable, it justifies, or at any rate excuses, his literary innovation.

But if, on the other hand, it is of a common quality, with nothing new about it but its manners, the public will judge the writer harshly. The most that can be said of Mr Whitman's vaticinations is, that, cast in a fluent and familiar manner, the average substance of them might escape unchallenged. But we have seen that Mr Whitman prides himself especially on the substance – the life – of his poetry. It may be rough, it may be grim, it may be clumsy – such we take to be the author's argument – but it is sincere, it is sublime, it appeals to the soul of man, it is the voice of a people. He tells us, in the lines quoted, that the words of his book are nothing. To our perception they are everything, and very little at that. A great deal of verse that is nothing but words has, during the war, been sympathetically sighed over and cut out of newspaper corners, because it has possessed a certain simple melody. But Mr Whitman's verse, we are confident, would have failed even of this triumph, for the simple reason that no triumph, however small, is won but through the exercise of art, and that this volume is an offense against art. It is not enough to be grim and rough and careless; common sense is also necessary, for it is by common sense that we are judged. There exists in even the commonest minds, in literary matters, a certain precise instinct of conservatism, which is very shrewd in detecting wanton eccentricities. To this instinct Mr Whitman's attitude seems monstrous. It is monstrous because it pretends to persuade the soul while it slights the intellect; because it pretends to gratify the feelings while it outrages the taste. The point is that it does this *on theory*, wilfully, consciously, arrogantly. It is the little nursery game of 'open your mouth and shut your eyes'. Our hearts are often touched through a compromise with the artistic sense, but never in direct violation of it. Mr Whitman sits down at the outset and counts out the intelligence. This were indeed a wise precaution on his part if the intelligence were only submissive! But when she is deliberately insulted, she takes her revenge by simply standing erect and open-eyed. This is assuredly the best she can do. And if she could find a voice she would probably address Mr Whitman as follows: 'You came to woo my sister, the human soul. Instead of giving me a kick as you approach, you should either greet me courteously, or, at least, steal in unobserved. But now you have me on your hands. Your chances are poor. What the human heart desires above all is sincerity, and you do not appear to me sincere. For a lover you talk entirely too much about yourself. In one place you threaten to absorb Kanada. In another you call upon the city of New York to incarnate you, as you have incarnated it. In another you inform us that neither youth pertains to you nor "delicatesse", that you are awkward in the parlor, that you do not dance, and that you have neither bearing, beauty, knowledge, nor fortune. In another place, by an allusion to your "little songs", you seem to identify yourself with the third person of the Trinity. For a poet who claims to sing "the idea of all", this is tolerably egotistical. We look in vain, however, through your book for a single idea. We find nothing but flashy imitations of ideas. We find a medley of extravagances and commonplaces. We find art, measure, grace, sense sneered at on every page, and nothing positive given us in their stead. To be positive one must have something to say; to be positive requires reason, labor, and art; and art requires, above all things, a suppression of one's self, a subordination of one's self to an idea. This will never do for you, whose plan is to adapt the scheme of the universe to your own limitations. You cannot entertain and exhibit ideas; but, as we have seen, you are prepared to incarnate them. It is for this reason, doubtless, that when once you have planted yourself squarely before the public, and in view of the great service you have done to the ideal, have become, as you say, "accepted everywhere", you can afford to deal exclusively in words. What would be bald nonsense and dreary platitudes in any one else becomes sublimity in you. But all this is a mistake. To become adopted as a national poet, it is not enough to discard everything in particular and to accept everything in general, to amass crudity upon crudity, to discharge the undigested contents of your blotting-book into the lap of the public. You must respect the public which you address; for it has taste, if you have not. It delights in the grand, the heroic, and the masculine; but it delights to see these conceptions cast into worthy form. It is indifferent to brute sublimity. It will never do for you to thrust your hands into your pockets and cry out that, as the research of form is an intolerable bore, the shortest and most economical way for the public to embrace its idols – for the nation to realize its genius – is in your own person. This democratic, liberty-loving, American populace, this stern and war-tried people, is a great civilizer. It is devoted to refinement. If it has sustained a monstrous war, and practised human nature's best in so many ways for the last five years, it is not to put up with spurious poetry afterwards. To sing aright our battles and our glories it is not enough to have served in a hospital (however praiseworthy the task in itself), to be aggressively careless, inelegant, and ignorant, and to be constantly preoccupied with yourself. It is not enough to be rude, lugubrious, and grim. You must also be serious. You must forget yourself in your ideas. Your personal qualities – the vigor of your temperament, the manly independence of your nature, the tenderness of your heart – these facts are impertinent. You must be *possessed*, and you must strive to possess your possession. If in your striving you break into divine eloquence, then you are a poet. If the idea which possesses you is the idea of your country's greatness, then you are a national poet; and not otherwise.'

(625–6)

William Dean Howells

Review of *Drum-Taps*, *The Round Table* November 1865

Will saltpeter explode? Is Walt Whitman a true poet? Doubts to be solved by the wise futurity which shall pay off our national debt. Poet or not, however, there was that in Walt Whitman's first book which compels attention to his second. There are obvious differences between the two: this is much smaller than that; and whereas you had at times to hold your nose (as a great sage observed) in reading *Leaves of Grass*, there is not an indecent thing in *Drum-Taps*. The artistic method of the poet remains, however, the same, and we must think it mistaken. The trouble about it is that it does not give you sensation in a portable shape; the thought is as intangible as aroma; it is no more put up than the atmosphere.

We are to suppose that Mr Whitman first adopted his method as something that came to him of its own motion. This is the best possible reason, and only possible excuse, for it. In its way, it is quite as artificial as that of any other poet, while it is unspeakably inartistic. On this account it is a failure. The method of talking to one's self in rhythmic and ecstatic prose is one that surprises at first, but, in the end, the talker can only have the devil for a listener, as happens in other cases when people address their own individualities; not, however, the devil of the proverb, but the devil of reasonless, hopeless, all-defying egotism. An ingenious French critic said very acutely of Mr Whitman that he made you partner of the poetical enterprise, which is perfectly true; but no one wants to share the enterprise. We want its effect, its success; we do not want to plant corn, to hoe it, to drive the crows away, to gather it, husk it, grind it, sift it, bake it, and butter it, before eating it, and then take the risk of its being at last moldy in our mouths. And this is what you have to do in reading Mr Whitman's rhythm.

At first, a favorable impression is made by the lawlessness of this poet, and one asks himself if this is not the form which the unconscious poetry of American life would take, if it could find a general utterance. But there is really no evidence that such is the case. It is certain that among the rudest peoples the lurking sublimity of nature has always sought expression in artistic form, and there is no good reason to believe that the sentiment of a people with our high average culture would seek expression more rude and formless than that of the savagest tribes. Is it not more probable that, if the passional principle of American life could find utterance, it would choose the highest, least dubious, most articulate speech? Could the finest, most shapely expression be too good for it?

If we are to judge the worth of Mr Whitman's poetic theory (or impulse, or possession) by its popular success, we must confess that he is wrong. It is already many years since he first appeared with his claim of poet, and in that time he has employed criticism as much as any literary man in our country, and he has enjoyed the fructifying extremes of blame and praise. Yet he is, perhaps, less known to the popular mind, to which he has attempted to give an utterance, than the newest growth of the magazines and the newspaper notices. The people fairly rejected his former revelation, letter and spirit, and those who enjoyed it were readers with a cultivated taste for the quaint and the outlandish. The time to denounce or to ridicule Mr Whitman for his first book is past. The case of *Leaves of Grass* was long ago taken out the hands of counsel and referred to the great jury. They have pronounced no audible verdict; but what does their silence mean? There were reasons in the preponderant beastliness of that book why a decent public should reject it; but now the poet has cleansed the old channels of their filth, and pours through them a stream of blameless purity, and the public has again to decide, and this time more directly, on the question of his poethood. As we said, his method remains the same, and he himself declares that, so far as concerns it, he has not changed nor grown in any way since we saw him last:

Beginning my studies, the first step pleased me so much,
The mere fact, consciousness – these forms – the power of
  motion,
The least insect or animal – the senses – eye-sight;
The first step, I say, aw'd me and pleas'd me so much,
I have never gone, and never wish'd to go, any further,
But stop and loiter all my life to sing it in ecstatic songs.

(1865, Beginning my Studies)

Mr Whitman has summed up his own poetical theory so well in these lines, that no criticism could possibly have done it better. It makes us doubt, indeed, if all we have said in consideration of him has not been said idly, and certainly releases us from further explanation of his method.

In *Drum-Taps*, there is far more equality than in *Leaves of Grass*, and though the poet is not the least changed in purpose, he is certainly changed in fact. The pieces of the new book are nearly all very brief, but generally his expression is freer and fuller than ever before. The reader understands, doubtless, from the title, that nearly all these pieces relate to the war; and they celebrate many of the experiences of the author in the noble part he took in the war. One imagines the burly tenderness of the man who went to supply the

– lack of woman's nursing

that there was in the hospitals of the field, and woman's tears creep unconsciously to the eyes as the pity of his heart communicates itself to his reader's. No doubt the pathos of many of the poems gains something from the quaintness of the poet's speech. One is touched in reading them by the same inarticulate feeling as that which dwells in music; and is sensible that the poet conveys to the heart certain emotions which the brain cannot analyse, and only remotely perceives. This is especially true of his inspirations from nature; memories and yearnings come to you folded, mute, and motionless in his verse, as they come in the breath of a familiar perfume. They give a strange, shadowy sort of pleasure, but they do not satisfy, and you rise from the perusal of this man's book as you issue from the presence of one whose personal magnetism is very subtle and strong, but who has not added to this tacit attraction the charm of spoken ideas. We must not mistake this fascination for a higher quality. In the tender eyes of an ox lurks a melancholy, soft and pleasing to the glance as the pensive sweetness of a woman's eyes; but in the orb of the brute there is no hope of expression, and in the woman's look there is the endless delight of history, the heavenly possibility of utterance.

Art cannot greatly employ itself with things in embryo. The instinct of the beast may interest science; but poetry, which is nobler than science, must concern itself with natural instincts only as they can be developed into the sentiments and ideas of the soul of man. The mind will absorb from nature all that is speechless in her influences; and it will demand from kindred mind those higher things which can be spoken. Let us say our say here against the nonsense, long current, that there is, or can be, poetry *between the lines*, as is often sillily asserted. *Expression* will always suggest; but mere *suggestion* in art is unworthy of existence, vexes the heart, and shall not live. Every man has tender, and beautiful, and lofty emotions; but the poet was sent into this world to give these a tangible utterance, and if he do not this, but only give us back dumb emotion for dumb emotion, he is a cumberer of the earth. There is a yearning, almost to agony at times, in the human heart, to throw off the burden of inarticulate feeling, and if the poet will not help it in this effort, if, on the contrary, he shall seek to weigh it and sink it down under heavier burdens, he has not any reason to be.

So long, then, as Mr Whitman chooses to stop at mere consciousness, he cannot be called a true poet. We all have consciousness; but we ask of art an utterance. We do not so much care in what way we get this expression; we will take it in ecstatic prose, though we think it is better subjected to the laws of prosody, since every good thing is subject to some law; but the expression we must have. Often, in spite of himself, Mr Whitman grants it in this volume, and there is some hope that he will hereafter grant it more and more. There are such rich possibilities in the man that it is lamentable to contemplate his error of theory. He has truly and thoroughly absorbed the idea of our American life, and we say to him as he says to himself, 'You've got enough in you, Walt; why don't you get it out?' A man's greatness is good for nothing folded up in him, and if emitted in barbaric yawps, it is not more filling than Ossian or the east wind.

(147–8)

Matthew Arnold

from a letter to W. D. O'Connor 16 September 1866

As to the general question of Mr Walt Whitman's poetical achievement, you will think that it savours of our decrepit old Europe when
I add that while you think it is his highest merit that he is so unlike
anyone else, to me this seems to be his demerit; no one can afford in
literature to trade merely on his own bottom and to take no account
of what the other ages and nations have acquired: a great original
literature America will never get in this way, and her intellect must
inevitably consent to come, in a considerable measure, into the
European movement. That she may do this and yet be an independent
intellectual power, not merely as you say an intellectual colony of
Europe, I cannot doubt; and it is on her doing this, and not on her
displaying an eccentric and violent originality that wise Americans
should in my opinion set their desires.

John Burroughs

from a review of *Drum-Taps*, *Galaxy* December 1866

The poem [*When Lilacs Last in the Dooryard Bloom'd*] may disappoint
on the first perusal. The treatment of the subject is so unusual – so
unlike the direct and prosy style to which our ears have been educated
– that it seems to want method and purpose. It eludes one; it hovers
and hovers and will not be seized by the mind, though the soul feels
it. But it presently appears that this is precisely the end contemplated by the poet. He would give as far as possible the analogy of
music, knowing that in that exalted condition of the sentiments at the
presence of death in a manner so overwhelming, the mere facts or
statistics of the matter are lost sight of, and that it is not a narrative
of the great man's death, done into rhyme, however faultless, or an
eulogy upon his character, however just and discriminating, that
offers an opportunity for the display of the highest poetic art, or that
would be the most fitting performance of an occasion so august and
solemn. Hence the piece has little or none of the character of the usual

productions on such occasions. It is dramatic, yet there is no procession of events or development of plot, but a constant interplay – a turning and re-turning of images and sentiments, so that the section in which is narrated how the great shadow fell upon the land occurs far along in the piece. It is a poem that may be slow in making admirers, yet it is well worth the careful study of every student of literature. . . .

The gravity and seriousness of this book and its primitive untaught ways are entirely new in modern literature. With all our profuse sentimentalism, there is no deep human solemnity – the solemnity of a strong, earnest, affectionate, unconventional man – in our literature. There are pathos and tears and weeds of mourning; but we would indicate an attitude or habit of the soul which is not expressed by melancholy – which is no sudden burst, or fit, or spasm – which is not inconsistent with cheerfulness and good nature, but which is always coupled with these – a state or condition induced by large perceptions, faith, and deep human sympathies. It may be further characterized as impatient of trifles and dallyings, tires even of wit and smartness, dislikes garrulity and fiction and all play upon words, and is but one remove from silence itself. The plainness and simplicity of the biblical writers afford the best example.

Contemplation, without love or sympathy, of the foibles, follies, and fashions of men and women and of their weaknesses and oddities begets the punning, scoffing, caricaturing habit we deprecate; contemplation of the laws and movements of society, the shows and processes of nature and the issues of life and death, begets the rugged faith and sweet solemnity we would describe in *Drum-Taps*.

The reader perceives that the quality of these poems is not in any word, or epithet, or metaphor, or verbal and labial felicity whatever; but in the several atmospheres they breathe and exhale. The poet does not aim to load his pages with sweets – he makes no bouquets, distils no perfumes – whatever flower-scents there are, are lost in a smell as of the earth, the shore, the woods. Fine writing, with him, goes for naught. He seeks neither to please nor startle, nor even convince, any more than nature does; and beauty follows, if at all, never as the aim, always as the result. There are none of the generally sought for, and, when found, much applauded, delicate fancies or poetical themes – but a large and loving absorption of whatever the earth holds. And this leads us to our final remark upon this subject, in making which we mean discredit to none.

It seems to us that Walt Whitman possesses almost in excess, a quality in which every current poet is lacking. We mean the faculty of being in entire sympathy with nature, and the objects and shows of nature, and of rude, abysmal man; and appalling directness of utterance therefrom, without any intermediate agency or modification.

The influence of books and works of art upon an author may be seen in all respectable writers. If knowledge alone made literature, or culture genius, there would be no dearth of these things among the moderns. But we feel bound to say that there is something higher and deeper than the influence or perusal of any or all books, or all other productions of genius – a quality of information which the masters can never impart, and which all the libraries do not hold. This is the absorption by an author, previous to becoming so, of the spirit of nature, through the visible objects of the universe, and his affiliation with them subjectively and objectively. The calm, all-permitting, wordless spirit of nature yet so eloquent to him who hath ears to hear! The sunrise, the heaving sea, the woods and mountains, the storm and the whistling winds, the gentle Summer day, the Winter sights and sounds, the night and the high dome of stars – to have really perused these, especially from childhood onward, till what there is in them so impossible to define finds its full mate and echo in the mind – his only is the lore which breathes the breath of life into all the rest. Without it, literary productions may have the superb beauty of statues, but with it only can they have the beauty of life.

(613–15)

Algernon Charles Swinburne

from *Under the Microscope* 1872

Effeminate therefore I suppose the modern poetry of England must be content to remain; but there is a poet alive of now acknowledged eminence, not hitherto assailed on this hand, about whom the masked or barefaced critics of the minute are not by any means of one mind –

if mind we are to call the organ which forms and produces their opinions. To me it seems that the truth for good and evil has never yet been spoken about Walt Whitman. There are in him two distinct men of most inharmonious kinds; a poet and a formalist. Of the poet I have before now done the best I could to express, whether in verse or prose, my ardent and sympathetic admiration. Of the formalist I shall here say what I think; showing why (for example) I cannot for my own part share in full the fiery partisanship of such thoughtful and eloquent disciples as Mr Rossetti and Dr Burroughs. It is from no love of foolish paradox that I have chosen the word 'formalist' to express my sense of the radical fault in the noble genius of Whitman. For truly no scholar and servant of the past, reared on academic tradition under the wing of old-world culture, was ever more closely bound in with his own theories, more rigidly regulated by his own formularies, than this poet of new life and limitless democracy. Not Pope, not Boileau, was more fatally a formalist than Whitman; only Whitman is a poet of a greater nature than they. It is simply that these undigested formulas which choke by fits the free passage of his genius are to us less familiar than theirs; less real or less evident they are not. Throughout his great book, now of late so nobly completed, you can always tell at first hearing whether it be the poet who speaks or the formalist. Sometimes in the course of two lines the note is changed, either by the collapse of the poet's voice into the tuneless twang of the formalist, or by the sudden break and rise of released music from the formalist's droning note into the clear sincere harmonies of the poet. Sometimes for one whole division of the work either the formalist intones throughout as to order, or the poet sings high and true and strong without default from end to end. It is of no matter whatever, though both disciples and detractors appear to assume that it must be at least in each other's eyes, whether the subject treated be conventionally high or low, pleasant or unpleasant. At once and without fail you can hear whether the utterance of the subject be right or wrong; this is the one thing needful; but then this one thing is needful indeed. Disciples and detractors alike seem to assume that if you object to certain work of Whitman's it must be because you object to his choice of topic and would object equally to any man's choice or treatment of it; if you approve, it must be that you approve of the choice of topic and would approve equally of any

poem that should start for the same end and run on the same lines. It
is not so in the least. Let a man come forward as does Whitman with
prelude of promise that he is about to sing and celebrate certain things,
fair or foul, great or small, these being as good stuff for song and
celebration as other things, we wait, admitting that, to hear if he will
indeed celebrate and sing them. If he does, and does it well and duly,
there is an end; *solvitur ambulando*; the matter is settled once for all by
the invaluable and indispensable proof of the pudding. Now whenever
the pure poet in Whitman speaks, it is settled by that proof in his
favour; whenever the mere theorist in him speaks, it is settled by the
same proof against him. What comes forth out of the abundance of his
heart rises at once from that high heart to the lips on which its thoughts
take fire, and the music which rolls from them rings true as fine gold
and perfect; what comes forth by the dictation of doctrinal theory
serves only to twist aside his hand and make the written notes run
foolishly awry. What he says is well said when he speaks as of himself
and because he cannot choose but speak; whether he speak of a small
bird's loss or a great man's death, of a nation rising for battle or a
child going forth in the morning. What he says is not well said when
he speaks not as though he must but as though he ought; as though
it behoved one who would be the poet of American democracy to do
this thing or to be that thing if the duties of that office were to be
properly fulfilled, the tenets of that religion worthily delivered. Never
before was high poetry so puddled and adulterated with mere doctrine
in its crudest form. Never was there less assimilation of the lower
dogmatic with the higher prophetic element. It so happens that the
present writer (*si quid id est*) is, as far as he knows, entirely at one with
Whitman on general matters not less than on political; if there be in
Whitman's works any opinion expressed on outward and social or
inward and spiritual subjects which would clash or contend with his
own, or with which he would feel his own to be incapable of concord
or sympathy, he has yet to find the passage in which that opinion is
embodied. To him the views of life and of death set forth by Whitman appear thoroughly acceptable and noble, perfectly credible and
sane. It is certainly therefore from no prejudice against the doctrines
delivered that he objects in any case to the delivery of them. What he
objects – to take two small instances – is that it is one thing to sing the
song of all trades, and quite another thing to tumble down together

the names of all possible crafts and implements in one unsorted heap; to sing the song of all countries is not simply to fling out on the page at random in one howling mass the titles of all divisions of the earth, and so leave them. At this rate, to sing the song of the language it should suffice to bellow out backwards and forwards the twenty-four letters of the alphabet. And this folly is deliberately done by a great writer, and ingeniously defended by able writers, alike in good faith, and alike in blind bondage to mere dogmatic theory, to the mere formation of foregone opinion. They cannot see that formalism need not by any means be identical with tradition: they cannot see that because theories of the present are not inherited they do not on that account become more proper than were theories of the past to suffice of themselves for poetic or prophetic speech. Whether you have to deliver an old or a brand-new creed, alike in either case you must first insure that it be delivered well; for in neither will it suffice you to deliver it simply in good faith and good intent. The poet of democracy must sing all things alike? let him sing them then, whether in rhyme or not is no matter, but in rhythm he must needs sing them. What is true of all poets is among them all most markedly true of Whitman, that his manner and his matter grow together; that where you catch a note of discord there you will find something wrong inly, the natural source of that outer wrongdoing; wherever you catch a note of good music you will surely find it came whence only it could come, from some true root of music in the thought or thing spoken. There never was and will never be a poet who had verbal harmony and nothing else; if there was in him no inner depth or strength or truth, then that which men took for music in his mere speech was no such thing as music.

By far the finest and truest thing yet said of Walt Whitman has been said by himself, and said worthily of a great man. 'I perceive in clear moments,' he said to his friend Dr Burroughs, 'that my work is not the accomplishment of perfections, but destined, I hope, always to arouse an unquenchable feeling and ardour for them.' A hope, surely, as well grounded as it is noble. But it is in those parts of his work which most arouse this feeling and this ardour that we find him nearest that accomplishment. At such times his speech has a majestic harmony which hurts us by no imperfection; his music then is absolutely great and good. It is when he is thinking of his part, of the duties and properties of a representative poet, an official democrat, that the strength forsakes his hand and the music ceases at his lips. It is then that he sets himself to define what books, and to what purpose, the scriptural code of democracy must accept and reject; to determine, Pope himself and council in one, what shall be the canons and articles of the church, which except a democrat do keep whole and undefiled, without doubt he shall perish everlastingly. With more than Athanasian assurance, with more than Calvinistic rigour, it is then that he pronounces what things are democratic and of good report, what things are feudal and of evil report, in all past literature of the world. There is much in these canonical decrees that is consonant with truth and reason; there is not a little that is simply the babbling of a preacher made drunk with his own doctrine. For instance, we find that 'the Democratic requirements' substantially and curiously fulfilled in the best Spanish literature are not only not fulfilled in the best English literature, but are insulted in every page. After this it appears to us that in common consistency the best remaining type of actual democracy in Europe here must be sought among French or Austrian Legitimists, if not on some imperial Russian or German throne. But Shakespeare is not only 'the tally of Feudalism', he is 'incarnated, uncompromising Feudalism in literature.' Now Shakespeare has doubtless done work which is purely aristocratic in tone. The supreme embodiment in poetic form of the aristocratic idea is *Coriolanus*. I cannot at all accept the very good special pleading of M. François-Victor Hugo against this the natural view of that great tragedy. Whether we like it or not, the fact seems to me undeniable that Shakespeare has here used all his art and might to subdue the many to the one, to degrade the figure of the people, to enhance and exalt the figure of the people's enemy. Even here, though, he has not done as in Whitman's view he does always; he has not left without shades the radiant figure, he has not left the sombre figure without lights; there are blemishes here and there on the towering glory of Coriolanus, redeeming points now and then in the grovelling ignominy of the commons. But what if there were none? Is this play the keynote of Shakespeare's mind, the keystone of his work? If the word Democracy mean anything – and to Whitman it means much – beyond the mere profession of a certain creed, the mere iteration of a certain shibboleth; if it signify first the cyclic life and truth of equal and various humanity, and secondly the form of principles and relations, the code of duties and of rights, by which alone adult society can walk straight; surely in the first and greatest sense there has never been and never can be a book so infinitely democratic as the Plays of Shakespeare.

These among others are reasons why I think it foolish to talk of Whitman as the probable founder of a future school of poetry unlike any other in matter as in style. He has many of the qualities of a re-former; he has perhaps none of the qualities of a founder. For one thing, he is far too didactic to be typical; the prophet in him too frequently subsides into the lecturer. He is not one of the everlasting models; but as an original and individual poet, it is at his best hardly possible to overrate him; as an informing and reforming element, it is absolutely impossible. Never did a country need more than America such an influence as his. We may understand and even approve his reproachful and scornful fear of the overweening 'British element' when we see what it has hitherto signified in the literature of his country. Once as yet, and once only, has there sounded out of it all one pure note of original song – worth singing, and echoed from the singing of no other man; a note of song neither wide nor deep, but utterly true, rich, clear, and native to the singer; the short exqui-site music, subtle and simple and sombre and sweet, of Edgar Poe. All the rest that is not of mocking-birds is of corncrakes, varied but at best for an instant by some scant-winded twitter of linnet or of wren.

(45–55)

Walt Whitman

'Nature and Democracy – Morality', *Specimen Days and Collect* 1882

Democracy most of all affiliates with the open air, is sunny and hardy and sane only with Nature – just as much as Art is. Something is required to temper both – to check them, restrain them from excess, morbidity. I have wanted, before departure to bear special testimony to a very old lesson and requisite. American Democracy, in its myriad personalities, in factories, work-shops, stores, offices – through the dense streets and houses of cities, and all their manifold sophisticated life – must either be fibred, vitalized, by regular contact with outdoor light and air and growths, farm-scenes, animals, fields, trees, birds, sun-warmth and free skies, or it will certainly dwindle and pale. We cannot have grand races of mechanics, work people, and com-monalty, (the only specific purpose of America,) on any less terms. I conceive of no flourishing and heroic elements of Democracy in the United States, or of Democracy maintaining itself at all, without the Nature-element forming a main part – to be its health-element and beauty-element – to really underlie the whole politics, sanity, religion and art of the New World.

Finally, the morality: 'Virtue,' said Marcus Aurelius, 'what is it, only a living and enthusiastic sympathy with Nature?' Perhaps in-deed the efforts of the true poets, founders, religions, literatures, all ages, have been, and ever will be, our time and times to come, essentially the same – to bring people back from their persistent strayings and sickly abstractions, to the costless average, divine, original concrete.

(200)

Walt Whitman

'Ventures, on an Old Theme : Notes Left Over', *Specimen Days and Collect* 1882

NEW POETRY – *California, Canada, Texas* – In my opinion the time has arrived to essentially break down the barriers of form between prose and poetry. I say the latter is henceforth to win and maintain its character regardless of rhyme, and the measurement-rules of iambic, spondee, dactyl, etc., and that even if rhyme and those measurements continue to furnish the medium for inferior writers and themes, (especially for persiflage and the comic, as there seems henceforward, to the perfect taste, something inevitably comic in rhyme, merely in itself, and anyhow,) the truest and greatest *Poetry*, (while subtly and necessarily always rhythmic, and distinguishable easily enough,) can never again, in the English language, be expressed in arbitrary and rhyming metre, any more than the greatest eloquence, or the truest power and passion. While admitting that the venerable and heavenly forms of chiming versification have in their time played great and fitting parts – that the pensive complaint, the ballads, wars, amours, legends of Europe, etc., have, many of them, been inimitably rendered in rhyming verse – that there have been very illustrious poets whose shapes the mantle of such verse has beautifully and appropriately enveloped – and though the mantle has fallen, with perhaps added beauty, on some of our own age – it is, notwithstanding, certain to me, that the day of such conventional rhyme is ended. In America, at any rate, and as a medium of highest aesthetic practical or spiritual expression, present or future, it palpably fails, and must fail, to serve. The Muse of the Prairies, of California, Canada, Texas, and of the peaks of Colorado, dismissing the literary, as well as social etiquette of oversea feudalism and caste, joyfully enlarging, adapting itself to comprehend the size of the whole people, with the free play, emotions, pride, passions, experiences, that belong to them, body and soul – to the general globe, and all its relations in astronomy, as the savans portray them to us – to the modern, the busy nineteenth century, (as grandly poetic as any, only different,) with steamships, railroads, factories, electric telegraphs, cylinder presses – to the thought of the solidarity of nations, the brotherhood and sisterhood of the entire earth – to the dignity and heroism of the practical labor of farms, factories, foundries, workshops, mines, or on shipboard, or on lakes and rivers – resumes that other medium of expression, more flexible, more eligible – soars to the freer, vast, diviner heaven of prose.

Of poems of the third or fourth class, (perhaps even some of the second), it makes little or no difference who writes them – they are good enough for what they are; nor is it necessary that they should be actual emanations from the personality and life of the writers. The very reverse sometimes gives piquancy. But poems of the first class, (poems of the depth, as distinguished from those of the surface,) are to be sternly tallied with the poets themselves, and tried by them and their lives. Who wants a glorification of courage and manly defiance from a coward or a sneak? – a ballad of benevolence or chastity from some rhyming hunks, or lascivious, glib *roué*?

In these States, beyond all precedent, poetry will have to do with actual facts, with the concrete States, and – for we have not much more than begun – with the definitive getting into shape of the Union. Indeed I sometimes think *it* alone is to define the Union, (namely, to give it artistic character, spirituality, dignity). What American humanity is most in danger of is an overwhelming prosperity, 'business' worldliness, materialism: what is most lacking, east, west, north, south, is a fervid and glowing Nationality and patriotism, cohering all the parts into one. Who may fend that danger, and fill that lack in the future, but a class of loftiest poets?

If the United States havn't grown poets on any scale of grandeur, it is certain they import, print, and read more poetry than any equal number of people elsewhere – probably more than all the rest of the world combined.

Poetry (like a grand personality) is a growth of many generations – many rare combinations.

To have great poets, there must be great audiences, too.

(322–4)

Gerard Manley Hopkins

Letter to Robert Bridges   18 October 1882

Stonyhurst College, Blackburn

Dearest Bridges,

I have read of Whitman's (1) 'Pete' [*Come up from the Fields, Father*] in the library at Bedford Square (and perhaps something else; if so I forget), which you pointed out; (2) two pieces in the *Athenaeum* or *Academy*, one on the Man-of-War Bird, the other beginning 'Spirit that formed this scene'; (3) short extracts in a review by Saintsbury in the *Academy*: this is all I remember. I cannot have read more than a half dozen pieces at most.

This, though very little, is quite enough to give a strong impression of his marked and original manner and way of thought and in particular of his rhythm. It might be even enough, I shall not deny, to originate or, much more, influence another's style: they say the French trace their whole modern school of landscape to a single piece of Constable's exhibited at the Salon early this century.

The question then is only about the fact. But first I may as well say what I should not otherwise have said, that I always knew in my heart Walt Whitman's mind to be more like my own than any other man's living. As he is a very great scoundrel this is not a pleasant confession. And this also makes me the more desirous to read him and the more determined that I will not.

Nevertheless I believe that you are quite mistaken about this piece and that on second thoughts you will find the fancied resemblance diminish and the imitation disappear.

And first of the rhythm. Of course I saw that there was to the eye something in my long lines like this, that the one would remind people of the other. And both are in irregular rhythms. There the likeness ends. The pieces of his I read were mostly in an irregular rhythmic prose: that is what they are thought to be meant for and what they seemed to me to be. Here is a fragment of a line I remember: 'or a handkerchief designedly dropped'. This is in a dactylic rhythm – or let us say anapaestic; for it is a great convenience in English to assume that the stress is always at the end of the foot; the consequence of which assumption is that in ordinary verse there are only two English feet possible, the iamb and the anapaest, and even in my regular sprung rhythm only one additional, the fourth paeon: for convenience' sake assuming this, then the above fragment is ana-paestic –

'or a hánd | kerchief . . . | . design | edly drópped'

– and there is a break down, a designed break of rhythm, after 'hand-kerchief', done no doubt that the line may not become downright verse, as it would be if he had said 'or a handkerchief purposedly dropped'. Now you can of course say that he meant pure verse and that the foot is a paeon –

'or a hánd | kerchief design | edly drópped';

or that he means, without fuss, what I should achieve by looping the syllable *de* and calling that foot an outriding foot – for the result might be attained either way. Here then I must make the answer which will apply here and to all like cases and to the examples which may be found up and down the poets of the use of sprung rhythm – *if they could have done it they would*: sprung rhythm, once you hear it, is so eminently natural a thing and so effective a thing that if they had known of it they would have used it. Many people, as we say, have been 'burning', but they all missed it; they took it up and mislaid it again. So far as I know – I am inquiring and presently I shall be able to speak more decidedly – it existed in full force in Anglo-Saxon verse and in great beauty; in a degraded and doggrel shape in *Piers Ploughman* (I am reading that famous poem and am coming to the conclusion that it is not worth reading); Greene was the last who employed it at all consciously and he never continuously; then it disappeared – for one cadence in it here and there is not sprung rhythm and one swallow does not make a spring. (I put aside Milton's case, for it is altogether singular.) In a matter like this a thing does not exist, is not *done* unless it is wittingly and willingly done; to recognize the form you are employing and to mean it is everything. To apply this: there is (I suppose, but you will know) no sign that Whitman means to use paeons or outriding feet where these breaks in rhythm occur; it seems to me a mere extravagance to think he means people to understand of themselves what they are slow to understand even when marked or pointed out. If he does not mean it then he does not do it; or in short what he means to write – and writes – is rhythmic prose and that only. And after all, you probably grant this.

Good. Now prose rhythm in English is always one of two things (allowing my convention about scanning upwards or from slack to stress and not from stress to slack) – either iambic or anapaestic. You may make a third measure (let us call it) by intermixing them. One of these three simple measures then, all iambic or all anapaestic or mingled iambic and anapaestic, is what he in every case means to write. He dreams of no other and he *means* a rugged or, as he calls it in that very piece 'Spirit that formed this scene' (which is very instructive and should be read on this very subject), a 'savage' art and rhythm.

Extremes meet, and (I must for truth's sake say what sounds pride) this savagery of his art, this rhythm in its last ruggedness and decomposition into common prose, comes near the last elaboration of mine. For that piece of mine is very highly wrought. The long lines are not rhythm run to seed: everything is weighed and timed in them. Wait till they have taken hold of your ear and you will find it so. No, but what it *is* like is the rhythm of Greek tragic choruses or of Pindar: which is pure sprung rhythm. And that has the same changes of cadence from point to point as this piece. If you want to try it, read one till you have settled the true places of the stress, mark these, then read it aloud, and you will see. Without this these choruses are prose bewitched; with it they are sprung rhythm like that piece of mine.

Besides, why did you not say *Binsey Poplars* was like Whitman? The present piece is in the same kind and vein, but developed, an advance. The lines and the stanzas (of which there are two in each poem and having much the same relation to one another) are both longer, but the two pieces are greatly alike: just look. If so how is this a being untrue to myself? I am sure it is no such thing.

The above remarks are not meant to run down Whitman. His 'savage' style has advantages, and he has chosen it; he says so. But you cannot eat your cake and keep it: he eats his offhand, I keep mine. It makes a very great difference. Neither do I deny all resemblance. In particular I noticed in *Spirit that Formed this Scene* a preference for the alexandrine. I have the same preference: I came to it by degrees, I did not take it from him.

About diction the matter does not allow me so clearly to point out my independence as about rhythm. I cannot think that the present piece owes anything to him. I hope not, here especially, for it is not even spoken in my own person but in that of St Winefred's maidens. It ought to sound like the thoughts of a good but lively girl and not at all like – not at all like Walt Whitman. But perhaps your mind may have changed by this.

I wish I had not spent so much time in defending the piece.

Believe me your affectionate friend

Gerard

Walt Whitman

'Slang in America', *North American Review* November 1885 (reprinted in *November Boughs*, 1888)

Viewed freely, the English language is the accretion and growth of every dialect, race, and range of time, and is both the free and compacted composition of all. From this point of view, it stands for Language in the largest sense, and is really the greatest of studies. It involves so much; is indeed a sort of universal absorber, combiner, and conqueror. The scope of its etymologies is the scope not only of man and civilization, but the history of Nature in all departments, and of the organic Universe, brought up to date; for all are comprehended in words, and their backgrounds. This is when words become vitalized, and stand for things, as they unerringly and soon come to do, in the mind that enters on their study with fitting spirit, grasp, and appreciation.

Slang, profoundly considered, is the lawless germinal element, below all words and sentences, and behind all poetry, and proves a certain perennial rankness and protestantism in speech. As the United States inherit by far their most precious possession – the language they talk and write – from the Old World, under and out of its feudal institutes, I will allow myself to borrow a simile even of those forms farthest removed from American Democracy. Considering Language then as some mighty potentate, into the majestic audience-hall of the monarch ever enters a personage like one of Shakespeare's clowns, and takes position there, and plays a part even in the stateliest ceremonies. Such is Slang, or indirection, an attempt of common humanity to escape from bald literalism, and express itself illimitably, which in highest walks produces poets and poems, and doubtless in prehistoric times gave the start to, and perfected, the whole immense tangle of the old mythologies. For, curious as it may appear, it is strictly the same impulse-source, the same thing. Slang, too, is the wholesome fermentation or eructation of those processes eternally active in language, by which froth and specks are thrown up, mostly to pass away; though occasionally to settle and permanently crystallize.

To make it plainer, it is certain that many of the oldest and solidest words we use, were originally generated from the daring and license of slang. In the processes of word-formation, myriads die, but here and there the attempt attracts superior meanings, becomes valuable and indispensable, and lives forever. Thus the term *right* means literally only straight. *Wrong* primarily meant twisted, distorted. *Integrity* meant oneness. *Spirit* meant breath, or flame. A *supercilious* person was one who raised his eyebrows. To *insult* was to leap against. If you *influenced* a man, you but flowed into him. The Hebrew word which is translated *prophesy* meant to bubble up and pour forth as a fountain. The enthusiast bubbles up with the Spirit of God within him, and it pours forth from him like a fountain. The word prophecy is misunderstood. Many suppose that it is limited to mere prediction;

that is but the lesser portion of prophecy. The greater work is to reveal God. Every true religious enthusiast is a prophet.

Language, be it remembered, is not an abstract construction of the learned, or of dictionary-makers, but is something arising out of the work, needs, ties, joys, affections, tastes, of long generations of humanity, and has its bases broad and low, close to the ground. Its final decisions are made by the masses, people nearest the concrete, having most to do with actual land and sea. It impermeates all, the Past as well as the Present, and is the grandest triumph of the human intellect. 'Those mighty works of art,' says Addington Symonds, 'which we call languages, in the construction of which whole peoples unconsciously co-operated, the forms of which were determined not by individual genius, but by the instincts of successive generations, acting to one end, inherent in the nature of the race – Those poems of pure thought and fancy, cadenced not in words, but in living imagery, fountain-heads of inspiration, mirrors of the mind of nascent nations, which we call Mythologies – these surely are more marvellous in their infantine spontaneity than any more mature production of the races which evolved them. Yet we are utterly ignorant of their embryology; the true science of Origins is yet in its cradle.

Daring as it is to say so, in the growth of Language it is certain that the retrospect of slang from the start would be the recalling from their nebulous conditions of all that is poetical in the stores of human utterance. Moreover, the honest delving, as of late years, by the German and British workers in comparative philology, has pierced and dispersed many of the falsest bubbles of centuries; and will disperse many more. It was long recorded that in Scandinavian mythology the heroes in the Norse Paradise drank out of the skulls of their slain enemies. Later investigation proves the word taken for skulls to mean *horns* of beasts slain in the hunt. And what reader had not been exercised over the traces of that feudal custom, by which *seigneurs* warmed their feet in the bowels of serfs, the abdomen being open'd for the purpose? It now is made to appear that the serf was only required to submit his unharmed abdomen as a foot cushion while his lord supped, and was required to chafe the legs of the seigneur with his hands.

It is curiously in embryons and childhood, and among the illiterate, we always find the groundwork and start, of this great science, and its noblest products. What a relief most people have in speaking of a man not by his true and formal name, with a 'Mister' to it, but by some odd or homely appellative. The propensity to approach a meaning not directly and squarely, but by circuitous styles of expression, seems indeed a born quality of the common people every where, evidenced by nick-names, and the inveterate determination of the masses to bestow sub-titles, sometimes ridiculous, sometimes very apt. Always among the soldiers during the Secession War, one heard of 'Little Mac' (Gen. McClellan), or of 'Uncle Billy' (Gen. Sherman). 'The old man' was, of course, very common. Among the rank and file, both armies, it was very general to speak of the different States they came from by their slang names. Those from Maine were called Foxes; New Hampshire, Granite Boys; Massachusetts, Bay Staters; Vermont, Green Mountain Boys; Rhode Island, Gun Flints; Connecticut, Wooden Nutmegs; New York, Knickerbockers; New Jersey, Clam Catchers; Pennsylvania, Logher Heads; Delaware, Muskrats; Maryland, Claw Thumpers; Virginia, Beagles; North Carolina, Tar Boilers; South Carolina, Weasels; Georgia, Buzzards; Louisiana, Creoles; Alabama, Lizzards; Kentucky, Corn Crackers; Ohio, Buckeyes; Michigan, Wolverines; Indiana, Hoosiers; Illinois, Suckers; Missouri, Pukes; Mississippi, Tad Poles; Florida, Fly up the Creeks; Wisconsin, Badgers; Iowa, Hawkeyes; Oregon, Hard Cases. Indeed I am not sure but slang names have more than once made Presidents. 'Old Hickory', (Gen. Jackson) is one case in point. 'Tippecanoe, and Tyler too', another.

I find the same rule in the people's conversations everywhere. I heard this among the men of the city horse-cars, where the conductor is often called a 'snatcher' (i.e. because his characteristic duty is to constantly pull or snatch the bell-strap, to stop or go on). Two young fellows are having a friendly talk, amid which, says 1st conductor, 'What did you do before you was a snatcher?' Answer of 2d conductor, 'Nail'd.' (Translation of answer: 'I work'd as carpenter.') What is a 'boom'? says one editor to another. 'Esteem'd contemporary,' says the other, 'a boom is a bulge.' 'Barefoot whiskey' is the Tennessee name for the undiluted stimulant. In the slang of the New York common restaurant waiters a plate of ham and beans is known as 'stars and stripes', codfish balls as 'sleeve-buttons', and hash as 'mystery'.

The Western States of the Union are, however, as may be supposed, the special areas of slang, not only in conversation, but in names of localities, towns, rivers, etc. A late Oregon traveller says:

On your way to Olympia by rail, you cross a river called the Shookum-Chuck; your train stops at places named Newaukum, Tumwater, and Toutle; and if you seek further you will hear of whole counties labell'd Wahkiakum, or Snohomish, or Kitsar, or Klikatat; and Cowlitz, Hookium, and Nenolelops greet and offend you. They complain in Olympia that Washington Territory gets but little immigration; but what wonder? What man, having the whole American continent to choose from, would willingly date his letters from the county of Snohomish or bring up his children in the city of Nenolelops? The village of Tumwater is, as I am ready to bear witness, very pretty indeed; but surely an emigrant would think twice before he establish'd himself either there or at Toutle. Seattle is sufficiently barbarous; Stelicoom is no better; and I suspect that the Northern Pacific Railroad terminus has been fixed at Tacoma because it is one of the few places on Puget Sound whose name does not inspire horror.

Then a Nevada paper chronicles the departure of a mining party from Reno: 'The toughest set of roosters that ever shook the dust off any town left Reno yesterday from the new mining district of Cornucopia. They came here from Virginia. Among the crowd were four New York cock-fighters, two Chicago murderers, three Baltimore bruisers, one Philadelphia prize-fighter, four San Francisco hoodlums, three Virginia beats, two Union Pacific roughs, and two check guerrillas.' Among the far-west newspapers, have been, or are, *The Fairplay* (Colorado) *Flume*, *The Solid Muldoon*, of Ouray, *The Tombstone Epitaph*, of Nevada, *The Jimplecute*, of Texas, and *The Bazoo*, of Missouri. Shirttail Bend, Whiskey Flat, Puppytown, Wild Yankee Ranch, Squaw Flat, Rawhide Ranch, Loafer's Ravine, Squitch Gulch, Toenail Lake, are a few of the names of places in Butte county, Cal.

Perhaps indeed no place or term gives more luxuriant illustrations of the fermentation processes I have mentioned, and their froth and specks, than those Mississippi and Pacific coast regions, at the present day. Hasty and grotesque as are some of the names, others are of an appropriateness and originality unsurpassable. This applies to the

Indian words, which are often perfect. Oklahoma is proposed in Congress for the name of one of our new Territories. Hog-eye, Lick-skillet, Rake-pocket and Steal-easy are the names of some Texan towns. Miss Bremer found among the aborigines the following names: *Men's*, Horn-point; Round-Wind; Stand-and-look-out; The Cloud-that-goes-aside; Iron-toe; Seek-the-sun; Iron-flash; Red-bottle; White-spindle; Black-dog; Two-feathers-of-honor; Gray-grass; Bushy-tail; Thunder-face; Go-on-the-burning-sod; Spirits-of-the-dead. *Women's*, Keep-the-fire; Spiritual-woman; Second-daughter-of-the-house; Blue Bird.

Certainly philologists have not given enough attention to this element and its results, which, I repeat, can probably be found working every where today, amid modern conditions, with as much life and activity as in far-back Greece or India, under prehistoric ones. Then the wit – the rich flashes of humor and genius and poetry – darting out often from a gang of laborers, railroad-men, miners, drivers or boatmen! How often have I hovered at the edge of a crowd of them, to hear their repartees and impromptus! You get more real fun from half an hour with them than from the books of all 'the American humorists'.

The science of language has large and close analogies in geological science, with its ceaseless evolution, its fossils, and its numberless submerged layers and hidden strata, the infinite go-before of the present. Or, perhaps Language is more like some vast living body, or perennial body of bodies. And slang not only brings the first feeders of it, but is afterward the start of fancy, imagination and humor, breathing into its nostrils the breath of life.

(68–72)

Walt Whitman

'A Backward Glance O'er Travel'd Roads', *November Boughs* 1888

Perhaps the best of songs heard, or of any and all true love, or life's fairest episodes, or sailors', soldiers' trying scenes on land or sea, is the *résumé* of them, or any of them, long afterwards, looking at the actualities away back past, with all their practical excitations gone. How the soul loves to float amid such reminiscences!

So here I sit gossiping in the early candle-light of old age – I and my book – casting backward glances over our travel'd road. After completing, as it were, the journey – (a varied jaunt of years, with many halts and gaps of intervals – or some lengthened ship-voyage, wherein more than once the last hour had apparently arrived, and we seemed certainly going down – yet reaching port in a sufficient way through all discomfitures at last) – After completing my poems, I am curious to review them in the light of their own (at the time uncon-scious, or mostly unconscious) intentions, with certain unfoldings of the thirty years they seek to embody. These lines, therefore, will probably blend the weft of first purposes and speculations, with the warp of that experience afterwards, always bringing strange developments.

Result of seven or eight stages and struggles extending through nearly thirty years, (as I nigh my three-score-and-ten I live largely on memory,) I look upon *Leaves of Grass*, now finished to the end of its opportunities and powers, as my definitive *carte visite* to the coming generations of the New World,[1] if I may assume to say so. That I have not gained the acceptance of my own time, but have fallen back on fond dreams of the future – anticipations – ('still lives the song, though Regnar dies') – That from a worldly and business point of view *Leaves of Grass* has been worse than a failure – that public criticism on the book and myself as author of it yet shows marked anger and contempt more than anything else – ('I find a solid line of enemies to you everywhere', – letter from W. S. K., Boston, 28 May 1884) – And that solely for publishing it I have been the object of two or three pretty serious special official buffetings – is all probably no more than I ought to have expected. I had my choice when I commenced. I bid neither for soft eulogies, big money returns, nor the approbation of existing schools and conventions. As fulfilled or partially fulfilled, the best comfort of the whole business (after a small band of the dearest friends and upholders ever vouchsafed to man or cause – doubtless all the more faithful and uncompromising – this little phalanx! – for being so few) is that, unstopped and unwarped by any influence outside the soul within me, I have had my say entirely

1 When Champollion, on his death-bed, handed to the printer the revised proof of his *Egyptian Grammar*, he said gayly, 'Be careful of this – it is my *carte de visite* to posterity.'

my own way, and put it unerringly on record – the value thereof to be decided by time.

In calculating that decision, William O'Connor and Dr Bucke are far more peremptory than I am. Behind all else that can be said, I consider *Leaves of Grass* and its theory experimental – as, in the deepest sense, I consider our American republic itself to be, with its theory. (I think I have at least enough philosophy not to be too absolutely certain of anything, or any results.) In the second place, the volume is a *sortie* – whether to prove triumphant, and conquer its field of aim and escape and construction, nothing less than a hundred years from now can fully answer. I consider the point that I have positively gained a hearing, to far more than make up for any and all other lacks and withholdings. Essentially, *that* was from the first, and has remained throughout, the main object. Now it seems to be achieved, I am certainly contented to waive any otherwise momentous draw-backs, as of little account. Candidly and dispassionately reviewing all my intentions, I feel that they were creditable – and I accept the result, whatever it may be.

After continued personal ambition and effort, as a young fellow, to enter with the rest into competition for the usual rewards, business, political, literary, etc. – to take part in the great *mêlée*, both for victory's prize itself and to do some good – After years of those aims and pursuits, I found myself remaining possessed, at the age of thirty-one to thirty-three, with a special desire and conviction. Or rather, to be quite exact, a desire that had been flitting through my previous life, or hovering on the flanks, mostly indefinite hitherto, had steadily advanced to the front, defined itself, and finally dominated every-thing else. This was a feeling or ambition to articulate and faithfully express in literary or poetic form, and uncompromisingly, my own physical, emotional, moral, intellectual, and aesthetic Personality, in the midst of, and tallying, the momentous spirit and facts of its im-mediate days, and of current America – and to exploit that Personality, identified with place and date, in a far more candid and comprehen-sive sense than any hitherto poem or book.

Perhaps this is in brief, or suggests, all I have sought to do. Given the nineteenth century, with the United States, and what they furnish as area and points of view, *Leaves of Grass* is, or seeks to be, simply a faithful and doubtless self-willed record. In the midst of all, it gives one man's – the author's – identity, ardors, observations, faiths, and thoughts, colored hardly at all with any decided coloring from other faiths or other identities. Plenty of songs had been sung – beautiful, matchless songs – adjusted to other lands than these – another spirit and stage of evolution; but I would sing, and leave out or put in, quite solely with reference to America and today. Modern science and democracy seemed to be throwing out their challenge to poetry to put them in its statements in contradistinction to the songs and myths of the past. As I see it now (perhaps too late,) I have unwittingly taken up that challenge and made an attempt at such statements – which I certainly would not assume to do now, knowing more clearly what it means.

For grounds for *Leaves of Grass* as a poem, I abandoned the conventional themes, which do not appear in it: none of the stock ornamentation, or choice plots of love or war, or high, exceptional personages of Old-World song; nothing, as I may say, for beauty's sake – no legend, or myth, or romance, nor euphemism, nor rhyme. But the broadest average of humanity and its identities in the now ripening nineteenth century, and especially in each of their countless examples and practical occupations in the United States today.

One main contrast of the ideas behind every page of my verses, compared with established poems, is their different relative attitude towards God, towards the objective universe, and still more (by reflection, confession, assumption, etc.) the quite changed attitude of the ego, the one chanting or talking, towards himself and towards his fellow-humanity. It is certainly time for America, above all, to begin this readjustment in the scope and basic point of view of verse; for everything else has changed. As I write, I see in an article on Wordsworth, in one of the current English magazines, the lines, 'A few weeks ago an eminent French critic said that, owing to the special tendency to science and to its all-devouring force, poetry would cease to be read in fifty years.' But I anticipate the very contrary. Only a firmer, vastly broader, new area begins to exist – nay, is already formed – to which the poetic genius must emigrate. Whatever may have been the case in years gone by, the true use for the imaginative faculty of modern times is to give ultimate vivification to facts, to science, and to common lives, endowing them with the glows and glories and final illustriousness which belong to every real thing, and to real things only. Without that ultimate vivification – which the poet or other artist alone can give – reality would seem incomplete, and science, democracy, and life itself, finally in vain.

Few appreciate the moral revolutions, our age, which have been profounder far than the material or inventive or war-produced ones. The nineteenth century, now well towards its close (and ripening into fruit the seeds of the two preceding centuries[1]) – the uprisings of national masses and shiftings of boundary-lines – the historical and other prominent facts of the United States – the war of attempted Secession – the stormy rush and haste of nebulous forces – never can future years witness more excitement and din of action – never completer change of army front along the whole line, the whole civilized world. For all these new and evolutionary facts, meanings, purposes, new poetic messages, new forms and expressions, are inevitable.

My book and I – what a period we have presumed to span! those thirty years from 1850 to '80 – and America in them! Proud, proud indeed may we be, if we have culled enough of that period in its own spirit to worthily waft a few live breaths of it to the future!

Let me not dare, here or anywhere, for my own purposes, or any purposes, to attempt the definition of Poetry, nor answer the question what it is. Like Religion, Love, Nature, while those terms are indispensable, and we all give a sufficiently accurate meaning to them, in my opinion no definition that has ever been made sufficiently encloses the name Poetry; nor can any rule or convention ever so absolutely obtain but some great exception may arise and disregard and overturn it.

Also it must be carefully remembered that first-class literature does not shine by any luminosity of its own; nor do its poems. They grow of circumstances, and are evolutionary. The actual living light is always curiously from elsewhere – follows unaccountable sources, and is lunar and relative at the best. There are, I know, certain controling themes that seem endlessly appropriated to the poets – as war, in the past – in the Bible, religious rapture and adoration – always

---

1 The ferment and germination even of the United States today, dating back to and in my opinion mainly founded on, the Elizabethan age in English history, the age of Francis Bacon and Shakespeare. Indeed, when we pursue it, what growth or advent is there that does not date back, back, until lost – perhaps its most tantalizing clues lost – in the receded horizons of the past?

love, beauty, some fine plot, or pensive or other emotion. But, strange as it may sound at first, I will say there is something striking far deeper and towering far higher than those themes for the best elements of modern song.

Just as all the old imaginative works rest, after their kind, on long trains of presuppositions, often entirely unmentioned by themselves, yet supplying the most important bases of them, and without which they could have had no reason for being, so *Leaves of Grass*, before a line was written, presupposed something different from any other, and, as it stands, is the result of such presupposition. I should say, indeed, it were useless to attempt reading the book without first carefully tallying that preparatory background and quality in the mind. Think of the United States today – the facts of these thirty-eight or forty empires soldered in one – sixty or seventy millions of equals, with their lives, their passions, their future – these incalculable, modern, American, seething multitudes around us, of which we are inseparable parts! Think, in comparison, of the petty environage and limited area of the poets of past or present Europe, no matter how great their genius. Think of the absence and ignorance in all cases hitherto, of the multitudinousness, vitality, and the unprecedented stimulants of today and here. It almost seems as if a poetry with cosmic and dynamic features of magnitude and limitlessness suitable to the human soul, were never possible before. It is certain that a poetry of absolute faith and equality for the use of the democratic masses never was.

In estimating first-class song, a sufficient Nationality, or, on the other hand, what may be called the negative and lack of it (as in Goethe's case, it sometimes seems to me,) is often, if not always, the first element. One needs only a little penetration to see, at more or less removes, the material facts of their country and radius, with the coloring of the moods of humanity at the time, and its gloomy or hopeful prospects, behind all poets and each poet, and forming their birthmarks. I know very well that my *Leaves* could not possibly have emerged or been fashioned or completed, from any other era than the latter half of the nineteenth century, nor any other land than democratic America, and from the absolute triumph of the National Union arms.

And whether my friends claim it for me or not, I know well

enough, too, that in respect to pictorial talent, dramatic situations, and especially in verbal melody and all the conventional technique of poetry, not only the divine works that today stand ahead in the world's reading, but dozens more, transcend (some of them immeasurably transcend) all I have done, or could do. But it seemed to me, as the objects in Nature, the themes of aestheticism, and all special exploitations of the mind and soul, involve not only their own inherent quality, but the quality, just as inherent and important, of *their point of view*,[1] the time had come to reflect all themes and things, old and new, in the lights thrown on them by the advent of America and democracy – to chant those themes through the utterance of one, not only the grateful and reverent legatee of the past, but the born child of the New World – to illustrate all through the genesis and ensemble of today; and that such illustration and ensemble are the chief demands of America's prospective imaginative literature. Not to carry out, in the approved style, some choice plot of fortune or misfortune, or fancy, or fine thoughts, or incidents, or courtesies – all of which has been done overwhelmingly and well, probably never to be excelled – but that while in such aesthetic presentation of objects, passions, plots, thoughts, etc., our lands and days do not want, and probably will never have, anything better than they already possess from the bequests of the past, it still remains to be said that there is even towards all those a subjective and contemporary point of view appropriate to ourselves alone, and to our new genius and environments, different from anything hitherto; and that such conception of current or gone-by life and art is for us the only means of their assimilation consistent with the Western world.

Indeed, and anyhow, to put it specifically, has not the time arrived when, (if it must be plainly said, for democratic America's sake, if for no other) there must imperatively come a readjustment of the whole theory and nature of Poetry? The question is important, and I may turn the argument over and repeat it: Does not the best thought of our day and Republic conceive of a birth and spirit of song superior to anything past or present? To the effectual and moral consolidation of our lands (already, as materially established, the greatest factors in known history, and far, far greater through what they prelude and

1 According to Immanuel Kant, the last essential reality, giving shape and significance to all the rest.

necessitate, and are to be in future) – to conform with and build on the concrete realities and theories of the universe furnished by science, and henceforth the only irrefragable basis for anything, verse included – to root both influences in the emotional and imaginative action of the modern time, and dominate all that precedes or opposes them – is not either a radical advance and step forward, or a new verteber of the best song indispensable?

The New World receives with joy the poems of the antique, with European feudalism's rich fund of epics, plays, ballads – seeks not in the least to deaden or displace those voices from our ear and area – holds them indeed as indispensable studies, influences, records, comparisons. But though the dawn-dazzle of the sun of literature is in those poems for us of today – though perhaps the best parts of current character in nations, social groups, or any man's or woman's individuality, Old World or New, are from them – and though if I were asked to name the most precious bequest to current American civilization from all the hitherto ages, I am not sure but I would name those old and less old songs ferried hither from east and west – some serious words and debits remain; some acrid considerations demand a hearing. Of the great poems received from abroad and from the ages, and today enveloping and penetrating America, is there one that is consistent with these United States, or essentially applicable to them as they are and are to be? Is there one whose underlying basis is not a denial and insult to democracy? What a comment it forms, anyhow, on this era of literary fulfillment, with the splendid day-rise of science and resuscitation of history, that our chief religious and poetical works are not our own, nor adapted to our light, but have been furnished by far-back ages out of their arriere and darkness, or, at most, twilight dimness! What is there in those works that so imperiously and scornfully dominates all our advanced civilization, and culture?

Even Shakespeare, who so suffuses current letters and art (which indeed have in most degrees grown out of him,) belongs essentially to the buried past. Only he holds the proud distinction for certain important phases of that past, of being the loftiest of the singers life has yet given voice to. All, however, relate to and rest upon conditions, standards, politics, sociologies, ranges of belief, that have been quite eliminated from the Eastern hemisphere, and never existed at all in the Western. As authoritative types of song they belong in

America just about as much as the persons and institutes they depict.
True, it may be said, the emotional, moral, and aesthetic natures of
humanity have not radically changed – that in these the old poems
apply to our times and all times, irrespective of date; and that they
are of incalculable value as pictures of the past. I willingly make those
admissions and to their fullest extent; then advance the points here-
with as of serious, even paramount importance.

I have indeed put on record elsewhere my reverence and eulogy
for those never-to-be-excelled poetic bequests and their indescribable
preciousness as heirlooms for America. Another and separate point
must now be candidly stated. If I had not stood before those poems
with uncovered head, fully aware of their colossal grandeur and
beauty of form and spirit, I could not have written *Leaves of Grass*.
My verdict and conclusions as illustrated in its pages are arrived at
through the temper and inculcation of the old works as much as
through anything else – perhaps more than through anything else. As
America fully and fairly construed is the legitimate result and evolutionary outcome of the past, so I would dare to claim for my verse.
Without stopping to qualify the averment, the Old World has had
the poems of myths, fictions, feudalism, conquest, caste, dynastic
wars, and splendid exceptional characters and affairs, which have
been great; but the New World needs the poems of realities and
science and of the democratic average and basic equality, which shall
be greater. In the centre of all, and object of all, stands the Human
Being, towards whose heroic and spiritual evolution poems and everything directly or indirectly tend, Old World or New.

Continuing the subject, my friends have more than once suggested
– or may be the garrulity of advancing age is possessing me – some
further embryonic facts of *Leaves of Grass*, and especially how I
entered upon them. Dr Bucke has, in his volume, already fully and
fairly described the preparation of my poetic field, with the particular
and general plowing, planting, seeding, and occupation of the ground,
till everything was fertilized, rooted, and ready to start its own way
for good or bad. Not till after this, did I attempt any serious acquaintance with poetic literature. Along in my sixteenth year I had become
possessor of a stout, well-crammed one thousand page octavo volume
(I have it yet,) containing Walter Scott's poetry entire – an inexhaust-

ible mine and treasury of poetic forage (especially the endless forests and jungles of notes) – has been so to me for fifty years, and remains so to this day.[1]

Later, at intervals, summers and falls, I used to go off, sometimes for a week at a stretch, down in the country, or to Long Island's sea-shores – there, in the presence of outdoor influences, I went over thoroughly the Old and New Testaments, and absorbed (probably to better advantage for me than in any library or indoor room – it makes such difference *where* you read,) Shakespeare, Ossian, the best translated versions I could get of Homer, Aeschylus, Sophocles, the old German Nibelungen, the ancient Hindoo poems, and one or two other masterpieces, Dante's among them. As it happen'd, I read the latter mostly in an old wood. The *Iliad* (Buckley's prose version) I read first thoroughly on the peninsula of Orient, northeast end of Long Island, in a sheltered hollow of rocks and sand, with the sea on each side. (I have wondered since why I was not overwhelmed by those mighty masters. Likely because I read them, as described, in the full presence of Nature, under the sun, with the far-spreading land-scape and vistas, or the sea rolling in.)

Toward the last I had among much else looked over Edgar Poe's poems – of which I was not an admirer, though I always saw that beyond their limited range of melody (like perpetual chimes of music bells, ringing from lower *b* flat up to *g*) they were melodious expressions, and perhaps never excelled ones, of certain pronounced phases of human morbidity. (The Poetic area is very spacious – has room for all – has so many mansions!) But I was repaid in Poe's prose by the idea that (at any rate for our occasions, our day) there can be no such thing as a long poem. The same thought had been haunting my mind before, but Poe's argument, though short, worked the sum and proved it to me.

Another point had an early settlement, clearing the ground greatly.

1 Sir Walter Scott's *Complete Poems*; especially including *Border Minstrelsy*; then *Sir Tristrem*; *Lay of the Last Minstrel*; *Ballads from the German*; *Marmion*; *Lady of the Lake*; *Vision of Don Roderick*; *Lord of the Isles*; *Rokeby*; *Bridal of Triermain*; *Field of Waterloo*; *Harold the Dauntless*; all the Dramas; various Introductions, endless interesting Notes, and Essays on Poetry, Romance, Etc.

Lockhart's 1833 (or '34) edition with Scott's latest and copious revisions and annotations. (All the poems were thoroughly read by me, but the ballads of the *Border Ministrelsy* over and over again.)

I saw, from the time my enterprise and questionings positively shaped themselves (how best can I express my own distinctive era and surroundings, America, Democracy ?) that the trunk and centre whence the answer was to radiate, and to which all should return from straying however far a distance, must be an identical body and soul, a personality – which personality, after many considerations and ponderings I deliberately settled should be myself – indeed could not be any other. I also felt strongly (whether I have shown it or not) that to the true and full estimate of the Present both the Past and the Future are main considerations.

These, however, and much more might have gone on and come to naught (almost positively would have come to naught,) if a sudden, vast, terrible, direct and indirect stimulus for new and national declamatory expression had not been given to me. It is certain, I say, that, although I had made a start before, only from the occurrence of the Secession War, and what it showed me as by flashes of lightning, with emotional depths it sounded and aroused (of course, I don't mean in my own heart only, I saw it just as plainly in others, in millions) – that only from the strong flare and provocation of that war's sights and scenes the final reasons-for-being of an autochthonic and passionate song definitely came forth.

I went down to the war fields in Virginia (end of 1862), lived thenceforward in camp – saw great battles and the days and nights afterward – partook of all the fluctuations, gloom, despair, hopes again aroused, courage evoked – death readily risked – *the cause*, too – along and filling those agonistic and lurid following years, 1863–'64–'65 – the real parturition years (more than 1776–'83) of this henceforth homogeneous Union. Without those three or four years and the experiences they gave, *Leaves of Grass* would not now be existing.

But I set out with the intention also of indicating or hinting some point-characteristics which I since see (though I did not then, at least not definitely) were bases and object-urgings toward those *Leaves* from the first. The word I myself put primarily for the description of them as they stand at last, is the word Suggestiveness. I round and finish little, if anything; and could not, consistently with my scheme. The reader will always have his or her part to do, just as much as I have had mine. I seek less to state or display any theme or thought, and more to bring you, reader, into the atmosphere of the theme or thought – there to pursue your own flight. Another impetus-word is Comradeship as for all lands, and in a more commanding and acknowledged sense than hitherto. Other word signs would be Good Cheer, Content, and Hope.

The chief trait of any given poet is always the spirit he brings to the observation of Humanity and Nature – the mood out of which he contemplates his subjects. What kind of temper and what amount of faith report these things? Up to how recent a date is the song carried? What the equipment, and special raciness of the singer – what his tinge of coloring? The last value of artistic expressers, past and present – Greek aesthetes, Shakespeare – or in our own day Tennyson, Victor Hugo, Carlyle, Emerson – is certainly involved in such questions. I say the profoundest service that poems or any other writings can do for their reader is not merely to satisfy the intellect, or supply something polished and interesting, nor even to depict great passions, or persons or events, but to fill him with vigorous and clean manliness, religiousness, and give him *good heart* as a radical posses-sion and habit. The educated world seems to have been growing more and more ennuyed for ages, leaving to our time the inheritance of it all. Fortunately there is the original inexhaustible fund of buoyancy, normally resident in the race, forever eligible to be appealed to and relied on.

As for native American individuality, though certain to come, and on a large scale, the distinctive and ideal type of Western character (as consistent with the operative political and even money-making features of United States' humanity in the nineteenth century as chosen knights, gentlemen and warriors were the ideals of the centuries of European feudalism) it has not yet appeared. I have allowed the stress of my poems from beginning to end to bear upon American individuality and assist it – not only because that is a great lesson in Nature, amid all her generalizing laws, but as counterpoise to the leveling tendencies of Democracy – and for other reasons. Defiant of ostensible literary and other conventions, I avowedly chant 'the great pride of man in himself', and permit it to be more or less a *motif* of nearly all my verse. I think this pride indispensable to an American. I think it not inconsistent with obedience, humility, defer-ence, and self-questioning.

Democracy has been so retarded and jeopardized by powerful personalities that its first instincts are fain to clip, conform, bring in
stragglers, and reduce everything to a dead level. While the ambitious
thought of my song is to help the forming of a great aggregate
Nation, it is, perhaps, altogether through the forming of myriads of
fully developed and enclosing individuals. Welcome as are equality's
and fraternity's doctrines and popular education, a certain liability
accompanies them all, as we see. That primal and interior something in man, in his soul's abysms, coloring all, and, by exceptional
fruitions, giving the last majesty to him – something continually
touched upon and attained by the old poems and ballads of feudalism,
and often the principal foundation of them – modern science and
democracy appear to be endangering, perhaps eliminating. But that
forms an appearance only; the reality is quite different. The new
influences, upon the whole, are surely preparing the way for grander
individualities than ever. Today and here personal force is behind
everything, just the same. The times and depictions from the *Iliad*
to Shakespeare inclusive can happily never again be realized – but the
elements of courageous and lofty manhood are unchanged.

Without yielding an inch the working-man and working-woman
were to be in my pages from first to last. The ranges of heroism and
loftiness with which Greek and feudal poets endowed their god-like
or lordly born characters – indeed prouder and better based and with
fuller ranges than those – I was to endow the democratic averages of
America. I was to show that we, here and today, are eligible to the
grandest and the best – more eligible now than any times of old were.
I will also want my utterances (I said to myself before beginning)
to be in spirit the poems of the morning. (They have been founded
and mainly written in the sunny forenoon and early mid-day of my
life.) I will want them to be the poems of women entirely as much
as men. I have wished to put the complete Union of the States in my
songs without any preference or partiality whatever. Henceforth, if
they live and are read, it must be just as much South as North – just as
much along the Pacific as Atlantic – in the valley of the Mississippi, in
Canada, up in Maine, down in Texas, and on the shores of Puget Sound.

From another point of view *Leaves of Grass* is avowedly the song
of Sex and Amativeness, and even Animality – though meanings that
do not usually go along with those words are behind all, and will

duly emerge; and all are sought to be lifted into a different light and atmosphere. Of this feature, intentionally palpable in a few lines, I shall only say the espousing principle of those lines so gives breath of life to my whole scheme that the bulk of the pieces might as well have been left unwritten were those lines omitted. Difficult as it will be, it has become, in my opinion, imperative to achieve a shifted attitude from superior men and women towards the thought and fact of sexuality, as an element in character, personality, the emotions, and a theme in literature. I am not going to argue the question by itself; it does not stand by itself. The vitality of it is altogether in its relations, bearings, significance – like the clef of a symphony. At last analogy the lines I allude to, and the spirit in which they are spoken, permeate all *Leaves of Grass*, and the work must stand or fall with them, as the human body and soul must remain as an entirety.

Universal as are certain facts and symptoms of communities or individuals all times, there is nothing so rare in modern conventions and poetry as their normal recognizance. Literature is always calling in the doctor for consultation and confession, and always giving evasions and swathing suppressions in place of that 'heroic nudity'[1] on which only a genuine diagnosis of serious cases can be built. And in respect to editions of *Leaves of Grass* in time to come (if there should be such) I take occasion now to confirm those lines with the settled convictions and deliberate renewals of thirty years, and to hereby prohibit, as far as word of mine can do so, any elision of them.

Then still a purpose enclosing all, and over and beneath all. Ever since what might be called thought, or the budding of thought, fairly began in my youthful mind, I had had a desire to attempt some worthy record of that entire faith and acceptance ('to justify the ways of God to man' is Milton's well-known and ambitious phrase) which is the foundation of moral America. I felt it all as positively then in my young days as I do now in my old ones; to formulate a poem whose every thought or fact should directly or indirectly be or connive at an implicit belief in the wisdom, health, mystery, beauty of every process, every concrete object, every human or other existence, not only considered from the point of view of all, but of each.

While I cannot understand it or argue it out, I fully believe in a clue and purpose in Nature, entire and several; and that invisible

1 *Nineteenth Century*, July 1883.

spiritual results, just as real and definite as the visible, eventuate all concrete life and all materialism, through Time. My book ought to emanate buoyancy and gladness legitimately enough, for it was grown out of those elements, and has been the comfort of my life since it was originally commenced.

One main genesis-motive of the *Leaves* was my conviction (just as strong today as ever) that the crowning growth of the United States is to be spiritual and heroic. To help start and favor that growth – or even to call attention to it, or the need of it – is the beginning, middle and final purpose of the poems. (In fact, when really ciphered out and summed to the last, plowing up in earnest the interminable average fallows of humanity – not 'good government' merely, in the common sense – is the justification and main purpose of these United States.)

Isolated advantages in any rank or grace or fortune – the direct or indirect threads of all the poetry of the past – are in my opinion distasteful to the republican genius, and offer no foundation for its fitting verse. Established poems, I know, have the very great advantage of chanting the already performed, so full of glories, reminiscences dear to the minds of men. But my volume is a candidate for the future. 'All original art,' says Taine, anyhow, 'is self-regulated, and no original art can be regulated from without; it carries its own counterpoise, and does not receive it from elsewhere – lives on its own blood' – a solace to my frequent bruises and sulky vanity.

As the present is perhaps mainly an attempt at personal statement or illustration, I will allow myself as further help to extract the following anecdote from a book, *Annals of Old Painters*, conned by me in youth. Rubens, the Flemish painter, in one of his wanderings through the galleries of old convents, came across a singular work. After looking at it thoughtfully for a good while, and listening to the criticisms of his suite of students, he said to the latter, in answer to their questions, (as to what school the work implied or belonged,) 'I do not believe the artist, unknown and perhaps no longer living, who has given the world this legacy, ever belonged to any school, or ever painted anything but this one picture, which is a personal affair – a piece out of a man's life.'

Leaves of Grass indeed (I cannot too often reiterate) has mainly been the outcropping of my own emotional and other personal nature –

an attempt, from first to last, to put *a Person*, a human being (myself, in the latter half of the nineteenth century, in America,) freely, fully and truly on record. I could not find any similar personal record in current literature that satisfied me. But it is not on *Leaves of Grass* distinctively as *literature*, or a specimen thereof, that I feel to dwell, or advance claims. No one will get at my verses who insists upon viewing them as a literary performance, or attempt at such performance, or as aiming mainly toward art or aestheticism.

I say no land or people or circumstances ever existed so needing a race of singers and poems differing from all others, and rigidly their own, as the land and people and circumstances of our United States need such singers and poems today, and for the future. Still further, as long as the States continue to absorb and be dominated by the poetry of the Old World, and remain unsupplied with autochthonous song, to express, vitalize and give color to and define their material and political success, and minister to them distinctively, so long will they stop short of first-class Nationality and remain defective.

In the free evening of my day I give to you, reader, the foregoing garrulous talk, thoughts, reminiscences,

As idly drifting down the ebb,
Such ripples, half-caught voices, echo from the shore.

Concluding with two items for the imaginative genius of the West, when it worthily rises – First, what Herder taught to the young Goethe, that really great poetry is always (like the Homeric or Biblical canticles) the result of a national spirit, and not the privilege of a polished and select few; Second, that the strongest and sweetest songs yet remain to be sung.

(5–18)

Walt Whitman

in conversation 1888–9 (from Horace Traubel's *Conversations with Walt Whitman*, vols. 1 and 2, 1908; vol. 3, 1914; vol. 4, 1953)

Wednesday, 16 May 1888

. . . [Whitman:] 'But let me tell you a little more about [Ernest] Rhys. He is very interesting to me. We talked of the poetic lilt. Rhys insists on it; insists on it, come good or bad. Well – the lilt is all right: yes, right enough: but there's something anterior – more imperative. The first thing necessary is the thought – the rest may follow if it chooses – may play its part – but must not be too much sought after. The two things being equal I should prefer to have the lilt present with the idea, but if I got down my thought and the rhythm was not there I should not work to secure it. I am very deliberate – I take a good deal of trouble, with words: yes, a good deal: but what I am after is the content not the music of words. Perhaps the music happens – it does no harm; I do not go in search of it. Two centuries back or so much of the poetry passed from lip to lip – was oral: was literally made to be sung: then the lilt, the formal rhythm, may have been necessary. The case is now somewhat changed: now, when the poetic work in literature is more than nineteen-twentieths of it by print, the simply tonal aids are not so necessary, or if necessary, have considerably shifted their character.'

(1, 163)

Thursday, 17 May 1888

... [Whitman] naturally diverted to [Sidney] Lanier. 'The recent published adverse reference to me from Lanier as reported in the Memorial volume was objected to by his wife, I am told, on the ground of its unfairness, not only to me but to Lanier, since other things said by Lanier about me, reflecting a more favorable mood, should also have been given. I know nothing about that myself and care less. I had several letters from Lanier – very warm letters. One of them is still about here somewhere: I want you to have it some day: the severely critical paragraphs in the book were therefore rather a surprise to me. I suppose we will all survive the anomaly. Lanier was tragic in life and death. He had the soul of the musician – was a flute player: indeed, in the accounts, was phenomenally fine. This extreme sense of the melodic, a virtue in itself, when carried into the art of the writer becomes a fault. Why? Why, because it tends to place the first emphasis on tone, sound – on the lilt as Rhys so often puts it. Study Lanier's choice of words – they are too often fit rather for sound than for sense. His ear was over-sensitive. He had a genius – a delicate, clairvoyant genius: but this over-tuning of the ear, this

extreme deference paid to oral nicety, reduced the majesty, the solid
worth, of his rhythms.'

(1, 170–71)

Wednesday, 6 June 1888

. . . [Whitman was led] to some reflections upon the character of these
latest poems. 'I often ask myself, is this expression of the life of an
old man consonant with the fresher, earlier, delvings, faiths, hopes,
stated in the original Leaves? I have my doubts – minor doubts – but
somehow I decide the case finally on my own side. It belongs to the
scheme of the book. As long as I live the Leaves must go on. Am I, as
some think, losing grip? – taking in my horns? No – no – no: I am
sure that could not be. I still wish to be, am, the radical of my stronger
days – to be the same uncompromising oracle of democracy – to
maintain undimmed the light of my deepest faith. I am sure I have
not gone back on that – sure, sure. The Sands [*Sands at Seventy*, an
'annex' of the 1880s] have to be taken as the utterances of an old man
– a very old man. I desire that they may be interpreted as confirma-
tions, not denials, of the work that has preceded. [William Dean]
Howells, [Henry] James and some others appear to think I rest my
philosophy, my democracy, upon braggadocio, noise, rough assertion, such integers. While I would not be afraid to assent to this as a
part of the truth I still insist that I am on the whole to be thought of
in other terms. I recognize, have always recognized, the importance
of the lusty, strong-limbed, big-bodied American of the Leaves: I do
not abate one atom of that belief now, today. But I hold to something
more than that, too, and claim a full, not a partial, judgment upon my
work – I am not to be known as a piece of something but as a totality.'

(1, 271–2)

Monday, 2 July 1888

. . . I will copy here the sheet of pencilled paper. It had had a headline
– 'The question of form' – which was marked out. [The sheet was
apparently composed by Whitman in the early 1870s.]

'The want for something finished, completed, and technically
beautiful will certainly not be supplied by this writer, as it is by existing esthetic works. For the best poems both the old ones and later

ones now accepted as first class are polished, rhymed regular, with all the elegance of fine conceits, carefully elaborated, showing under all the restraints of art, language and phrase chosen after very much has been rejected, and only the best admitted, and then all joined and cemented together, and finally presenting the beauty of some architectural temple – some palace, proudly rising in proportions of marble, entered from superb porticos and adorned with statuary satisfying the art sense and that of form, fulfilling beauty and inviting criticism. Not so his poetry. Its likeness is not the solid stately palace, nor the sculpture that adorns it, nor the paintings on its walls. Its analogy is *the Ocean*. Its verses are the liquid, billowy waves, ever rising and falling, perhaps sunny and smooth, perhaps wild with storm, always moving, always alike in their nature as rolling waves, but hardly any two exactly alike in size or measure (meter), never having the sense of something finished and fixed, always suggesting something beyond.'

(1, 414–15)

Thursday, 2 August 1888

... Returned him [W. E.] Henley's poems. Told him I had read the book through. He exclaimed: 'All through ? Why, I had no idea anybody was capable of that. I read only the fore part of it – the hospital pieces – was peculiarly, intensely, interested in that – but as for the rest –' After a pause: 'It struck me as extremely deliberate verse – verse written of malice prepense – all laid out, designed, on mathematical principles. Did you get that impression of it ? Or did it carry you right along as if you could not help it?'

(2, 77)

Friday, 24 August 1888

I found a poem by [Algernon Charles] Swinburne – *A Double Ballad of August*. [Whitman] said: 'Oh yes, I did see that. And if Swinburne had a few grains of thought with all his music wouldn't he be the greatest charmer of all? I never liked him from the first – Swinburne – from the very first: could not take him in, adapt myself to him. I know of nothing I think of so little account as pretty words, pretty thoughts, pretty china, pretty arrangements.'

(2, 188)

Monday, 24 September 1888

... [Whitman:] 'If there is anything whatever in *Leaves of Grass* – anything that sets it apart as a fact of any importance – that thing must be its totality – its massings. I respond to no other explanation: no other explanation comes up to my purpose – tallies the long steady pull of my many years of adhesion to a first purpose. I chose the fundamentals for *Leaves of Grass* – heart, spirit: the initiating passions of character: chose that it should stand for, be, a human being, with all the impulses, desires, aspirations, gropings, triumphs, that go with human life: comprehended at no time by its parts, at all times by its unity.' He was very earnest. Then he went on: '*Leaves of Grass* is not intellectual alone (I do not despise the intellectual – far from it: it is not to be despised – has its uses) nor sympathetic alone (though sympathetic enough, too) nor yet vaguely emotional – least of all this. I have always stood in *Leaves of Grass* for something higher than qualities, particulars. It is atmosphere, unity: it is never to be set down in traits but as a symphony: is no more to be stated by superficial criticism than life itself is to be so stated: is not to be caught by a smart definition or all given up to any one extreme statement.'

(2, 373)

Monday, 22 October 1888

[During a discussion of Edmund Gosse, the British critic:] Gosse had remarked Poe's great influence upon English writers. [Whitman] said: 'He means in technique – of all things, metrical niceties! Gosse's applause of Poe is like admiration for a shop window crowded with delicacies: is like a polite Episcopal preacher's estimate, analysis, of a Catholic priest.'

(2, 518)

Wednesday, 31 October 1888

... [Whitman:] 'The best gift to our age so far is what we have come to know as the scientific spirit ... It is the crowning glory of our time that this new evangel has appeared. There is no salvation if not in that: it is an appeal to nature, an appeal to final meanings – to facts, to the sun itself: it is an absolute surrender to the truth: it never asks us: Do you want this thing to be true? or, Is it ugly, hateful? but,

Is it true, and if it is true that settles it. That's all there is to it – that's all there needs to be to it; that's enough. Here science and literature are one, as they everywhere and always should be one in fact, and it is here, in such a noble equipment, that [Heinrich] Heine lustrously shines. Brilliants, gems, crystallizations, in the requisites of a writer – bright epigrams, splendid learning, eloquent roundings-off of phrase – all these, I can see, have an importance, too, though second-rate, third-rate, at the best. But in all imaginative work, all pure poetic work, there must especially come in a primal quality, not to be mentioned, named, described, but always felt when present: the direct off-throwing of nature, parting the ways between formal, conventional, borrowed expression and the fervor of genuine spirit. Heine had it – so do all the big fellows have it. More than any other agent, science has been furthering it.' Was it not also in *Leaves of Grass*? [Whitman] exclaimed fervidly: 'Oh! I hope so, I believe so: it has been in the air: I have sucked it in as the breath of life: unconsciously, not by determination, but with full recognition now of its great value, of its wonderful significance. Yes, *Leaves of Grass* would lose much if it lost that, that [*sic*] is the ground underlying all: the fact, the fact: that alone: the fact devotedly espoused, sacred, uplifting! The whole mass of people are being leavened by this spirit of scientific worship – this noblest of religions coming after all the religions that came before. ... That's where science becomes religion – where the new spirit utters the highest truth – makes the last demonstration of faith: looks the universe full in the face – its bad in the face, its good – and says yes to it.'

(2, 562–3)

Tuesday, 6 November 1888

Reference having been made to Shakespeare, [Whitman] said: 'Shakespeare shows undoubted defects: he often uses a hundred words where a dozen would do: it is true that there are many pithy terse sentences everywhere: but there are countless prolixities: though as for the overabundances of words more might be said: as, for instance, that he was not ignorantly prolific; that he was like nature itself: nature, with her trees, the oceans: nature, saying "there's lots of this, infinitudes of it – therefore, why spare it? If you ask for ten I give you a hundred, for a hundred I give you a thousand, for a thousand I give you ten thousand." It may be that we should look at it in that way: not complain of it: rather understanding its amazing intimations.'

(3, 35–6)

Monday, 26 November 1888

... [Whitman:] 'I could never go Milton: he is turgid, heavy, overstately.' I said: 'Take *Paradise Lost*: doesn't its vogue come mainly from a sort of Christian theological self-interest rather than from pure delight in its beauty?' He responded at once: 'Oh! an immense lot! Besides, it seems to me that Milton is a copy, not only [of] Homer but the *Aeneid*: a sort of modern repetition of the same old story: legions of angels, devils; war is declared, waged: moreover, even as a story it enlists little of my attention: he seems to me like a bird – soaring yet overweighted: dragged down, as if burdened – too greatly burdened: a lamb in its beak: its flight not graceful, powerful, beautiful, satisfying, like the gulls we see over the Delaware in mid-winter – their simple motion a delight – attracting you when they first break upon your sight: soaring, soaring, irrespective of cold or storm. It is true, Milton soars, but with dull, unwieldy motion.'

(3, 185)

Sunday, 10 February 1889

... He [Whitman] continued: 'The trouble is that writers are too literary – too damned literary. There has grown up – Swinburne I think an apostle of it – the doctrine (you have heard of it? it is dinned everywhere), art for art's sake: think of it – art for art's sake. Let a man really accept that – let that be his ruling thought – and he is lost.' I suggested: 'If we say politics for politics' sake they get mad.' [Whitman:] 'So they do: that is very good: it's true: politics for politics' sake, church for church's sake, talk for talk's sake, government for government's sake: state it any way you choose it becomes offensive: it's all out of the same pit. Instead of regarding literature as only a weapon, an instrument, in the service of something larger than itself, it looks upon itself as an end – as a fact to be finally worshipped, adored. To me that's all a horrible blasphemy – a bad-smelling apostasy.'

(4, 121)

Monday, 11 March 1889

[Whitman:] '. . . it is that catalogue business that wrecks them all – that hauls them up short, that determines their opposition: they shudder at it.' He smiled: 'They call the catalogue names: but suppose they do? it *is* names: but what could be more poetic than names?' [Dr Richard Maurice] Bucke said: 'Yes: look at those lines of Indian names!' adding: 'It is one of the choice bits in *Leaves of Grass*.' [Whitman] said: 'I almost think so myself: at least I like it: I have often resolved within myself that I would write a book on names – simply names: it has been one of my pet ambitions never realized.'

(4, 324)

George Santayana

'Walt Whitman: A Dialogue', *Harvard Monthly*, vol. 10, no. 3   May 1890

McStout: Coming?
Van Tender: What, is it time?
McStout: Fifteen minutes before the game begins. We might take a stroll. It is such splendid weather!
Van Tender: Yes, and this is the best place to enjoy it. The warm wind blows in over you, and you can almost fancy how the trees feel when they thaw, and the sap begins to run, and the buds throb till they burst, and every leaf breathes and trembles. The plants don't have to move from their places to feel that it's spring.. Why should we? You know my motto:

Better than to stand to sit, better than to sit to lie,
Better than to dream to sleep, better than to sleep to die.

But you can't expect to attain the highest good at one bound from the depths of Philistia. You can't do better for the present than to come in and stretch your energetic self on the other half of the window seat. Isn't it delicious? What better apology for idlers? Here you can breathe the air and look at the fresh grass, while you read a poet and cut a lecture. He tells you how in another country, perhaps, he felt what you are feeling now, as he watched the spring of another year. That is the best part of the pleasure, to know that it's human, and that all men have had it in common, from Adam down.

McStout: And who is your poet now? Swinburne?

Van Tender: Oh, no.

McStout: Keats?

Van Tender: No, it's Walt Whitman. There is a time for everything, you know.

McStout: If, like you, one does nothing. No wonder you like Walt Whitman now and then for a change. You must be so tired of poetry.

Van Tender: Isn't this poetry? What is poetry?

McStout: A matter of words – more of words than matter. But if Walt Whitman is poetry, it isn't on account of the words. You don't pretend he can write English?

Van Tender: Not according to the English department. But that is a local standard. Could Homer pass an examination in Goodwin's moods and tenses? And doesn't he say Σμινθεῦ, which is a ἅπαξ λεγόμενον.[1]

McStout: I dare say Homer talked as it was the fashion to talk in his day. And when English becomes a dead language and nothing survives but the *Leaves of Grass*, Whitman's style will be above criticism. But now English has the misfortune of being in use. A man can't make it to suit his fancy, and if he won't trouble himself to write the language of his fellows he can't expect them to learn his. How can you endure a man who has neither the accent of Christians, nor the style of a Christian, pagan, nor man?

Van Tender: Precisely for that reason: he produces a new effect, he gives you a new sensation. If you will show me a well-written book that contains the same emotion, I agree to bind the leaves of grass into bundles and cast them into the furnace. If only a man could become an artist in his words, and yet retain the innocence of his feelings! But to learn a method of expression is to become insensible to all it can't express. The schools don't teach us to paint what we see, but to see what others have painted.

McStout: I've heard of an old master who used to say to his pupils, 'Copy if you want to be copied.' When people are fascinated by the

1 And doesn't he say 'Sminthean', which is a 'unique form'. [Ed.]

extravagant they show they haven't experience and training enough to appreciate what is sane and solid. Would you make no distinction between the normal and human and the eccentric and perverse? You toss sense and grammar to the Philistines, who ought to be correct since they can't be original. But your geniuses, you think, mustn't submit to standards; they create standards. If they didn't seem ridiculous to the vulgar, would they be truly sublime? You may say that if you like, but if originality is genius there are more great men at Somerville than at Cambridge. You can't get over the difference between sense and nonsense, between beauty and caprice. Any one can produce a new effect when fools are impressed by his blunders. You may like to hear Whitman's 'barbaric yawp over the roofs of the world', but you must confess it is a whim of yours, and that a yawp is one thing and a poem another.

VAN TENDER: Certainly, I admit that a barbarism is an annoyance. When I come upon one it gives me a little shock, and I wish for the moment that it wasn't there. But there are models of English enough. I don't read Whitman for his verbal graces, although he has them, after his own fashion. If you wrote me a letter it might not be a model of style either, yet I should read it with interest if it told me what I wanted to hear. And Whitman does that. He hasn't the merits of Keats or of Shakespeare, but he has merits of his own. His verses bring a message theirs couldn't bring, so I read theirs for their style and his for his inspiration. It is the voice of nature crying in the wilderness of convention.

MCSTOUT: I wish you could tell me what you mean by that. The only novelty I can see in him is that he mentions all sorts of things and says nothing about them. If you like pantheism and indecency, why aren't you satisfied with French novels and German philosophy? These are the same things in their genuine form.

VAN TENDER: It's not a theory or a description of things I get from Whitman. It's an attitude, a faculty of appreciation. You may laugh at his catalogues of objects, at his enumeration of places. But the hurrying of these images through the mind gives me a sense of space, of a multiplicity of things spread endlessly around me. I become aware of the life of millions of men, of great stretches of marsh, desert, and ocean. Have you never thought of the poetry of the planet? Fancy this little ball spinning along so fast, and yet so little in a hurry.

Imagine the film of blue-gray water and the flat patches of land, now green, now brown, and dim clouds creeping over all. And near the ocean, here and there, conceive the troops of men and animals darkening the earth like so many ants. And think how little the murmur of one thousand jargons ruffles the air, and how the praises of each god are drowned in the vaults of his temple!

McStout: But all that is very different from Walt Whitman. Astronomy may have its impressive side, and even geography, when you connect it with the fortunes of mankind. Science is interesting, and if you can manage to make poetry out of it we shall have the first poetry in the world not resting on illusion. It seems to me that the illusion is what is poetic, and the fact is so only when in fancy we assimilate it to the fiction. The migrations of men from one land to another, for instance, are important events, and you may cast the glamour of poetry over them for a moment by dramatizing them. You may call the Strait of Magellan a Hellespont and himself a Jason. You may say the whole world is a Troad and the history of civilization a war of heroes. But if you mention the heroes, and their real qualities, where is the poetry? And if you reverse the process and try to explain the fables as history symbolized, or what not, you degrade the ideal and distort the facts. The reason why Walt Whitman is ridiculous is that he talks of real objects as if they could enter into poetry at all. It isn't art to point to objects, nor poetry to turn out 'chants of Ohio, Indiana, Illinois, Wisconsin, Iowa, and Minnesota'. Poetry deals with sensuous attractions, found nowhere on the map. To see them you must have a passport into fairy land.

Van Tender: Ah, you are caught at last! You have defined poetry. Now I wouldn't for a moment defend metaphysical confusions. The trouble with the German sort of criticism is that it isn't satisfied with the fact, but goes in search of a theory, as if a theory could be anything real and ultimate, or more than the flight of the soul from perception to perception, from emotion to emotion, on which alone she can alight to find rest and truth.

Grau, teurer Freund, ist alle Theorie,
Und grün des Lebens goldner Baum.[1]

1 All theory, dear friend, is grey, but the golden tree of actual life springs ever green. [Ed.]

But what makes you think the essence poetry distils can't be extracted from every object? Why should one thing leave its type in the world of ideas, and not another! Trust me, beauty is everywhere, if we only had the genius to see it. If a man has the ability to make us feel the fitness, the necessity, the beauty of common things, he is a poet of the highest type. If some objects seem to you poetic rather than others, if Venice can be apostrophized and Oshkosh is unmentionable, it's because habit makes it easier to idealize them. This beauty has been pointed out so often that we know it by heart. But what merit is it to repeat the old tricks, and hum the old tunes? You add nothing to the beauty of the world. You see no new vision. You are the author of nothing, but merely an apprentice in the poetic guild, a little poet sucking the honey with which great poets have sweetened words. You are inspired by tradition and judged by convention. Yet this very convention must have been inspiration at first. The real objects about a man must have impressed him and he must have found words fit to communicate his impression. These words in that way became poetic, and afterwards any man who used them was an artist.

McStout: And you think literary tradition wholly arbitrary? You think it a mere accident that all hearts were touched by one man's words, and that all generations adopted his words and imitated his methods? Why was one poet's inspiration turned into a convention rather than another's? Evidently because he discovered and selected the truly interesting aspects of life, and dwelt upon those things which of themselves are beautiful. Don't you know how every age fancies it has a poet of original genius, that afterwards turns out to have been nothing but a fashionable mountebank? He had some trick that appealed to a particular mood or passion of the time, and his success in drawing attention for the moment is mistaken for a sign of greatness. That happens to Walt Whitman. The times are favorable to his vague pantheism, his formlessness, his confusion of values, his substitution of emotion for thought, his trust in impulse rather than in experience. Because we are too ignorant or too wilful to see the distinctions of things and of persons, we decree that there are no distinctions, and proceed to remodel literature and society upon that principle.

Van Tender: If the distinctions are real, there is no danger of their being destroyed. Things have different values, as one star differs from another star in brightness. All I insist on is that in all you can see light, if your eyes are open. Whitman would teach you, if you would only read him, to see in things their intrinsic nature and life, rather than the utility they may have for one another. That is his great merit, his sublime justice. It is a kind of profound piety that recognizes the life of every thing in nature, and spares it, and worships its intrinsic worth. There is something brutal and fatuous in the habit we commonly have of passing the parts of nature in review and pronouncing them good or bad according to the effect they have on our lives. Aren't they as real as ourselves? In practical life we have to override them, for if we waited for justice and the ultimate good to direct what we should do, we should die before we had done anything. But it's the privilege of contemplation to be just. Listen to what Whitman says here:

And do not call the tortoise unworthy because she is not something else,
And the jay in the woods never studied the gamut, yet trills pretty well to me,
And the look of the bay mare shames silliness out of me.

(Song of Myself, 13)

MCSTOUT: This justice of yours may be sublime, but isn't it a trifle dangerous? By admiring the beasts so much we may come to resemble them, – or perhaps the resemblance is the cause of the admiration. You may say it is brutal to make ourselves a standard for other creatures; yet a human standard is better than none at all, and can we have any other? But Walt Whitman, I understand, would think it a great improvement if men imitated the animals more than they do.
VAN TENDER: Undoubtedly, in some respects. Here he explains it perfectly:

I think I could turn and live with animals, they are so placid and self-contained,
I stand and look at them long and long.
They do not sweat and whine about their condition,
They do not lie awake in the dark and weep for their sins,
They do not make me sick discussing their duty to God,

Not one is dissatisfied, not one is demented with the mania of
   owning things,
Not one kneels to another, nor to his kind that lived thousands
   of years ago,
Not one is respectable or unhappy over the whole earth.

                     (*Song of Myself*, 32)

McStout: And not one writes bad prose or worse poetry, not one
is untrue to his instincts as all this talk is untrue to the better instincts
of man.

Van Tender: I knew it would came at last: Walt Whitman is
immoral!

McStout: It isn't immoral to call a spade a spade, but it is immoral
to treat life as a masquerade, as a magic pantomime in which acts have
no consequences and happiness and misery don't exist.

Van Tender: Ah, but Whitman is nothing if not a spectator, a
cosmic poet to whom the whole world is a play. And good and evil,
although not equally pleasant to experience, are equally interesting to
look at. Is it wrong to enjoy our misery when its distance from us
makes contemplation of it possible? How else can the gods have been
happy? To refuse us this pleasure is to deprive us of a consolation
without preventing our suffering. Or do you think the knowledge
of what life is would make us unfit to live? Should we be really more
wicked if the sun were not a Puritan and dared to look on the world
through the twenty-four hours?

McStout: Perhaps not, but the trouble with your contemplation
and impartiality is that it unnerves a man and makes him incapable
of indignation or enthusiasm. He goes into raptures over everything,
and accomplishes nothing. The world is so heavenly to him that he
finds nothing to do in it.

Van Tender: Except play his harp and wear his crown. Is it nothing
to perceive the beauty of the world, and help other men to perceive
it? I don't mean simply the pleasure of art itself. I mean the widening
of your sympathies, your reconciliation with nature. What better
thing is there for a man than to remember now and then that the
stars are laughing at him, to renounce his allegiance to his own
preferences and passions and by understanding to enter into those of
other men? We can't play at life without getting some knocks and

bruises, and without running some chance of defeat. But our best moments are the breathing spells when we survey the field and see what a glorious game it all is.

McSTOUT: I'm glad we may do that, especially as the other game is over.

VAN TENDER: What! is it possible we have been talking so long?

McSTOUT: There are the men coming back. We've won, though. You can tell by their faces.

VAN TENDER: So you see we weren't really needed. For all our philosophy, the world wags on.

(85–92)

Edward Dowden

from 'The Poetry of Democracy', *Studies in Literature 1789–1877* 1892

Men of every class then are interesting to Whitman. But no individual is pre-eminently interesting to him. His sketches of individual men and women, though wonderfully vivid and precise, are none of them longer than a page; each single figure passes rapidly out of sight, and a stream of other figures of men and women succeeds. Even in *Lincoln's Burial Hymn* he has only a word to say of 'the large sweet soul that has gone'; the chords of his nocturn, with their implicated threefold sweetness, odour and sound and light, having passed into his strain, really speak not of Lincoln but of death. George Peabody is celebrated briefly, because through him, 'a stintless, lavish giver, tallying the gifts of earth', a multitude of human beings have been blessed, and the true service of riches illustrated. No single person is the subject of Whitman's song, or can be; the individual suggests a group, and the group a multitude, each unit of which is as interesting as every other unit, and possesses equal claims to recognition. Hence the recurring tendency of his poems to become catalogues of persons and things. Selection seems forbidden to him; if he names one race of mankind the names of all other races press into his page; if he mentions one trade or occupation, all other trades and occupations follow. A long procession of living forms passes before him; each

several form, keenly inspected for a moment, is then dismissed. Men
and women are seen *en masse*, and the mass is viewed not from a
distance, but close at hand, where it is felt to be a concourse of individuals. Whitman will not have the people appear in his poems by
representatives or delegates; the people itself, in its undiminished
totality, marches through his poems, making its greatness and variety
felt. Writing down the headings of a Trades' Directory is not poetry;
but this is what Whitman never does. His catalogues are for the poet
always, if not always for the reader, *visions* – they are delighted – not
perhaps delightful – enumerations; when his desire for the perception
of greatness and variety is satisfied, not when a really complete
catalogue is made out, Whitman's enumeration ends; we may
murmur, but Whitman has been happy; what has failed to interest
our imaginations has deeply interested his; and even for us the impression of multitude, of variety, of equality is produced, as perhaps
it could be in no other way. Whether Whitman's habit of cataloguing
be justified by what has been said, or is in any way capable of justification, such at least is its true interpretation and significance.

One can perceive at a glance that these characteristics of Whitman's
work proceed directly from the democratic tendencies of the world
of thought and feeling in which he moves. It is curious to find De
Tocqueville, before there existed properly any native American
literature, describing in the spirit of philosophical prophecy what we
find realized in Whitman's *Leaves of Grass*:

He who inhabits a democratic country sees around him, on
every hand, men differing but little from each other; he cannot
turn his mind to any one portion of mankind without expanding
and dilating his thought till it embraces the whole world. . . .
The poets of democratic ages can never take any man in
particular as the subject of a piece, for an object of slender
importance, which is distinctly seen on all sides, will never lend
itself to an ideal conception. . . . As all the citizens who
compose a democratic community are nearly equal and alike, the
poet cannot dwell upon any one of them; but the nation itself
invites the exercise of his powers. The general similitude of
individuals which renders any one of them, taken separately,
an improper subject of poetry, allows poets to include them all

in the same imagery, and to take a general survey of the people itself. Democratic nations have a clearer perception than any other of their own aspect; and an aspect so imposing is admirably fitted to the delineation of the ideal.

The democratic poet celebrates no individual hero, nor does he celebrate himself. 'I celebrate myself,' sings Whitman, and the longest poem in *Leaves of Grass* is named by his own name; but the self-celebration throughout is celebration of himself as a man and an American; it is what he possesses in common with all others that he feels to be glorious and worthy of song, not that which differentiates him from others; manhood, and in particular American manhood, is the real subject of the poem *Walt Whitman*; and although Whitman has a most poignant feeling of personality, which indeed is a note of all he has written; it is to be remembered that in nearly every instance in which he speaks of himself the reference is as much impersonal as personal. In what is common he finds what is most precious. The true hero of the democratic poet is the nation of which he is a member, or the whole race of man to which the nation belongs. The mettlesome, proud, turbulent, brave, self-asserting young Achilles, lover of women and lover of comrades of Whitman's epic, can be no other than the American people; the Ulysses, the prudent, the 'cute, the battler with the forces of nature, the traveller in sea-like prairie, desolate swamp, and dense forest is brother Jonathan. But if the American nation is his hero, let it be observed that it is the American nation as the supposed leader of the human race, as the supposed possessor in ideas, in type of character, and in tendency if not in actual achievement of all that is most powerful and promising for the progress of mankind.

To the future Whitman looks to justify his confidence in America and in democracy. The aspect of the present he finds both sad and encouraging. The framework of society exists; the material civilization is rich and fairly organized. Without any transcendentalism or political mysticism about the principle of universal suffrage, not glossing over its 'appalling dangers', and for his own part content that until its time were come self-government should wait, and the condition of authoritative tutelage continue, he yet approves the principle as 'the only safe and preservative one for coming times', and sees in America its guardian. He dwells with inexhaustible delight upon certain elements in the yet unformed personal character of the average American man and woman. And his experience, and the experience of the nation during the Civil War – proving the faithfulness, obedience, docility, courage, fortitude, religious nature, tenderness, sweet affection of countless numbers of the unnamed, unknown rank and file of North and South – practically justifies democracy in Whitman's eyes 'beyond the proudest claims and wildest hopes of its enthusiasts'. But at the same time no one perceives more clearly, or observes with greater anxiety and alarm, the sore diseases of American society; and leaving us to reconcile his apparently contradictory statements he does not hesitate to declare that the New World democracy, 'however great a success in uplifting the masses out of their sloughs, in materialistic development, products, and in a certain highly deceptive superficial popular intellectuality, is so far an almost complete failure in social aspects, in any superb general personal character, and in really grand religious, moral, literary, and aesthetic results'. A vast and more and more thoroughly appointed body Whitman finds in the American world, and little or no soul. His senses are flattered, his imagination roused and delighted by the vast movement of life which surrounds him, its outward glory and gladness, but when he inquires, what is behind all this? the answer is of the saddest and most shameful kind. The following passage is in every way, in substance and in manner, highly characteristic of Whitman; but the reader must remember that in spite of all that he discerns of evil in democratic America, Whitman remains an American proud of his nationality, and a believer who does not waver in his democratic faith:

After an absence, I am now again (September, 1870) in New York city and Brooklyn, on a few weeks' vacation. The splendor, picturesqueness, and oceanic amplitude and rush of these great cities, the unsurpassed situation, rivers and bay, sparkling sea-tides, costly and lofty new buildings, the façades of marble and iron, of original grandeur and elegance of design, with the masses of gay color, the preponderance of white and blue, the flags flying, the endless ships, the tumultuous streets, Broadway, the heavy, low, musical roar, hardly ever intermitted even at night; the jobbers' houses, the rich shops, the wharves, the great Central Park, and the Brooklyn Park of hills (as I wander among them this beautiful fall weather, musing, watching, absorbing) – the assemblages of the citizens in their groups, conversations, trade, evening amusements, or along the by-quarters – these, I say, and the like of these, completely satisfy my senses of power, fulness, motion, etc., and give me, through such senses and appetites, and through my esthetic conscience, a continued exaltation and absolute fulfilment. Always, and more and more, as I cross the East and North rivers, the ferries, or with the pilots in their pilot-houses, or pass an hour in Wall Street, or the gold exchange, I realize (if we must admit such partialisms) that not Nature alone is great in her fields of freedom and the open air, in her storms, the shows of night and day, the mountains, forests, seas – but in the artificial, the work of man too is equally great – in this profusion of teeming humanity – in these ingenuities, streets, goods, houses, ships – these hurrying, feverish, electric crowds of men, their complicated business genius (not least among the geniuses), and all this mighty, many-threaded wealth and industry concentrated here.

But sternly discarding, shutting our eyes to the glow and grandeur of the general superficial effect, coming down to what is of the only real importance, Personalities, and examining minutely, we question, we ask, Are there, indeed, *men* here worthy the name? Are there athletes? Are there perfect women, to match the generous material luxuriance? Is there a pervading atmosphere of beautiful manners? Are there crops of fine youths and majestic old persons? Are there arts worthy freedom, and a rich people? Is there a great moral and religious civilization – the only justification of a great material one? Confess that to severe eyes, using the moral microscope upon humanity, a sort of dry and flat Sahara appears, these cities, crowded with petty grotesques, malformations, phantoms, playing meaningless antics. Confess that everywhere in shop, street, church, theatre, bar-room, official chair, are pervading flippancy and vulgarity, low cunning, infidelity – everywhere, the youth puny, impudent, foppish, prematurely ripe – everywhere an abnormal libidinousness, unhealthy forms, male, female, painted, padded, dyed, chignoned, muddy complexions, bad blood, the capacity for good motherhood deceasing or deceased, shallow notions of beauty, with a range of manners, or rather lack of manners, (considering the advantages enjoyed) probably the meanest to be seen in the world.

(*Democratic Vistas*, 1871)

Such a picture of the outcome of American democracy is ugly enough to satisfy the author of 'Shooting Niagara – and after?' [Thomas Carlyle] but such a picture only represents the worst side of the life of great cities. Whitman can behold these things, not without grief, not without shame, but without despair. He does not unfairly contrast the early years of confusion and crudity of a vast industrial and democratic era with the last and perfected results of an era of feudalism and aristocracy. He finds much to make him sad; but more to make him hopeful. He takes account of the evil anxiously, accurately; and can still rejoice. Upon the whole his spirit is exulting and prompt in cheerful action; not self-involved, dissatisfied, and fed by indignation. Contrast with the passage given above Whitman's preface to *Leaves of Grass* prefixed to Mr Rossetti's volume of Selections, with its joyous confidence and pride in American persons and things, or that very noble poem, *A Carol of Harvest, for 1867,* in which the armies of blue-clad conquering men are seen streaming North, and melt away and disappear, while in the same hour the heroes reappear, toiling in the fields, harvesting the products, glad and secure under the beaming sun, and under the great face of Her, the Mother, the Republic, without whom not a scythe might swing in security, 'not a maize-stalk dangle its silken tassels in peace'. If all enthusiasm about political principles be of the nature of *Schwärmerei*, Whitman's feeling towards the Republic deserves that name; but he would have the principles of democracy sternly tested by results – results however not only present but such prospective results as are logically inevitable, and he has faith in them not because they seem to him to favour freedom any more than because they seem to favour law and self-control, and security and order. He, as much as Mr Carlyle, admires 'disciplined men', and believes that with every disciplined man 'the arena of *Anti*-Anarchy, of God-appointed Order in this world' is widened; but he does not regard military service as the type of highest discipline, nor the drill-sergeant as the highest conceivable official person in the land. . . .

At times this optimism leads Whitman to the entire denial of evil; 'he contemplates evil as, in some sense, not existing, or, if existing, then as being of as much importance as anything else'; in some transcendental way, he believes, the opposition of God and Satan cannot really exist. Practically, however, he is not led astray by any such transcendental reducing of all things to the Divine. Any tendency of a mystical kind to ignore the distinction between good and evil, is checked by his strong democratic sense of the supreme importance of personal qualities, and the inevitable perception of the superiority of virtuous over vicious personal qualities.

By one who feels profoundly that the differences between men are determined, not by rank, or birth, or hereditary name or title, but simply by the different powers belonging to the bodies and souls of men, there is small danger of the meaning of *bad* and *good* being forgotten. And Whitman never really forgets this. The formation of a noble national character, to be itself the source of all literature, art, statesmanship, is that which above all else he desires. In that character the element of religion must, according to Whitman's ideal, occupy an important place, only inferior to that assigned to moral soundness, to conscience. 'We want, for These States, for the general character, a cheerful, religious fervour, imbued with the ever-present modifications of the human emotions, friendship, benevolence, with a fair field for scientific inquiry [to check fanaticism], the right of individual judgment, and always the cooling influences of material Nature.' These are not the words of one who moves the landmarks of right and wrong, and obscures their boundaries. For Whitman the worth of any man is simply the worth of his body and soul; each gift of nature, product of industry, and creation of art, is valuable in his eyes exactly in proportion to what it can afford for the benefit of body and soul. Only what belongs to these, and becomes a part of them, properly belongs to us – the rest is mere 'material'. This mode of estimating values is very revolutionary, but it is essentially just and moral. The rich man is not he who has accumulated unappropriated matter around him, but he who possesses much of what 'adheres, and goes forward, and is not dropped by death'.

Personality, character, is that which death cannot affect. Here again

Whitman's democratic feeling for personality overmasters his democratic tendency towards pantheism. He clings to his identity and his consciousness of it, and will not be tempted to surrender that consciousness in imagination by the attractions of any form of *nirvana*. Death, which is a name to him full of delicious tenderness and mystery not without some element of sensuousness curiously blended with it – ('O the beautiful touch of Death, soothing and benumbing a few moments, for reasons'), is but a solemn and immortal birth:

Dark Mother, always gliding near, with soft feet,
Have none chanted for thee a chant of fullest welcome?
Then I chant it for thee – I glorify thee above all;
I bring thee a song that when thou must indeed come, come
    unfalteringly.

> (1865 Sequel, *When Lilacs Last in
> the Dooryard Bloom'd*, 16)

From such indications as these, and others that have gone before, the reader must gather, as best as he can, the nature of Whitman's religious faith. But the chief thing to bear in mind is that Whitman cares far less to establish propositions than to arouse energy and supply a stimulus. His pupil must part from him as soon as possible, and go upon his own way.

I tramp a perpetual journey – (come listen all!)
My signs are a rain-proof coat, good shoes, and a staff cut from
    the woods;
No friend of mine takes his ease in my chair;
I have no chair, no church, no philosophy;
I lead no man to a dinner-table, library, or exchange!
But each man and each woman of you I lead upon a knoll,
My left hand hooking you round the waist,
My right hand pointing to landscapes of continents, and a plain
    public road.

> (*Song of Myself*, 46)

That plain public road each man must travel for himself.

Here we must end. We have not argued the question which many persons are most desirous to put about Walt Whitman – 'Is he a poet at all?' It is not easy to argue such a question in a profitable way. One thing only needs to be said, – no adequate impression of Whitman's poetical power can be obtained from this study. A single side of his mind and of his work has been examined, but such criticism as the present, narrowed and perhaps hardened by a tendency half doctrinaire, we attempt with an abiding remembrance of the truth expressed by Vauvenargues: 'Lorsque nous croyons tenir la vérité par un endroit, elle nous échappe par mille autres.'[1] To pass through and beyond a *view* of such a writer as Whitman, – a writer whose best function is to supply stimulus and energy, – and to enter into a vital personal contact with him is essential to true knowledge of his character. But views may help us on our way.

(493–523)

1 Just when we think we hold truth secure, it escapes us in a thousand ways. [Ed.]

Part Two **The Developing Debate**

Introduction

'I expected hell,' Whitman told Horace Traubel, 'and I got it.'
In spite of the remarkable serenity with which Whitman suffered
criticism, he was not indifferent to the kind of attack levelled at
him by Howells and James. Few major nineteenth-century poets
would have been humbled enough to say at the end of their lives
that 'in respect to pictorial talent, dramatic situations, and
especially in verbal melody and all the conventional technique of
poetry, not only the divine works that today stand ahead in the
world's reading, but dozens more, transcend . . . all that I have
done, or could do'. With his best friends assuring him that they
loved him whether he wrote in something called verse or prose,
it is no wonder that Whitman would conclude 'A Backward
Glance' by telling his audience his work offered a 'Person' rather
than 'literature', and therefore 'No one will get at my verses who
insists upon viewing them as a literary performance. . . .' But if
Whitman was rejected by America's men of letters he found
himself a hero nevertheless. The 'cosmic' Whitman admired by
his friend Dr Bucke, however, is not the author of *Democratic
Vistas*, the man who could write: 'Society, in these States, is
canker'd, crude, superstitious, and rotten . . . our New World
Democracy . . . [in spite of its] materialistic development . . . is,
so far, an almost complete failure in its social aspects. . . .' The
Whitman so much admired was the Whitman of 'high-
mindedness' (to use William James's phrase [p. 167]); the
emancipator of sexual freedom; or Van Wyck Brook's 'natural
affirmer', the optimistic spokesman for fresh air and democratic
culture. For twenty years testaments were written by men and
women for whom reading Whitman was a religious experience,
in spite of the fact that, like G. K. Chesterton (p. 169) or
Edwin Arlington Robinson, they were often unsympathetic to
both Whitman's language and his form. Such statements are
really a part of the history of morals rather than criticism, but
they account for Whitman's popularity during these years. Paul

Elmer More's essay (p. 171) stands out in that it acknowledges Whitman's total commitment to literary experience and, without condescension, tests his work against his contemporaries, Tennyson and Browning.

It is sometimes difficult in the essays collected here to distinguish Whitman's admirers from his detractors; but all are in opposition to the 'cosmic' Whitman whom Lawrence teases so relentlessly in his essay in *Studies in Classic American Literature*, the Whitman who 'aches with amorous love' and who in 'embracing All', leaves nothing of himself. 'Whitman's insight into man,' Santayana remarks, 'did not go beyond a sensuous sympathy; it consisted in a vicarious satisfaction in their pleasures, and instinctive love of their persons. It never approached a scientific or imaginative knowledge of their hearts' (p. 165). Santayana's accusation anticipates Lawrence's condemnation of Whitman's failure of nerve, his reluctance to pursue as a writer as well as a human being, the logic of the 'individual soul' (p. 196). Both Santayana and John Jay Chapman (p. 152) acknowledge Whitman's power, but in describing Whitman as a poet who offered 'an abundance of detail without organization' and a 'wealth of perception without intelligence', they were only confirming the deep-rooted prejudices of a younger generation about to admire Joyce and Eliot. Pound, extending his hand to Whitman, could admire the spirit of his defiance, but not his craft:

I make a pact with you, Walt Whitman –
I have detested you long enough.
I come to you as a grown child
Who has had a pig-headed father;
I am old enough now to make new friends,
It was you that broke the new wood,
Now it is a time for carving.

We have one sap and one root –
Let there be commerce between us.

Pound's note of 1900 on Whitman (unpublished until 1955)
suggests that he had other thoughts (p. 183). It is unfortunate
that Pound took no further occasion to write on Whitman's
poetry, since Pound acknowledged the 'deliberate artistry' behind
the apparent freedom in Whitman's line and caught his
insinuating rhythms. To the followers of Pound and Eliot,
Whitman's verse seemed antithetical to all that was ironic,
impersonal, allusive and well-wrought. As Amy Lowell smugly
put it, the moderns were 'positively trying to do something',
Whitman was 'negatively trying not to do something else' (p. 207).

For long after the shock of Whitman's subject wore off, there
still remained the problem of his form. Perhaps Eliot's confusion
reflects most dramatically the difficulty his generation had with
Whitman's line. Writing in the *Nation and Athenaeum* in June 1927,
Eliot remarked that Whitman 'was a great master of versification,
though much less reliable than Tennyson. It is, in fact, as a verse
maker that he deserves to be remembered; for his intellect was
decidedly inferior to that of Tennyson.' In his Introduction to
the *Selected Poems of Ezra Pound* (1928), Eliot reversed himself:
'Whitman's originality is both genuine and spurious. It is
genuine in so far as it is a logical development of certain English
prose; Whitman was a great prose writer. It is spurious in so far
as Whitman wrote in a way that asserted that his great prose was
a new form of verse.' Whitman's indebtedness to the parallelism
of Biblical poetry, to the rhetoric of oratory and to the prose of
Emerson had been pointed out almost from the beginning. The
real question, as Bliss Perry (p. 180) and Basil de Selincourt (p. 185)
noted, was not how much Whitman's verse resembled prose, but
exactly in what ways it differed from prose. De Selincourt shows
us how we are asked by the speaker in Whitman's poetry to
'stray upon the borderland of prose and poetry by a guide confident

of his power to keep us on the right side of the border'.

Thirty years after Whitman's death a new generation of poets wrote him off as a 'magnificent failure'. Like William Carlos Williams, whose opinion of Whitman was never to change (p. 329), younger poets wanted to separate their own poetry from 'those fitful risings and fallings' they felt characterized Whitman's verse. 'Free verse – if ever it existed – is out', Williams wrote in 1932:

[Whitman] in his later stages showed all the terrifying defects of his own method. Whitman to me is one broom stroke and that is all. He could not go on. Nature, the Rousseauists who foreshadowed Whitman, the imitation of the sounds of the sea *per se*, are a mistake. Poetry has nothing to do with that. It is not nature. It is poetry. Whitman grew into senseless padding, bombast, bathos. His invention ended where it began. He is almost a satirist of his era, when his line itself is taken as the criterion. He evaporates under scrutiny – crumbling not into sand, surely, but into a moraine, sizeable and impressive because of that.

(Letter to Kay Boyle)

The central claims of Whitman's reputation – his contribution to the poetic line and his role as the poet of democracy – come under careful scrutiny in the two essays which conclude this section. If the Whitman who emerges from the pages of Dimitri Mirsky (p. 238) and Amy Lowell is less revolutionary than the figure who went before – making poetry 'out of a system of prosody to which he is in principle opposed' and speaking a language which is 'that of the newspapers rather than that of colloquial speech' – he emerges as a poet and not something else. Both essays remind us that the only way to get at Whitman is to look at particular poems.

In the thirty years which followed his death, Whitman acquired an international reputation, but much of the interest in his work continued to remain biographical rather than critical. Edward Carpenter's *Days with Walt Whitman* (1906) was the first book to reprint Whitman's letter to Arthur Symonds denying homoerotic love in *Leaves of Grass*. Carpenter is one of many critics writing during these years who try to penetrate the mask of Whitman's normality. The best biography to appear was Emory Holloway's *Walt Whitman* (1926), here reviewed by T. S. Eliot (p. 205). Holloway's book remained the standard biography until Gay Wilson Allen's *The Solitary Singer* (1955). While wrong on some factual counts, Holloway was able nevertheless to write a persuasive account of a working poet and to save the human from the prophetic Whitman. Of the major figures writing during these years, only Lawrence could openly admire Whitman's ability to prune away the 'cliché of rhythm' as well as of phrase, but two critical studies of Whitman need no apology. In the work of Bliss Perry and Basil de Selincourt, Whitman acquired two readers who were, as the selections included here suggest, adept at both explication and the analysis of style.

The work of some European critics deserves special mention. In 1933 the Danish critic Frederik Schyberg (p. 231) furthered the pioneering psychological studies of Jean Catel (*Walt Whitman: la naissance du poète*, 1926) and undertook a penetrating analysis of the successive editions of *Leaves of Grass*. I have included a section from his chapter on the *Calamus* poems as the best analysis of the emotions expressed in those poems and the most reasonable statement that can be made concerning the erotic in Whitman's verse. The essay by Dimitri Mirsky is one of two admirable surveys of Whitman's verse included in this section (the other is by Amy Lowell). It originally served as the introduction to the 1935 translation of *Leaves of Grass* by K. I. Chukovsky. Mirsky's essay is all the more remarkable for being the work of a famous convert to Marxism who is able to cut through the political cant and to see Whitman as a thoroughly bourgeois poet.

Henry James

from a review of *Calamus: Walt Whitman's Letters to Peter Doyle*, *Literature*, vol. 2 16 April 1898

What sense shall I speak of as affected by the series of letters published, under the title of *Calamus*, by Dr R. M. Bucke, one of the literary executors of Walt Whitman? The democratic would be doubtless a prompt and simple answer, and as an illustration of democratic social conditions their interest is lively. The person to whom, from 1868 to 1880, they were addressed was a young labouring man, employed in rough railway work, whom Whitman met by accident – the account of the meeting, in his correspondent's own words, is the most charming passage in the volume – and constituted for the rest of life a subject of a friendship of the regular 'eternal', the legendary sort. The little book appeals, I daresay, mainly to the Whitmanite already made, but I should be surprised if it has actually failed of power to make a few more. I mean by the Whitmanite those for whom the author of *Leaves of Grass* is, with all his rags and tatters, an upright figure, a *successful* original. It has in a singular way something of the same relation to poetry that may be made out in the luckiest – few, but fine – of the writer's other pages; I call the way singular because it squeezes through the narrowest, humblest gate of prose.

There is not even by accident a line with a hint of style – it is all flat, familiar, affectionate, illiterate colloquy. If the absolute natural be, when the writer is interesting, the supreme merit of letters, these, accordingly, should stand high on the list. (I am taking for granted, of course, the interest of Whitman.) The beauty of the natural is, here, the beauty of the particular nature, the man's own overflow in the deadly dry setting, the personal passion, the love of life plucked like a flower in a desert of innocent, unconscious ugliness. To call the whole thing vividly American is to challenge, doubtless, plenty of dissent – on the ground, presumably, that the figure in evidence was no less queer a feature of Camden, New Jersey, than it would have been of South Kensington. That may perfectly be; but a thousand images of patient, homely, American life, else undistinguishable, are what its queerness – however startling – happened to express. In this little book is an audible New Jersey voice, charged thick with such impressions, and the reader will miss a chance who does not find in it many odd and pleasant human harmonies. Whitman wrote to his friend of what they both saw and touched, enormities of the common, sordid occupations, dreary amusements, undesirable food; and the record remains, by a mysterious marvel, a thing positively delightful. If we ever find out why, it must be another time. The riddle meanwhile is a neat one for the sphinx of democracy to offer.

(453)

John Jay Chapman

from 'Walt Whitman', *Emerson and Other Essays* 1898

... Whitman is representative. He is a real product, he has a real and most interesting place in the history of literature, and he speaks for a class and type of human nature whose interest is more than local, whose prevalence is admitted, – a type which is one of the products of the civilization of the century, perhaps of all centuries, and which has a positively planetary significance.

There are, in every country, individuals who, after a sincere attempt to take a place in organized society, revolt from the drudgery of it, content themselves with the simplest satisfactions of the grossest need of nature, so far as subsistence is concerned, and rediscover the infinite pleasures of life in the open air.

If the roadside, the sky, the distant town, the soft buffeting of the winds of heaven, are a joy to the aesthetic part of man, the freedom from all responsibility and accountability is Nirvana to his moral nature. A man who has once tasted these two joys together, the joy of being in the open air and the joy of being disreputable and unashamed, has touched an experience which the most close-knit and determined nature might well dread. Life has no terrors for such a man. Society has no hold on him. The trifling inconveniences of the mode of life are as nothing compared with its satisfactions. The worm that never dies is dead in him. The great mystery of consciousness and of effort is quietly dissolved into the vacant happiness of sensation, – not base sensation, but the sensation of the dawn and the sunset, of the mart and the theatre, and the stars, the panorama of the universe.

To the moral man, to the philosopher or the business man, to any one who is a cog in the wheel of some republic, all these things exist for the sake of something else. He must explain or make use of them, or define his relation to them. He spends the whole agony of his existence in an endeavor to docket them and deal with them. Hampered as he is by all that has been said and done before, he yet feels himself driven on to summarize, and wreak himself upon the impossible task of grasping this cosmos with his mind, of holding it in his hand, of subordinating it to his purpose.

The tramp is freed from all this. By an act as simple as death, he has put off effort and lives in peace.

It is no wonder that every country in Europe shows myriads of these men, as it shows myriads of suicides annually. It is no wonder, though the sociologists have been late in noting it, that specimens of the type are strikingly identical in feature in every country of the globe.

The habits, the physique, the tone of mind, even the sign-language and some of the catchwords, of tramps are the same everywhere. The men are not natally outcasts. They have always tried civilized life. Their early training, at least their early attitude of mind towards life, has generally been respectable. That they should be criminally inclined goes without saying, because their minds have been freed from the sanctions which enforce law. But their general innocence is, under the circumstances, very remarkable, and distinguishes them from the criminal classes.

When we see one of these men sitting on a gate, or sauntering down a city street, how often have we wondered how life appeared to him; what solace and what problems it presented. How often have we longed to know the history of such a soul, told, not by the police-blotter, but by the poet or novelist in the heart of the man!

Walt Whitman has given utterance to the soul of the tramp. A man of genius has passed sincerely and normally through this entire experience, himself unconscious of what he was, and has left a record of it to enlighten and bewilder the literary world.

In Whitman's works the elemental parts of a man's mind and the fragments of imperfect education may be seen merging together, floating and sinking in a sea of insensate egotism and rhapsody, repellent, divine, disgusting, extraordinary.

Our inability to place the man intellectually, and find a type and reason for his intellectual state, comes from this: that the revolt he represents is not an intellectual revolt. Ideas are not at the bottom of it. It is a revolt from drudgery. It is the revolt of laziness.

There is no intellectual coherence in his talk, but merely pathological coherence. Can the insulting jumble of ignorance and effrontery, of scientific phrase and French paraphrase, of slang and inspired adjective, which he puts forward with the pretence that it represents thought, be regarded, from any possible point of view, as a philosophy, or a system, or a belief? Is it individualism of any statable kind? Do the thoughts and phrases which float about in it have a meaning which bears any relation to the meaning they bear in the language of thinkers? Certainly not. Does all the patriotic talk, the talk about the United States and its future, have any significance as patriotism? Does it poetically represent the state of feeling of any class of American citizens towards their country? Or would you find the nearest equivalent to this emotion in the breast of the educated tramp of France, or Germany, or England? The speech of Whitman is English, and his metaphors and catchwords are apparently American, but the emotional content is cosmic. He put off patriotism when he took to the road.

The attraction exercised by his writings is due to their flashes of reality. Of course the man was a *poseur*, a most horrid mountebank and ego-maniac. His tawdry scraps of misused idea, of literary smartness, of dog-eared and greasy reminiscence, repel us. The world of men remained for him as his audience, and he did to civilized society the continuous compliment of an insane self-consciousness in its presence.

Perhaps this egotism and posturing is the revenge of a stilled conscience, and we ought to read in it the inversion of the social instincts. Perhaps all tramps are *poseurs*. But there is this to be said for Whitman, that whether or not this posing was an accident of a personal nature, or an organic result of his life, he was himself an authentic creature. He did not sit in a study and throw off his saga of balderdash, but he lived a life, and it is by his authenticity, and not by his poses, that he has survived.

The descriptions of nature, the visual observation of life, are first-hand and wonderful. It was no false light that led the Oxonians to call some of his phrases Homeric. The pundits were right in their curiosity over him; they went astray only in their attempt at classification.

It is a pity that truth and beauty turn to cant on the second delivery, for it makes poetry, as a profession, impossible. The lyric poets have always spent most of their time in trying to write lyric poetry, and the very attempt disqualifies them.

A poet who discovers his mission is already half done for; and even Wordsworth, great genius though he was, succeeded in half drowning his talents in his parochial theories, in his own self-consciousness and self-conceit.

Walt Whitman thought he had a mission. He was a professional poet. He had purposes and theories about poetry which he started out to enforce and illustrate. He is as didactic as Wordsworth, and is thinking of himself the whole time. He belonged, moreover, to that class of professionals who are always particularly self-centred, autocratic, vain, and florid, – the class of quacks. There are, throughout society, men, and they are generally men of unusual natural powers, who, after gaining a little unassimilated education, launch out for themselves and set up as authorities on their own account. They are, perhaps, the successors of the old astrologers, in that what they seek to establish is some personal professorship or predominance. The old occultism and mystery was resorted to as the most obvious device for increasing the personal importance of the magician; and the chief difference today between a regular physician and a quack is, that the quack pretends to know it all.

Brigham Young and Joseph Smith were men of phenomenal capacity, who actually invented a religion and created a community by the apparent establishment of supernatural and occult powers. The phrenologists, the venders of patent medicine, the Christian Scientists, the single-taxers, and all who proclaim panaceas and nostrums make the same majestic and pontifical appeal to human nature. It is this mystical power, this religious element, which floats them, sells the drugs, cures the sick, and packs the meetings.

By temperament and education Walt Whitman was fitted to be a prophet of this kind. He became a quack poet, and hampered his talents by the imposition of a monstrous parade of rattletrap theories and professions. If he had not been endowed with a perfectly marvellous capacity, a wealth of nature beyond the reach and plumb of his rodomontade, he would have been ruined from the start. As it is, he has filled his work with grimace and vulgarity. He writes a few lines of epic directness and cyclopean vigor and naturalness, and then obtrudes himself and his mission.

He has the bad taste bred in the bone of all missionaries and palmists, the sign-manual of a true quack. This bad taste is nothing more than the offensive intrusion of himself and his mission into the matter in hand. As for his real merits and his true mission, too much can hardly be said in his favor. The field of his experience was narrow, and not in the least intellectual. It was narrow because of his isolation from human life. A poet like Browning, or Heine, or Alfred de Musset deals constantly with the problems and struggles that arise in civilized life out of the close relationships, the ties, the duties and desires of the human heart. He explains life on its social side. He gives us some more or less coherent view of an infinitely complicated matter. He is a guidebook or a notebook, a highly trained and intelligent companion.

Walt Whitman has no interest in any of these things. He was fortunately so very ignorant and untrained that his mind was utterly incoherent and unintellectual. His mind seems to be submerged and to have become almost a part of his body. The utter lack of concentration which resulted from living his whole life in the open air has left him spontaneous and unaccountable. And the great value of his work is, that it represents the spontaneous and unaccountable functioning of the mind and body in health.

It is doubtful whether a man ever enjoyed life more intensely than Walt Whitman, or expressed the physical joy of mere living more completely. He is robust, all tingling with health and the sensations of health. All that is best in his poetry is the expression of bodily well-being.

A man who leaves his office and gets into a canoe on a Canadian river, sure of ten days' release from the cares of business and housekeeping, has a thrill of joy such as Walt Whitman has here and there thrown into his poetry. One might say that to have done this is the greatest accomplishment in literature. Walt Whitman, in some of his lines, breaks the frame of poetry and gives us life in the throb.

It is the throb of the whole physical system of a man who breathes the open air and feels the sky over him. *When Lilacs Last in the Dooryard Bloom'd* is a great lyric. Here is a whole poem without a trace of self-consciousness. It is little more than a description of nature. The allusions to Lincoln and to the funeral are but a word or two – merest suggestions of the tragedy. But grief, overwhelming grief, is in every line of it, the grief which has been transmuted into this sensitiveness to the landscape, to the song of the thrush, to the lilac's bloom, and the sunset.

Here is truth to life of the kind to be found in King Lear or Guy Mannering, in Aeschylus or Burns.

Walt Whitman himself could not have told you why the poem was good. Had he had any intimation of the true reason, he would have spoiled the poem. The recurrence and antiphony of the thrust, the lilac, the thought of death, the beauty of nature, are in a balance and dream of natural symmetry such as no cunning could come at, no conscious art could do other than spoil.

It is ungrateful to note Whitman's limitations, his lack of human passion, the falseness of many of his notions about the American people. The man knew the world merely as an observer, he was never a living part of it, and no mere observer can understand the life about him. Even his work during the war was mainly the work of an observer, and his poems and notes upon the period are picturesque. As to his talk about comrades and Manhattanese car-drivers, and brass-founders displaying their brawny arms round each other's brawny necks, all this gush and sentiment in Whitman's poetry is false to life. It has a lyrical value, as representing Whitman's personal feelings, but no one else in the country was ever found who felt or acted like this.

In fact, in all that concerns the human relations Walt Whitman is as unreal as, let us say, William Morris, and the American mechanic would probably prefer Sigurd the Volsung, and understand it better than Whitman's poetry.

This falseness to the sentiment of the American is interwoven with such wonderful descriptions of American sights and scenery, of ferryboats, thoroughfares, cataracts, and machine-shops that it is not strange the foreigners should have accepted the gospel.

On the whole, Whitman, though he solves none of the problems of life and throws no light on American civilization, is a delightful appearance, and a strange creature to come out of our beehive. This man committed every unpardonable sin against our conventions, and his whole life was an outrage. He was neither chaste, nor industrious, nor religious. He patiently lived upon cold pie and tramped the earth in triumph.

He did really live the life he liked to live, in defiance of all men, and this is a great desert, a most stirring merit. And he gave, in his writings, a true picture of himself and of that life, – a picture which the world had never seen before, and which it is probable the world will not soon cease to wonder at.

(116–28)

George Santayana

from 'The Poetry of Barbarism', *Interpretations of Poetry and Religion*
1900

The classic and the Christian systems were both systems of ideas, attempts to seize the eternal morphology of reality and describe its unchanging constitution. The imagination was summoned thereby to contemplate the highest objects, and the essence of things being thus described, their insignificant variations could retain little importance and the study of these variations might well seen superficial. Mechanical science, the science of causes, was accordingly neglected, while the science of values, with the arts that express these values, was exclusively pursued. The reverse has now occurred and the spirit of life, innocent of any rationalizing discipline and deprived of an authoritative and adequate method of expression, has relapsed into miscellaneous and shallow exuberance. Religion and art have become short winded. They have forgotten the old maxim that we should copy in order to be copied and remember in order to be remembered. It is true that the multiplicity of these incompetent efforts seems to many a compensation for their ill success, or even a ground for asserting their absolute superiority. Incompetence, when it flatters the passions, can always find a greater incompetence to approve of it. Indeed, some people would have regarded the Tower of Babel as the best academy of eloquence on account of the variety of oratorical methods prevailing there.

It is thus that the imagination of our time has relapsed into barbarism. But discipline of the heart and fancy is always so rare a thing that the neglect of it need not be supposed to involve any very terrible or obvious loss. The triumphs of reason have been few and partial at any time, and perfect works of art are almost unknown. The failure of art and reason, because their principle is ignored, is therefore hardly more conspicuous than it was when their principle, although perhaps acknowledged, was misunderstood or disobeyed. Indeed, to one who fixes his eye on the ideal goal, the greatest art often seems the greatest failure, because it alone reminds him of what it should have been. Trivial stimulations coming from vulgar objects, on the contrary, by making us forget altogether the possibility of a deep satisfaction, often succeed in interesting and in winning applause. The pleasure they give us is so brief and superficial that the wave of essential disappointment which would ultimately drown it has not time to rise from the heart.

The poetry of barbarism is not without its charm. It can play with sense and passion the more readily and freely in that it does not aspire to subordinate them to a clear thought or a tenable attitude of the will. It can impart the transitive emotions which it expresses; it can find many partial harmonies of mood and fancy; it can, by virtue of its red-hot irrationality, utter wilder cries, surrender itself and us to more absolute passion, and heap up a more indiscriminate wealth of images than belong to poets of seasoned experience or of heavenly inspiration. Irrational stimulation may tire us in the end, but it excites us in the beginning; and how many conventional poets, tender and prolix, have there not been, who tire us now without ever having excited anybody? The power to stimulate is the beginning of greatness, and when the barbarous poet has genius, as he well may have, he stimulates all the more powerfully on account of the crudity of his methods and the recklessness of his emotions. The defects of such art – lack of distinction, absence of beauty, confusion of ideas, incapacity permanently to please – will hardly be felt by the contemporary public, if once its attention is arrested; for no poet is so undisciplined that he will not find many readers, if he finds readers at all, less disciplined than himself.

These considerations may perhaps be best enforced by applying them to two writers of great influence over the present generation who seem to illustrate them on different planes – Robert Browning and Walt Whitman. They are both analytic poets – poets who seek to reveal and express the elemental as opposed to the conventional; but the dissolution has progressed much farther in Whitman than in Browning, doubtless because Whitman began at a much lower stage of moral and intellectual organization; for the good will to be radical was present in both. The elements to which Browning reduces experience are still passions, characters, persons; Whitman carries the disintegration further and knows nothing but moods and particular images. The world of Browning is a world of history with civilization for its setting and with the conventional passions for its motive forces. The world of Whitman is innocent of these things and contains only far simpler and more chaotic elements. In him the barbarism is much more pronounced; it is, indeed, avowed, and the 'barbaric yawp' is sent 'over the roofs of the world' in full consciousness of its inarticulate character; but in Browning the barbarism is no less real though disguised by a literary and scientific language, since the passions of civilized life with which he deals are treated as so many 'barbaric yawps', complex indeed in their conditions, puffings of an intricate engine, but aimless in their vehemence and mere ebullitions of lustiness in adventurous and profoundly ungoverned souls.

Irrationality on this level is viewed by Browning with the same satisfaction with which, on a lower level, it is viewed by Whitman; and the admirers of each hail it as the secret of a new poetry which pierces to the quick and awakens the imagination to a new and genuine vitality. It is in the rebellion against discipline, in the abandonment of the ideals of classic and Christian tradition, that this rejuvenation is found. Both poets represent, therefore, and are admired for representing, what may be called the poetry of barbarism in the most accurate and descriptive sense of this word. For the barbarian is the man who regards his passions as their own excuse for being; who does not domesticate them either by understanding their cause or by conceiving their ideal goal. He is the man who does not know his derivations nor perceive his tendencies, but who merely feels and acts, valuing in his life its force and its filling, but being careless of its purpose and its form. His delight is in abundance and vehemence; his art, like his life, shows an exclusive respect for quantity and splendour of materials. His scorn for what is poorer and weaker than himself is only surpassed by his ignorance of what is higher.

Walt Whitman

The works of Walt Whitman offer an extreme illustration of this phase of genius, both by their form and by their substance. It was the singularity of his literary form – the challenge it threw to the conventions of verse and of language – that first gave Whitman notoriety: but this notoriety has become fame, because those incapacities and solecisms which glare at us from his pages are only the obverse of a profound inspiration and of a genuine courage. Even the idiosyncrasies of his style have a side which is not mere perversity or affectation; the order of his words, the procession of his images, reproduce the method of a rich, spontaneous, absolutely lazy fancy. In most poets such a natural order is modified by various governing motives – the thought, the metrical form, the echo of other poems in the memory. By Walt Whitman these conventional influences are resolutely banished. We find the swarms of men and objects rendered as they might strike the retina in a sort of waking dream. It is the most sincere possible confession of the lowest – I mean the most primitive – type of perception. All ancient poets are sophisticated in comparison and give proof of longer intellectual and moral training. Walt Whitman has gone back to the innocent style of Adam, when the animals filed before him one by one and he called each of them by its name.

In fact, the influences to which Walt Whitman was subject were as favourable as possible to the imaginary experiment of beginning the world over again. Liberalism and transcendentalism both harboured some illusions on that score; and they were in the air which our poet breathed. Moreover he breathed this air in America, where the newness of the material environment made it easier to ignore the fatal antiquity of human nature. When he afterward became aware that there was or had been a world with a history, he studied that world with curiosity and spoke of it not without a certain shrewdness. But he still regarded it as a foreign world and imagined, as not a few Americans have done, that his own world was a fresh creation, not amenable to the same laws as the old. The difference in the condi-

tions blinded him, in his merely sensuous apprehension, to the identity
of the principles.

His parents were farmers in central Long Island and his early years
were spent in that district. The family seems to have been not too
prosperous and somewhat nomadic; Whitman himself drifted through
boyhood without much guidance. We find him now at school, now
helping the labourers at the farms, now wandering along the beaches
of Long Island, finally at Brooklyn working in an apparently desultory way as a printer and sometimes as a writer for a local newspaper.
He must have read or heard something, at this early period, of the
English classics; his style often betrays the deep effect made upon
him by the grandiloquence of the Bible, of Shakespeare, and of
Milton. But his chief interest, if we may trust his account, was
already in his own sensations. The aspects of Nature, the forms and
habits of animals, the sights of cities, the movement and talk of common people, were his constant delight. His mind was flooded with
these images, keenly felt and afterward to be vividly rendered with
bold strokes of realism and imagination.

Many poets have had this faculty to seize the elementary aspects of
things, but none has had it so exclusively; with Whitman the surface
is absolutely all and the underlying structure is without interest and
almost without existence. He had had no education and his natural
delight in imbibing sensations had not been trained to the uses of
practical or theoretical intelligence. He basked in the sunshine of
perception and wallowed in the stream of his own sensibility, as
later at Camden in the shallows of his favourite brook. Even during
the civil war, when he heard the drum-taps so clearly, he could only
gaze at the picturesque and terrible aspects of the struggle, and linger
among the wounded day after day with a canine devotion; he could
not be aroused either to clear thought or to positive action. So also
in his poems; a multiplicity of images pass before him and he yields
himself to each in turn with absolute passivity. The world has no
inside; it is a phantasmagoria of continuous visions, vivid, impressive,
but monotonous and hard to distinguish in memory, like the waves
of the sea or the decorations of some barbarous temple, sublime only
by the infinite aggregation of parts.

This abundance of detail without organization, this wealth of
perception without intelligence and of imagination without taste,

makes the singularity of Whitman's genius. Full of sympathy and receptivity, with a wonderful gift of graphic characterization and an occasional rare grandeur of diction, he fills us, with a sense of the individuality and the universality of what he describes – it is a drop in itself yet a drop in the ocean. The absence of any principle of selection or of a sustained style enables him to render aspects of things and of emotion which would have eluded a trained writer. He is, therefore, interesting even where he is grotesque or perverse. He has accomplished, by the sacrifice of almost every other good quality, something never so well done before. He has approached common life without bringing in his mind any higher standard by which to criticize it; he has seen it, not in contrast with an ideal, but as the expression of forces more indeterminate and elementary than itself; and the vulgar, in this cosmic setting, has appeared to him sublime.

There is clearly some analogy between a mass of images without structure and the notion of an absolute democracy. Whitman, inclined by his genius and habits to see life without relief or organization, believed that his inclination in this respect corresponded with the spirit of his age and country, and that Nature and society, at least in the United States, were constituted after the fashion of his own mind. Being the poet of the average man, he wished all men to be specimens of that average, and being the poet of a fluid Nature, he believed that Nature was or should be a formless flux. This personal bias of Whitman's was further encouraged by the actual absence of distinction in his immediate environment. Surrounded by ugly things and common people, he felt himself happy, ecstatic, overflowing with a kind of patriarchal love. He accordingly came to think that there was a spirit of the New World which he embodied, and which was in complete opposition to that of the Old, and that a literature upon novel principles was needed to express and strengthen this American spirit.

Democracy was not to be merely a constitutional device for the better government of given nations, not merely a movement for the material improvement of the lot of the poorer classes. It was to be a social and a moral democracy and to involve an actual equality among all men. Whatever kept them apart and made it impossible for them to be messmates together was to be discarded. The literature of democracy was to ignore all extraordinary gifts of genius or virtue, all distinction drawn even from great passions or romantic adventures. In Whitman's works, in which this new literature is foreshadowed, there is accordingly not a single character nor a single story. His only hero is Myself, the 'single separate person', endowed with the primary impulses, with health, and with sensitiveness to the elementary aspects of Nature. The perfect man of the future, the prolific begetter of other perfect men, is to work with his hands, chanting the poems of some future Walt, some ideally democratic bard. Women are to have as nearly as possible the same character as men: the emphasis is to pass from family life and local ties to the friendship of comrades and the general brotherhood of man. Men are to be vigorous, comfortable, sentimental, and irresponsible.

This dream is, of course, unrealized and unrealizable, in America as elsewhere. Undeniably there are in America many suggestions of such a society and such a national character. But the growing complexity and fixity of institutions necessarily tends to obscure these traits of a primitive and crude democracy. What Whitman seized upon as the promise of the future was in reality the survival of the past. He sings the song of pioneers, but it is in the nature of the pioneer that the greater his success the quicker must be his transformation into something different. When Whitman made the initial and amorphous phase of society his ideal, he became the prophet of a lost cause. That cause was lost, not merely when wealth and intelligence began to take shape in the American Commonwealth, but it was lost at the very foundation of the world, when those laws of evolution were established which Whitman, like Rousseau, failed to understand. If we may trust Mr Herbert Spencer, these laws involve a passage from the homogeneous to the heterogeneous, and a constant progress at once in differentiation and in organization – all, in a word, that Whitman systematically deprecated or ignored. He is surely not the spokesman of the tendencies of his country, although he describes some aspects of its past and present condition: nor does he appeal to those whom he describes, but rather to the dilettanti he despises. He is regarded as representative chiefly by foreigners, who look for some grotesque expression of the genius of so young and prodigious a people.

Whitman, it is true, loved and comprehended men; but this love and comprehension had the same limits as his love and comprehension of Nature. He observed truly and responded to his observation with genuine and pervasive emotion. A great gregariousness, an innocent tolerance of moral weakness, a genuine admiration for bodily health and strength, made him bubble over with affection for the generic human creature. Incapable of an ideal passion, he was full of the milk of human kindness. Yet, for all his acquaintance with the ways and thoughts of the common man of his choice, he did not truly understand him. For to understand people is to go much deeper than they go themselves; to penetrate to their characters and disentangle their inmost ideals. Whitman's insight into man did not go beyond a sensuous sympathy; it consisted in a vicarious satisfaction in their pleasures, and an instinctive love of their persons. It never approached a scientific or imaginative knowledge of their hearts.

Therefore Whitman failed radically in his dearest ambition: he can never be a poet of the people. For the people, like the early races whose poetry was ideal, are natural believers in perfection. They have no doubts about the absolute desirability of wealth and learning and power, none about the worth of pure goodness and pure love. Their chosen poets, if they have any, will be always those who have known how to paint these ideals in lively even if in gaudy colours. Nothing is farther from the common people than the corrupt desire to be primitive. They instinctively look toward a more exalted life, which they imagine to be full of distinction and pleasure, and the idea of that brighter existence fills them with hope or with envy or with humble admiration.

If the people are ever won over to hostility to such ideals, it is only because they are cheated by demagogues who tell them that if all the flowers of civilization were destroyed its fruits would become more abundant. A greater share of happiness, people think, would fall to their lot could they destroy everything beyond their own possible possessions. But they are made thus envious and ignoble only by a deception: what they really desire is an ideal good for themselves which they are told they may secure by depriving others of their pre-eminence. Their hope is always to enjoy perfect satisfaction themselves; and therefore a poet who loves the picturesque aspects of labour and vagrancy will hardly be the poet of the poor. He may have described their figure and occupation, in neither of which they are much interested; he will not have read their souls. They will prefer to him any sentimental story-teller, any sensational dramatist, any moralizing poet; for they are hero-worshippers by temperament, and are too wise or too unfortunate to be much enamoured of themselves or of the conditions of their existence.

Fortunately, the political theory that makes Whitman's principle of literary prophecy and criticism does not always inspire his chants, nor is it presented, even in his prose works, quite bare and unadorned. In *Democratic Vistas* we find it clothed with something of the same poetic passion and lighted up with the same flashes of intuition which we admire in the poems. Even there the temperament is finer than the ideas and the poet wiser than the thinker. His ultimate appeal is really to something more primitive and general than any social aspirations, to something more elementary than an ideal of any kind. He speaks to those minds and to those moods in which sensuality is touched with mysticism. When the intellect is in abeyance, when we would 'turn and live with the animals, they are so placid and self-contained', when we are weary of conscience and of ambition, and would yield ourseves for a while to the dream of sense, Walt Whitman is a welcome companion. The images he arouses in us, fresh, full of light and health and of a kind of frankness and beauty, are prized all the more at such a time because they are not choice, but drawn perhaps from a hideous and sordid environment. For this circumstance makes them a better means of escape from convention and from that fatigue and despair which lurk not far beneath the surface of conventional life. In casting off with self-assurance and a sense of fresh vitality the distinctions of tradition and reason a man may feel, as he sinks back comfortably to a lower level of sense and instinct, that he is returning to Nature or escaping into the infinite. Mysticism makes us proud and happy to renounce the work of intelligence, both in thought and in life, and persuades us that we become divine by remaining imperfectly human. Walt Whitman gives a new expression to this ancient and multiform tendency. He feels his own cosmic justification and he would lend the sanction of his inspiration to all loafers and holiday-makers. He would be the congenial patron of farmers and factory hands in their crude pleasures and pieties, as Pan was the patron of the shepherds of Arcadia: for he is sure that in spite of his hairiness and animality, the gods will acknowledge him as one of themselves and smile upon him from the serenity of Olympus.

(172–87)

William James

from 'The Religion of Healthy-Mindedness', *The Varieties of Religious Experience* 1902

Walt Whitman owes his importance in literature to the systematic expulsion from his writings of all contractile elements. The only sentiments he allowed himself to express were of the expansive order; and he expressed these in the first person, not as your mere monstrously conceited individual might so express them, but vicariously for all men, so that a passionate and mystic ontological emotion suffuses his words, and ends by persuading the reader that men and women, life and death, and all things are divinely good.

Thus it has come about that many persons today regard Walt Whitman as the restorer of the eternal natural religion. He has infected them with his own love of comrades, with his own gladness that he and they exist. Societies are actually formed for his cult; a periodical organ exists for its propagation, in which the lines of orthodoxy and heterodoxy are already beginning to be drawn; hymns are written by others in his peculiar prosody; and he is even explicitly compared with the founder of the Christian religion, not altogether to the advantage of the latter.

Whitman is often spoken of as a 'pagan'. The word nowadays means sometimes the mere natural animal man without a sense of sin; sometimes it means a Greek or Roman with his own peculiar religious consciousness. In neither of these senses does it fitly define this poet. He is more than your mere animal man who has not tasted of the tree of good and evil. He is aware enough of sin for a swagger to be present in his indifference towards it, a conscious pride in his freedom from flexions and contractions, which your genuine pagan in the first sense of the word would never show.

... I could turn and live with animals, they are so placid and
    self-contained,
I stand and look at them long and long.

They do not sweat and whine about their condition,
They do not lie awake in the dark and weep for their sins.

· · · · · ·

Not one is dissatisfied, not one is demented with the mania of
   owning things,
Not one kneels to another, nor to his kind that lived thousands
   of years ago,
Not one is respectable or unhappy over the whole earth.
                              (*Song of Myself*, 32)

No natural pagan could have written these well-known lines. But
on the other hand Whitman is less than a Greek or Roman; for their
consciousness, even in Homeric times, was full to the brim of the sad
mortality of this sunlit world, and such a consciousness Walt Whitman
resolutely refuses to adopt. When, for example, Achilles, about to slay
Lycaon, Priam's young son, hears him sue for mercy, he stops to
say:

Ah, friend, thou too must die: why thus lamentest thou?
Patroclos too is dead, who was better far than thou. . . . Over
me too hang death and forceful fate. There cometh morn or
eve or some noonday when my life too some man shall take
in battle, whether with spear he smite, or arrow from the
string.
                    (*Iliad*, XXI; E. Myer's translation)

Then Achilles savagely severs the poor boy's neck with his sword,
heaves him by the foot into the Scamander, and calls to the fishes of
the river to eat the white fat of Lycaon. Just as here the cruelty and
the sympathy each ring true, and do not mix or interfere with one
another, so did the Greeks and Romans keep all their sadnesses and
gladnesses unmingled and entire. Instinctive good they did not
reckon sin; nor had they any such desire to save the credit of the
universe as to make them insist, as so many of *us* insist, that what
immediately appears as evil must be 'good in the making', or something equally ingenious. Good was good, and bad just bad, for the
earlier Greeks. They neither denied the ills of nature – Walt Whitman's
verse, 'What is called good is perfect and what is called bad is just as
perfect,' would have been mere silliness to them – nor did they, in
order to escape from those ills, invent 'another and a better world' of
the imagination, in which, along with the ills, the innocent goods of
sense would also find no place. This integrity of the instinctive

reactions, this freedom from all moral sophistry and strain, gives a pathetic dignity to ancient pagan feeling. And this quality Whitman's outpourings have not got. His optimism is too voluntary and defiant; his gospel has a touch of bravado and an affected twist, and this diminishes its effect on many readers who yet are well disposed towards optimism, and on the whole quite willing to admit that in important respects Whitman is of the genuine lineage of the prophets.

(84–6)

G. K. Chesterton

'Conventions and the Hero' 1904 (in *Lunacy and Letters*, 1958)

The cynics (pretty little lambs) tell us that experience and the advance of years teach us the hollowness and artificiality of things. In our youth, they say, we imagine ourselves among roses, but when we pluck them they are red paper. Now, I believe everybody alive knows that the reverse of this is the truth. We grow conservative as we grow old, it is true. But we do not grow conservative because we have found so many new things spurious. We grow conservative because we have found so many old things genuine. We begin by thinking all conventions, all traditions, false and meaningless. Then one convention after another, one tradition after another, begins to explain itself, begins to beat with life under our hand. We thought these things were simply stuck on to human life; we find that they are rooted. We thought it was only a tiresome regulation that we should take off our hats to a lady; we find it is the pulse of chivalry and the splendour of the West. We thought it was artificial to dress for dinner. We realize that the festive idea, the idea of the wedding garment, is more natural than Nature itself. As I say, the precise opposite of the cynical statement is the truth. Our ardent boyhood believes things to be dead; and graver manhood discovers them to be alive. We waken in our infancy and believe ourselves surrounded by red paper. We pluck at it and find that it is roses.

A good instance may be found in the case of a great man who has been the sole spiritual support of me and many others, who will remain one of our principal spiritual supports. Walt Whitman is, I suppose, beyond question the ablest man America has yet produced. He also happens to be, incidentally, one of the greatest men of the nineteenth century. Ibsen is all very well, Zola is all very well and Maeterlinck is all very well; but we have begun already to get to the end of them. And we have not yet begun to get to the beginning of Whitman. The egoism of which men accuse him is that sense of human divinity which no one has felt since Christ. The baldness of which men accuse him is simply that splendidly casual utterance which no sage has used since Christ. But all the same, this gradual and glowing conservatism which grows upon us as we live leads us to feel that in just those points in which he violated the chief conventions of poetry, in just those points he was wrong. He was mistaken in abandoning metre in poetry; not because in forsaking it he was forsaking anything ornamental or anything civilized, as he himself thought. In forsaking metre he was forsaking something quite wild and barbarous, something as instinctive as anger and as necessary as meat. He forgot that all real things move in a rhythm, that the heart beats in harmony, that the seas rise and ebb in harmony. He forgot that any child who shouts falls into some sort of repetition and assonance, that the wildest dancing is at the bottom monotonous. The whole of Nature moves in a recurrent music; it is only with a considerable effort of civilization that we can contrive to be other than musical. The whole world talks poetry; it is only we who, with elaborate ingenuity, manage to talk prose.

The same that is true of Whitman's violation of metre is true, though in a minor degree, of his violation of what is commonly called modesty. Decorum itself is of little social value; sometimes it is a sign of social decay. Decorum is the morality of immoral societies. The people who care most about modesty are often those who care least about chastity; no better examples could be given than oriental Courts or the west-end drawing-rooms. But all the same Whitman was wrong. He was wrong because he had at the back of his mind the notion that modesty or decency was in itself an artificial thing. This is quite a mistake. The roots of modesty, like the roots of mercy or of any other traditional virtue, are to be found in all fierce and primitive things. A wild shyness, a fugitive self-possession, belongs to all simple creatures. It belongs to children; it belongs to savages; it belongs even to animals.

171 Paul Elmer More

To conceal something is the first of Nature's lessons; it is far less elaborate than to explain everything. And if women are, as they certainly are, much more dignified and much more modest than men, if they are more reticent, and, in the excellent current phrase, 'keep themselves to themselves' much more, the reason is very simple; it is because women are much more fierce and much more savage than men. To be thoroughly immodest is an exceedingly elaborate affair. To have complete self-revelation one must have complete self-consciousness. Thus it is that while from the beginning of the world men have had the most exquisite philosophies and social arrangements, nobody ever thought of complete indecency, indecency on principle, until we reached a high and complex state of civilization. To conceal some things came to us like eating bread. To talk about everything never appeared until the age of the motor-car.

(62–5)

Paul Elmer More

from 'Walt Whitman', *Shelburne Essays* 1906

... When he succeeds, Whitman stands naturally with the great and not the minor poets. Take, for instance, these three familiar poems by Browning and Tennyson and Whitman on the same theme, and Whitman, though not at his highest here, is still not out of place:

Fear death? – to feel the fog in my throat,
    The mist in my face,
When the snows begin, and the blasts denote
    I am nearing the place,
The power of the night, the press of the storm,
    The post of the foe;
Where he stands, the Arch Fear in a visible form,
    Yet the strong man must go. . . .
I was ever a fighter, so – one fight more,
    The best and the last!
I would hate that death bandaged my eyes, and forbore,
    And bade me creep past!

No! let me taste the whole of it, fare like my peers
   The heroes of old,
Bear the brunt, in a minute pay glad life's arrears
   Of pain, darkness and cold.
For sudden the worst turns the best to the brave,
   The black minute's at end,
And the elements' rage, the fiend-voices that rave,
   Shall dwindle, shall blend,
Shall change, shall become first a peace out of pain,
   Then a light, then thy breast,
O thou soul of my soul! I shall clasp thee again,
   And with God be the rest!

Sunset and evening star,
   And one clear call for me!
And may there be no moaning of the bar,
   When I put out to sea,

But such a tide as moving seems asleep,
   Too full for sound and foam,
When that which drew from out the boundless deep
   Turns again home.

Twilight and evening bell,
   And after that the dark!
And may there be no sadness of farewell
   When I embark;

For tho' from out our bourne of Time and Place
   The flood·may bear me far,
I hope to see my Pilot face to face
   When I have crossed the bar.

Whispers of heavenly death murmur'd I hear,
Labial gossip of night, sibilant chorals,
Footsteps gently ascending, mystical breezes wafted soft and low,
Ripples of unseen rivers, tides of a current flowing, forever flowing,
(Or is it the plashing of tears? the measureless waters of human
   tears?)

I see, just see skyward, great cloud-masses,
Mournfully slowly they roll, silently swelling and mixing,
With at times a half-dimm'd sadden'd far-off star,
Appearing and disappearing.

(Some parturition rather, some solemn immortal birth;
On the frontiers to eyes impenetrable,
Some soul is passing over.)

(*Whispers of Heavenly Death*)

Browning's lines are beaten out with a superb vigour, but in substance they express only the crude individualism of a man who sees nothing beyond his personal emotions, who will contend for these face to face with the Arch Fear, that great contemner of persons, and thinks to carry them into the silence of the grave. Tennyson, the poet of universal law, has caught up into one luminous throbbing image the merging of the soul into the great tides of being from whence it sprung, while still the idea of personality is not entirely lost, but changed into a kind of mystic symbol. It is notable that Whitman, who posed before the world as the upholder of rank egotism, shows less of this quality in the presence of death than either of his great contemporaries. Here all thought of self is lost in a vague *rapport*, as he would say, with the dim suggestions of whispering, cloud-wrapped night; here is a perception of spiritual values far above the anthropomorphism of Browning, and a power of evoking a poetical mood, when once we have trained our ear to bring out his rhythms, as strong, though not as permanent, as Tennyson's. In this note of almost pantheistic revery, the lines may represent a departure from Whitman's earlier manner, but in another respect they exhibit the most constant and characteristic of his qualities – the sense of ceaseless indistinct motion, intimated in the sound of ascending footsteps and of the unseen flowing rivers, expressed more directly in the shifting clouds and the far off appearing and disappearing star.

And this sense of indiscriminate motion is, I think, the impression left finally by Whitman's work as a whole, – not the impression of wind-tossed inanities that is left by Swinburne, but of realities, solid and momentous, and filled with blind portents for the soul. Now the observer seems to be moving through clustered objects beheld vividly for a second of time and then lost in the mass, and, again, the observer himself is stationary while the visions throng past him in almost dizzy rapidity; but in either case we come away with the feeling of having been merged in unbroken processions, whose beginning and end are below the distant horizon, and whose meaning we but faintly surmise:

All is a procession,
The universe is a procession with measured and perfect motion.
(*I Sing the Body Electric*, 6)

The explanation of this effect is in part simple. The aspect of nature never forgotten by Whitman in town or field is the sea, and always the sea in motion. He is on the beach listening 'As the old mother sways her to and fro singing her husky song', and looking out upon the 'troops of white-maned racers racing to the goal'. The endless rush of the ferries is in the substance of his verse as it formed a part of his life, and the quick pulsations of Broadway are equally there:

Thou of the endless sliding, mincing, shuffling feet!
Thou, like the parti-coloured world itself – like infinite teeming,
    mocking life!
Thou visor'd, vast, unspeakable show and lesson!
(*Broadway*)

And the world itself is an Open Road, – 'the long brown path before me,' he calls it, 'leading wherever I choose.' Only as adding to the freedom and spaciousness of this sliding panorama can the 'cataloguing' portions of Whitman's book find any justification.

From these material images it is an easy transition to the vision 'Of the progress of the souls of men and women along the grand roads of the universe.' Out of the infinite past he beholds himself climbing, as it were, up the long gradations of time:

Rise after rise bow the phantoms behind me,
Afar down I see the huge first Nothing, I know I was even there,
I waited unseen and always, and slept through the lethargic mist,
And took my time, and took no hurt from the fetid carbon. . . .

Cycles ferried my cradle, rowing and rowing like cheerful
    boatmen,

For room to me stars kept aside in their own rings,
They sent influences to look after what was to hold me.
(Song of Myself, 44)

And in the future, the soul, like Columbus dreaming of ever new worlds, perceives for itself other unending voyages:

As if some miracle, some hand divine unseal'd my eyes,
Shadowy vast shapes smile through the air and sky,
And on the distant waves sail countless ships,
And anthems in new tongues I hear saluting me.
(Prayer of Columbus)

It was the same symbolism in the *Passage to India* ('Passage to more than India!' as the refrain becomes) which led Whitman to speak of that poem to Mr Traubel as containing, in the jargon of Mickle Street, 'the essential ultimate me' and 'the unfolding of cosmic purposes'.

To most men, when their eyes within are opened, that spectacle brings a feeling of painful doubt. The mere physical perception of innumerable multitudes jostling forward with no apparent goal, contains an element of intellectual bewilderment for the observer. His own identity is suddenly threatened, and the meaning of his existence becomes as obscure to him as that of the alien individualities that crowd his path. And when this spectacle, as it does with some men, passes into an intuition of vast shadowy fluctuations in the invisible world, the bewilderment grows to a sense of terror, even of despair. It is the tonic quality of Whitman – the quality for which his sane readers return to him again and again – that his eyes were opened to this vision, and that he remained unafraid. All the vociferousness of his earlier poems is little more than a note of defiance against the thronging shapes that beset him. But I think it was something more than his obstreperous individualism that saved him in the end. Look into his face, especially in the noble war-time picture of him called the Hugo portrait, and you will be struck by that veiled brooding regard of the eyes which goes with the vision of the seer. He felt not only his personal identity entrenched behind walls of inexpugnable egotism, but he was conscious, also, of another kind of identity, which made him one with every living creature, even with the inanimate elements.

He was no stranger in the universe. The spirit that gazed out of his own eyes into the unresting multitude looked back at him with silent greeting from every passing face. And it was chiefly through this higher identity, or sympathy, that he cast away fear. He chants its power in a hundred different ways – now crudely pronouncing himself this person and that, and again merely declaring that all persons are the same and equally good to him, now denying all distinctions whatsoever. He gave it a mystical name:

Through me the afflatus surging and surging, through me the
  current and index.

I speak the *pass-word primeval*; I give the sign of *democracy* . . .[1]
  (*Song of Myself*, 24)

The word has been caught up by certain of his disciples and made the pass-word for admission into Whitman clubs and the key to unlock the society of the future. As the poet of democracy he is supposed to have relegated all preceding literatures and religions to the dust heap, and to have inaugurated a new era of civilization. Now, undoubtedly he did represent in a way the political and physical aspects of America before the war – its large fluctuations of population, its sense of unfulfilled destiny. But for the problems confronting the actual militant democracy I cannot see that his poems have any answer. 'Salvation can't be legislated' was the phrase with which he warned off the labour agitators and heralds of reform who sought his assistance in the later years. I fear that the working-man today who should undertake to follow his doctrine of insouciance would soon learn that loafing may be something very different from an invitation to the soul. There may be inspiration for the self-reliant individual in Whitman, but even more than Emerson's his philosophy is one of fraternal anarchy, leaving no room for the stricter ties of marriage or the state. It is curious that throughout his works you will find scarcely an intimation of the more exclusive forms of love or friendship which furnish the ordinary theme of poetry. In that universe of un-resting motion into which he gazed he could discover neither time nor place for the knitting of those more enduring unions. Camerado! was his word, the cry from one man to another as they meet in the

1 Paul Elmer More's italics. [Ed.]

streaming procession, walk together for a little way with clasped hands, and then with the kiss of parting separate, each to his own end. This, and no political programme, is, as I understand it, the meaning of the pass-word primeval, democracy.

Only with Whitman's experience of the war, and his daily familiarity with death, do we catch the first note of that deeper mysticism which looks through the illusion of change into the silence of infinite calm. I have been struck by the fact that it was the battle-fields of Virginia that first revealed to him the stars and their infinite contrast with this life of ours. He is describing 'these butchers' shambles' in his *Specimen Days*, when suddenly he seems to have become aware of the full glory of the sky:

Such is the camp of the wounded – such a fragment, a reflection afar off of the bloody scene – while over all the clear, large moon comes out at times softly, quietly shining. Amid the woods, that scene of flitting souls – amid the crack and crash and yelling sounds – the impalpable perfume of the woods – and yet the pungent, stifling smoke – the radiance of the moon, looking from heaven at intervals so placid – the sky so heavenly – the clear-obscure up there, those buoyant upper oceans – a few large placid stars beyond, coming silently and languidly out, and then disappearing – the melancholy, draperied night above, around.

It was out of such material as this, written hastily in little pocket note-books, that the *Drum-Taps* were later constructed. One of the poems, the earliest in which this pathetic fallacy of the sky appears, connects Whitman with Homer:

I see before me now a travelling army halting,
Below a fertile valley spread, with barns and the orchards of
    summer,
Behind, the terraced sides of a mountain, abrupt, in places rising
    high,
Broken, with rocks, with clinging cedars, with tall shapes
    dingily seen,
The numerous camp-fires scatter'd near and far,
    some away up on the mountain,
The shadowy forms of men and horses, looming, large-sized,
    flickering,

And over all the sky – the sky! far, far out of reach, studded,
  breaking out, the eternal stars.

(Bivouac on a Mountain Side)

It is a picture, roughly-limned, yet comparable in its own way with
that scene in the *Iliad* which Tennyson has translated so magni-
ficently:

And these all night upon the bridge of war
Sat glorying; many a fire before them blazed:
As when in heaven the stars about the moon
Look beautiful, when all the winds are laid,
And every height comes out, and jutting peak
And valley, and the immeasurable heavens
Break open to their highest, and all the stars
Shine.

    Almost, in such passages as these, it would seem as if the familiarity
with death had drawn for Whitman the last curtain of initiation;
almost he stands like Emerson's young mortal in the hall of the
firmament,

On the instant, and incessantly, fall snow-storms of illusions.
He fancies himself in a vast crowd which sways this way and that.
... Every moment, new changes, and new showers of
deceptions, to baffle and distract him. And when, by and by, for
an instant, the air clears, and the cloud lifts a little, there are the
gods still sitting around him on their thrones, – they alone with
him alone.

To that diviner glimpse Whitman never quite attained, and this is
well, for in attaining it he would have passed beyond the peculiar
inspiration which makes him what he is. He had been haunted by the
idea of death as a boy, and had associated it with the breaking of the
sea-waves on the beach. It was the supreme symbol of change, beautiful and beneficent, purging and renewing, yet still a gateway into
new roads, and never a door opening into the chambers of home.
    Such a character it retains, indeed, in the later poems, but its minis-
tration strikes nearer the heart of things:

Word over all, beautiful as the sky,
Beautiful that war and all its carnage must in time be utterly lost,

That the hands of the sisters Death and Night incessantly softly
    wash again, and ever again, this soil'd world;
For my enemy is dead, a man divine as myself is dead,
I look where he lies white-faced and still in the coffin – I draw
    near,
Bend down and touch lightly with my lips the white face in the
    coffin.

                    (*Reconciliation*)

Even in his chant, *When Lilacs Last in the Dooryard Bloom'd*, it is
notable that he instinctively chooses for his picture the dead President
on that long westward journey, with the crowds thronging to behold
the passing train. He is still haunted by the thought of endless progress
and procession, although in the same poem is to occur that wonderful
hymn to the Deliverer:

Come lovely and soothing death,
Undulate round the world, serenely arriving, arriving,
In the day, in the night, to all, to each,
Sooner or later delicate death.

Prais'd be the fathomless universe,
For life and joy, and for objects and knowledge curious,
And for love, sweet love – but praise! praise! praise!
For the sure-enwinding arms of cool-enfolding death.

Dark mother always gliding near with soft feet,
Have none chanted for thee a chant of fullest welcome?
Then I chant it for thee, I glorify thee above all.

                      (14)

    He lacked the rare and unique elevation of Emerson from whom so
much of his vision was unwittingly derived, but as a compensation
his temperament is richer than the New England poet's, and his
verbal felicity at its best more striking. I do not see why Americans
should hesitate to accept him, with all his imperfections and incom-
pleteness, and with all his vaunted pedantry of the pavement, as one
of the most original and characteristic of their poets; but to do this
they must begin by forgetting his disciples.

                      (200–211)

Bliss Perry

from *Walt Whitman* 1906

It was evident that, however freely Whitman made use of lines or paragraphs of sheer prose, the closing cadences of most of the poems had been constructed with the utmost care. Very characteristic are these final lines:

Smile, for your lover comes!

(Song of Myself, 21)

It is nearer and further than they.

(A Song for Occupations, 4)

And that was a jet black sunrise.

Yet the rhythmical structure of *Leaves of Grass* is scarcely to be apprehended through the metrical analysis of single lines. Whitman composed – and in this respect, at least, he resembled the great masters of blank verse – with reference to the group, or paragraph of lines, and not merely to the single unit. If read aloud, page after page, the general rhythmic type makes itself felt. It is highly individual, and yet it is clearly related to other well-recognized modes of impassioned literary expression.

On one side it touches the 'prose poetry' of Carlyle and Emerson, De Quincey and Poe, writers with whom Whitman was familiar, and some of whom he had imitated in his earlier productions. Passages from *Sartor Resartus* and from Emerson's *Essays* have frequently been rearranged typographically, without any verbal alteration whatever, so as to look and sound like passages from *Leaves of Grass*. It is well known that Ruskin, for example, brought this rhythm of 'prose poetry' so near to actual metre, that the transposition of a few words, and the addition or subtraction of a syllable here and there would turn his prose into verse. William Cairns has pointed out in the London *Chronicle* how easily the following passage from Ruskin's *Notes on Turner* resolves itself into hexameters:

Morning breaks as I write, along those Coniston Fells, and the
level mists, motionless and gray beneath the rose of the moorlands,
veil the lower woods, and the sleeping village, and the long lawns

by the lake shore. Oh, that some one had but told me in my youth, when all my heart seemed to be set on these colours and clouds, that appear for a little while, and then vanish away, how little my love of them would serve me, when the silence of lawn and wood in the dews of morning should be completed; and all my thoughts should be of those whom, by neither, I was to meet more.

Morning breaks as I write, o'er the Coniston Fells, and the level,
Motionless mists lie gray beneath the rose of the moorlands,
Veiling the lower woods, the lake, and the slumbering village.
Oh, had some friend in the days when my heart, in youthful emotion,
Seemed to be set on these colours and clouds which appear but to vanish,
Warned me how little my love of their fast-fading beauty would serve, when
Deep and profound over woodland and lake in the dews of the morning,
Rested a silence complete; and the thoughts which beset me should ever
Dwell on those I should never meet more, or by lake or by woodland.

The ease of this transition from skilful, if dangerous, prose to mediocre verse proves the delicacy of Ruskin's ear, and the sharp aesthetic differentiation between rhythmical effect and metrical effect.

Again, the heightened passages of oratory tend, in proportion to their impassioned quality, to fall into regular stress. The natural orators to whom Whitman loved to listen were fond of the heavily accented periods, which, like the cadences of prose poetry, approximate, without quite reaching, metrical regularity. Often, indeed, in orators of florid taste – precisely as in the pathetic passages of Dickens – the rhythm slips over into unconscious iambics. Whitman's friend, Robert G. Ingersoll, a well-known popular orator, once described the old classic myths, in a glowing sentence which has been printed without change as verse:

They thrilled the veins of Spring with tremulous desire;
Made tawny Summer's billowed breast the throne and home of Love;

Filled Autumn's arms with sun-kissed grapes and gathered sheaves;
And pictured Winter as a weak old king,
Who felt, like Lear, upon his withered face, Cordelia's tears.

Whitman utilized freely the characteristic effects of both 'prose poetry' and oratory, but he varied these effects not only with prose rhythms, but with the tunes of lyric poetry. He admitted, furthermore, his indebtedness to music as suggesting rhythmical variations. He told Mrs Fanny Raymond Ritter that more of his poems were actually inspired by music than he himself could remember. He frequently compared his interweaving of lyric with descriptive passages to the alternating aria and recitative of an oratorio. That his senses were peculiarly responsive to all suggestions of movement seems clear. Professor F. N. Scott notes 'his delicate susceptibility to certain modes of motion and sequences of sound,' particularly the free, swaying, 'urging', motions of the ferry-boat, the railroad train, the flight of birds; and, among sounds, those of the wind, the locusts in the tree-tops and the sea.

In endeavoring to analyse his own metrical system Whitman selected the analogy of the waves. In a striking self-criticism, ... he declared:

He dismisses without ceremony all the orthodox accoutrements, tropes, verbal haberdashery, 'feet' and the entire stock in trade of rhyme-talking heroes and heroines and all the lovesick plots of customary poetry, and constructs his verse in a loose and free metre of his own, of an irregular length of lines, apparently lawless at first perusal, although on closer examination a certain regularity appears, like the recurrence of lesser and larger waves on the seashore, rolling in without intermission, and fitfully rising and falling.

(83–8)

... His own essential model, after all is said, was the rhythmical patterns of the English Bible. Here was precisely that natural stylistic variation between the 'terrific', the 'gentle', and the 'inferior' parts, so desired by William Blake. Here were lyric fragments, of consummate beauty, imbedded in narrative or argumentative passages. The parallelism which constituted the peculiar structural device of Hebrew poetry gave the English of the King James version a heightened rhythm without destroying the flexibility and freedom natural to prose. In this strong, rolling music, this intense feeling, these concrete words expressing primal emotions in daring terms of bodily sensation,[1] Whitman found the charter for the book he wished to write.

As a whole, therefore, *Leaves of Grass* belonged to no one accepted type of poetry. It was a hybrid, with something of the hybrid's exotic and disturbing charm. Whitman spoke of it afterwards as 'a new and national declamatory expression', and of his three adjectives the last is the most weighty. *Leaves of Grass* – whatever else it may have been – was superb declamation. It was so full of poetry that to deny it the name of 'poem' is pedantic; yet 'rhapsody' is a more closely descriptive word. To interpret as formal song what was intended for rhapsodical speech is to misread Walt Whitman. Here was no born maker of poetry, like Shelley, transforming his thought and emotions into a new medium and scarcely conscious of the miracle he is achieving; but rather a man burdened with sensations, wrestling with language, and forcing it into accents that are like the beating of his own tumultuous heart. Both Shelley and Whitman 'communicate' passion; but in one case we are listening to a pure aria that might conceivably issue from a violin or a skylark, while in the other we are listening to a declaimer with 'Tears in his eyes, distraction in's aspect.' Not to apprehend *Leaves of Grass* as a *man speaking* is to miss its purport.

(96–7)

Ezra Pound

'What I Feel About Walt Whitman' 1909

From this side of the Atlantic I am for the first time able to read Whitman, and from the vantage of my education and – if it be permitted a man of my scant years – my world citizenship: I see him America's poet. The only Poet before the artists of the Carmen-

---

1 Compare Thoreau's dictum: 'The poet writes the history of his body' (Thoreau's *Journal* for 29 September 1851).

Hovey [sic] period, or better, the only one of the conventionaly recognized 'American Poets' who is worth reading.

He *is* America. His crudity is an exceeding great stench, but it *is* America. He is the hollow place in the rock that echos with his time. He *does* 'chant the crucial stage' and he is the 'voice triumphant'. He is disgusting. He is an excedingly nauseating pill, but he acomplishes his mission.

Entirely free from the renaissance humanist ideal of the complete man or from the Greek idealism, he is content to be what he is, and he is his time and his people. He is a genius because he has vision of what he is and of his function. He knows that he is a beginning and not a classicaly finished work.

I honor him for he prophesied me while I can only recognize him as a forebear of whom I ought to be proud.

In America there is much for the healing of the nations, but woe unto him of the cultured palate who attempts the dose.

As for Whitman, I read him (in many parts) with acute pain, but when I write of certain things I find myself using his rythms. The expression of certain things related to cosmic consciousness seems tainted with this maramis.

I am (in common with every educated man) an heir of the ages and I demand my birth-right. Yet if Whitman represented his time in language acceptable to one accustomed to my standard of intellectual-artistic living he would belie his time and nation. And yet I am but one of his 'ages and ages' encrustations' or to be exact an encrustation of the next age. The vital part of my message, taken from the sap and fibre of America, is the same as his.

Mentaly I am a Walt Whitman who has learned to wear a colar and a dress shirt (although at times inimical to both). Personaly I might be very glad to conceal my relationship to my spiritual father and brag about my more congenial ancestry – Dante, Shakespeare, Theocritus, Villon, but the descent is a bit difficult to establish. And, to be frank, Whitman is to my fatherland (*Patriam quam odi et amo*[1] for no uncertain reasons) what Dante is to Italy and I at my best can only be a strife for a renaissance in America of all the lost or temporarily mislaid beauty, truth, valor, glory of Greece, Italy, England and all the rest of it.

1 The fatherland I love and hate so much. [Ed.]

And yet if a man has written lines like Whitmans to the *Sunset Breeze* one has to love him. I think we have not yet paid enough attention to the deliberate artistry of the man, not in details but in the large.

I am immortal even as he is, yet with a lesser vitality as I am the more in love with beauty (If I realy do love it more than he did). Like Dante he wrote in the 'vulgar tongue', in a new metric. The first great man to write in the language of his people.

Et ego Petrarca in lingua vetera scribo,[1] and in a tongue my people understood not.

It seems to me I should like to drive Whitman into the old world. I sledge, he drill – and to scourge America with all the old beauty. (For Beauty *is* an accusation) and with a thousand thongs from Homer to Yeats, from Theocritus to Marcel Schwob. This desire is because I am young and impatient, were I old and wise I should content myself in seeing and saying that these things will come. But now, since I am by no means sure it would be true prophecy, I am fain set my own hand to the labour.

It is a great thing, reading a man to know, not 'His Tricks are not as yet my Tricks, but I can easily make them mine' but 'His message is my message. We will see that men hear it.'

Basil de Selincourt

from *Walt Whitman: A Critical Study* 1914

Clearly Whitman's refusal of metre was the refusal of innocence, not of experience. One must doubt whether his ear was capable of receiving the disciplined music of such verse as Milton's, whether, in fact, the verse of all the greatest poets did not seem sing-song to him. Certainly, whatever determined his choice of irregularity, his perception of the meaning of conventional forms, his instinct and practice in the use of them, were at a primitive level. He is far from being unsusceptible to the charms of metre. But they are Circe charms to him. Crying out for an ideal of nonchalance and ease he escapes a temptress.

1 And I, Petrarch, write in an ancient tongue. [Ed.]

It is true of all commanding poetry that its form is only perfect when it is secondary, when it is an instrument, a vessel:

The words of the true poems give you more than poems ...
They do not seek beauty, they are sought,
Forever touching them or close upon them follows beauty,
    longing, fain, love-sick.

(*Song of the Answerer, 2*)

To none does the truth apply more accurately than to Walt Whitman's. The echoes of cultivated verse exercised a considerable influence upon him, and this influence, as far as it went, was damaging. His own wild music, ravishing, unseizable, like the song of a bird, came to him, as by his own principles it should have come, when he was not searching for it. And his greatness as a poet, when we regard his poetry on its formal side, is that conventional echoes damaged him so little, that in spite of unavoidable elements of wilfulness and reaction in his poetry, he was able to achieve so real an independence.

Independence, it is necessary to remember, was in his case essential to artistic success. For he had to find the forms which would be appropriate to a specific purpose. He set out to discover a means of direct personal appeal, capable of ranging from the levels of a merely conversational tone, familiar but always ardent, along the broad and copious lower slopes of vivid description and specification, and up by the steps and steeps of impassioned argument and persuasion to those heights of prophetic ecstasy and assurance where speech itself is a song. And this he actually achieves. He gives us poems which represent severally all the different stages of the ascent; he gives us other poems – and these perhaps are the most characteristic of him – in the course of which we pass imperceptibly from one stage to another, now rising, now falling as the development of the theme requires.

In all, the determining condition of the form is this direct personal impulse. The poem, as Whitman conceives it, is to remain fundamentally a conversation. It is to be the expression by me to you of the feelings which are as much yours as mine, and would undoubtedly have been expressed by you to me but for the accident of my being the more garrulous fellow of the two. It is to act in the field of spiritual needs much as the more modern kind of advertisement does in the field of material needs, button-holing its client, assuring him that he is a brother, and confiding to him its knowledge of the common perplexities of the life of man. How easily this atmosphere of confidence and familiarity raises a smile! It subsists largely upon illusions; but the illusions are harmless, for they deceive nobody; and they are really worth entertaining, even if they are a little wearisome and over-persistent at times; for with them come large reinforcements of that genuine raciness and diffused good feeling which are part of America's contribution to the civilization of the world. There was more of strength and perception and courage than there was of weakness in Whitman's determination to turn this unpromising stuff to poetic uses. The impromptu confab, in which equal takes equal aside for a few words (or not so few!), this he felt to be typical not only of his country but also of his country's ideals. And it is in poems where a conversational tone is the most apparent that he is most completely himself.

As I lay with my head in your lap camerado,
The confession I made I resume, what I said to you and the open
   air I resume,
I know I am restless and make others so,
I know my words are weapons full of danger, full of death,
For I confront peace, security, and all the settled laws, to
   unsettle them,
I am more resolute because all have denied me than I could ever
   have been had all accepted me,
I heed not and have never heeded either experience, cautions,
   majorities, nor ridicule,
And the threat of what is call'd hell is little or nothing to me,
And the lure of what is call'd heaven is little or nothing to me;
Dear camerado! I confess I have urged you onward with me,
   and still urge you, without the least idea what is our destination,
Or whether we shall be victorious, or utterly quell'd and defeated.
             (*As I Lay With My Head in Your*
             Lap Camerado)

It is tempting at first sight to argue that this, being mere prose, would be more sensible and straightforward as a continuous paragraph. Little, indeed, seems to be added to the composition by the scanty formalities in virtue of which it claims the name of a poem. But the question is not whether there is much or little, but whether there is enough. For what, after all, is the artist's essential quality, if not to know how much exactly is enough and to give no more? 'O', sings the forsaken mocking bird, with whom Whitman identifies himself in perhaps the loveliest of his poems:

... O I think you could give me my mate back again if you only
   would,
For I am almost sure I see her dimly whichever way I look.

(*Out of the Cradle Endlessly Rocking*)

'I am *almost* sure I see her *dimly*'; that quaver of uncertainty in the words is the source of their power. The sentimentalist would have been quite sure he saw her clearly, and would have demanded instant restitution! Only passion can afford to take gradations, to admit its doubts. The poem *As I Lay* exemplifies power of a similar kind. The theme resolves itself into a series of autobiographical reflections; yet, in their total effect, these reflections touch us intimately; and the effect, so far as form contributes to it, results from the fact that we have been asked to stray upon the borderland of prose and poetry by a guide confident of his power to keep us on the right side of the border.

The beauty of the poem, formally, is that it is content to hang its existence upon a thread. Each line is a single contributory thought floated to us on a contributory breath. The single impulse which produced the whole has divided itself into a succession of waves of impulse, which vary in height and volume, each, whether by sympathy or by contrast, affecting the height and volume of the rest. Take one instance only of the workings of these subtle compensations: who can read the words 'Dear camerado' at the beginning of the last line but one, without an instinctive recovery of the cadence of the first line of the piece, with the blending emotions of intimate affection, calm concession, confiding resignation, which were expressed in that and the line following? The intervening lines, it is equally obvious, have been, as waves, a kind of complementary reaction. The tide has been stationary; there has been a retirement, a back-wash. But the water as it continues to move continues to prepare us for a new pressure of advance; and in the last two lines this new pressure has arrived. Swiftly and smoothly it spreads over a fresh stretch of sand and leaves us at the end with an exquisite sob or falter as, in its completion, it disappears.

Dear camerado! I confess I have urged you onward with me, and
    still urge you, without the least idea what is our destination,
Or whether we shall be victorious, or utterly quell'd and defeated.

We must note further as an essential feature of the form at which Whitman is aiming that each poem he writes has to be judged by an intrinsic standard. Most of the conventional forms with which we are familiar have their fixed possibilities and limitations; to adopt the sonnet form, the *In Memoriam* quatrain or that of Omar Khayyám, is to entitle the reader to more or less specific expectations, and he will judge a poem written in these metres according to the degree in which it fulfils what he expects of them or replaces his expectation by something better. The form of Whitman's conversational poem depends on the course the conversation takes and the temper which has initiated it; and whether the form is perfect or not in a particular case we can decide only by familiarizing ourselves with the unique requirements of the case in point. Thus, in the example that follows, the tone of conversation has passed into that of soliloquy; the mood is too intimate, too remote, to admit of the idea of any but an impersonal utterance; we picture the soul of the poet addressing as it were some shadow of itself:

Tears! tears! tears!
In the night, in solitude, tears,
On the white shore dripping, dripping, suck'd in by the sand,
Tears, not a star shining, all dark and desolate,
Moist tears from the eyes of a muffled head;
O who is that ghost? that form in the dark, with tears?
What shapeless lump is that, bent, crouch'd there on the sand?
Streaming tears, sobbing tears, throes, choked with wild cries;
O storm, embodied, rising, careering with swift steps along the
    beach!
O wild and dismal night storm, with wind – O belching and
    desperate!

O shade so sedate and decorous by day, with calm countenance
　and regulated pace,
But away at night as you fly, none looking – O then the
　unloosen'd ocean,
Of tears! tears! tears!

(*Tears*)

The form here is of such exquisite sensitiveness that it is with an effort
we remember the offences its author could commit. The lines 'O
who is that ghost' and 'What shapeless lump is that' serve just to
maintain the air of realistic familiarity that Whitman loves. He takes
advantage of the ballast they provide to soar up into heights of
suggestion and impressionism where he is equally at home. The
storm, the human creature out in it, exchange forces, appearance,
personality almost, from line to line. The tears are the rain, but who
is it that is weeping? The night, the tempest, the seashore are part of
the solitude and the despair they cover, part of the outpouring of
passion and sorrow which they liberate, echo and absorb. And how
does language take the impress of hints so vague and so conflicting
and of an integration so profound? All through the piece alliteration,
though never obtruding itself, and indeed never appearing till it is
sought out, adds significance to the choice of the words by coaxing
the reader to dwell upon them and so helping him to pass naturally
over gaps whether of grammar or idea which might otherwise check
him; he may observe next how every line, sensitive to the cadence of
the first, divides itself sympathetically into a succession of lesser
impulses, of which there are usually, but not always, three; and
finally, as the sign of a still more vital sensitiveness, he will note the
repetition of the keynote of the piece, the word 'tears'. The word is
not only repeated, but variously placed in successive lines, so that by
maintenance of the emphasis upon it its structural significance may be
fully brought out. Then, at what is structurally the centre of the piece,
there is a cessation; four lines of release and tumult follow which are
silent of it; and so we are prepared for the beauty and inevitability
of the final cadence in which it returns.

(72–81)

D. H. Lawrence

'Poetry of the Present', Introduction to the American edition of
New Poems 1920

It seems when we hear a skylark singing as if sound were running
forward into the future, running so fast and utterly without consideration, straight on into futurity. And when we hear a nightingale, we
hear the pause and the rich, piercing rhythm of recollection, the
perfected past. The lark may sound sad, but with the lovely lapsing
sadness that is almost a swoon of hope. The nightingale's triumph is
a paean, but a death-paean.

So it is with poetry. Poetry is, as a rule, either the voice of the far
future, exquisite and ethereal, or it is the voice of the past, rich,
magnificent. When the Greeks heard the *Iliad* and the *Odyssey*, they
heard their own past calling in their hearts, as men far inland sometimes hear the sea and fall weak with powerful, wonderful regret,
nostalgia; or else their own future rippled its time-beats through
their blood, as they followed the painful, glamorous progress of the
Ithacan. This was Homer to the Greeks; their Past, splendid with
battles won and death achieved, and their Future, the magic wandering
of Ulysses through the unknown.

With us it is the same. Our birds sing on the horizons. They sing
out of the blue, beyond us, or out of the quenched night. They sing
at dawn and sunset. Only the poor, shrill, tame canaries whistle
while we talk. The wild birds begin before we are awake, or as we
drop into dimness out of waking. Our poets sit by the gateways,
some by the east, some by the west. As we arrive and as we go out
our hearts surge with response. But whilst we are in the midst of life,
we do not hear them.

The poetry of the beginning and the poetry of the end must have
that exquisite finality, perfection which belongs to all that is far off.
It is in the realm of all that is perfect. It is of the nature of all that is
complete and consummate. This completeness, this consummateness,
the finality and the perfection are conveyed in exquisite form: the
perfect symmetry, the rhythm which returns upon itself like a dance
where the hands link and loosen and link for the supreme moment of
the end. Perfected bygone moments, perfected moments in the glim-

mering futurity, these are the treasured gem-like lyrics of Shelley and Keats.

But there is another kind of poetry: the poetry of that which is at hand: the immediate present. In the immediate present there is no perfection, no consummation, nothing finished. The strands are all flying, quivering, intermingling into the web, the waters are shaking the moon. There is no round, consummate moon on the face of running water, nor on the face of the unfinished tide. There are no gems of the living plasm. The living plasm vibrates unspeakably, it inhales the future, it exhales the past, it is the quick of both, and yet it is neither. There is no plasmic finality, nothing crystal, permanent. If we try to fix the living tissue, as the biologists fix it with formation, we have only a hardened bit of the past, the bygone life under our observation.

Life, the ever-present, knows no finality, no finished crystallization. The perfect rose is only a running flame, emerging and flowing off, and never in any sense at rest, static, finished. Herein lies its transcendent loveliness. The whole tide of all life and all time suddenly heaves, and appears before us as an apparition, a revelation. We look at the very white quick of nascent creation. A water-lily heaves herself from the flood, looks round, gleams, and is gone. We have seen the incarnation, the quick of the ever-swirling flood. We have seen the invisible. We have seen, we have touched, we have partaken of the very substance of creative change, creative mutation. If you tell me about the lotus, tell me of nothing changeless or eternal. Tell me of the mystery of the inexhaustible, forever-unfolding creative spark. Tell me of the incarnate disclosure of the flux, mutation in blossom, laughter and decay perfectly open in their transit, nude in their movement before us.

Let me feel the mud and the heavens in my lotus. Let me feel the heavy, silting, sucking mud, the spinning of sky winds. Let me feel them both in purest contact, the nakedness of sucking weight, nakedly passing radiance. Give me nothing fixed, set, static. Don't give me the infinite or the eternal: nothing of infinity, nothing of eternity. Give me the still, white seething, the incandescence and the coldness of the incarnate moment: the moment, the quick of all change and haste and opposition: the moment, the immediate present, the Now. The immediate moment is not a drop of water running downstream. It is the source and issue, the bubbling up of the stream. Here, in this very instant moment, up bubbles the stream of time, out of the wells of futurity, flowing on to the oceans of the past. The source, the issue, the creative quick.

There is poetry of this immediate present, instant poetry, as well as poetry of the infinite past and the infinite future. The seething poetry of the incarnate Now is supreme, beyond even the everlasting gems of the before and after. In its quivering momentaneity it surpasses the crystalline, pearl-hard jewels, the poems of the eternities. Do not ask for the qualities of the unfading timeless gems. Ask for the whiteness which is the seethe of mud, ask for that incipient putrescence which is the skies falling, ask for the never-pausing, never-ceasing life itself. There must be mutation, swifter than iridescence, haste, not rest, come-and-go, not fixity, inconclusiveness, immediacy, the quality of life itself, without dénouement or close. There must be the rapid momentaneous association of things which meet and pass on the forever incalculable journey of creation: everything left in its own rapid, fluid relationship with the rest of things.

This is the unrestful, ungraspable poetry of the sheer present, poetry whose very permanency lies in its wind-like transit. Whitman's is the best poetry of this kind. Without beginning and without end, without any base and pediment, it sweeps past for ever, like a wind that is forever in passage, and unchainable. Whitman truly looked before and after. But he did not sigh for what is not. The clue to all his utterance lies in the sheer appreciation of the instant moment, life surging itself into utterance at its very well-head. Eternity is only an abstraction from the actual present. Infinity is only a great reservoir of recollection, or a reservoir of aspiration: man-made. The quivering nimble hour of the present, this is the quick of Time. This is the immanence. The quick of the universe is the *pulsating, carnal self*, mysterious and palpable. So it is always.

Because Whitman put this into his poetry, we fear him and respect him so profoundly. We should not fear him if he sang only of the 'old unhappy far-off things', or of the 'wings of the morning'. It is because his heart beats with the urgent, insurgent Now, which is even upon us all, that we dread him. He is so near the quick.

From the foregoing it is obvious that the poetry of the instant present cannot have the same body or the same motion as the poetry of the before and after. It can never submit to the same conditions. It is never finished. There is no rhythm which returns upon itself, no serpent of eternity with its tail in its own mouth. There is no static perfection, none of that finality which we find so satisfying because we are so frightened.

Much has been written about free verse. But all that can be said, first and last, is that free verse is, or should be, direct utterance from the instant, whole man. It is the soul and the mind and body surging at once, nothing left out. They speak all together. There is some confusion, some discord. But the confusion and the discord only belong to the reality as noise belongs to the plunge of water. It is no use inventing fancy laws for free verse, no use drawing a melodic line which all the feet must toe. Free verse toes no melodic line, no matter what drill-sergeant. Whitman pruned away his clichés – perhaps his clichés of rhythm as well as of phrase. And this is about all we can do, deliberately, with free verse. We can get rid of the stereotyped movements and the old hackneyed associations of sound or sense. We can break down those artificial conduits and canals through which we do so love to force our utterance. We can break the stiff neck of habit. We can be in ourselves spontaneous and flexible as flame, we can see that utterance rushes out without artificial foam or artificial smoothness. But we cannot positively prescribe any motion, any rhythm. All the laws we invent or discover – it amounts to pretty much the same – will fail to apply to free verse. They will only apply to some form of restricted, limited unfree verse.

All we can say is that free verse does *not* have the same nature as restricted verse. It is not of the nature of reminiscence. It is not the past which we treasure in its perfection between our hands. Neither is it the crystal of the perfect future, into which we gaze. Its tide is neither the full, yearning flow of aspiration, nor the sweet, poignant ebb of remembrance and regret. The past and the future are the two great bournes of human emotion, the two great homes of the human days, the two eternities. They are both conclusive, final. Their beauty is the beauty of the goal, finished, perfected. Finished beauty and measured symmetry belong to the stable, unchanging eternities.

But in free verse we look for the insurgent naked throb of the instant moment. To break the lovely form of metrical verse, and to dish up the fragments as a new substance, called *vers libre*, this is what most of the free-versifiers accomplish. They do not know that free verse has its own *nature*, that it is neither star nor pearl, but instantaneous like plasm. It has no goal in either eternity. It has no finish. It has no satisfying stability, satisfying to those who like the immutable. None of this. It is the instant; the quick; the very jetting source of all will-be and has-been. The utterance is like a spasm, naked contact with all influences at once. It does not want to get anywhere. It just takes place.

For such utterance any externally-applied law would be mere shackles and death. The law must come new each time from within. The bird is on the wing in the winds, flexible to every breath, a living spark in the storm, its very flickering depending upon its supreme mutability and power of change. Whence such a bird came: whither it goes: from what solid earth it rose up, and upon what solid earth it will close its wings and settle, this is not the question. This is a question of before and after. Now, *now*, the bird is on the wing in the winds.

Such is the rare new poetry. One realm we have never conquered: the pure present. One great mystery of time is *terra incognita* to us: the instant. The most superb mystery we have hardly recognized: the immediate, instant self. The quick of all time is the instant. The quick of all the universe, of all creation, is the incarnate, carnal self. Poetry gave us the clue: free verse: Whitman. Now we know.

The ideal – what is the ideal? A figment. An abstraction. A static abstraction, abstracted from life. It is a fragment of the before or the after. It is a crystallized aspiration, or a crystallized remembrance: crystallized, set, finished. It is a thing set apart, in the great storehouse of eternity, the storehouse of finished things.

We do not speak of things crystallized and set apart. We speak of the instant, the immediate self, the very plasm of the self. We speak also of free verse.

(i–ix)

D. H. Lawrence

'Whitman', *The Nation and the Athenaeum* 23 July 1921

Whitman is the greatest of the Americans. One of the greatest poets of the world, in him an element of falsity troubles us still. Something is wrong: we cannot be quite at ease in his greatness.

This may be our own fault. But we sincerely feel that something is overdone in Whitman; there is something that is too much. Let us get over our quarrel with him first.

All the Americans, when they have trodden new ground, seem to have been conscious of making a breach in the established order. They have been self-conscious about it. They have felt that they were trespassing, transgressing, or going very far, and this has given a certain stridency, or portentousness, or luridness to their manner. Perhaps that is because the steps were taken so rapidly. From Franklin to Whitman is a hundred years. It might be a thousand.

The Americans have finished in haste, with a certain violence and violation, that which Europe began two thousand years ago or more. Rapidly they have returned to lay open the secrets which the Christian epoch has taken two thousand years to close up.

With the Greeks started the great passion for the ideal, the passion for translating all consciousness into terms of spirit and ideal or idea. They did this in reaction from the vast old world which was dying in Egypt. But the Greeks, though they set out to conquer the animal or sensual being in man, did not set out to annihilate it. This was left for the Christians.

The Christians, phase by phase, set out actually to *annihilate* the sensual being in man. They insisted that man was in his reality *pure spirit*, and that he was perfectible as such. And this was their business, to achieve such a perfection.

They worked from a profound inward impulse, the Christian religious impulse. But their proceeding was the same, in living extension, as that of the Greek esoterics, such as John the Evangel or Socrates. They proceeded, by will and by exaltation, to overcome *all* the passions and all the appetites and prides.

Now, so far, in Europe, the conquest of the lower self has been objective. That is, man has moved from a great impulse within himself, unconscious. But once the conquest has been effected, there is a temptation for the conscious mind to return and finger and explore, just as tourists now explore battlefields. This self-conscious *mental* provoking of sensation and reaction in the great affective centres is what we call sentimentalism or sensationalism. The mind returns upon the affective centres, and sets up in them a deliberate reaction.

And this is what all the Americans do, beginning with Crèvecoeur, Hawthorne, Poe, all the transcendentalists, Melville, Prescott, Wendell Holmes, Whitman, they are all guilty of this provoking of mental reactions in the physical self, passions exploited by the mind. In Europe, men like Balzac and Dickens, Tolstoy and Hardy, still act direct from the passional motive, and not inversely, from mental provocation. But the aesthetes and symbolists, from Baudelaire and Maeterlinck and Oscar Wilde onwards, and nearly all later Russian, French, and English novelists set up their reactions in the mind and reflect them by a secondary process down into the body. This makes a vicious living and a spurious art. It is one of the last and most fatal effects of idealism. Everything becomes self-conscious and spurious, to the pitch of madness. It is the madness of the world of today. Europe and America are all alike; all the nations self-consciously provoking their own passional reactions from the mind, and *nothing* spontaneous.

And this is our accusation against Whitman, as against the others. Too often he deliberately, self-consciously *affects* himself. It puts us off, it makes us dislike him. But since such self-conscious secondariness is a concomitant of all American art, and yet not sufficiently so to prevent that art from being of rare quality, we must get over it. The excuse is that the Americans have had to perform in a century a curve which it will take Europe much longer to finish, if ever she finishes it.

Whitman has gone further, in actual living expression, than any man, it seems to me. Dostoevsky has burrowed underground into the decomposing psyche. But Whitman has gone forward in life-knowledge. It is he who surmounts the grand climacteric of our civilization.

Whitman enters on the last phase of spiritual triumph. He really arrives at that stage of infinity which the seers sought. By subjecting the *deepest centres* of the lower self, he attains the maximum consciousness in the higher self: a degree of extensive consciousness greater, perhaps, than any man in the modern world.

We have seen Dana and Melville, the two adventurers, setting out to conquer the last vast *element*, with the spirit. We have seen Melville touching at last the far end of the immemorial, prehistoric Pacific civilization, in *Typee*. We have seen his terrific cruise into universality.

Now we must remember that the way, even towards a state of infinite comprehension, is through the externals towards the quick. And the vast elements, the cosmos, the big things, the universals, these are always the externals. These are met first and conquered first. That is why science is so much easier than art. The quick is the living being, the quick of quicks is the individual soul. And it is here, at the quick, that Whitman proceeds to find the experience of infinitude, his vast extension, or concentrated intensification into All-ness. He carries the conquest to its end.

If we read his paeans, his chants of praise and deliverance and accession, what do we find? All-embracing, indiscriminate, passional acceptance; surges of chaotic vehemence of invitation and embrace, catalogues, lists, enumerations. 'Whoever you are, to endless announcements. . . .' 'And of these one and all I weave the song of myself.' 'Lovers, endless lovers.'

Continually the one cry: 'I am everything and everything is me. I accept everything in my consciousness; nothing is rejected':

I am he that aches with amorous love;
Does the earth gravitate? does not all matter, aching, attract all
   matter?
So the body of me to all I meet or know.
                              (*I am He that Aches with Love*)

At last everything is conquered. At last the lower centres are conquered. At last the lowest plane is submitted to the highest. At last there is nothing more to conquer. At last all is one, all is love, even hate is love, even flesh is spirit. The great oneness, the experience of infinity, the triumph of the living spirit, which at last includes everything, is here accomplished.

It is man's accession into wholeness, his knowledge in full. Now he is united with everything. Now he embraces everything into himself in a oneness. Whitman is drunk with the new wine of this new great

experience, really drunk with the strange wine of infinitude. So he
pours forth his words, his chants of praise and acclamation. It is man's
maximum state of consciousness, his highest state of spiritual being.
Supreme spiritual consciousness, and the divine drunkenness of
supreme consciousness. It is reached through embracing love. 'And
whoever walks a furlong without sympathy walks to his own funeral
dressed in his own shroud.' And this supreme state, once reached,
shows us the One Identity in everything, Whitman's cryptic *One
Identity*.

Thus Whitman becomes in his own person the whole world, the
whole universe, the whole eternity of time. Nothing is rejected.
Because nothing opposes him. All adds up to one in him. Item by
item he identifies himself with the universe, and this accumulative
identity he calls Democracy, En Masse, One Identity, and so on.

But this is the last and final truth, the last truth is at the quick. And
the quick is the single individual soul, which is never more than itself,
though it embrace eternity and infinity, and never *other* than itself,
though it include all men. Each vivid soul is unique, and though one
soul embrace another, and include it, still it cannot *become* that other
soul, or livingly dispossess that other soul. In extending himself,
Whitman still remains himself; he does not become the other man,
or the other woman, or the tree, or the universe: in spite of Plato.

Which is the maximum truth, though it appears so small in contrast to all these infinites, and En Masses, and Democracies, and
Almightynesses. The essential truth is that a man is himself, and only
himself, throughout all his greatnesses and extensions and intensifi-
cations.

The second truth which we must bring as a charge against Whitman
is the one we brought before, namely, that his Allness, his One
Identity, his En Masse, his Democracy, is only a half-truth – an
enormous half-truth. The other half is Jehovah, and Egypt, and
Sennacherib: the other form of Allness, terrible and grand, even as in
the Psalms.

Now Whitman's way to Allness, he tells us, is through endless
sympathy, merging. But in merging you must merge away from
something, as well as towards something, and in sympathy you must
depart from one point to arrive at another. Whitman lays down this
law of sympathy as the one law, the direction of merging as the one

direction. Which is obviously wrong. Why not a right-about-turn? Why not turn slap back to the point from which you started to merge? Why not *that* direction, the reverse of merging, back to the single and overweening self? Why not, instead of endless dilation of sympathy, the retraction into isolation and pride?

Why not? The heart has its systole diastole, the shuttle comes and goes, even the sun rises and sets.We know, as a matter of fact, that all life lies between two poles. The direction is twofold. Whitman's *one direction* becomes a hideous tyranny once he has attained his goal of Allness. His One Identity is a prison of horror, once realized. For identities are manifold and each jewel-like, different as a sapphire from an opal. And the motion of merging becomes at last a vice, a nasty degeneration, as when tissue breaks down into a mucous slime. There must be the sharp retraction from isolation, following the expansion into unification, otherwise the integral being is overstrained and will break, break down like disintegrating tissue into slime, imbecility, epilepsy, vice, like Dostoevsky.

And one word more. Even if you reach the state of infinity, you can't sit down there. You just physically can't. You either have to strain still further into universality and become vaporish, or slimy: or you have to hold your toes and sit tight and practise Nirvana; or you have to come back to common dimensions, eat your pudding and blow your nose and be just yourself; or die and have done with it. A grand experience is a grand experience. It brings a man to his maximum. But even at his maximum a man is not more than himself. When he is infinite he is still himself. He still has a nose to wipe. The state of infinity is *only* a state, even if it be the supreme one.

But in achieving this state Whitman opened a new field of living. He drives on to the very centre of life and sublimates even this into consciousness. Melville hunts the remote white whale of the deepest passional body, tracks it down. But it is Whitman who captures the whale. The pure sensual body of man, at its deepest remoteness and intensity, this is the White Whale. And this is what Whitman captures.

He seeks his consummation through one continual ectasy: the ecstasy of *giving himself*, and of being taken. The ecstasy of his own reaping and merging with another, with others; the sword-cut of sensual death. Whitman's motion is always the motion of *giving himself.* This is my body – take, and eat. It is the great sacrament. He knows nothing of the other sacrament, the sacrament in pride, where the communicant envelops the victim and host in a flame of ecstatic consuming, sensual gratification, and triumph.

But he is concerned with others beside himself: with woman, for example. But what is woman to Whitman? Not much: she is a great function – no more. Whitman's 'athletic mothers of these States' are depressing. Muscles and wombs: functional creatures – no more.

As I see my soul reflected in Nature,
As I see through a mist, One with inexpressible completeness,
    sanity, beauty,
See the bent head, and arms folded over the breast, the Female
    I see.

(I Sing the Body Electric, 5)

That is all. The woman is reduced, really, to a submissive function. She is no longer an individual being with a living soul. She must fold her arms and bend her head and submit to her functioning capacity. Function of sex, function of birth.

This the nucleus – after the child is born of woman, man is born
    of woman,
This is the bath of birth, this the merge of small and large, and the
    outlet again –

(I Sing the Body Electric, 5)

Acting from the last and profoundest centres, man acts womanless. It is no longer a question of race continuance. It is a question of sheer, ultimate being, the perfection of life, nearest to death. Acting from these centres, man is an extreme being, the unthinkable warrior, creator, mover, and maker.

And the polarity is between man and man. Whitman alone of all moderns has known this positively. Others have known it negatively, *pour épater les bourgeois.* But Whitman knew it positively, in its tremendous knowledge, knew the extremity, the perfectness, and the fatality.

Even Whitman becomes grave, tremulous, before the last dynamic truth of life. In *Calamus* he does not shout. He hesitates: he is reluctant, wistful. But none the less he goes on. And he tells the mystery of manly love, the love of comrades. Continually he tells us the same truth: the new world will be built upon the love of comrades, the new great dynamic of life will be manly love. Out of this inspiration the creation of the future.

The strange Calamus has its pink-tinged root by the pond, and it sends up its leaves of comradeship, comrades at one root, without the intervention of woman, the female. This comradeship is to be the final cohering principle of the new world, the new Democracy. It is the cohering principle of perfect soldiery, as he tells in *Drum-Taps*. It is the cohering principle of final *unison* in creative activity. And it is extreme and alone, touching the confines of death. It is something terrible to bear, terrible to be responsible for. It is the soul's last and most vivid responsibility, the responsibility for the circuit of final friendship, comradeship, manly love.

Yet, you are beautiful to me you faint-tinged roots, you make
    me think of death,
Death is beautiful from you, (what indeed is finally beautiful
    except death and love?).
I think it is not for life I am chanting here my chant of lovers, I
    think it must be for death,
For how calm, how solemn it grows to ascend to the atmosphere
    of lovers,
Death or life I am then indifferent, my soul declines to prefer,
    (I am not sure but the high soul of lovers welcomes death most),
Indeed, O death, I think now these leaves mean precisely the same
    as you mean –

(*Scented Herbage of my Breast*)

Here we have the deepest, finest Whitman, the Whitman who knows the extremity of life, and of the soul's responsibility. He has come near now to death, in his creative life. But creative life must come near to death, to link up the mystic circuit. The pure warriors must stand on the brink of death. So must the men of a pure creative nation. We shall have no beauty, no dignity, no essential freedom otherwise. And so it is from Sea-Drift, where the male bird sings the lost female:

not that she is lost, but lost to him who has had to go beyond her, to
sing on the edge of the great sea, in the night. It is the last voice on the
shore.

Whereto answering, the sea
Delaying not, hurrying not,
Whispered me through the night, and very plainly before daybreak,
Lisp'd to me the low and delicious word death,
And again death, death, death, death,
Hissing melodious, neither like the bird nor like my aroused
    child's heart,
But edging near as privately for me rustling at my feet,
Creeping thence steadily up to my ears and laving me softly all
    over,
Death, death, death, death, death –
                    (*Out of the Cradle Endlessly Rocking*)

What a great poet Whitman is: great like a great Greek. For him
the last enclosures have fallen, he finds himself on the shore of the last
sea. The extreme of life: so near to death. It is a hushed, deep responsibility. And what is the responsibility? It is for the new great era of
mankind. And upon what is this new era established? On the perfect
circuits of vital flow between human beings. First, the great sexless
normal relation between individuals, simple sexless friendships, unison
of family, and clan, and nation, and group. Next, the powerful sex
relation between man and woman, culminating in the eternal orbit
of marriage. And, finally, the sheer friendship, the love between
comrades, the manly love which alone can create a new era of life.

The one state, however, does not annul the other: it fulfils the other.
Marriage is the great step beyond friendship, and family, and
nationality, but it does not supersede these. Marriage should only give
repose and perfection to the great previous bonds and relationships. A
wife or husband who sets about to annul the old, pre-marriage
affections and connexions ruins the foundations of marriage. And so
with the last, extremest love, the love of comrades. The ultimate
comradeship which sets about to destroy marriage destroys its own
raison d'être. The ultimate comradeship is the final progression from
marriage; it is the last seedless flower of pure beauty, beyond purpose.
But if it destroys marriage it makes itself purely deathly. In its beauty,

the ultimate comradeship flowers on the brink of death. But it flowers from the root of all life upon the blossoming tree of life.

The life-circuit now depends entirely upon the sex-unison of marriage. This circuit must never be broken. But it must be still surpassed. We cannot help the laws of life.

If marriage is sacred, the ultimate comradeship is utterly sacred, since it has no ulterior motive whatever, like procreation. If marriage is eternal, the great bond of life, how much more is this bond eternal, being the great life-circuit which borders on death in all its round. The new, extreme, the sacred relationship of comrades awaits us, and the future of mankind depends on the way in which this relation is entered upon by us. It is a relation between fearless, honorable, self-responsible men, a balance in perfect polarity.

The last phase is entered upon, shakily, by Whitman. It will take us an epoch to establish the new, perfect circuit of our being. It will take an epoch to establish the love of comrades, as marriage is really established now. For fear of going on, forwards, we turn round and destroy, or try to destroy, what lies behind. We are trying to destroy marriage, because we have not the courage to go forward from marriage to the new issue. Marriage must never be wantonly attacked. *True* marriage is eternal; in it we have our consummation and being. But the final consummation lies in that which is beyond marriage.

And when the bond, or circuit of perfect comrades is established, what then, when we are on the brink of death, fulfilled in the vastness of life? Then, at last, we shall know a starry maturity.

Whitman put us on the track years ago. Why has no one gone on from him? The great poet, why does no one accept his greatest word? The Americans are not worthy of their Whitman. They take him like a cocktail, for fun. Miracle that they have not annihilated every word of him. But these miracles happen.

The greatest modern poet! Whitman, at his best, is purely himself. His verse springs sheer from the spontaneous sources of his being. Hence its lovely, lovely form and rhythm: at the best. It is sheer, perfect *human* spontaneity, spontaneous as a nightingale throbbing, but still controlled, the highest loveliness of human spontaneity, undecorated, unclothed. The whole being is there, sensually throbbing, spiritually quivering, mentally, ideally speaking. It is not, like Swinburne, an exaggeration of the one part of being. It is perfect and whole. The whole soul speaks at once, and is too pure for mechanical assistance of rhyme and measure. The perfect utterance of a concentrated spontaneous soul. The unforgettable loveliness of Whitman's lines!

Out of the cradle endlessly rocking.
Ave America!

(616–18)

T. S. Eliot

'Whitman and Tennyson', a review of Emory Holloway's *Whitman: An Interpretation in Narrative*, The Nation and the Athenaeum 18 December 1926

This book is in no way a critical examination of Whitman's work; it has nothing to say – thank God! – about Whitman's influence upon *vers libre* and contemporary American verse; it is silent about Whitman's present standing in American literature. Mr Van Wyck Brooks would have made the subject the occasion for an elegy, Mr Mencken for a diatribe upon democracy. Mr Holloway's subject is 'Whitman the Man' and his environment, and he keeps to the matter in hand. The book is written in an artless style, which ends by pleasing; and in the end we think of all the things the book might have been and is not, and give the author thanks. It is, I should suppose, as good a *biography* of Whitman as has been written, or is likely to be. For it makes us realize (and I am sure that this is a token of its merit) that a critical appreciation of Whitman's poetry must take account of place and time. And this the book does without pretending to make any critical estimate itself. It is a modest and efficient book.

The time, of course, is the epoch of American history known to readers of *Martin Chuzzlewit*. To most Europeans, I imagine, this is a time which hardly exists; its difference, that is, from the Colonial Period (which we may say ended in 1829 with the defeat of Adams by Jackson) on the one hand, and the Age of Jazz on the other. But with relation to Whitman, it must be recognized that his was a time with a character of its own, and one in which it was possible to hold certain notions, and many illusions, which are now untenable. Now Whitman was (and this Mr Holloway's book makes abundantly clear) a 'man with a message', even if that message was sometimes badly mutilated in transmission; he was interested in what he had to say; he did not think of himself primarily as the inventor of a new technique of versification. His 'message' must be reckoned with, and it is a very different message from that of Mr Carl Sandburg.

The world of the American voyage in *Martin Chuzzlewit* is the same. Dickens knew best what it looked like, but Whitman knew what it felt like. There is another interesting parallel: *Leaves of Grass* appeared in 1856, *Les fleurs du mal* in 1857: could any age have produced more heterogeneous leaves and flowers? The contrasts should be noted. But perhaps more important than these contrasts is the similarity of Whitman to another master, one whose greatness he always recognized and whose eminence he always acknowledged generously – to Tennyson. Between the ideas of the two men, or, rather, between the relations of the ideas of each to his place and time, between the ways in which each held his ideas, there is a fundamental resemblance. Both were born laureates. Whitman, of course, fought hard against corruption, against Press servility, against slavery, against alcohol (and I dare say Tennyson would have done so under the same conditions); but essentially he was satisfied – too satisfied – with things as they are. His labourers and pioneers (at that date all Anglo-Saxon, or at least North European, labourers and pioneers) are the counterpart to Tennyson's great broad-shouldered Englishman at whom Arnold pokes fun; Whitman's horror at the monarchical tyranny of Europe is the counterpart to Tennyson's comment on the revolutions of French politics, no 'graver than a schoolboy's barring out'. Baudelaire, on the other hand, was a disagreeable person who was rarely satisfied with anything: *je m'ennuie en France*, he wrote, *où tout le monde ressemble à Voltaire*.

I do not mean to suggest that all discontent is divine, or that all self-righteousness is loathesome. On the contrary, both Tennyson and Whitman made satisfaction almost magnificent. It has not the best aspect of their verse; if neither of them had more, neither of them would be still a great poet. But Whitman succeeds in making America as it was, just as Tennyson made England as it was, into something grand and significant. You cannot quite say that either was deceived, and you cannot at all say that either was insincere, or the victim of popular cant. They had the faculty – Whitman perhaps more prodigiously than Tennyson – of transmuting the real into an ideal. Whitman had the ordinary desires of the flesh; for him there was no chasm between the real and the ideal, such as opened before the horrified eyes of Baudelaire. But this, and the 'frankness' about sex for which he is either extolled or mildly reproved, did not spring from any particular honesty or clearness of vision: it sprang from what may be called either 'idealization' or a faculty for make-believe, according as we are disposed. There is, fundamentally, no difference between the Whitman frankness and the Tennyson delicacy, except in its relation to public opinion of the time. And Tennyson liked monarchs, and Whitman liked presidents. Both were conservative, rather than reactionary or revolutionary; that is to say, they believed explicitly in progress, and believed implicitly that progress consists in things remaining much as they are.

If this were all there is to Whitman, it would still be a great deal; he would remain a great representative of America, but emphatically of an America which no longer exists. It is not the America of Mr Scott Fitzgerald, or Mr Dos Passos, or Mr Hemmingway – to name some of the more interesting of contemporary American writers. If I may draw still one more comparison, it is with Hugo. Beneath all the declamations there is another tone, and behind all the illusions there is another vision. When Whitman speaks of the lilacs or of the mocking-bird, his theories and beliefs drop away like a needless pretext.

(426)

Amy Lowell

'Walt Whitman and the New Poetry', *Yale Review*, n.s., vol. 16 1926–7

Whitman's is a very curious case in the long line of expressive geniuses. His message was given entire in his first book, and for thirty years he merely added to it. His was not a career of phases in the literary meaning of that term. His first phase, one of complete conformity and banality, if we are to believe his contemporaries as well as himself on the subject, was got over in the pages of ephemeral journalism; he was already in his second and final phase when he printed *Leaves of Grass* in 1855.

But, if his main attitude was invariable, his practice underwent some modifications. For instance, in the matter of titles. I suppose no man ever perpetrated worse titles than those in his first volumes. He changed many of these later; they became more literary, but less forceful, peculiar, original. *Poem of the Road* is now *Song of the Open Road*, *Broad-Axe Poem* is *Song of the Broad Axe*, *Poem of Salutation* attitudinizes as *Salut au Monde!* and *Poem of Wonder at the Resurrection of the Wheat* is diluted into *This Compost*. Occasionally, however, he succeeded in making a possible new title. The awkward *Poem of the Daily Work of the Workmen and Workwomen of These States* is shortened into *A Song for Occupations*; and the *Poem of the Sayers of the Words of the Earth* is not seriously injured by becoming *A Song of the Rolling Earth*. Yet I think the very clumsiness of the early titles is intriguing, and the word 'song' has a painfully Victorian ring. Only rarely has he made an indubitable improvement. *Poem of Many in One* is certainly better, if a trifle vague, as *By Blue Ontario's Shore*, and *I Sing the Body Electric* was a burst of inspiration for which we must be grateful; it is hard to wish to read anything which announces itself as *Poem of the Body*.

When his working over is followed into the text, the changes are usually happy. They are, on the whole, more effective and less brutal, or perhaps I mean vulgar; at any rate, less purely animal in connotation. The first stanza of *Poem of the Body* begins:

The bodies of men and women engirth me, and I engirth them,
They will not let me off nor I them till I go with them respond
    to them love them.

In the later version this is changed to:

I sing the body electric,
The armies of those I love engirth me and I engirth them,
They will not let me off till I go with them, respond to them,
And discorrupt them, and charge them full with the charge of the
    soul.

In other words, Walt Whitman's development was a constant march towards a greater preoccupation with form. And here I wish to make a statement which I fear will be somewhat startling. I believe that Walt Whitman fell into his own peculiar form through ignorance, and not, as is commonly supposed, through a high sense of fitness; in this point he is at complete issue with the moderns who are supposed to derive from him, since they are perfectly conscious artists writing in a medium not less carefully ordered because it is based upon cadence and not upon metre. Whitman never had the slightest idea of what cadence is, and I think it does not take much reading to force the conviction that he had very little rhythmical sense.

Whitman was a great poet whether he invented his form consciously or whether he stumbled into it while endeavoring to avoid the obvious pitfalls of an older practice; and that he was not what Dr Patterson would call 'aggressively rhythmic', I think I can, without much difficulty, show. I am perfectly aware that he has given reasons, and cogent reasons, for writing as he did in 'A Backward Glance O'er Travel'd Roads', but it is by these very utterances that I intend to prove my point.

First and foremost, Whitman was chiefly propagandist and only afterwards poet. He admits so much himself when he says: 'I say the profoundest service that poems or any other writings can do for their reader is not merely to satisfy the intellect, or supply something polished and interesting, nor even to depict great passions, or persons or events, but to fill him with vigorous and clean manliness, religiousness, and give him *good heart* as a radical possession and habit.'

That is merely a splendidly virile re-statement of the Victorian theory that the chief end of art is a moral one. There is nothing in it which would not have met with the hearty accord of both Longfellow and Tennyson. For, after all, far-seeing though he was, Whitman was fundamentally of his age, and this odd fact confronts us again and again. It is true that, among modern poets, there is one group which holds somewhat to this opinion, but by far the most important poets believe art to be an entity, a saving entity, one which in itself contains the other, but nevertheless something of supreme value as it is. A work of art is not static, but dynamic. It carries within itself the power of growth and change. Its moral effect is not direct, but insidious and persistent.

A man does not love his wife because it improves his character to do so, he loves her because he must, his spiritual nature requires such functioning; but it is undeniable that the feeling serves a moral end as well. At moments Whitman dimly apprehended this, but generally his mind was of too harsh and primitive a texture to grasp it fully. He had a curiously limited way of viewing life principally from the outside: 'Whatever may have been the case in years gone by, the true use for the imaginative faculty of modern times is to give ultimate vivification to facts, to science, and to common lives, endowing them with the glows and glories and final illustriousness which belong to every real thing, and to real things only.' There is his vision, in the last line, and that is his bequest to the new world.

Whitman was like a prophet straying in a fog and shouting half-truths with a voice of great trumpets. He was seeking something, but he never knew quite what, and he never found it. He vanishes in the mist, and his words float back, dim, superb, to us behind him.

Whitman was artist enough, even in the beginning, to perceive that the type of verse current in his day would not fit the sublime and raucous message which meant poetry to him. He sought and sought, but what he reached was not through a process of creation, but through one of elimination.

For grounds of *Leaves of Grass*, as a poem, I abandoned the conventional themes, which do not appear in it: none of the stock ornamentation, or choice plots of love or war, or high, exceptional personages of Old-World song; nothing, as I may say, for beauty's sake – no legend, or myth, or romance, nor euphemism, nor rhyme. But the broadest average of humanity and its identities in the now ripening nineteenth century, and especially in each of their countless examples and practical occupations in the United States today.

('A Backward Glance O'er Travel'd Roads')

One can imagine him being read centuries hence for his lists of occupations, much as we find Virgil's *Georgics* greatly delightful for its catalogue of agricultural labors. But Virgil's catalogues are scarcely Whitman's. Those interminable bald statements of trades. Flat, flat, flat, seldom a pregnant word, scarcely a relieving gesture. In four hundred pages, I found so few, here they are:

Earth of the vitreous pour of the full moon, just tinged with blue!
(*Song of Myself, 21*)

O for the voices of animals – O for the swiftness and balance of
   fishes!
O for the dropping of raindrops in a song!
O for the sunshine and motion of waves in a song!
(*A Song of Joys*)

   I do not say there are not others, only that I have not found them.
Beauty of another kind there is, but just now I am speaking of the
alleviation of such passages as:

The usual routine . . . the workshop, factory, yard, office, store,
   or desk;
The jaunt of hunting or fishing, or the life of hunting or fishing,
Pasturelife, foddering, milking and herding, and all the personnel
   and usages;
The plum-orchard and apple-orchard . . . gardening . . . seedlings,
   cuttings, flowers and vines . . .
(1855, 'Come closer to me', p. 61.[1])

   This is by no means the beginning of the passage, and it continues
uninterrupted for six pages! The only hint at artistic selection in them
is in the assonance and alliteration of 'hinge, flange, band, bolt'
varying into the soft 'o' and changed consonants of 'throttle'.
   In the passage from 'A Backward Glance O'er Travel'd Roads'
which I have just quoted, it will be noticed that rhyme is considered
a beauty and eschewed. Nothing at all is said about rhythm, but the
inclusion of rhyme is significant, and bears out my opinion that
Whitman had a decided liking for conventional verse although he did
not consider it an appropriate medium for what he wanted to say.
He was probably not among those who take to rhyme naturally, and
so, being somewhat of a labor, it handicapped the pure expression
of his thought, but I think he would have smiled considerably at the
arrogant and one-idea'd young persons who condemn it wholesale.
That he could rhyme, the first stanza of the *Song of the Broad-Axe*
proves:

1 This was later called *A Song for Occupations*. [Ed.]

Weapon shapely, naked, wan,
Head from the mother's bowels drawn,
Wooded flesh and metal bone, limb only one and lip only one,
Grey-blue leaf by red-heat grown, helve produced from a little
    seed sown,
Resting the grass amid and upon,
To be lean'd and to lean on.

A purist might object that there were a good many false rhymes in that passage, but let us not be purists, let us be people of taste and understanding. Now, if Whitman could write so fine a passage in rhyme, why does he think the use of rhyme improper to the bulk of his poetry? Frankly, flatly, unpedantically, because it was only occasionally that he could make rhyme 'go' as well as that. He was in the urgent haste of creation, the necessary rhyme stumbled and lagged, he must get on, the thought would not wait. So he got on; that is the long and short of the matter.

So much for Whitman's form and the cause of it. It sprang, not from a positive desire to give substance to a new conception of beauty, but from a negative one not to incorporate in his work any existing beauties whatsoever.

Here, at once, is a cleavage with the moderns. They are positively trying to do something; he is negatively trying not to do something else.

The layman is fond of calling all verse not based upon metre 'free verse'. It does not in the least trouble him that there is not, and cannot be, any such thing. The term is, obviously, derived from a mistaken translation of the French term *vers libre*. Now *vers*, in French, means line; and *vers libre* meant a line which was not obliged to contain a given number of feet. The true English equivalent would be 'free line', but a better term is 'cadenced verse', or a type of verse based upon cadence. We all know how difficult it is to correct terms already in current use. We grandiloquently employ the word 'hangar' to denote the building used to house a dirigible balloon, but a 'hangar' is simply a shed. Speak to nine people out of ten about a balloon shed, however, and they will gently set you right by assuring you that the technical name is 'hangar'.

So the term *vers libre* seems to be with us to stay, and it is most unfortunate. Still, I do not despair, we may succeed in pushing 'cadenced verse' to the front before long. But here is the point, cadence is rhythm. Modern *vers libre*, far from being non-rhythmical as some people have supposed, is entirely based upon rhythm. Its rhythms differ from those of metre by being less obvious and more subtle, but rhythm is, nevertheless, the very ground and root of its structure. *Vers libre* looks easy to write, and bad *vers libre* is easy; but when it is bad it is not *vers libre* at all, but prose cut into arbitrary lines. The lines of good *vers libre* are not arbitrary, they are determined by the interrelating circles of the rhythm. Every word is placed in relation to the whole, and a change of a syllable will often throw a line quite out, in absolutely the same way that a change of a syllable would throw out a line of metre.

Here is a point to be carefully considered and understood. Walt Whitman did not write in metre (I exclude for the moment his occasional metrical pieces), and neither did he write *vers libre*. What he did write was a highly emotional prose, rising at times into genuine rhythmical prose, the *prose rythmée* of our Gallic neighbors.

His poems are true poetry, however, not only because of their essence, but because he approaches his subject from the poetic point of view. For what makes a literary work prose or poetry is not a matter of typography; it is a matter of approach and of return. By return I mean some device by which a poem is brought continually back to its starting place. Something which keeps the basic emotional symbol constantly reappearing throughout the poem. All nations have recognized this, and they have achieved this quality of return in diverse ways. Our own most usual form employs metre and rhyme, our Anglo-Saxon ancestors made use of alliteration, the Hebrews wrote in double images, the Chinese have a scheme of alternating tones which only their language could be capable of, the Japanese alternate lines of seven and five syllables, and so on. There are as many ways of achieving 'return' as there are prosodies, but in every one it is the determining factor of the technique of poetry. Now Whitman returns with a dominant thought, often with a specific set of words.

I am not going to labor the point. That what Whitman wrote was poetry, I think no longer admits of discussion, but that much of it had precious little rhythm is quite easily demonstrable. I am far from

saying he never had it. There are superb instances to the contrary –
for example, the lyric parts of *Out of the Cradle Endlessly Rocking*,
the whole poem *Tears*, much of *Passage to India* – and I think they are
his finest work; but that he could have let so much pass which was
quite innocent of any rhythmical pattern, would seem to imply that
he did not consider rhythm as of paramount importance. Again, he
does not eschew rhythm with the other beauties, the conclusion being
that he did not regard rhythm as a beauty.

Often and often I read in the daily, weekly, and monthly press, that
the modern *vers libre* writers derive their form from Walt Whitman.
As a matter of fact, most of them got it from the French Symbolist
poets, they were nearest to our time; but in spite of its French name,
vers libre was written in England long before it was thought of in
France; Milton wrote it in his choruses to *Samson Agonistes*, Blake
wrote it in various of the prophetic books, Matthew Arnold wrote it
in *The Nightingale*, Henley wrote it in *London Voluntaries*. And all
these poems are true *vers libre,* poems based upon cadence.

But why did not Whitman try this form instead of taking metrical
verse as a base and dropping things out of it ? I believe for two reasons:
one was that he did not read, or like, these poems; the other, that he
did not feel any vital urge towards rhythm. I believe that another
reason for his poems taking the form they did was because of his
habit of reading the heroic poems of Greece and Rome and Italy and
the East in translations, and most of the translations of his day, with
the exception of the Bible, were either in strict metre or in prose.
Since he had cast out metre, heroic poetry in his mind unconsciously
fell into the form of prose. Had he read Butcher and Lang's translation
of Homer, or Waley's rendering of Chinese poems, he might have
got a hint of cadence as a genre by itself, for he was quite capable of
adopting modes of writing; he took things when they seemed to him
suitable – like the Oriental return by repetition:

Houses and rooms are full of perfumes, the shelves are crowded
　with perfumes.

(*Song of Myself*, 2)

It would not take much knowledge of Oriental practice to get that.
He might have found it in the *Psalms* or *Isaiah*, but it is on record that

he had read translations of Eastern works. In *Specimen Days* he quotes some lines from an old Hindu poem.

No, the moderns, even the modern practitioners of 'cadenced verse', with the possible exception of Carl Sandburg, owe very little of their form to Whitman. What they do owe is an attitude, to determine which we must first consider what was this vision of the world that Whitman had. It is not difficult to find out. The whole of *Leaves of Grass* shouts it to us, and he has also explained it in page after page of prose. He hands it to us like a nut wrapped in a shell. The shell is his speech – the nut? Well, as I have said, I doubt whether he himself had ever really seen it. Here is his brief, final summary:

As long as the States continue to absorb and be dominated by the poetry of the Old World, and remain unsupplied with autochthonous song, to express, vitalize and give color to and define their material and political success, and minister to them distinctively, so long will they stop short of first-class Nationality and remain defective.

('A Backward Glance')

Walt Whitman proposed to give them this autochthonous song. He would make a poetry of America, he would make it of the lives of the great even strata of work-people. He would include all activities, all trades, he would be the voice of the whole continent from coast to coast, he would be North, and South, and Middle, he would laud his country and believe in her; nothing should be beneath him, nothing above. It was a magnificent aim, and in great part he did exactly what he set out to do.

He saw that science had changed the face of the world; he knew that we must adjust. He believed in the poet's mission of seer. It was the poet who must proclaim not only the moment, but its future. He had read the words of a French critic who said that 'owing to the special tendency to science and its all-devouring force, poetry would cease to be read in fifty years.' He took up the challenge, and set himself to the task of refutation. He saw himself as America. In a curious, detached kind of way, he lifted himself, for purposes of expression, into the role of American superman. He took himself, and what he knew of America, and deified them into an ideal.

It was a great and noble thing to have someone sing for America, America as a base, a home land, not as a colony. The other poets of Whitman's day read far too much like colonials; only Lowell touched a native savor, the others, for all their Water-Fowls and Barbara Frietchies and Paul Reveres were (in a literary sense) directly sprung from British loins. We needed Whitman's message; we need it today. We need it as he meant it, rather than as he said it; much of it is in our blood, unnoticed but invigorating. But the letter of his speech – ah, there is the crux! Ill-digested, his message may be as dangerous as a Bolshevik *pronunciamento*. Walt Whitman was a law-abiding citizen, a bit of a dreamer, a grand, nebulous soul, a fine, intuitive poet. The last ignominy to him would be the usage of his words as pickaxes to tear down the governmental structure he loved. It is perhaps somewhat sadly significant that the three modern poets who most loudly acknowledge his leadership are all of recent foreign extraction. For the native breed is doing what? It is going back, back, slowly learning, seeing beauty as its ancestors saw it. Following, not Whitman only, but Langland, and Chaucer, and Wordsworth, and Robert Burns, seeing beauty in today, their day. Clinging to the fundamental human meanings which outlast mere tools and occasions. Is it time or Whitman which has caused us to cease our colonial habit? I believe both. Raw Whitman appeals to our late arrivals; modified Whitman is in us all.

Ah, but he was really American, the good gray poet, he not only dared the complete vision of his early manhood; later, when age had opened troubled vistas, he did not flinch from leaving a record of them:

Modern science and democracy seemed to be throwing out their challenge to poetry to put them in its statements in contradistinction to the songs and myths of the past. As I see it now (perhaps too late) I have unwittingly taken up that challenge and made an attempt at such statements – which I certainly would not assume to do now, knowing more clearly what it means.

('A Backward Glance')

An inkling of his poetic lapses comes to him in old age also: 'I have probably not been afraid of careless touches from the first – and am not now – nor of parrot-like repetitions – nor platitudes and the commonplace. Perhaps I am too democratic for such avoidances.'

If that last sentence be true, democracy carries the coffin of art upon her shoulders. But I do not believe it. It is not by levelling down, but up, that democracy can ever succeed in adequately containing life. And even then, it will be with it as with the human race itself: the upward shoots thrusting above the even plane prove finally of the most importance.

Whitman was right when he declared that 'No one will get at my verses who insists upon viewing them as a literary performance, or attempt at such performance, or as aiming mainly toward art or aestheticism.' He has put it more succinctly in a poem:

. . . a book I have made,
The words of my book nothing, the drift of it everything.
(*Shut not Your Doors*)

His whole is more important than his parts. Some obscure feeling for fitness prompted him to put all his poems together, at the last, under his first generic title: *Leaves of Grass*. His work was not manifold, but single. It was all cut from one piece – himself. But, after all, he wrote; and we today also write. We have his poetic practice left to examine. How did he treat his poems; how do we treat ours?

In the first place, the modern has one frightful bugbear, the cliché. It pursues him relentlessly, and sometimes it catches him. Now, Whitman says that he has not been afraid of platitudes nor the commonplace. How very differently Mr Sandburg manages his catalogues from the way that Walt Whitman managed his. Here is a passage; if you were to hear it without the slightest possibility of knowing who wrote it, in what particular pigeon-hole of literary history would you place it, do you think?

Blow trumpeter free and clear, I follow thee,
Where at thy liquid prelude, glad, serene,
The fretting world, the streets, the noisy hours of the day
    withdraw,
A holy calm descends like dew upon me,
I walk in cool refreshing night the walks of Paradise,

I scent the grass, the moist air and the roses;
The song expands my numb'd imbonded spirit, thou freest,
    launchest me,
Floating and basking upon Heaven's lake.

I think that proves my contention that when the prophet was off
duty, the poet was very much a man of his time.

And this prophet – Whitman is called the voice of his period, but
here is a forward gaze which is almost uncanny:

I see not America only, not only Liberty's nation but other nations
    preparing,
I see tremendous entrances and exits, new combinations, the
    solidarity of races . . .
I see men marching and countermarching by swift millions,
I see the frontiers and boundaries of the old aristocracies broken,
I see the landmarks of European kings removed,
I see this day the People beginning their landmarks . . .
                              (*Years of the Modern*)

The extreme left wing of poetry might take those lines as a battle
slogan were they unrelated to their whole. But the people in Whitman's eyes was no rapacious plunderer, it was a good quiet village
folk, well able, because slow to conclude yet firm in conclusion, to
govern itself. The poem goes on:

I see Freedom, completely arm'd and victorious and very haughty,
    with Law on one side and Peace on the other.

Law and Peace, but Whitman was no pacifist. Try as our literary
aliens may to force him into the role of tutelary god to the conscientious objector, he resists. We shall all know that he resisted, that
he was bone and sinew of resistance in what he believed a righteous
cause, if we read him instead of books about him. *Drum-Taps* is
scarcely the volume of a pacifist. And this man knew war. He followed the armies; in the hospital tents – the terrible hospitals of those
days with practically no anaesthetics and no antiseptics at all – he
saw suffering with naked eyes. He walked battlefields in the red sun-
sets of days of conflict:

Look down fair moon and bathe this scene,
Pour softly down night's nimbus floods on faces ghastly, swollen,
    purple,
On the dead on their backs with arms toss'd wide,
Pour down your unstinted nimbus sacred moon.

                    (*Look Down Fair Moon*)

Reading this poem, we are instantly reminded of another poet who
has seen war, Siegfried Sassoon. His book, *Counter-Attack*, is full of
just such scenes.

The modern poet is bitter. He has lost his old vision in the reek of
war. He is not sad and merciful, he hates. Hates the waste and useless
horror of war. The setting back of the clock of civilization is always
in his consciousness. It is so with all the sincere writers of the present
day. This consciousness of waste is minimized to Whitman by his
far-seeing outlook of a present necessity. Besides, once more I
reiterate that he was a man of his time. Not yet the day when dreamers
dared proclaim their hope a possible reality. We are more self-
conscious today. It may be a gain; it may be a loss; but it is a fact.
Besides, not in all the ranks of modern poetry has there yet appeared
a seer.

Was Whitman's vision a true one? This America which he so
loved, has she that within her through which she can rise victorious
above all catastrophes? It is all in his poem, *Thou Mother with thy
Equal Brood*:

In many a smiling mask death shall approach beguiling thee, thou in
    disease shalt swelter,
The livid cancer spread its hideous claws, clinging upon thy
    breasts, seeking to strike thee deep within,
Consumption of the worst, moral consumption, shall rouge thy
    face with hectic,
But thou shalt face thy fortunes, thy diseases, and surmount them
    all . . .

                            (6)

He could write so because it was only a vision. In security he could
gaze clear-eyed at chaos, for the future has its perspective as well as
the past. Do not expect such utterance from modern poets. The

disease is here; haply we may preserve our sanity. To keep on going, to see beauty still beyond the red night, that is the awful task before our poets today. Granted that all are not worthy to be taken seriously, why, every age has had this same difficulty – clouds of gnats buzzing about the falcons. But gnats are short-lived creatures, while the falcons endure. It is confusing; but make no mistake, it has always been confusing.

Whitman is not always on the mountain peak of prophecy. Sometimes he is unexpectedly the poet of pure beauty. Nothing could be more modern, nothing more akin to the point of view of our contemporaries, than this:

To me every hour of the light and dark is a miracle,
Every cubic inch of space is a miracle,
Every square yard of the surface of the earth is spread with the
    same,
Every foot of the interior swarms with the same;
Every spear of grass – the frames, limbs, organs, of men and
    women, and all that concerns them,
All these to me are unspeakably perfect miracles.
                                        (1881, *Miracles*)

And this is the very essence of that type of poetry which we have learnt to call Imagistic:

Through the ample open door of the peaceful country barn,
A sunlit pasture field with cattle and horses feeding,
A haze and vista, and the far horizon fading away.
                                        (*Farm Picture*)

There are many such pictures: *Cavalry Crossing a Ford*, *Bivouac on a Mountain Side*, *An Army Corps on the March*, and others; yet it would be utter folly to consider that the vignettes in modern work derive from Whitman, when, in his own day, this sort of thing was being done, and much better done, by Emily Dickinson. In almost all such cases, the moderns have found their prototype elsewhere than in Whitman, although it is undeniable that Whitman hints at many of the ways of modern practice. 'Away with love verses sugar'd in rhyme' might be taken as a slogan by some of our younger lyrists. 'The indirect is just as much as the direct' has a sympathetic sound to various of our present-day groups, and Whitman calls this indirectness 'Suggestiveness'. The modern term scarcely differs, it is 'Suggestion'. He analyses it exactly as we do:

I round and finish little, if anything; and could not, consistently with my scheme. The reader will always have his or her part to do, just as much as I have had mine. I seek less to state or display any theme or thought, and more to bring you, reader, into the atmosphere of the theme or thought – there to pursue your own flight.

('A Backward Glance')

Yet how far Whitman was from the indirectness of present-day methods!

To compare what is near and yet very far is always a delightful occupation. Here are two poems built upon almost the same theme. One is Whitman's O *Magnet-South*.

O magnet-South! O glistening perfumed South! my South!
O quick mettle, rich blood, impulse and love! good and evil, O
    all dear to me!
O dear to me my birth-things – all moving things and the trees
    where I was born – the grains, plants, rivers,
Dear to me my own slow sluggish rivers where they flow, distant
    over flats of silvery sands or through swamps,
Dear to me the Roanoke, the Savannah, the Altamahaw, the
    Pedee, the Tombigbee, the Santee, the Coosa and the Sabine,
O pensive, far away wandering, I return with my soul to haunt
    their banks again.

This is from Carl Sandburg's *Prairie*:

I was born on the prairie and the milk of its wheat, the red of its
    clover, the eyes of its women, gave me a song and a slogan.
Here the water went down, the icebergs slid with gravel, the gaps
    and the valleys hissed, the black loam came, and the yellow
    sandy loam,
Here between the sheds of the Rocky Mountains and the
    Appalachians, here now a morning star fixes a fire sign over the
    timber claims and cow pastures, the corn belt, the cotton belt,
    the cattle ranches.

Here the gray geese go five hundred miles and back with a wind
    under their wings honking the cry for a new home.
Here I know I will hanker after nothing so much as one more
    sunrise or a sky moon of fire doubled to a river moon of water.
The prairie sings to me in the forenoon and I know in the night
    I rest easy in the prairie arms, on the prairie heart.

Both those passages are mere fragments of the poems to which
they belong, but they show a great deal. For instance, the sentimentality which underlay Whitman's coarseness; the complete absence of
it in Sandburg. It is the difference of sixty years. The world is no
longer the same.

I might make more of these comparisons. For instance, *The Song
of the Redwood Tree* with Vachel Lindsay's *Golden Whales of California*, although, to be sure, the latter is ironical; or, again, Whitman's
group of poems about Lincoln, with John Gould Fletcher's *Abraham
Lincoln*, by far the finest modern poem on the subject. Since I may
not do this, I must content myself with citing a few differences. I have
mentioned the modern horror of the cliché. Another nightmare is the
inversion; but so far removed from our point of view was Whitman,
that he could calmly produce this very type and model of the dreadful thing:

O little shells, so curious-convolute, so limpid-cold and voiceless,
Will you not little shells to the tympans of temples held,
Murmurs and echoes still call up, eternity's music faint and far.
                    (*As Consequent*)

Whitman, like all poets, felt a pleasure in mere words, and particularly, it would seem, in foreign words. They are a constant source
of misery in reading him, for his use of them is frequently ill-judged.
One thing is very marked today: a large number of the poets are fair
linguists. I think scarcely one of them could be guilty of such an
amazing grammatical blunder as the following:

Now I absorb immortality and peace,
I admire death and test proportions.

How plenteous! how spiritual! how resumé!
                    (*Night on the Prairies*)

It is dangerous to use foreign words when you do not even know whether they are parts of verbs, or nouns, or adjectives. Even in his own tongue what can one think of the taste which would perpetrate such a line as 'The rich man's elegant villa'!

That kind of thing could not find a lodgment anywhere in print now, but it was rife in Whitman's day, and Whitman was – he was several things – a great voice, and a silly, flattered old man; a conceited, ardent young fellow spattered with genius, and a primitive being teased by violent animal reactions. He was a powerful original poet, with a somewhat disconcerting dash of the *poseur*. Singer, prophet, orator, lover of beauty, sentimentalist and often slovenly workman, his poems are that splendid paradox – himself. Magnificence punctuated with 'the things no fellow can do'; in substance, technique, fact, it is the same. To follow him is merely to imitate the pattern of his cloak. His time is past, we have ours. It is (to use the sort of language affected by his closest imitators) 'up to us.' Let us be thankful for him as we are thankful for Theocritus, and Dante, and Chaucer, and Browning. But our skies are not his, and he would be the first to wish us 'God speed' under them. Has he not written:

Let me not dare, here or anywhere, for my own purposes, or for any purposes, to attempt the definition of Poetry, nor answer the question what it is. Like Religion, Love, Nature, while those terms are indispensable, and we all give a sufficiently accurate meaning to them, in my opinion no definition that has ever been made sufficiently encloses the name Poetry; nor can any rule or convention ever so absolutely obtain but some great exception may arise and disregard and overturn it.
('A Backward Glance')

Sane and wise words, but indeed the writing of books is dust unless we can also say with him:

Camerado, this is no book,
Who touches this touches a man.
(*So Long*)

(502–19)

Constance Rourke

from 'I Hear America Singing', *American Humor* 1931

Whitman stressed the personal intention, insisting that it belonged to all his poetry.

Leaves of Grass indeed (I cannot too often reiterate) has been mainly the outcropping of my own emotional and other personal nature – an attempt, from first to last, to put a *Person*, a human being (myself, in the latter half of the nineteenth century of America) freely, fully and truly on record.

('A Backward Glance O'er
Travel'd Roads')

Yet Whitman's emotion was rarely the personal emotion; it always included others who swiftly become the subject or even in a sense the singer. The 'I' or 'Me' of Whitman is no more personal in final content than was that of the rhapsodic backwoodsman: it has the urgency of many people. The gesture is open-handed, the framework that of autobiography: yet this poetry constantly slips into another realm. Once he acknowledged this escape or evasion:

... before all my arrogant poems the real Me stands yet untouch'd, untold, altogether unreach'd.

(*As I Ebb'd with the Ocean of
Life*, 2)

In the end Whitman went far beyond that transcending of the merely personal which must occur if poetry is to be created. For the first time in American literature, perhaps for the first time in all literature, he created a generic and inclusive 'I' who embraces many minds and many experiences.

Passsage after passage in his poems begins with the personal experience or mood only to drop these for the generic. In the first few lines of *Starting from Paumanok* Whitman is briefly himself: he then quickly becomes that being who was his great subject, that mythical American who had not only known Manhattan but had been a pioneer in Dakota and a miner in California, who had roamed the entire continent and had comprised all its typical experiences.

I am of old and young, of the foolish as much as the wise,
Regardless of others, ever regardful of others,
Maternal as well as paternal, a child as well as a man,
Stuff'd with the stuff that is coarse and stuff'd with the stuff that is fine,
One of the Nation of many nations, the smallest the same and the largest the same,
A Southerner soon as a Northerner, a planter nonchalant and hospitable down by the Oconee I live,
A Yankee bound my own way ready for my trade, my joints the limberest joints on earth and the sternest joints on earth,
A Kentuckian walking the vale of the Elkhorn in my deerskin leggings, a Louisianian or Georgian,
A boatman over lakes and bays or along coasts, a Hoosier, Badger, Buckeye –

(*Song of Myself*, 16)

He was a Yankee sailor aboard a clipper; he was a farmer in a country barn, among the dried grasses of harvest-time. Whitman was not only full of this great theme but aware of queries which might arise in relation to it, often humorously aware:

Do I contradict myself?
Very well then I contradict myself,
(I am large, I contain multitudes).

(*Song of Myself*, 51)

His inclusions might be grossly made: but by the scope of his view and the urgency of his consideration he evoked a large and comprehensive figure not unlike that inclusive character toward which the types of popular comedy had seemed to merge.

Often this figure went beyond the bounds of nationalism, as in portions of the *Song of Myself* and in *Children of Adam*. Whitman could leave the nationalistic for the purely human. Yet the body of his thought was nationalistic: his iterated theme was the American – was the nation. 'The ambitious thought of my song is to help the forming of a great aggregate Nation,' he declared, frankly leaving the

purpose to transcribe a *Person* altogether. With an exuberance like that
of the fable of the contrast he shouted, 'I chant America the mistress,
I chant a greater supremacy.' His notions of the older countries were
closely linked with those of the fable. Whitman's warmest conception
of the older nations was that of pity. 'Once powerful,' he called them,
'now reduced, withdrawn or desolate.' In a less temperate mood he
could talk of 'Europe's old dynastic slaughter-house, Area of murder-
plots of thrones, with scent yet left of wars and scaffolds everywhere.'
In a nobler measure he queried:

> Have the elder races halted?
> Do they droop and end their lesson, wearied over there beyond
>   the seas?
> We take up the task eternal, and the burden and the lesson,
>   Pioneers! O pioneers!
>   (*Pioneers! O Pioneers!*)

He carried the theme into a hitherto untouched sphere, the consideration of poetry:

> Shrouded bards of other lands, you may rest, you have done your
>   work.
>   (*Pioneers! O Pioneers!*)

He passed to a visionary scheme for perfection which America was to
crown:

> And thou America,
> For the scheme's culmination, its thought and reality,
> For these (not for thyself) thou hast arrived.
>   (*Song of the Universal*, 4)

Whitman was filled as well with themes which he might have
caught from those strolling exponents of the divine comedy who
reached a crest of their ecstasy in the decade before he began to write.
Like them he declared that he meant to 'inaugurate a religion'. They
had often denied evil, announcing that perfection was at hand. 'I say
in fact there is no evil.' He declared that 'only the good is universal',
and that he meant 'to formulate a poem whose every thought or fact
should directly or indirectly be or connive at the implicit belief in the
wisdom, health, mystery, beauty of every process, every concrete

object, every human or other existence. . . .' He was constantly occupied with the theme of perfection:

In this broad earth of ours,
Amid the measureless grossness and the slag,
Enclosed and safe within its central heart,
Nestles the seed perfection.

(*Song of the Universal*, 1)

In America he expected to find 'a world primal again'. From America 'in vistas of glory incessant and branching' he expected perfection to spread.

Some of Whitman's convictions may have been gained from austere statements of similar themes by Emerson: but his large impetus seems to have come from popular sources, particularly in the West. In that highly sensitized period just before he began the writing of *Leaves of Grass* Whitman went over the Cumberland Gap by the wagon-road which many pioneers had followed, and down the Ohio and the Mississippi by boat. The physical imprint of the West appears throughout his poetry. Even in that long soliloquy in which he considers the place of his birth on the Atlantic shore he is soon 'singing in the West', singing 'chants of the prairies, chants of the long-running Mississippi . . .' He mentions the mocking-bird again and again. 'Flatboatmen make fast toward dusk near cotton-wood or pecan-trees.' He wrote of soft afternoon airs that blow from the southwest. 'I saw in Louisiana a live oak growing.' 'O magnet South!' he cried – the South which was the old Southwest. The imagery in the phrase *Leaves of Grass* may have come from the prairie lands and great meadows of the West. His stress upon physical prowess and strength was western, as was his resilient good humor. 'Henceforth I ask not good fortune, I myself am good fortune.'

At times Whitman achieved a serene and ineffaceable and tender strain of feeling which seemed a final residium of humor; this belonged to his finest poetry. At others he followed only the wildest of western comic boastings – often with unconscious comedy. The rhapsodic, leaping, crowing backwoodsman had long since come into the popular view, adopting the phrase 'child of nature'. Whitman in turn celebrated 'spontaneous me', or described himself as an acutely self-conscious 'child of nature' under the title *Me Imperturbe*:

Me Imperturbe, standing at ease in Nature,
Master of all or mistress of all, aplomb in the midst of irrational
    things –

His famous 'I sound my barbaric yawp over the roofs of the world'
might have been shouted by the gamecock of the wilderness, even
though the image belongs to the cities. In his early *Boston Ballad*
Whitman joined in the classic comic warfare between the backwoodsman and the Yankee. Half gravity, half burlesque, in its swift slipping
from the foothold of reality the poem is not far from the pattern of
the tall tales or from the familiar extravagant form of mock-oratory.

In later years Whitman could fall into that rough-hewn grotesquerie
of language which the backwoodsman had exhibited in moments of
exhilarated comedy.

In fact, here I am these current years 1890 and '91, (each successive
year getting stiffer and stuck deeper) much like some hard-cased
dilapidated grim ancient shell-fish or time-banged conch (no legs,
utterly non-locomotive) cast up high and dry on the shore-sands,
helpless to move anywhere – nothing left but to behave myself
quiet. . . .

>   (Preface note to
>   *Good-Bye My Fancy*)

He noted the Negro dialect, and found there hints of 'a modification
of all words of the English language, for musical purposes, for a
native grand opera in America.' He theorized about language. 'In
America an immense number of new words are needed,' he declared.

This subject of language interests me – interests me: I never quite
get it out of my mind. I sometimes think the *Leaves* is only a
language experiment – that it is an attempt to give the spirit, the
body, the man, new words, new potentialities of speech – an
American, a cosmopolitan (the best of America is the best cosmo-
politanism) range of expression. The new world, the new times,
the new peoples, the new vista, need a tongue according – yes,
what is more will have such a tongue – will not be satisfied until
it is evolved.

>   (*An American Primer*)

He freely used plain words, 'farmer's words', 'sea words', 'the likes of you', and much of the jargon of the time. Whitman, in short, used language as a new and plastic and even comical medium, as it had long since been used in native folk-lore.

To enter the world of Whitman is to touch the spirit of American popular comedy, with its local prejudices, its national prepossessions, its fantastic beliefs; many phases of comic reaction are unfolded there. Nothing is complete, nothing closely wrought; often Whitman's sequences are incoherent, like sudden movements of undirected thought or feeling. 'No one will get at my verses who insists upon viewing them as literary performances,' he said. The scale was large; Whitman possessed that sense of a whole civilization which must belong to the epic; his sweeping cadences could have held the heroic form; and though he lacked the great theme of gods and men his awareness of the country had a stirring animism, and his prototypical American was of far greater than human stature. Yet Whitman did not achieve the heroic, or only rarely, in broken or partial passages. Like those popular story-tellers who had often seemed on the verge of wider expression, he failed to draw his immeasurable gift into the realm of great and final poetry. For the most part he remained an improviser of immense genius, unearthing deep-lying materials in the native mind, in a sense 'possessed' by the character of that mythical and many-sided American whom he often evoked. He was indeed the great improviser of modern literature. He had turned the native comic rhapsody, abundant in the backwoods, to broad poetic forms.

Whitman achieved the epical scale; at the same time he remained within a sphere which, along with a movement toward the epical, had been defined in popular comedy – that of the acutely self-aware. At the end of *Me Imperturbe* he uttered a brief prayer that the supreme naturalness which he desired might be achieved, as if he knew that the shadow of himself stood in his way. Elsewhere he was revealed as acutely self-conscious, when like any backwoodsman on the rivers and levees he picturized himself in a costume conspicuous by its negation of color. He was self-aware in the promotion of his own work, in his summaries of purpose. But with all this, with all his forced awkwardness and flamboyance, he achieved an ultimate culmination of the conscious in the richness and fullness of his finer soliloquies. The free mind was there, turned inward, truly conscious and indwelling, yet flowing naturally into speech. That movement toward the soliloquy which had appeared in popular modes and again in the writings of Emerson and Thoreau reached a culmination in Whitman. His finest poems are cast in the deep and delicate form: *When Lilacs Last in the Dooryard Bloom'd*, the rhapsodic *Crossing Brooklyn Ferry*, the long and sometimes cryptic *Starting from Paumanok*, the reflective songs in *Children of Adam*. The monologue or rhapsody was turned inward, without analysis or introspection: moods, shades of feeling, fragments of thought, pour out in an untrammeled stream which is often not far from the so-called stream of consciousness. Whitman anticipated by many years the modern mode of inner revelation with its broken sequences, its irrelevant changes, its final move into the realm of soliloquy.

It was on this level that Whitman touched the great theme which had so deeply underlain the experience of the pioneer, the theme of death, touched it with an emotion that belongs to the finer aspects of comedy. 'And to die is different from what any one supposed, and luckier,' he said. 'And I will show that nothing can happen more beautiful than death.' *When Lilacs Last in the Dooryard Bloom'd* is a poem of reconcilement with death of profound tenderness, embracing the widening theme of the farm-lands and the cities, 'the large unconscious scenery of my land with its lakes and forests', as if there in warmth and sunlight and a common life lay an ultimate answer. The simplest flow of feeling is kept, like that of some archaic ceremonial:

O what shall I hang on the chamber walls,
And what shall the pictures be that I hang on the walls,
To adorn the burial-house of him I love?

Always this feeling deepens, so that the poem becomes a poem of reconcilement not only for the death of Lincoln but for all death within a beloved land.

Whitman had circled from the generic and inclusive and national-istic 'I' to the realm of inner feeling; and the inner world which he discovered was that which had been opened by comedy; it was of the mind; that is, it was reflective rather than emotional. Sorrow occupied him greatly only once, in *When Lilacs Last in the Dooryard Bloom'd*. The verses in *Drum-Taps* were written less in sorrow than in tenderness or assuagement. Emotion in Whitman most often meant deep tenderness; its quality was indwelling. With all his direct improvisation and outpouring the simple emotions were far from belonging to him. His most ardent feelings were those which he could share with a crowd; his sense of identity with other human beings seemed to stir him more deeply than any other experience. On the theme of sexual passion he was sometimes direct, but the emotion which he expressed was likely to be strange and inverted, or to move quickly outside the realm of feeling altogether into a consideration of the many divergent forms of passion, or to sweep into argument. Again the conscious superseded the emotional.

In literature the scope was new and strange which could include the epical scale in free expression and at the same time reveal the conscious and indwelling mind. To these biases, which had belonged to American popular comedy, was added another, likewise of that province. Neither Whitman – nor Thoreau – for all their inclusions of the outer world was primarily concerned with outer circumstance. Thoreau stood, as he said, at the meeting of two eternities; Whitman's true world was wholly visionary even when it included the touch and color of earth.

(168–79)

Frederik Schyberg

from 'Leaves of Grass 1855–89', *Walt Whitman* 1933 (translated from the Danish by E. A. Allen, 1951)

Though we are so decidedly lacking in biographical information about Whitman, though he has himself cleverly and consistently destroyed every trace which could help with a historical explanation, nevertheless we have in the *Calamus* poetry – from which he himself said that we must get clues for a real understanding of him – plain evidence of a tragic love affair, probably about 1859, when, according to Holloway's statement, the poems were written. If, therefore, we used the term 'Romance' for any part of his life, it must be this. By studying the book alone, in its changing phases, it becomes clear and obvious that it was between the second and the third editions that the crisis in his life took place. Holloway and Catel have exploded the New Orleans myth, but neither of them was concerned with a closer investigation of this second and more decisive period. Holloway makes the laconic concession that 'surely some lover had died', and afterwards talks of Whitman's love affair as 'a passion so tragically powerful' and of *Calamus* as 'born out of a mood . . . but it is an unhealthy mood'. He does not engage in a more careful definition of Whitman's personality as it is here revealed.

Earlier I mentioned the adolescent and effeminate traits in Whitman's erotic psychology. At the climax of the first and second editions his eroticism merges with his religious emotion in a fashion not unfamiliar in world literature. Certain effeminate medieval mystics such as Heinrich Suso and the Persian poet Rumi expressed themselves in similar fashion. Divinity and the longed-for beloved are one and the same person. The theme is developed in the third edition in *Proto-Leaf*.[1]

Not he, adhesive, kissing me so long with his daily kiss,
Has winded and twisted around me that which holds me to him,
Any more than I am held to the heavens, to the spiritual world.

In *Tilskueren*, January, 1919, a Danish translator rendered 'he' as 'nogen' (some one), and later as 'ham eller hende', Whitman's peculiar dual 'him or her', which significantly enough is *not* found in this passage. It is important that Whitman's whole concept of the divinity is so closely united to his ideal of 'manly attachment'. We have seen how his great longing for an answer, an echo, a release, was not satisfied by his reception as a poet. Thus, on the *first* attempt his verse was no emancipation, it was just 'cries of unsatisfied love', it was the old question of his youthful story, 'Wherefore is there no response?' Therefore, in the years immediately after 1856, everything was stored up and waiting for a *personal* outpouring of his need for love. We see what kind of outcry it was, but it comes out more clearly in the 1860 edition, because there it was not impeded. Afterwards Whitman deleted the two poems which disclosed most intimately and most personally what had happened to him. Since they are not in modern editions of *Leaves of Grass*, I quote the complete poems.

1 This was later called *Starting from Paumanok*. [Ed.]

In the introduction to the first (No. 8 of the *Calamus* group) Whitman describes the various stages of his development.

Long I thought that knowledge alone would suffice me – O if I
    could but obtain knowledge!
Then my lands engrossed me – Lands of the prairies, Ohio's land,
    the southern savannas, engrossed me – For them I would live –
    I would be their orator;
Then I met the examples of old and new heroes – I heard of
    warriors, sailors, and all dauntless persons – And it seemed to
me that I too had it in me to be as dauntless as any – and would
    be so;
And then, to enclose all, it came to me to strike up the songs of
    the New World – And then I believed my life must be spent in
    singing; . . .

Then he continues by telling what happened.

But now take notice, land of the prairies, land of the south
    savannas, Ohio's land,
Take notice, you Kanuck woods – and you Lake Huron – and all
    that with you roll toward Niagara – and you Niagara also,
And you, Californian mountains – That you each and all find
    somebody else to be your singer of songs,
For I can be your singer of songs no longer – One who loves me
    is jealous of me, and withdraws me from all but love,
With the rest I dispense – I sever from what I thought would
    suffice me, for it does not – it is now empty and tasteless to me,
I heed knowledge, and the grandeur of The States, and the
    example of heroes, no more,
I am indifferent to my own songs – I will go with him I love,
It is to be enough for us that we are together [N.B.] – We never
    separate again.

This poem is absolutely astounding. We cannot question the beauty and vigor of the contents and treatment; its genuine passion is unmistakable. More arresting is *its complete disagreement with the program of the volume in which it appears*. Suddenly the poet no longer cares for his land, his poetry, the greatness of which was a fixed belief, his hold on existence. Now he celebrates something entirely different, which makes other interests superficial, because his passion does not need any outlet except the natural one.

This poem with its pretended contents of passionate happiness is beyond analysis, because we are left with no evidence except the poem itself. But it is supplemented immediately by the second poem, No. 9, which is, perhaps, the most poignant of the *Calamus* poems. It is impossible to misunderstand the note of despair.

Hours continuing long, sore and heavy-hearted,
Hours of the dusk, when I withdraw to a lonesome and
  unfrequented spot, seating myself, leaning my face in my hands;
Hours sleepless, deep in the night, when I go forth, speeding
  swiftly the country roads, or through the city streets, or pacing
  miles and miles, stifling plaintive cries;
Hours discouraged, distracted – for the one I cannot content
  myself without, soon I saw him content himself without me;
Hours when I am forgotten, (O weeks and months are passing,
  but I believe I am never to forget!)
Sullen and suffering hours! (I am ashamed – but it is useless – I am
  what I am;)
Hours of my torment – I wonder if other men ever have the like,
  out of the like feelings?
Is there even one other like me – distracted – his friend, his lover,
  lost to him?
Is he too as I am now? Does he still rise in the morning, dejected,
  thinking who is lost to him? and at night, awaking, think who
  is lost?
Does he too harbor his friendship silent and endless? harbor his
  anguish and passion?
Does some stray reminder, or the casual mention of a name, bring
  the fit back upon him, taciturn and deprest?
Does he see himself reflected in me? In these hours, does he see the
  face of his hours reflected?

This is probably the most poignant love poem in the whole collection, and its omission in 1867 was an artistic loss. But from Whitman's point of view it is clear why the omission was made. The content of the poem could not be misunderstood. No explanation or misinterpretation is possible. The poet speaks frankly of his shipwreck, his

despair and loneliness. That gives us the private foreground of all the
Calamus poems. Like all love poetry, they have come from loving
another person in whom he can see 'his hours reflected'. But in my
opinion this poem is also something like a rough draft or sketch for
Out of the Cradle, in which the story of his lover having left him and
'contented himself with another' has been poetically transmuted into
the lonely bird's song to the sea and the moon – and the personal
intimate pain has thus achieved a richer, fuller tone. It seems to me
that in the artistic shaping and artistic result these two poems parallel
the real experience. The change of sex must be regarded as a far more
innocent change of 'he' and 'she' than in the poem *Once I Pass'd*,
also originally a *Calamus* poem, but 'for reasons' put under *Children
of Adam*. At the same time, there are in the omitted poems the first
traces in *Calamus* of a realization of the abnormality of the emotion.
The question of whether 'other men ever have the like' is an appre-
hensive development of the question asked in the first edition by the
poet as a half-grown boy when in doubt as to 'where he stood',
childhood or manhood, and the gnawing hunger on the bridge
between. We are repelled by it, and by the naïveté of the big 'lubberly
fellow', but we cannot deny that there is something sublime in its
expression, as there always is when a real poet yields to a sincere
emotion, whether it is love or wonder. Whitman's 'wonder at the
world', which Carpenter mentions, is nowhere more apparent than
in his love poems.

Whitman's great emotion, his 'manly attachment', his erotic
burden, with its peculiar characteristic, influenced and colored his
whole interpretation of the world around him, as we have observed
in his earlier poetry. As Nietzsche says, 'the degree and kind of a
person's sexuality penetrates every corner of his being.' For a long
time it was certainly Whitman's belief that it was a normal, healthy
emotion which he nourished, although of abnormal warmth and
strength; and in any case it was his dream to sanctify it in his poems.

You bards of ages hence! . . .

Publish my name and hang up my picture as that of the tenderest
      lover,
The friend, the lover's portrait, of whom his friend, his lover, was
      fondest,

Who was not proud of his songs, but of the measureless ocean of
   love within him – and freely poured it forth.
                                    (1860, *Calamus*, No. 10)

Instead he found his emotion was misunderstood, elicited scorn,
and aroused opposition. Even he realized that there was a darker, more
daemonic side, in No. 36 (*Earth! My Likeness*), probably from the
period of falling in love, and therefore in the chronology of the love
affair it should be inserted between the two omitted poems.

Earth! my likeness!
Though you look so impassive, ample and spheric there,
I now suspect that is not all;
I now suspect there is something fierce in you, eligible to burst forth;
For an athlete is enamoured of me – and I of him,
But toward him there is something fierce and terrible in me,
   eligible to burst forth,
I dare not tell it in words – not even in these songs.

The blending of emotions and moods, of heedless confession and
poetic interpretation, is extraordinary in this section of *Leaves of Grass*.
It stretches from requited to unrequited love, from confidence and
arrogance to insecurity and shame, from bold shout and frank court-
ship to a wondering desperate confession that love is a dangerous,
inconstant passion which will not bring happiness, for example, No. 12:

Are you the new person drawn toward me? . . .
To begin with, take warning, . . .

Thus, in spite of the conflicting emotions, it is as tenderly expressed
as any collection of love poetry in world literature. But we cannot
deny that at times its diversity includes completely irreconcilable
contradictions. Side by side with the bashful confessions of love and
devotion, along with the poetically inspired expression of ideal
friendship and comradeship, are poems suddenly and completely
erotomaniac in character, in which the poet's insatiable longing for
new faces, new experiences, makes us involuntarily doubt the
sincerity and honesty of his experiences. As always when love becomes
a purely lyrical emotion, it becomes universal, all-embracing, because it is directed at no one in particular – other than the poet himself.
It is necessary to insist on the erotomaniac trait in Whitman's lyrics,

because now and then we get the impression that, as he himself says, he is not capable of remaining long in one place, he must go on to new experiences, new sensations. If, therefore, Whitman in his own life did not establish a permanent love connexion, he was prevented by his own nature; it would not have suited him. But as world literature has witnessed, this defect *was a part of his genius; the constant flitting and wandering of his emotion was all-pervading in his lyricism*. In modern literature we find the great German lyricist Richard Dehmel parallel-ing the erotomania of Whitman. But this trait of volatility and in-satiability does not make the tragedy in the poet's heart or the tragic personal experience of 1859 less bitter or less significant. The less that actually happened, the more clearly the secretly desired relationship was revealed as impossible and hopeless; then the more surely was the erotically aroused lover to believe that this was the only real love. To the erotic psyche mirrored in these *Calamus* poems it is really the unsuccessful love which will be transformed into the great love; whereas the successful love will last but a day or two and will then be displaced by a yearning for new faces, new experiences. All of this was revealed in the 1860 *Calamus* – a single experience and at the same time characteristic of his whole erotic type. *Calamus* is, therefore, the central nervous system of the book. In *Roots and Leaves*, No. 13, Whitman says that only he who brings like emotions to the reading of these poems will see them unfold themselves as the sun and rain make flowers and leaves unfold. For all others they are the poet's avowals, a confession, and thus a clue to all *Leaves of Grass*, and at the same time a spectacular unveiling of a yearning, emotional man who has to sing the song of the passions to give vent to his own passion.

In spite of a few moments of happiness that Whitman may possibly have had in a love affair in the autumn of 1859, it is highly probable that after all *he was not talking of any erotic relationship*, that it never actually developed that far; moreover *I suspect that, after all, Whitman never actually had any such experience during his whole life, in spite of his homosexual bent*. That is where the mistake in judging the homosexuals of world literature is always made. The question has always been an ethical one: How guilty is he? Never: To what spiritual or physical group does he belong? It is no longer a secret that just that dangerous blending of sex in human nature produces artists. Greater information and greater tolerance will probably result in a more open and frank discussion in literary history of this difficult subject. It will be to the advantage of the writers if it can be discussed with more freedom and sympathy. Many writers have undoubtedly produced their greatest work out of sublimated emotion, sublimated either voluntarily or because it was taboo. Just as in the work of Hans Andersen we can trace the artistic effects of an unexpressed sex life, so it is that Whitman's lyricism has gained in vigor and in emotional strength by his unfulfilled erotic longing. At the same time this unsatisfied yearning furnished an excellent excuse for his attitude when the Calamus question was brought up later in his life by Symonds. Hindered by the ignorance of the physiological and psychological aspects of the problem which prevailed until the beginning of this century, Whitman had a perfect right to deny his homosexuality if he had never indulged in homosexual practices. Probably he was totally unaware of the 'type', though in old age he revealed a concern about this characteristic of his, by deletions and omissions in *Calamus*. As he expurgated his book he tried to expurgate his life. Such a statement may seem to be an impertinent intrusion into Whitman's privacy, but the literary historian will not so regard it. To the modern literary historian the intrusion is necessary if he does not content himself merely with the individual, but wants to get at the 'type'.

(161–8)

D. Mirsky

from 'Poet of American Democracy' 1935 (translated from the Russian by Samuel Putnam, in Gay Wilson Allen (ed.), *Walt Whitman Abroad*, 1955)

Whitman is the poet of American democracy of the Fifties and Sixties, in all of its organic strength. He gives poetic voice to democracy's illusion that a new humanity has already been born, one that has but to grow and develop normally; his is the highest expression that we have of such illusions. But with all of his genius, he bears the indelible brand of that democracy's anti-revolutionary and provincial character.

The individual quality of Whitman's poetry derives in good part from the strange and even weird combination that we find in it of originality and inspired daring, in a choice of themes never before treated by poets, with a provincial naïveté that is utterly incapable of beholding itself through the eyes of others. Out of this provincialism comes a break with the culture of the past and the poet's obstinate depiction of himself as prophet and preacher. Such a provincialism, obviously tinged by and akin to religious sectarianism, enabled Whitman to build up out of the illusions of American democracy a system which to him presented the same appearance as had that historic order which was based upon the religions of the past. If on the one hand Whitman is a brother spirit to Dante and Goethe, his other affinities would include such individuals as Brigham Young, leader of the Mormon sect, and the founder of 'Christian Science', Mrs. Eddy.

Being a systematization of far-flung illusions, pointing to a luminous future to be evolved out of a present that was bubbling with life and energy, Whitman's ideology was a reasoned admixture of materialistic and mystical elements. Taking an environment that was ready at hand, in the fulness of its sweep and scope, with all of its material and practical implications, as a high and authentic reality, Whitman was unable to grasp that reality in its true revolutionary unfoldment. His optimism was not based upon a correct and active comprehension of what lay wrapped up in all this energy, and so, had need of a 'higher' strength by way of support. While his point of departure was materialism, he could not avoid falling back upon mystic pantheism. He felt the need of an imminent god, the 'soul' of matter. This soul was in the nature of a pledge, to the effect that all was making for a brighter future, that all was right with the world and moving in a necessary direction, one that would assure a better order of things. Whitman's mystical pantheism was an expression not alone of that illusory character of his ideals, but of their anti-revolutionary character as well. Animate nature might be left to see to the progress of her off-spring.

At the same time, however, it is Whitman's democratic pantheism, which underlying that cult of the common man, constitutes the fundamental pathos of his poetry. In his pantheism, he is not highly original, nor does he stand alone among democratic (and pseudo-democratic) ideologists of the nineteenth and twentieth centuries. Optimistic in outlook this pantheism is sharply inimical to the old dogmatic religions; but it is nonetheless definitely religious in mental attitude and definitely mystical in world-view; in substance, it is above all a popularization of the philosophy of bourgeois democracy. The kernel is from the contemplative Rousseau, while Hugo, in his historiosophic poems, supplies an embodiment which in poetic strength is second only to Whitman's own. A plain traveller, this, in that stream of petty bourgeois thought that gravitates toward socialism, one which, in our own time, was to be given a notably vulgarized, though for a wide circle of the petty bourgeoisie, an extremely effective expression in the *Saint Joan* of Bernard Shaw.

The mystical basis of Whitman's system will be found set forth with the utmost clarity in the fifth section of the poem, *Walt Whitman*[1], in a language which is quite familiar to all who possess an acquaintance with the 'classics' of mysticism.

Whitman's mysticism, however, was not uprooted from material- ism; just as democratic illusions regarding the future still had their roots in the reality of present-day democracy. It was a spontaneous, idealistic outgrowth of materialistic premises that were true enough, even as the illusions were swift-growing, optimistic offshoot of real conditions. Whitman very definitely extols science and that know- ledge of the world which it affords. But science was not sufficient. In addition to it, there must be a 'higher knowledge': in the Foreword to the edition of 1876, he wrote:

Only (for me, at any rate, in all my prose and poetry) joyfully accepting modern science, and loyally following it without the slightest hesitation, there remains ever recognized still a higher flight, a higher fact, the eternal soul of man (of all else too) the spiritual, the religious ...

One can no more shut his eyes to the anti-revolutionary character of Whitman's ideology than one can to his mysticism. His position in American democracy was not on the extreme Left. If a man like John Brown, striving with a handful of companions to stage a slave uprising, is an exceptional and well-nigh solitary figure, the Whit- man of before the war stands definitely apart, not only from a John Brown, but from the abolition movement of the world, which was fighting to do away with slavery by legal means.

1 Later called *Song of Myself*. [Ed.]

Whitman's democracy, organically and in deepest essence, was nationalistic. Democracy for him was something specifically American. He accepted it as something already existent in the nature of the American people and needing only to be brought to light. At the beginning, he believed – as a present-day prophet – that the publication of *Leaves of Grass* would be the signal for the discovery of a true democracy. Later on, in the Seventies, he had to confess that America of the present was yet far from the ideal; but all the same, he continued to assert that

... the morbid facts of American politics and society everywhere are but passing incidents and flanges of our unbounded impetus of growth ... weeds, annuals, of the rank, rich soil – not central, enduring, perennial things ...

(Preface to 1876, Leaves of Grass)

At the same time, he had learned that

... the true growth-characteristic of the democracy of the New World are henceforth to radiate in superior literary, artistic and religious expressions, far more than in its republican forms, universal suffrage and frequent elections. ...

(Preface to 1876, Leaves of Grass)

Thus it was, Whitman was led to that assertion of the inferiority of politics, its lack of worth as compared to 'higher values', which is to be met with in Shelley, and which is so characteristic for the whole of non-democratic humanism. His historic world-view will be found expressed, in extremely concise form, in the following verses, bearing the curious sub-title, 'After Reading Hegel' (the title is *Roaming in Thought*):

Roaming in thought over the Universe, I saw the little that is
    Good steadily hastening toward immortality,
And the vast all that is call'd Evil I saw hastening to merge itself
    and become lost and dead.

In America, the 'little that is Good' was already at work and might be left to complete its task to the fullest extent. As for other peoples, Whitman, like American democracy as a whole, sympathized with them in their struggle with kings and feudal barons. He occasionally sings the praises of the French Revolution, and he extends greetings to the émigré rebel of 1848 (for Whitman, 'The 72d and 73d Years of These States'). But his sympathy is purely a passive one, and the class war never comes within the range of Whitman's themes. If the Southern slaveholders were his enemies, it was not because they were slaveholders, but for the reason that they had wanted to cease being Americans.

Human brotherhood meant for Whitman, depending upon the direction it took, two very different things. In the one case, it was something wholly concrete and related to life, an emotional brotherhood with the 'mass' of 'average' Americans round about him. In the other case, it was a pantheistic feeling of fraternal sympathy with each and every human being, and – what is more – with every living creature and with all matter. This latter sentiment is thoroughly passive, and is unaccompanied by any arduous desire to struggle for a real, democratic brotherhood of peoples. It is measureably nearer to Christian brotherhood than it is to a communistic solidarity of workers. If there was in Whitman, in relation to his brother Americans, an active 'love of comrades', one that is given an inspired lyric expression in his verse and a practical application in his hospital work during the years 1861–5, his feeling of brotherhood, on the other hand, toward mankind, in general, toward men of another race or class than his own (e.g. the slave), was no more than a 'survival', no more than an 'inner experience'. He is conscious of a fraternal, pantheistic identity with the fugitive slave; indeed, he migrates into the slave's body and soul (*Song of Myself*, section 33); and the verses he has given us on this subject are among the strongest that we have from his pen. Yet, earlier in this same poem (section 16), speaking of his sense of universal identity, he is equally one with the slaveholder:

A southerner soon as a northerner – a planter nonchalant and
     hospitable; down by the Oconee I live.

In his no less inspired *I Sing the Body Electric*, he speaks thus of the sale of a slave at auction:

A man's body at auction;
I help the auctioneer – the sloven does not half know his business.
Gentlemen, look on this wonder!

Whatever the bids of the bidders, they cannot be high enough
  for it . . .

  Back of man's vileness and degradation, Whitman beholds his
native grandeur, but in such a manner that the vileness and degradation is skimmed off, as an inferior and unauthentic reality, and so,
ceasing to exist, is no longer an occasion for struggle. This is precisely
the path followed by Christian thought, which announces that 'there
is neither slave nor free man, Greek nor Jew, but that all are children
of the heavenly father and the partakers of his glory.'
  It is not possible to disavow or gloss over these aspects of Whitman's as being the inconsistencies and contradictions of an insuffi-
ciently thought out system of reasoning. For Whitman's ideology is
fully thought out and rounded. Its contradictions are the organic and
unavoidable ones to be found in all bourgeois thinking. It is one that
is still held, in the full force of its implications, by all social idealists
and left-revolutionists. We are, accordingly, obliged to adopt a
critical attitude toward it. For it would be a gross distortion to attempt
to cover over its anti-revolutionary and mystical aspects, and to
behold in Whitman a seer with the brain of a proletarian revolutionist,
looking forward to a classless society of the future. If his ideology is a
democratic one, his brand of democracy is thoroughly bourgeois.
  However, we do not judge writers and thinkers of the past by their
ideologies, nor by that element of the ephemeral and the nationalistic
which is inevitably to be met with in each of them; we judge them
rather by what is progressive and enduring in their work. This
progressive and enduring element in the case of Whitman is his
poetry.

The basis of Whitman's art lies in a vanquishing of Romanticism upon
its own ground, that of 'exalted' poetry. Arising out of a protest
against the realistic path taken by the French Revolution and by
capitalism in its development, Romanticism affirmed a break between
knowledge and the ideal. Leading poetry out of the concrete real of
today, it proceeded to confer upon it a heavenly-incorporal or
retrospective character. This attitude was a widespread one; it is to
be found not merely in a few Romanticists, but throughout the whole
of nineteenth-century poetry in Europe. The contemporary scene –

political, economic, and technological – might make its way into the poet's pages only when symbolically transmuted, only when trigged out in a more or less precapitalistic garb. Even where, as in *Faust*, poetry was an expression of underlying forces at work in the present, its gaze was turned aside from the element of concrete falsity inherent in those forces. Only in the field of satire did it remain realistic in style, preserving a bond of union with the prose of the literary realists. In Russia, Whitman's contemporary, Nekrasov, was at work here, broadening the scope of satire and creating a new poetry. But satire as a whole was looked down upon, as being of a lower order; and even when they sympathized with its ideas, Nekrasov's countrymen deemed his work of little value from the poetic point of view, holding it to be nothing more than 'prose in verse'. This orientation of poetry in the direction of realistic prose was marked by a repudiation of the great philosophic themes dealt with by bards of a more exalted kind, and by an abandonment of free lyricism.

In this orientation lay, too, an avowal of the triumph of prose over poetry, of the poet's subdual by capitalistic reality. *Don Juan* and *Germania* were not capitulations to a 'century hostile to poetry'; they represented a forced understanding to the effect that the century in question was to be combatted on its own field, that of prose.

Whitman, breaking sharply with all nineteenth-century poetry, brought a new affirmation of reality, by creating a lofty, lyric interpretation of the present. This it is which is basic and central in his work, rendering it a forerunner of the poetry of socialism. And this affirmation, needless to say, is inseparably bound up with the poet's democratic illusions, with his system of thought. These twin phases of Whitman are wholly different in value. His system provided a logically complete, abstract generalization of environing reality and that future which was reared upon it. His poetry afforded a true and concrete reflection of that same reality. The system put a false estimate upon the internal tendencies of bourgeois democracy. The poems laid bare in the bourgeois–democratic consciousness that humanity which could come to full bloom only under socialism. And that which was false when given an abstract-theoretic generalization thanks to the saving concreteness of art was left standing as a truth.

That reality which Whitman affirmed was a bourgeois reality. But in his affirmation, the poet stressed not that which was essentially bourgeois, but that which was creative and progressive. This spark of the creatively progressive was one that he fanned and nursed; and if in his system the result was a crude distortion of perspectives, in his poetry the same impulse went to enrich a hyperbolism that is legitimately and organically present in the domain of science.

Whitman keeps telling us, over and over again, that 'I celebrate myself'. One of his bold and original 'sorties' is the calling of himself by his full name in the course of a sustained lyric poem (*Song of Myself*). But in essence, Whitman is as genuine a specimen as any that there is of the impersonal type of poet; the poet in this case is no 'lyric hero'; he is without lyric biography; he but gives 'choric' expression to feelings and ideas that are not dependent upon any personal destiny. Another especially good example of such a poet in modern times is Schiller; but in contrast to him, Whitman stands out brilliantly by reason of his originality and his innovations. The contemporary scene enters into Schiller's poetry only after it has been abstractly purged of its concrete aspect. In Whitman's it is all there, with all of its everyday, prosaic topicality, in all its grime and mire. It is lifted and generalized into poetry, not through any process of abstraction or catharsis, but by means of a symbolic expansion, predicating the importance of the discovery of types and their significance in the scene's lowest and most trivial elements.

Whitman's poetry is profoundly realistic. And like all enduring art of the kind, it is based upon a disclosure of the typical in the individual. Whitman's realism, however, does not consist in an unfoldment of plots and characters such as we know from our reading of the classic realities in the form of the novel.

This is a realism that is achieved by separate strokes, with subjects and incidents neither described nor depicted, but simply and swiftly listed, listed with a definitive concreteness. From the conjunction of these strokes springs Whitman's essential, generalized poetic form – which is, at the same time, that of American democracy.

The quality of Whitman's verse is very uneven. When the poet loses his realistic concreteness, it degenerates into a noisy rhetoric, crude and monotonous in rhythm and yet cruder and more monotonous in its tone, which is like a prolonged, continuous shout. Here belong many declamatory lines which come not so much from the poet as from the prophet and system-builder. Under this head are those verses where Whitman, striving to remain concrete, is led to speak of things that he knows nothing about, inasmuch as they exceed the bounds of his American horizon. Such clumsily rhetorical passages are sometimes redeemed by their unconscious humor. This, for example, may be said to be true of the celebrated poem, *Salut au Monde*, constructed in accordance with his favorite method, that of cataloguing. Whitman's provincialism and lack of cultural background are here evidenced in a fortuitous piling up of appellations for objects and incidents taken from a popular geography and compelled to yield a grandiose and vulgarized picture of present-day humanity in the bulk.

The core of Whitman's work, its rock-bottom, so to speak, will bear comparison with the best poetry that the world has produced. One may mention here such poems as *Song of Myself*, *I Sing the Body Electric*, *The Sleepers*, *Crossing Brooklyn Ferry*, *Song of the Broad-Axe*, *Out of the Cradle Endlessly Rocking*, *Pioneers! O Pioneers*, *When Lilacs Last in the Dooryard Bloom'd* (on the death of President Lincoln), and a whole series of shorter poems, including one so notable for its lyric qualities as *Tears* (from the group, *Sea-Drift*), and *Drum-Taps*, which is almost a whole collection dealing with the Civil War, 1860–66. All the pieces mentioned belong to the Fifties and Sixties, which witnessed the simultaneous dawn of American democracy and of democracy's great poet. In 1873, Whitman suffered a paralytic stroke, which definitely shattered his health. This coincided with America's rapid capitalistic decline and the crushing of that objective optimism which had marked the preceding decades. It was in this period of depression that Whitman's work made its appearance. The last two decades of his life added little to the substance of that work, although those years do include so surprising a poem as *The Dalliance of the Eagles*, which contains, it may be, the concentrated essence of his genius, of all that he wrote.

The 'Walt Whitman' whom Whitman 'celebrated' was not an individual endowed with a definite biography, a definite personality differentiating him from others; he was a metonymical type, the average man, the average American, bringing from out the American masses the sum and substance of the contemporary scene. The individuality that Whitman hymns is crystallized with precision in the opening lines of the first poem (first in the final group) of his collected verse,

One's Self I Sing. This untranslatable blending of an impersonal 'one' with a recurring 'self' might be rendered as 'the self of everyman', or 'everyman's self'; it has a light to throw upon bourgeois democracy, and upon democracy's poet.

The pathos of Whitman's poetry is the pathos of union, equality, human dignity and progress. The artistic expression of these themes in verse is not to be identified with their theoretic development in the ideologic system; the former is not to be viewed in the light of the latter. In thinking out, intellectually, the subjects that he took for his verse, Whitman was led to abandon a poetic concreteness of imagery for a false and one-sided process of abstract generalization which comes as a break in the true pathos of his work. It is Whitman the prophet acting as self-interpreter for Whitman the poet. Inasmuch as it is difficult to demarcate one from the other with exactitude, we should proceed from the premise that the prophet's interpretations not only are not binding upon us, but that they actually interfere with a proper understanding of the poet.

Thus, in connection with the theme of unity, there is no need for us to accept, naively and unquestioningly, the 'prophetic' explanation of it, as pantheism. The sentiment of unity with respect to the nation, humanity, the world order is in Whitman a direct lyric expansion of the vital sympathy he felt for the democratic masses. It receives an incarnation in the form of a feeling for the political unity of 'These States', as expressed in the war poems, in a concrete feeling of brotherhood with the American who is one of the people – in the theme of 'comradeship', as democracy's basic cement. As for the theme of unity as a common link embracing all humanity, while it is given a glowing expression in certain isolated instances (the fugitive slave in *Song of Myself*, the episode of the mother and the Indian squaw in *The Sleepers*), it is in general set forth in verses that are abstract rather than realistic. But at the other pole, the theme unfolds in an opulent lyric bloom, in the form of verses on the oneness of nature, the sea and the universe. This motive, indeed, that of a union with material nature, is accorded in Whitman a simpler, more direct and immediately lyric treatment than in any other poet of modern times.

The idea of an actual union with the whole of things attains a highly original peak in the theme of death. In the Whitmanic acceptation, death is a 'cool' and happy fusion with the material universe, a conception in which there is no room for weariness or decay. It is a thoroughly optimistic feeling, this, and one that springs from an animating sense of identity of direction, the feeling that each man is traveling a path along which others will continue after him – the classic sense of succession and survival. Nor is it strange if the theme in question stands out with especial clarity in the notable poem written on the death of Abraham Lincoln, leader and hero of American democracy, *When Lilacs Last in the Dooryard Bloom'd* (in particular, the song of the hermit thrush).

The theme of equality, likewise, enters into Whitman's poetry, as one of its organic and organizing constituents. This it is which at bottom explains the poet's passion for bestowing an exalted lyric treatment upon everything which up to his time had been looked upon as vile and 'unworthy of the Muse'. Closely related to this are Whitman's realistic innovations and his cataloguing, a method of which he is so fond. With him, the sentiment of equality is especially directed against unilateral affirmation of the 'spiritual' man at the expense of the flesh-and-blood being. This theme comes, accordingly, to be closely interwoven with the exaltation of the body, which lends itself to the development of another, broader motive, the forceful revelation and assertion of human dignity. One of the nodal passages in all Whitman's poetry is the famous ninth section of *I Sing the Body Electric*, where he applies his inventory method to the parts of the body, from the head to the lower organs, all the way down to the heels, by way of affirming their equal worth with the human consciousness or 'soul'.

In this dignifying of humankind through the human body, Whitman aligns himself with the followers of Saint-Simon, bent upon a 'rehabilitation of the flesh'. But in working out the idea poetically, Whitman displays a maximum of originality. The rehabilitation of the flesh, as a counterpoise to Christian repression, had already been brilliantly dealt with by Goethe. Goethe, however, was unable to get along without stylization. Just as in *Faust* he had need of a Renaissance dress, so in his *Roman Elegies* and other erotic verse, he still was unable to dispense with antiquity. Like the men of the French Revolution, he felt the necessity of justifying and fortifying himself with the authority of the ancients. In essence, his eroticism comes close to the practical materialism of the Southern slaveholder. A woman for him is above all an object of enjoyment and possession. There is here, as well, a trace of that art for art's sake, an exaggerated development of which is to be seen in Théophile Gautier and – carried further yet – in Rémy de Gourmont. Whitman is free at once of artiness and of stylistic tricks. Beauty to the latter is merely the complete unfoldment of man's nature, one mode of realizing human dignity to the utmost. Of the very warp and woof of Whitman's eroticism is the merging of the physical passions with a sentiment of equality and respect toward womankind, something that is absolutely new in world poetry, even though, ideologically speaking, the Saint-Simonians are the precursors here. Hung upon a lovely poetic thread in *I Sing the Body Electric*, this theme is expressed with a definitive concision and in a truly inspired manner in that pearl among poems, *The Dalliance of the Eagles*.

And then, finally, there is Whitman's fourth theme, that of the inorganic possibilities unfolding to man's view through a conquest of nature, the theme of democratic expansion and democratic construction, the principal embodiment of which is to be found in the *Song of the Broad-Axe* and in *Pioneers! O Pioneers!* (1856 and 1865, respectively).

One cannot but be struck by the parallel between this motive and our own socialist construction. There are, needless to say, sharp contrasts which are equally striking. Not to speak of the fact that American democratic expansion was essentially predatory, so far as Indians and Mexicans were concerned (a circumstance of which, naturally, no notice is taken in Whitman's poetry), democratic construction, both in reality and in the pages of its bard, was an elementary, one-man affair. But for all of that, in his handling of the theme, Whitman is the undoubted forerunner of the poetry of Socialism. The chief thing that goes to make him such a harbinger is the fact that he was the first to introduce the theme of *labor* into poetry, in the form of a creative, lyric statement. Amid all his work, Whitman's poems on the subject of democratic construction come the nearest of all to the *ode* form. But these are odes of an utterly new kind.

It is not the idea of labor, not labor in general, that finds a place in Whitman's verse, but rather, labor's realistic, concrete, and technical processes. The *Song of the Broad-Axe* may be compared to Schiller's *Song of the Bells*, one of the rare instances in bourgeois poetry where such processes are treated in the concrete. In the first place, Schiller singles out work as a theme for the reason that it bears, to begin with, the stamp of religious approval in this case – the labor of casting the bells; in the second place, work is here, in a special sense, pre-capitalistic, being closely associated with the guild organizations; and lastly, the work of the bell-founders is no more than an allegory, symbolizing a prudent bourgeois progress that knows how to ward off revolutions.

In place of one traditional process, Whitman takes the work of construction in all its range, all the infinite variety of its applications, processes and products. There is no allegory within. No antithesis between the construction of the material object, on the one hand, and, on the other hand, the social construction of democracy. Out of isolated fragmentary images, the *Song of the Broad-Axe* is built up, an endless succession of images, metaphors, instances, fashioned out of the same stuff as constructive democracy. Inventoried with the greatest conciseness and the utmost concreteness, objects and incidents form an impressive generalized image of the whole of democratic America.

Based upon the favored Whitman method, of inventory and cata-logue, the poem consists of a number of successive strophes of a cumulative intensity. Following a lyric introduction, the third section serves as a sort of index, being made up of a series of nouns (alluding to objects or actions) with their attributive definitions. This is done in such a way, creatively, that objects and actions stand out in a delimiting sharpness, as if they were parts of a poetic encyclopedia of carpentry that is to function as a symbol of democratic construction in America.

This is followed by a fresh catalogue of objects created by the broad-axe. The construction here is a parallel and again a cumulative one, ranging verbally from monosyllabic nouns like 'hut' and 'tent' to lengthy adjectives, and ideationally, from the same hut and tent to 'Manhattan steamboats and clippers, taking the measure of all seas.'

In a third movement, we have the enumeration of no end of objects having to do with the builder's trade, saturated, all of them, with a complex and elevated social content. Starting from simple terms ('factories, arsenals'), the poet goes on to build up a picture out of objects taken as points of departure for incidents replete with social meaning:

The shape of the step-ladder for the convicted and sentenced
    murderer, the murderer with haggard face and pinion'd arms, . . .
The door whence the son left home, confident and puff'd up;
The door he enter'd again from a long and scandalous absence,
    diseas'd, broken down, without innocence, without means.

This movement is rounded off with the significant and unifying 'shapes' that mark the national scene – American democracy and its accompaniments.

And thus is constructed a new and unprecedented type of realistic ode, one springing out of an everyday and prosaic reality and catching up the myriad artistic threads of a highly variegated American life.

On the side of form, Whitman shows himself to be a thorough-going innovator, breaking completely with an older poetry of a 'feudal' Europe and Asia (and its American imitators) and building up a new poetic art from the very beginning. Assuredly, in all the history of art there is no other case of so absolute a break; we shall have to acknowledge that Whitman was a truly great innovator, the greatest that the world of poetry has known.

His innovations in form are directly derived from his novelty of content. This is a fundamental point, involving a liquidation of the dignity of the disparity between the conventional, stylized and retro-spective idiom of elevated poetry and the language of the present. Whitman's language is that of the prosaic and democratic scene about him. His democratic speech, however, is of a different order from that of a Mayakovsky or – to stay within Anglo-American precincts – of a Kipling or a Vachel Lindsay. The prose idiom that Whitman employed in bringing new life to poetry was not the colloquial tongue of the street, the factory or the barracks; it was, rather, the language of printed prose, of newspapers and of popular science. Today, when American colloquial speech is at so very far a remove from that of literature, and when, at the same time, it is making such enormous gains in the literary field, the difference between Whitman's poetic vocabulary and that of his contemporaries, such as Emerson and Longfellow, is less noticeable. The truth is, Whitman avoided not only jargon and slang, but, in general, any tendency to colloquial syntax. The linguistic novelty of his poems springs from a new store of themes; the new words that we find there are for the most part the names of objects which up to his time had been held to be unpoetic.

To a considerably less degree dependent upon novelty of content is another fundamental tenet of Whitman's stylistic credo, namely, the avoidance of rhyme and metrics for the sake of rhythm and cadence. The poet's contempt for such 'feudal playthings' is an immediate result of the *one-sided character* of the bond that held him to the democratic masses. Whitman gave expression to the masses, but he did not speak *for* them. He spoke in their name, but not to them. This was because he failed to realize that poetry written for the masses must first of all be easy-flowing, readily memorizable, and that therefore it must possess a rhythmic transparency of form. Now, in the English language (as in the vast majority of contemporary European tongues, including the Russian), this calls for rhyme. But Whitman – in his own eyes – was first of all a prophet. The important thing was not that the masses should memorize the words of his poems, but that they should adopt his teachings. He was writing, not songs, but books of sermons, scriptures.

To commit to memory Whitman's poetry is a difficult thing, but to appraise the artistic worth of his complex rhythms, a practiced ear will suffice. It is an obvious but not unnatural paradox that Whitman should first have been appreciated, not by the masses from whom he came and to whom he was so close, but by cultured and fastidious readers of the study, by an Emerson in America, by Tennyson and the Pre-Raphaelites in England.

Whitman's poems have the general coherency of the usual 'free' verse, without rhyme or meter; they display a close syntax, which does not admit of such variations as arise from a carrying-over of the thought from one stanza to another. But within these limitations, Whitman achieves a truly great variety indeed. It is true, as I have said before, that a good part of his verse is rhythmically crude and monotonous; but on his own poetic ground, he is an inspired and unsurpassed master of rhythm. At times, as he draws near to the summit of his powers, he at the same time approaches a true and spontaneous meter, as for example, in his *Pioneers! O Pioneers!* or in the magnificent opening lines of *Song of the Broad-Axe*, with their metallic woodsman's rhythm and where the rhyme seems to be motivated by the recurring blows of the axe.

Weapon shapely, naked, wan,
Head from the mother's bowels drawn,
Wooded flesh and metal bone, limb only one and lip only one,
Gray-blue leaf by red-heat grown, helve produced from a little
    seed sown,
Resting the grass amid and upon,
To be lean'd and to lean on.

But such approaches to rhyme and meter are comparatively rare in Whitman. However, in his commonly free and outwardly 'formless' verse he exhibits no less strength and an equal variety.

His rhythm may achieve a high degree of spring-like compression and energy, as in the poem which I have mentioned once or twice already, *The Dalliance of the Eagles*, and may take on a complicated flexibility and delicacy in comparison with which even Shelley's finest-spun efforts are somewhat arid-seeming, and schematic, as in these lines from *I Sing the Body Electric*:

Bridegroom night of love working surely and softly into the
    prostrate dawn,
Undulating into the willing and yielding day,
Lost in the cleave of the clasping and sweet-flesh'd day.

Out of a system of prosody to which he is in principle opposed, he is able to create such admittedly incomparable pieces as the song of the thrush in *When Lilacs Last in the Dooryard Bloom'd*.

Whitman's command over the vowels and (especially) the consonants of the English language has no little to do with his rhythmic artistry as a whole, and this is something which even the most skilful translation cannot hope to bring out. Like Shakespeare, Whitman is to be appreciated in all his beauty only by those who read him in the original and whose ears are capable of catching his rhythmic vitality in English.

In connexion with Whitman, we are vividly reminded of what Marx had to say of the capitalistic era's hostility to poetry. Here, we have a poet of genius, bringing us a veracious, substantial, deep-rooted expression of American bourgeois democracy; yet that same democracy did not take him in. He himself, of course, was in part to blame for this, in so far as his poetic form was distinctly anti-popular. But though Whitman may have grievously erred on this question, despite the fact that he was possessed of a profound and structural acquaintance with, and understanding of, the society in which he lived, this but serves to cast into deeper relief the fact that, on all questions save that of poetry, he spoke the same language as democracy's self.

Bourgeois democracy could not accept a poetics such as his. Poetry for it meant 'fine' poetry, of the sort purveyed by a Longfellow. Of great poetry, a poetry related to life, it felt no slightest need.

If the unpopularity of Whitman's poetic form was but the fruit of a thoroughly anti-poetic attitude on the part of the bourgeois-democratic masses, this was not any the less of an obstacle to its acceptance by the proletariat. A popular proletarian poet Whitman was not. Instead, he was the favorite of a sufficiently wide circle of the petty bourgeois intelligentsia. His enormous growth in popularity and influence at the close of the nineteenth and the beginning of the twentieth century was closely associated with the growth of those democratic illusions that marked the rise of imperialism.

Notwithstanding all the really new elements that he brought into poetry, it was not possible to appraise Whitman at the start of the new era. As for the history of poetry after Whitman, it is one of degeneration and decline. Verhaeren stands to Whitman in the same relation that European democracy of the imperialistic epoch does to American democracy of the Civil War years. Whitman's direct descendants – the Unanimists in France, Carl Sandburg in America, – have taken above all the weaker sides of his poetry, the rhetoric and abstraction of his worst pieces; they have carried these phases still further and have given to the Whitmanic forms yet more of an unpopular character. Whitman is for them Whitman the prophet, not Whitman the poet.

These abstract and rhetorical blemishes go to explain the place that Whitman occupies in proletarian poetry. He is integrally a part of an earlier stage of that poetry's development, when abstractions alike rule with regard to the revolution and to the cosmic process, a view of the world dependent for expression upon a rhetorical form. He was not able to open up a new poetic era in bourgeois society, for the very good reason that, in such a society, there could be no such new era. Down to this day, he does not succeed in reaching the proletariat, inasmuch as he is handed to the masses by petty bourgeois disciples who have taken from him precisely that which is of least worth.

If Whitman did not succeed in inaugurating a new era, he did create a poetry containing much that is not to be found in any of the classic bards of old, and which, without a doubt, brings him near to the proletariat and to socialist man. It was through a statement of environing reality that he did this; and if that reality, as stated by him, is a bourgeois one, he for all of that selected what was most worthwhile and progressive in it – democracy, labor, the conquest of nature. He brought to poetry a new concreteness, a new feeling for the material object, not as an owner aesthetically sensing it, but as the man who works with his hands and who has an interest in the product of his labor. He it was who created the poetry of human dignity, a practical vision of that full man whose fulness is only to be realized under socialism.

It is not as to a prophet with a system that we should come to Whitman, but as to an artist. The important thing is not his views, with their resulting false and theoretic concatenation of ideas, but rather those concrete forms to which he brought all the depth and strength of his emotion, all that he as an artist had learned from the American scene. This is the Whitman who occupies an honorable place with the great poets of the past, who have afforded us – I repeat – a vision of that full man who in reality is only able to exist as, at once the builder and the creator of constructive socialism.

(169–85)

Part Three Modern Views

Introduction

As far as the thirties are concerned, it might be more instructive
to report on who did *not* write on Whitman. The reader will
look in vain for critical essays by Blackmur, Tate, Eliot, Leavis,
Ransom or Penn Warren. In the warfare between Henry James,
the organized 'paleface', and Walt Whitman, the formless 'redskin',
as defined by Philip Rahv in the pages of *The Kenyon Review*
('Paleface and Redskin' is reprinted in *Image and Idea*), Walt
Whitman was bound to be treated more as a portent than a poet.
Whitman was not read by the major literary critics; he was used.
He became a straw man in critical attacks against 'transcendental
individualism', one more of the followers of the 'Lucifer of
Concord' (the phrase is Allen Tate's), whose programme, when
pursued in opposition to 'tradition', supposedly made poetry
impossible. These wars have a certain 'strategic value', as Leslie
Fiedler has remarked, 'so long as we remember that the causes for
which they are fought are not really the poets who bear the same
names, but merely their images, tricked out to horrify or allure.
Whitman is no more devil than messiah. He is a poet whom we
must begin now to rescue from parody as well as apotheosis.'
Mr Fiedler's essay 'Images of Walt Whitman' appeared in a volume
celebrating the one hundredth anniversary of *Leaves of Grass*. His
urgency, and the general tone of the volume, suggests how much
Whitman's reputation needed shoring up.

Whitman required the kind of criticism that would cut through
both the aesthetic and political propaganda, propaganda which
prompted Rahv to assert, à propos Whitman, that the political
counterpart of a literary redskin is a mindless democrat, 'a vulgar
anti-intellectual, combining aggression with conformity and
reverting to the crudest forms of frontier psychology.' Whitman
may have left himself open to such charges but there was clearly
another side to his nature. As Lionel Trilling observed, 'Whitman
is always showing himself as a more complex intelligence than
perhaps he wanted to be, or than many of his readers want him to

be.' Writers like Trilling (p. 291) and Newton Arvin (p. 263) and
F. O. Matthiessen (p. 275) established a precedent for the useful
study of Whitman. Arvin's work is usually described as 'politically-
minded', but it would be more accurate to characterize it as a
study of that 'long foreground' about which Emerson was so
curious. By setting Whitman apart from the Transcendentalists,
both Arvin and Matthiessen touch upon that peculiar blend of the
concrete and the ideal which is a quality of Whitman's mind and
style.

The most recent criticism of Whitman begins in scepticism and
ends in belief. It has taken the whole of Whitman without taking
Whitman whole. It has accepted Whitman as a bundle of
contradictions – that 'powerful, original poet' with the 'disconcerting dash of the *poseur*' – and has attempted to sort out (in
works like Gay Wilson Allen's *The Solitary Singer*) not only the
facts of Whitman's life, but the best of Whitman's poetry. Recent
critics of Whitman would be willing to settle for a body of verse
both smaller and different from that which Whitman's earliest
admirers proposed; they have rejected Whitman the rhetorician,
the 'bard of democratic society', and looked instead at the self-
exploring, hesitating poet. R. W. B. Lewis characterizes Whitman
as the spokesman of the self and the self's swaying motion –
outward into a teeming world where objects were 'strung like
beads of glory' on his sight; backward into private communion
with the "real Me"' (p. 450). In the work of writers like Constance
Rourke (p. 224) and Richard Chase (p. 331), criticism has tried to
get behind some of those public images Whitman devised for
himself and explore the various 'selves' in Whitman's poetry;
it has been attracted to a more ironic, detached Whitman, not
confusing the hero of Whitman's poems with 'the Whitman of
daily life'. Behind the exuberant Whitman of such poems as
Song of Myself, Chase has described an alienated, lonely figure who
reattaches himself to the world by 'aggressive poetic assertions';

suggesting, in fact, that when Whitman refused to explore his
loneliness and created extra-poetic selves ('the hospital visitor',
the 'sage and master') that his end as a poet was in sight. When
Yeats remarked that poets like Emerson and Whitman seemed to
him to have become 'superficial' because they lacked the 'Vision of
Evil', he was saying farewell to some heroes of his youth and not
adequately characterizing Walt Whitman. In poems like *The
Sleepers* and *Hours Continuing Long, Sore and Heavy-Hearted*,
modern readers have discovered enough anxiety and guilt to satisfy
the most anguished taste.

The poems which have most engaged modern critics of
Whitman are those written before 1871. In spite of Malcolm
Cowley's claim that *Song of Myself* is Whitman's 'greatest poem',
most readers have preferred the elegiac Whitman, the 'laureate of
death'. This is the Whitman that Eliot himself admired, the poet
of the lilac and the mocking-bird. It is no coincidence that
Whitman's three greatest odes – *As I Ebb'd With the Ocean of Life*,
Out of the Cradle Endlessly Rocking and *When Lilacs Last in the
Dooryard Bloom'd* – are meditations on both death and the poetic
act. The great love affair of Whitman's life has turned out to be his
devotion to his art. 'The work of my life is making poems', he
told Emerson, and modern critics have taken him at his word. In
doing so, they have come to feel that like Wordsworth, Emerson
or Stevens, Whitman's great subject is the confrontation of the
imagination and Nature; that, for Whitman, the poetic imagination
begins in the recognition of loss; and that the greatest loss is the
separation of the poetic imagination from the self as it is overwhelmed by reality. Few poets would dare to presume, as
Whitman did at the end of his career, that heaven is but another
step in the imagination's ascent:

Long indeed have we lived, slept, filter'd, become really blended
    into one;

Then if we die we die together, (yes, we'll remain one,)
If we go anywhere we'll go together to meet what happens,
May-be we'll be better off and blither, and learn something,
May-be it is yourself now really ushering me to the true songs,
  (who knows?)
May-be it is you the mortal knob really undoing, turning – so
  now finally,
Good-bye – and hail! my Fancy.

                                    (*Good-Bye My Fancy*)

It would be false to leave the impression, however, that Whitman
is now universally admired. A sceptical response to Whitman and
to the criticism which surrounds him (reflected here in the essays
by Yvor Winters (p. 299) and Martin Green (p. 424)) is more
common than Whitman's readers are likely to admit. The case
of Whitman, however, is frequently reopened. As Randall Jarrell
discovered (p. 303), Walt Whitman is a better poet than he
ought to be.

Whitman excluded very few poems from *Leaves of Grass* and
his revisions, as Roger Asselineau in his essay 'From Mysticism
to Art' points out, were not always made to disguise his true
feelings. But Whitman *did* reshuffle his poems, and in doing so,
chose to emphasize the prophetic rather than the human in his
verse, to present himself, as Leslie Fiedler once remarked, as the
poet Laureate of America, rather than the self-doubting, troubled
writer that he was. The road to Whitman, as Roy Harvey Pearce
put it, is not 'impassable', but working with the edition of 1891–2
is both 'tedious' and 'misleading'. By making the editions of 1855
and 1860 easily available to readers of Whitman, both Malcolm
Cowley (who is interested almost exclusively in the expansive poet
of *Song of Myself* and is represented here by a selection from the
'Introduction' to his edition) and Pearce (who writes about the
more introspective poet in 'Walt Whitman Justified: The Poet in

1860') did much to restore the poet to his poetry.

It is not surprising that some of the best essays on Whitman written since the thirties served (like Leslie Fiedler's) as introductions to anthologies, or that general surveys of Whitman's art, like those of Denis Donoghue (p. 427) and Randall Jarrell, are written with a sense of discovery. Younger critics, further removed from Eliot's influence, began to look at Whitman again. As the Romantics in general were restored to favour, it no longer seemed necessary to argue so exclusively the case for conventional forms. The more important question was – did Whitman succeed with the form he chose? That he did succeed is attested to in the essays included here which treat single poems: Malcolm Cowley (p. 347) provides a guide to the argument of *Song of Myself*, and in doing so answers those critics who have been unable to see any progression of thought in that poem; Richard Chase explores *Song of Myself*, *The Sleepers*, *Crossing Brooklyn Ferry* and *Out of the Cradle*; R. W. B. Lewis continues the discussion of Whitman in the sixties with his explication of *As I Ebb'd With the Ocean of Life*; and Charles Feidelson (p. 318) discusses Whitman as symbolist, with particular reference to *Starting from Paumanok* and *When Lilacs Last in the Dooryard Bloom'd*. In addition to the sympathetic treatment of Whitman's language provided here by F. O. Matthiessen, I have included Gay Wilson Allen's study of Whitman's use of Biblical forms, especially parallelism and repetition (p. 407). Together with Lawrence's 'Poetry of the Moment', they are the best apologics I know for Whitman's poetics.

Newton Arvin

from 'Science and the Unseen', *Walt Whitman* 1938

In an intellectual environment so full of contradictions as this – an environment bounded at one extreme by Volney and Darwin, at another by George Sand and Hegel – it is little wonder that so impressionable a temper as Whitman's should express itself artistically in a confusing and paradoxical manner. He was not a mere smooth and passive surface, reflecting mirror-like the images and the ideas cast upon him by his complicated age: his sensibility was too highly characterized and his plastic power too robust for that. But his sensibility itself was a complicated one and his plastic power had its natural limits: the result was a body of poetic work almost as divided within itself as the culture of Whitman's America was. Sincerely convinced that the poetry of the new day should bring itself into harmony with the most advanced thought and knowledge, Whitman was able to stride forward a certain distance – a remarkable distance – into the regions still so largely unexplored by men of letters; but he could outstrip his fellows, his audience, and one side of his own nature, so far and no further. Like Shelley, like Heine, like Baudelaire – and more than any of them – he was able to spell out the first invigorating syllables of a naturalistic credo; like them too, however, he recoiled from its full and final exactions, and fell back, if not upon Platonism or the Old Testament or Swedenborg, then upon an intuitionalist theism that was for him the more natural equivalent. As the bard of Scientism, he gave very generously with his right hand, and then took back with his left something of what he had given.

Something, but by no means all. Whitman had learned too much from the rationalists and the popularizers of science ever to forget his lesson entirely, and his work as a whole, verse and prose, could certainly not have been produced by a poet before the Englightenment. Its strain of bold and positive naturalism is too pervasive ever to be successfully minimized. For one thing, Whitman had early acquired a passionate anti-clericalism, a vehement antagonism to churches and 'preachers', and from this, in spite of the all-inclusiveness he later cultivated, he was never to recede. It reveals itself in *Leaves of Grass* rather by indirection than otherwise, but it is unmistakably there. No doubt Whitman had found encouragement toward a certain sort of religious heterodoxy even in Carlyle and Emerson, but the quality of his anti-clericalism is much less theirs than it is that of Paine and Volney; much less the romantic repudiation of the Transcendentalists than the fiery hostility of the Jacobins. It dated back to a period in his life before Transcendentalism had affected him in the slightest. At the end of the century old men on Long Island who remembered Whitman in his school-teaching days recalled that he had not been religious in any way, that he had never been seen inside a church, and that in fact he had had a local notoriety as an atheist or infidel. There was something about preachers, as a rule, said his brother George after Whitman's death, that seemed to repel Walt; and though the poet of *Leaves of Grass* usually refrained from denunciation here as elsewhere, that same poet, if he had realized his ambition to become a popular lecturer, might then have been less affirmative. That at least is what certain manuscript notes for lectures suggest to us:

Really [he asks in one of them] what has America to do with all this mummery of prayer and rituals and the rant of exhorters and priests? We are not at all deceived by this great show that confronts us of churches, priests and rituals – for piercing beneath, we find there is no life, no faith, no reality of belief, but that all is essentially a pretence, a sham.

(*Walt Whitman's Workshop*, p. 41)

Even in the publicity of print, the early Whitman was capable of a similar harshness of invective: in the open letter to Emerson in his second edition, he dared to denounce the churches of America as 'one vast lie,' a lie in which neither the people nor the churches themselves believed; and fifteen years later he was to return to the theme in one of the gloomier passages of *Democratic Vistas*: 'A lot of churches, sects, etc., the most dismal phantasms I know', he then wrote, 'usurp the name of religion.' The passage of time might mellow or weaken his feeling about many things, but nothing that appeared in the American churches of the seventies and eighties availed to tone down this early-acquired anti-clericalism. It was part of what lay at the base of his admiring friendship for the famous infidel, Robert Ingersoll, with whom he differed frankly at particular points, and it came out with all the heat of a youthful passion in his conversations with Horace Traubel. For the church as an institution, he told Traubel, he had 'the profoundest contempt', and it is clear from other conversations that this contempt, far from being merely Transcendental, still had the older political and social bias. On one occasion, when he had been denouncing the priests of religion and the priests of the arts, Traubel interjected: 'We still have the priests of commerce to contend with.' 'So we have,' answered Whitman: 'doubly so: the priests of commerce augmented by the priests of churches, who are everywhere the parasites, the apologists, of systems as they exist.' This was hardly the literal truth about the church and the priesthood everywhere, at all times – nor even of the American church and the American ministry in Whitman's day – but it testifies to the strength of his antagonism that he should have struck this old deistic note even in his latest years.

It was a note he had virtually never struck explicitly in *Leaves of Grass*, though even there, first in his original preface and then in the poem ultimately named *By Blue Ontario's Shore*, he had announced the disappearance of priesthoods in a line which he never dropped from the book: 'There will shortly be no more priests, I say their work is done.' With rather different phrasing Emerson or Carlyle might also have written that line, and certainly the poet who did write it had long since thrown in his lot with the romantic visionaries. The first thin copies of *Leaves of Grass* that reached the men in Concord made that clear enough to them: nevertheless, the new prophet-poet whom they welcomed so hospitably was to espouse, during his first phase of four or five years, an idealism in which the elements were not mingled quite as they had been by the idealists of the pure tradition. There was something singularly earthly and man-centered in the form of the spiritual philosophy expounded by the writer of the first preface and the earliest poems and certain lecture notes of the period. When this Whitman spoke of the supernatural, of God, of the soul, it was in a manner that might have led his readers to question the real bent of his idealism. He could reject supernaturalism with what was not really the Transcendentalist accent: 'The whole theory of the special and supernatural and all that was twined with it or educed out of it departs as a dream,' he wrote, in almost the vein of his earliest rationalistic teachers; and neither Carlyle nor Emerson would have described the supernatural, in language Whitman used, as 'of no account'. They might challenge the old simple dualism of matter and spirit, but it was always to assert the superior reality of what lay above and beyond the natural.

This was not quite Walt Whitman's way at the beginning, and when he spoke of deity it was not in the manner of Carlyle – 'Love not Pleasure; love God' – or of Emerson – 'Idealism sees the world in God.' On the contrary, he sometimes spoke at this stage in the tones of a kind of Transcendental atheism. Like Swinburne a few years later, Whitman began by exalting Man at the expense of any omnipotent Maker. The notes for lectures are particularly sweeping:

> The whole scene shifts – the relative positions change – Man comes forward inherent, superb, the soul, the judge, the common average man advances, ascends to place. God disappears – the whole idea of God, as hitherto presented in the religions of the world for the thousands of past years, or rather the scores of thousands of past years, for reasons disappears –
> *God abdicates.*
>
> *(Walt Whitman's Workshop*, p. 43)

It is true that he did not mean this apparent atheism as literally as Swinburne meant his: Whitman would never have cried out against 'the supreme evil, God,' and almost from the beginning there were the germs of a nebulous theism in what he wrote. His first inclination, nevertheless, was to humble and naturalize and humanize the thought of deity, not to sublimate it, and he came closer than he may have intended to an almost godless pantheism:

> I hear and behold God in every object, yet understand God not in the least,
> Nor do I understand who there can be more wonderful than myself.

> Why should I wish to see God better than this day?
> I see something of God each hour of the twenty-four, and each moment then,
> In the faces of men and women I see God, and in my own face in the glass.
>
> *(Song of Myself*, 48)

There is little even of the ideal and impersonal Oversoul or Absolute in lines like these, and just as little in the passage in which Whitman declares that the poet worthy of these states is silent in the dispute on God and eternity:

He sees eternity in men and women.

(*By Blue Ontario's Shore*, 10)

He certainly did not wish to be taken as denying either God or eternity, though half-wittingly he was emptying those words of most of their serious content, and he certainly did not wish to be taken as denying the soul. But the young poet of the early editions had too robust and too spontaneous a love of bodily life and 'this beautiful material world' to insist on the soul and the spiritual world at their expense, as the stricter idealists were always doing. He could not, at the beginning, see the universe of natural objects and physical bodies as a mere evocation of the thinking or willing ego, as only a lovely symbol of transcendent realities, or as the illusory vesture in which Spirit might choose to clothe itself fleetingly. On the contrary, his unschooled and unsophisticated 'metaphysics' led him to make spirituality and the soul depend upon the visible and the palpable in a manner that savored strongly of the materialism he disavowed. There is a curious manuscript note, evidently of an early date, in which Whitman charges himself to preserve in his work the balanced truth that the world of matter and its laws are as 'grand and superb' as that of spirit and its laws:

Most writers have disclaimed the physical world and they have not over-estimated the other, or soul, but have under-estimated the corporeal. How shall my eye separate the beauty of the blossoming buckwheat field from the stalks and heads of tangible matter? How shall I know what the life is except as I see it in the flesh?

(*Complete Writings*, 1902,
vol. ix, p. 5)

There were the germs of heresy, of course, in this very material ideality: it leaned much more toward a supernatural naturalism than toward Carlyle's 'Natural Supernaturalism'; and Whitman was later, in effect, to abjure it. But the poet of the fifties found no difficulty in having his metaphysical cake and eating it too. 'I will make the poems of materials,' he cried, 'for I think they are to be the most spiritual poems.' And there were even more radical implications in a passage of the *Sun-Down Poem* (*Crossing Brooklyn Ferry*) of 1856. The poet is addressing all the sparkling, stirring, flowing objects of Manhattan Bay at sunset:

We descend upon you and all things, we arrest you all,
We realize the soul only by you, you faithful solids and fluids,
Through you color, form, location, sublimity, ideality,
Through you every proof, comparison, and all the suggestions
    and determinations of ourselves.

He was to drop this passage from the poem many years later, and for obvious reasons; but fortunately he never reworked all the early poems from beginning to end, and he never rejected this equally revealing passage in *Starting from Paumanok* (1860):

Was somebody asking to see the soul?
See, your own shape and countenance, persons, substances,
    beasts, the trees, the running rivers, the rocks and sands ...

Behold, the body includes and is the meaning, the main concern,
    and includes and is the soul.

The poet who wrote this last line was the poet who also wrote the *Poem of the Many in One* (*By Blue Ontario's Shore*):

All comes by the body, only health puts you rapport with the
    universe.

and the *Song of Prudence*:

The spirit receives from the body just as much as it gives to the
    body, if not more.

and he was also, of course, the poet who composed the *Children of Adam* chants for the express purpose of re-vindicating, in the teeth of all corrupt asceticisms, the dignity – he himself said rather the 'sacredness' – of the human body, and the high worth – he himself said even the 'divinity' – of all its functions and acts. He might be bound not only by the vocabulary but by some of the old mental habits of supernaturalism when he spoke of these things, but the poet who quietly resisted Emerson's suggestion that he drop *I Sing the Body Electric* and its companion poems – this poet owed a heavier debt to the wholesome influences of modern science, of modern physiology and medicine, than to either the Quakers or the meta-physicians. There was a token of this in the very gusto with which he used such words as 'physiology' itself or 'physiognomy' or 'phrenology'; and certainly in all that frank celebration of sexuality Whitman was closer to what was rebelliously naturalistic in the poetry of his century – to Byron and his sensualism, to Heine's 'rehabilita-tion of matter', to Pushkin's defiant fleshliness – than he was to the ascetic Fichte or the attrabilious Carlyle. The biologist and his like would be more at home than the subjective idealist with these dithy-rambs of health and physical fitness and procreation.

Naturally there was a temperamental basis, quite as real as the ideological one, for such poems as *Spontaneous Me*; but naturally, too, the personal impulse could have expressed itself so boldly only in a certain environment of ideas and attitudes, and it would not be easy to say just how far *Children of Adam* was prepared for by the 'pagan' poets and just how far by the developments represented, however humbly, by Orson Fowler's *Physiology*. The two, of course, were but different aspects of one general earthward movement of men's thoughts and loyalties, and it was that movement – embodied in-differently, if one will, in Burns and Lyell, in Heine and Liebig, in Diderot and Cuvier – that lay behind all that was most affirmative and acceptant, in an earthly and even an earthy sense, in *Leaves of Grass*. It may have been 'Scientism' of the most general and undif-ferentiated sort, but it was Scientism and not metaphysical idealism that confirmed and abetted Whitman in his early passion for the 'divine soil' and the 'rolling earth', in the large healthy satisfaction he took in mere air and light and water, in his delighted sense of being in easy harmony with the natural elements, in his conviction that all things, even the meanest or vilest, are there 'for reasons' and are good 'in their place'. There were idealists, to be sure, like Schelling and Emerson, for whom objective nature was precious as the emblem of supernal reality, but for one thing the early Whitman did not speak so characteristically of an abstract 'Nature' as of the friendly and substantial 'earth', and besides he sometimes exalted it in a manner that would have seemed alarming, theoretically, to the others:

I swear there is no greatness or power that does not emulate those
  of the earth,
There can be no theory of any account unless it corroborate the
  theory of the earth,
No politics, song, religion, behaviour, or what not, is of account,
  unless it compare with the amplitude of the earth,
Unless it face the exactness, vitality, impartiality, rectitude of the
  earth.

(A Song of the Rolling Earth, 3)

A religion that has to compare with the amplitude and face the
impartiality of the earth – or be rejected as of no account – is not the
religion that Kant or Coleridge or Emerson had proposed to recon-
struct: for them, it would have signified a setting of all such things
on their heads, and certainly the 'earth' of these early passages is not
so much an emblem of anything as a criterion of everything. It is not
something flickering, fanciful, metaphorical, and transient, any more
than it is something base and sin-ridden: it is a thing immitigably real
and good and lasting, adequate in itself to all the physical and spiritual
needs of man. 'I conjure you, my brethren,' said Nietzsche, '*remain
true to the earth*'; and the early Whitman had anticipated him: 'The
earth,' he had written, 'that is sufficient.' He had spoken of it as no
really consistent Transcendentalist could have done:

What can the future bring me more than I have?
Do you suppose I wish to enjoy life in other spheres?

I say distinctly I comprehend no better sphere than this earth,
I comprehend no better life than the life of my body.

This passage too – from the *Clef Poem* of 1856 – was rejected after
twenty-five years, but it had said its say, in all the early editions, for
a very geocentric idealism. The emotion it expressed had been so
strong that, even after *more* than twenty-five years, the aged poet
could recur to it with magnificent unconcern for so much of what he
had said in the interval. The important thing, Whitman could say as
a very old man, is the present life and the people about us, 'the earth
struggle' itself; whatever may come later, we need not bother our
heads about it: 'our responsibilities are on the earth'.
  When he spoke in this strain, he was justifying, so far as that went,

his own claim that he had written in full sympathy with the findings of natural science. There were other respects too in which he was genuinely affected by the spirit of that tradition. 'Scientific' rather than Transcendental surely, was the vivid sense Whitman had, especially at the beginning, of the inexhaustible multiplicity of things and the delight he took in it; the outgoing love of variety that was sometimes so much stronger in him than his meditative conviction of unity; the thing that made him the poet of the Many at least as much as he was the poet of the One. It was in the naturalistic heritage, in the heritage that had celebrated 'the plurality of worlds,' that Whitman would have found a certain corroboration for his naïve satisfaction in numbers and the pleasure it gave him to contemplate a world pullulating with uncountable stars and comets, with stones and plants and animals, with cities, races, languages, trades, buildings: 'always,' as he wrote, 'the free range and diversity.' In the vastnesses of space that the astronomers had opened up, in the dizzy remotenesses of time evoked by the geologists and archaeologists, he found not terror or dejection but exhilaration:

See ever so far, there is limitless space outside of that,
Count ever so much, there is limitless time around that;
(Song of Myself, 45)

and with a similar zest:

We have thus far exhausted trillions of winters and summers,
There are trillions ahead, and trillions ahead of them.
(Song of Myself, 44)

Far from rebelling against space and time, indeed, or denying their reality, as the idealists did, Whitman could glorify them – even, paradoxically, in his mystical moments – as 'ties eternal'; and far from being obsessed with the Unchangeable, like the orthodox visionaries, he felt a profane enthusiasm for change. Was it not the 'tough' side of his mind that enabled him to feel it? Certainly he was no more depressed than a geologist or a chemist would be by the spectacle of a universe in constant motion, involved in a restless process of breaking down and building up:

Ever the mutable,
Ever materials, changing, crumbling, re-cohering;
(Eidólons)

on the contrary, the fact of change, of movement, of an endless procession of finite events was a congenial fact to the realistic Whitman; it braced him with a sense of the unweariable power and fecundity at the heart of things:

Urge and urge and urge,
Always the procreant urge of the world.

(*Song of Myself*, 3)

It was partly the tirelessness of the 'rolling earth' that inspired his paean to it, and in this virtue he elsewhere proposed to emulate it himself:

Let others finish specimens, I never finish specimens,
I start them by exhaustless laws as Nature does, fresh and
    modern continually.

(*Myself and Mine*)

What is the *Song of the Open Road* if not a call to men and women to rouse themselves from their lethargy, to refuse al lstops and stays, to move with the free and flexible movement of the world of objects, to 'know the universe itself as a road, as many roads, as roads for traveling souls'?

There was undoubtedly something in the idea of the mere flux that stirred Whitman happily in his healthiest years, but even at the beginning of his poetic career he had understood that for modern naturalistic thought the flux is no mere chaos but an orderly process – even if not 'designed' – and an intelligible one – even if not consciously intelligent. 'I have felt from the first,' he said to Traubel, 'that my own work must assume the essential truths of evolution, or something like them'; and although the qualifying phrase is more important than he may have realized, it is quite true that even before *The Origin of Species* Whitman, like Emerson, had had more than a glimpse of some of the things that were implied by what was then called the Development Theory. Inevitably all that pre-Darwinian speculation – by cosmogonists, by palaeontologists, by comparative anatomists – had seeped through to him along the public channels; however indirectly, and no doubt partly through the uproar over *The Vestiges of Creation*, he had made out more or less clearly what Buffon and Goethe, Lamarck and Geoffroy, Erasmus, Darwin and

Robert Chambers had been getting at. With all its rich implications of slow and patient growth, of increasingly complex development, of progressive change, the conception of evolution not only in its biological but in its vastest sense had captured the imagination of Walt Whitman almost from the beginning.

We know how the conception expressed itself most palpably in his verse – in images of a world emerging slowly and serenely out of 'deathly fire' and 'turbulent chaos', of the 'covering waters and gases' that overlay it 'before man had appear'd', of the 'long slow strata' that had accumulated for his own embryo to 'rest on', of the 'long-threaded moss' and 'esculent roots' he himself 'incorporated', and of the birds and quadrupeds with which he was 'stucco'd all over'. We know too that the 'evolutionism' Whitman considered himself to have voiced was of a highly teleological and sometimes egocentric sort; that he could say with a curious subjectivism, 'All forces have been steadily employ'd to complete and delight me'; and that his evolutionism was rather early given a bias that brought it nearer to Hegel than to Darwin. When all deductions are made, however, the idea of progressive development on the natural level is potent and productive in *Leaves of Grass*.

There is a final sense in which, more than any comparable book, Whitman's is affirmative of what physical science had made possible, if not of its philosophic substructure. Most of the poets of his time, even in America, were either indifferent to the machines which applied science had brought into being or bitterly hostile to them. It was an attitude that, in view of much that those machines had done to human life and human personality, it is easy enough to understand and condone. To distinguish between the necessary and the actual effects of the machine – under the social circumstances in which its use began – was evidently more than many men of great gifts were capable of doing. Unlike most of them, on the other hand, Whitman did feel that distinction, even if he had never made it consciously; and characteristically he saw in the machine not only a delight to the eye of the craftsman but an intrinsically constructive agent in the civilizing of mankind, the freeing of it from the primitive bonds of distance and inflexibility and weight. Thoreau's fear that the railroad might ride upon us instead of our riding upon it Whitman virtually never shared, though he sometimes said loosely comparable things;

and he told Traubel that he had no patience with such protests as Tennyson's against the introduction of a railroad near him on the Isle of Wight, or with Ruskin's thinking himself constituted to object to all modern improvements.

It was in a very different spirit from theirs, certainly, that the editor of the *Eagle* remarked, apropos of a visit to the engine-room of a ferry-boat, that 'there are few more magnificent pieces of handiwork than a powerful steam-engine, swiftly at work!' Or that, on another day, he gloatingly described a new printing-press the paper had acquired as 'about as pretty and clean-working a piece of machinery as a man might wish to look on'. This was the young writer whose verse, after a few years, was to be so unprecedentedly full of steam printing-presses, telegraph-wires, sewing-machines, forge-furnaces, steam-whistles, and even drain-pipes and gasometers. He was the poet for whom a locomotive was to be – not, as for the romantic poets generally, something ugly because it was useful, but – a 'fierce-throated beauty', a 'type of the modern'; the poet for whom steam-ships were to be 'splendid resistless black poems', and the reapers and threshers that crawled like monsters over the fields of the West to be 'human-divine inventions'. If he had done nothing else in *Leaves of Grass*, Whitman would have done an important service to culture by opening men's eyes to the unhackneyed if 'unromantic' beauty of the machine and to the imaginative grandeur of much that men of mechanical genius had achieved. Nothing came easier to him than to praise 'the strong light works of engineers', and it was quite in the spirit of a subsequent and, in this respect, bolder generation than his that Whitman proposed, in a late prose sketch, to take as a symbol of America 'some colossal foundry', flaming, smoky, dust-clouded, disordered, and clangorous. When he wrote in this vein – as in the others we have alluded to – Whitman was richly bearing out his proud claim to be the poet of modern Scientism.

(197–213)

F. O. Matthiessen

'Words! book-words! what are you?', *American Renaissance* 1941

One aspect of Whitman's work that has not yet received its due attention is outlined in *An American Primer*, notes for a lecture that he seems to have collected mainly between 1855 and 1860, using the paper covers of the unbound copies of the first edition of *Leaves of Grass* for his improvised sheets. This lecture, which, as he says, 'does not suggest the invention but describes the growth of an American English enjoying a distinct identity', remained, like most of Whitman's lectures, undelivered and unpublished at his death. But he often talked to Traubel about it in the late 1880s, telling him that he never quite got its subject out of his mind, that he had long thought of making it into a book, and adding: 'I sometimes think the *Leaves* is only a language experiment.' It will be interesting, therefore, to begin by seeing how much we can learn about Whitman just by examining his diction.

He understood that language was not 'an abstract construction' made by the learned, but that it had arisen out of the work and needs, the joys and struggles and desires of long generations of humanity, and that it had 'its bases broad and low, close to the ground'. Words were not arbitrary inventions, but the product of human events and customs, the progeny of folkways. Consequently he believed that the fresh opportunities for the English tongue in America were immense, offering themselves in the whole range of American facts. His poems, by cleaving to these facts, could thereby release 'new potentialities' of expression for our native character. When he started to develop his conviction that 'a perfect user of words uses things', and to mention some of the things, he unconsciously dilated into the loose beats of his poetry: 'they exude in power and beauty from him – miracles from his hands – miracles from his mouth . . . things, whirled like chain-shot rocks, defiance, compulsion, houses, iron, locomotives, the oak, the pine, the keen eye, the hairy breast, the Texan ranger, the Boston truckman, the woman that arouses a man, the man that arouses a woman.'

He there reveals the joy of the child or the primitive poet just in naming things. This was the quality in Coleridge that made Whitman speak of him as being 'like Adam in Paradise, and almost as free from artificiality' – though Whitman's own joy is far more naïve and relaxed than anything in Coleridge. Whitman's excitement carries weight because he realized that a man cannot use words so unless he has experienced the facts that they express, unless he has grasped them with his senses. This kind of realization was generally obscured in the nineteenth century, partly by its tendency to divorce education of the mind from the body and to treat language as something to be learned from a dictionary. Such division of the individual's wholeness, intensified by the specializations of a mechanized society, has become a chief cause of the neurotic strain oppressing present-day man, for whom the words that pour into him from headlines so infrequently correspond to a concrete actuality that he has touched at first hand. For Whitman it was axiomatic that the speakers of such words are merely juggling helplessly with a foreign tongue. He was already convinced by 1847 – as he recorded in the earliest of his manuscript notebooks that has been preserved – that 'a man only is interested in anything when he identifies himself with it.' When he came to observe in the *Primer* that 'a perfect writer would make words sing, dance, kiss ... or do any thing that man or woman or the natural powers can do', he believed that such a writer must have realized the full resources of his physical life, and have been immersed in the evolving social experience of his own time.

Thus instinctively, if crudely, he reached the conviction that 'only the greatest user of words himself fully enjoys and understands himself,' a conviction surprisingly close to Eliot's, that Racine and Baudelaire, the two chief French 'masters of diction are also the greatest two psychologists' among French poets. Whitman thought that all the talk in Racine was 'on stilts', and his sole mention of Baudelaire was to quote one of the few beliefs they shared, 'The immoderate taste for beauty and art leads men into monstrous excesses.' Noting that *Les fleurs du mal* appeared only two years after *Leaves of Grass*, Eliot has asked whether any age could have produced 'more heterogeneous leaves and flowers'? But his pronouncement that there was for Whitman 'no chasm between the real and the ideal, such as opened before the horrified eyes of Baudelaire', did not blind him to Whitman's prodigious faculty 'in making America as it was ... into something grand and significant', 'of transmuting the real into an ideal'.

Feeling that he had discovered the real America that had been

hidden behind the diction of a superficial culture which hardly
touched native life, Whitman exclaimed with delight: 'Monongahela
– it rolls with venison richness upon the palate.' He pursued the
subject of how 'words become vitaliz'd, and stand for things' in an
essay in his late *November Boughs* called 'Slang in America' (1885).
He grasped there the truth that language is the 'universal absorber
and combiner', the best index we have to the history of civilization.
In the *Primer* his cognizance that English had assimilated contributions
from every stock, that it had become an amalgamation from all
races, rejecting none, had led him to declare that he would never
allude to this tongue 'without exultation'. In the few pages of his
printed essay there is more exultation than clarity, particularly in his
conception of slang. His starting point is straightforward enough, the
statement that 'slang, profoundly consider'd, is the lawless germinal
element, below all words and sentences, and behind all poetry, and
proves a certain perennial rankness and protestantism in speech.' But
when he equates slang with 'indirection, an attempt of common
humanity to escape from bald literalism, and express itself illimitably',
we are reminded of Emerson's use of the term 'indirection' and need
recourse to other passages in Whitman for the elusive connotations
that he associated with this word.

When he said in his 1855 Preface that the expression of the American
poet was to be 'transcendent and new', 'indirect and not direct or
descriptive or epic', he had just been enumerating the kinds of things
the poet must incarnate if he was to be commensurate with his people:
the continent's geography and history, the fluid movement of the
population, the life of its factories and commerce and of the southern
plantations. He appears to have thought that the expression of this
surging newness must be 'indirect' in the sense that it could not find its
voice through any of the conventional modes, but must wait for the
poet who 'sees the solid and beautiful forms of the future where there
are now no solid forms.' Here Whitman's belief in the way in which the
organic style is called into being is seen to converge with his similar
understanding of the origin of words. He might have had in mind either
or both in his account of the creative process, in another early notebook:

All truths lie waiting in all things – They neither urge the opening of themselves nor resist it. For their birth you need not the

obstetric forceps of the surgeon. They unfold to you and emit
themselves more fragrant than roses from living buds, whenever
you fetch the spring sunshine moistened with summer rain –
But it must be in yourself – It shall come from your soul – It
shall be love.

(Uncollected Prose and Poetry,
vol. II, p. 80)

Living speech could come to a man only through his absorption
in the life surrounding him. He must learn that the final decisions of
language are not made by dictionary makers but 'by the masses,
people nearest the concrete, having most to do with actual land and
sea.' By such a route, illogical as it may be, Whitman came to think
of slang as indirection, as the power to embody in a vibrant word or
phrase 'the deep silent mysterious never to be examined, never to be
told quality of life itself.' When he tried to make his meaning plainer
by giving examples of how many 'of the oldest and solidest words
we use, were originally generated from the daring and license of
slang', he showed that what he was really thinking of was something
very like Emerson's first proposition about language – that words are
signs of natural facts. Whitman's examples are almost identical with
those in *Nature*: 'Thus the term *right* means literally only straight.
Wrong primarily meant twisted, distorted. *Integrity* meant oneness.
Spirit meant breath, or flame. A *supercilious* person was one who
raised his eyebrows. To *insult* was to leap against. If you *influenced* a
man, you but flowed into him.' Moreover, as Whitman continued, he
expanded into Emerson's next proposition – that natural facts are
symbols of spiritual facts – by launching from the word 'prophesy'
into an enunciation of the transcendental view of the poet: 'The
Hebrew word which is translated *prophesy* meant to bubble up and
pour forth as a fountain. The enthusiast bubbles up from the Spirit
of God within him, and it pours forth from him like a fountain. The
word prophecy is misunderstood. Many suppose that it is limited to
mere prediction; that is but the lesser portion of prophecy. The greater
work is to reveal God. Every true religious enthusiast is a prophet.'

In such a passage you come up against one of the most confusing
aspects of Whitman, the easy-hearted way he could shuttle back and
forth from materialism to idealism without troubling himself about

any inconsistency. Thinking of *Children of Adam* or of what Lawrence cared for in Whitman, 'the sheer appreciation of the instant moment, life surging itself at its very well-head', we tend to deny that his bond with transcendentalism could have been strong. But it is significant that his earliest quotation from one of Emerson's 'inimitable lectures', in a notice for *The Brooklyn Eagle* in 1847, is from 'Spiritual Laws' and begins, 'When the act of reflection takes place in the mind, when we look at ourselves in the light of thought, we discover that our life is embosomed in beauty.' Whitman's response to this kind of idealism was more than fleeting, as we may judge from his marginal note on an unidentified essay on 'Imagination and Fact,' which Bucke dated to the early fifties. The sentence that struck the poet reads: 'The mountains, rivers, forests and the elements that gird them round about would be only blank conditions of matter if the mind did not fling its own divinity around them.' Whitman commented: 'This I think is one of the most indicative sentences I ever read.'

The idealistic strain also runs through his conception of language. Although he asks in his *Song of the Banner at Daybreak*:

Words! book-words! what are you?

and affirms in *A Song of the Rolling Earth*:

... the substantial words are in the ground and sea,

nevertheless he proclaims on the first page of his *Primer*: 'All words are spiritual – nothing is more spiritual than words.' This is the Whitman who could say, 'The words of my book nothing, the drift of it every thing', the Whitman so concerned with the idea rather than the form that he could take flight into the vaguest undifferentiated generalizations about 'Democracy, ma femme', or could write on occasion even of 'the body electric' with no sensuous touch of his material:

O for you whoever you are your correlative body! O it, more than all else, you delighting!

(*From Pent-up Aching Rivers*)

This is the Whitman who has seemed to linguists as though he was trying to get beyond the limits of language altogether. In the view of Sapir, subscribed to by Ogden and Richards, he sometimes is moving so entirely in terms of abstractions that he appears to be 'striving for a generalized art language, a literary algebra.' In this quality of his work Sapir regarded him as an extreme example of the transcendental drift, an artist whose 'expression is frequently strained, it sounds at times like a translation from an unknown original – which, indeed, is precisely what it is.' We recall that Emerson's most idealized passages of verse struck Chapman in much the same way.

Thus Whitman seems to show the very dichotomy between the material and the ideal, the concrete and the abstract that we observed in Emerson's remarks on language. Nevertheless, when we look at their poems, it is obvious that Whitman often bridged the gap in a way that Emerson could not. The whole question of the relation of Whitman's theory and practice of art to Emerson's is fascinating, since, starting so often from similar if not identical positions, they end up with very different results. The extent of Emerson's influence has been obscured by Whitman's desire in his old age not to appear to have been too indebted to anyone. In his open letter to Emerson, which appeared in the second (1856) edition, though not subsequently, Whitman did not hesitate to address him as 'Master'. Speaking of 'that new moral American continent without which, I see, the physical continent remained incomplete,' he said: 'Those shores you found. I say you have led the States there – have led me there.' Long afterwards he told his disciples that he was referring to the experience of having read Emerson after receiving his tribute to the first edition of the *Leaves*, but a more likely account would seem to be the one he gave to J. T. Trowbridge. In this version, based on a conversation in 1860 – though not printed until after Whitman's death – the poet 'freely admitted that he could never have written his poems if he had not first "come to himself", and that Emerson helped him to "find himself". I asked him if he thought he would have come to himself without that help. He said, "Yes, but it would have taken longer."' Here Whitman dated the fecund reading to the summer of 1854 when he had been working at his trade of carpenter and had carried a book with him in his lunch pail. One day it 'chanced to be a volume of Emerson; and from that time he took with him no other writer.' As we know, he had been at least acquainted with Emerson's ideas for some years before that, and their working in him may well have been a slower fermentation. He gave his own characteristic expression to the process: 'I was simmering, simmering, simmering; Emerson brought me to a boil.'

It is not hard to find, for what they are worth, passages in Whitman running parallel to most of Emerson's major convictions about the nature of art. But it would always be salutary to head them with these two from *Self-Reliance* and *Song of Myself*: 'Suppose you should contradict yourself; what then? . . . With consistency a great soul has simply nothing to do'; and

Do I contradict myself?
Very well then I contradict myself,
(I am large, I contain multitudes.)

At the end of a long paragraph of appreciation of Emerson that Bucke places around 1850, Whitman had already observed that 'there is hardly a proposition in Emerson's poems or prose which you cannot find the opposite of in some other place.' Nevertheless, the main contours of Emerson's doctrine of expression, as we have seen it develop, are unmistakable, and unmistakably Whitman's as well. They can both compress it into headlines: Emerson, 'By God, it is in me, and must come forth of me'; Whitman, 'Walt, you contain enough, why don't you let it out then?' Again, whole essays of Emerson's, notably that on 'The Poet', speak eloquently about the very things from which Whitman made his poetry. The two share the same view of the poet as inspired seer, of his dependence for his utterance upon his moments of inner illumination. Yet looking back over forty years, though Whitman reaffirmed that his last word would be 'loyal, loyal', he admitted that Emerson's work had latterly seemed to him 'pretty thin', 'always a *make*, never an unconscious *growth*', and 'some ways short of earth'.

Whitman's language is more earthy because he was aware, in a way that distinguished him not merely from Emerson but from every other writer of the day, of the power of sex. In affirming natural passion to be 'the enclosing basis of everything', he spoke of its sanity, of the sacredness of the human body, using specifically religious terms: 'we were all lost without redemption, except we retain the sexual fibre of things.' In defending his insistence on this element in his poems (1856), he made clear his understanding of its immediate bearing upon a living speech: 'To the lack of an avowed, empowered, unabashed development of sex (the only salvation for the same), and to the fact of speakers and writers fraudulently assuming as always dead what every one knows to be always alive, is attributable the remarkable non-personality and indistinctness of modern productions in books.' Continuing in this vein he made almost the same observations about conventional society as were later to be expressed by Henry Adams, who, incidentally, found Whitman to be the only American writer who had drawn upon the dynamic force of sex 'as every classic had always done'. Both were agreed, though the phrasing here is Whitman's, that particularly among the so-called cultivated class the neuter gender prevailed, and that 'if the dresses were changed, the men might easily pass for women and the women for men'.

Emerson never gave up deploring the want of male principle in our literature, but one reason why it remained remote from his own pages is contained in his pronouncement (1834): 'I believe in the existence of the material world as the expression of the spiritual or real.' The continuation of his thought reveals the difference of his emphasis from that of the poet of *Crossing Brooklyn Ferry*: 'and so look with a quite comic and condescending interest upon the show of Broadway with the air of an old gentleman when he says, "Sir, I knew your father." Is it not forever the aim and endeavor of the real to embody itself in the phenomenal?' No matter how happily inconsistent Emerson might be on other matters, this basic position of the idealist was one from which he never departed. Whitman was far less consistent in his consideration of the relation between body and soul. He was impressed by a line of John Sterling's, which was also a favorite of Emerson's, 'Still lives the song tho' Regnar dies.' Whitman added this gloss to it: 'The word is become flesh.' Just what he implied in talking about language as incarnation, and how he diverged from Emerson, can be followed most briefly in his own words.

In the manuscript draft for the opening section of *Song of Myself*, he announced the equalitarian inclusiveness that was destined always to be part of his desire:

And I say that the soul is not greater than the body,
And I say that the body is not greater than the soul.

However, that arbitrary equilibrium between the two is far less characteristic of his accents of most intimate discovery than his exultant reckless feeling in *Children of Adam* that the body 'includes and is the soul',

And if the body were not the soul, what is the soul?

But in different moods, as in *A Song of Joys*, he veers towards the other pole and seems loosely to approximate Blake in saying that the real life of his senses transcends his senses and flesh, that it is not his material eyes that finally see, or his material body that finally loves. However, he does not pursue this strain very long, and says more usually that the soul achieves its 'identity' through the act of observing, loving, and absorbing concrete objects:

We realize the soul only by you, you faithful solids and fluids.

This particular kind of material ideality, suggestive in general of Fichte's, remains his dominant thought, so it is worth observing how he formulated it in one of his notebooks:

Most writers have disclaimed the physical world and they have
not over-estimated the other, or soul, but have under-estimated the
corporeal. How shall my eye separate the beauty of the blossoming
buckwheat field from the stalks and heads of tangible matter?
How shall I know what the life is except as I see it in the flesh?
I will not praise one without the other or any more than the other.
(*Complete Writings*, 1902, vol. IX,
p. 5)

In commenting on the mixture of his heritage, Whitman once remarked that 'like the Quakers, the Dutch are very practical and materialistic . . . but are terribly transcendental and cloudy too.' That mixture confronts and tantalizes you throughout his poetry. He is at his firmest when he says that 'imagination and actuality must be united'. But in spite of his enthusiasm for the natural sciences as well as for every other manifestation of progress, he never came very close to a scientific realism. When he enunciated, in the 1870s, that 'body and mind are one', he had then been led into this thought by his reading of – or about – the German metaphysicians. And he declared that 'only Hegel is fit for America', since in his system

'the human soul stands in the centre, and all the universes minister
to it'. Following the Civil War, and increasingly during the last
twenty years of his life, he kept saying that in his *Leaves*, 'One
deep purpose underlay the others – and that has been the religious
purpose.' He often posed variants of the question, 'If the spiritual is
not behind the material, to what purpose is the material?' Yet, even
then, his most natural way of reconciling the dichotomy between the
two elements, 'fused though antagonistic', was to reaffirm his earlier
anology: 'The Soul of the Universe is the Male and genital master and
the impregnating and animating spirit – Physical matter is Female and
Mother and waits . . .'

No arrangement or rearrangement of Whitman's thoughts on this
or any other subject can resolve the paradoxes or discover in them a
fully coherent pattern. He was incapable of sustained logic, but that
should not blind the reader into impatient rejection of the ebb and
flow of his antitheses. They possess a loose dialectic of their own, and
a clue of how to find it is provided by Engels' discussion of Feuerbach:
'One knows that these antitheses have only a relative validity; that
that which is recognized now as true has also its latent false side which
will later manifest itself, just as that which is now regarded as false has
also its true side by virtue of which it could previously have been
regarded as true.' Whitman's ability to make a synthesis in his poems
of the contrasting elements that he calls body and soul may serve as a
measure of his stature as a poet. When his words adhere to concrete
experience and yet are bathed in imagination, his statements become
broadly representative of humanity:

I am she who adorn'd herself and folded her hair expectantly,
My truant lover has come, and it is dark.
                                    (*The Sleepers*)

When he fails to make that synthesis, his language can break into the
extremes noted by Emerson when he called it 'a remarkable mixture
of the *Bhagavad Gita* and the *New York Herald*'. The incongruous
lengths to which Whitman was frequently carried in each direction
shows how hard a task he undertook. On the one hand, his desire to
grasp American facts could lead him beyond slang into the rawest
jargon, the journalese of the day. On the other, his attempts to pass
beyond the restrictions of language into the atmosphere it could

suggest often produced only the barest formulas. His inordinate and grotesque failures in both directions throw into clearer light his rare successes, and the fusion upon which they depend.

The slang that he relished as providing more fun than 'the books of all "the American humorists"' was what he heard in the ordinary talk of 'a gang of laborers, rail-road men, miners, drivers, or boatmen', in their tendency 'to approach a meaning not directly and squarely' but by the circuitous routes of lively fancy. This tendency expressed itself in their fondness for nicknames like Old Hickory, or Wolverines, or Suckers, or Buckeyes. Their inventiveness had sowed the frontier with many a Shirttail Bend and Toenail Lake. Current evasions of the literal transformed a horsecar conductor into a 'snatcher', straight whisky into 'barefoot', and codfish balls into 'sleeve buttons'. But even though Whitman held such slang to be the source of all that was poetical in human utterance, he was aware that its fermentation was often hasty and frothy, and, except for occasional friendly regional epithets like Hoosiers or Kanucks, he used it only sparingly in his poems. Indeed, in some notes during the period of the gestation of his first Leaves, he advised himself to use 'common idioms and phrases – Yankeeisms and vulgarisms – cant expressions, when very pat only'. In consequence, the diction of his poetry is seldom as unconventional as that in the advice he gave himself for an essay on contemporary writing: 'Bring in a sockdolager on the Dickens-fawners.' He gave examples of 'fierce words' in the Primer – 'skulk', 'shyster', 'doughface', 'mean cuss', 'backslider', 'lickspittle' – and sometimes cut loose in the talk that Traubel reported. But only on the rare occasions when he felt scorn did he introduce into his poems any expressions as savagely untrammelled as

This now is too lamentable a face for a man,
Some abject louse asking leave to be, cringing for it,
Some milk-nosed maggot blessing what lets it wrig to its hole.
(Faces, 2)

By contrast his most characteristic colloquialisms are easy and relaxed, as when he said 'howdy' to Traubel and told him that he felt 'flirty' or 'hunkydory', or fell into slang with no self-consciousness, but with the careless aplomb of a man speaking the language most natural to him:

I reckon I am their boss, and they make me a pet besides.
                              (*The Sleepers*)

And will go gallivant with the light and air myself.
                              (*The Sleepers*)

Shoulder your duds, dear son, and I will mine.
                              (*Song of Myself*, 46)

Earth! you seem to look for something at my hands,
Say, old top-knot, what do you want?
                              (*Song of Myself*, 40)

One of Whitman's demands in the *Primer* was that words should be brought into literature from factories and farms and trades, for he knew that 'around the markets, among the fish-smacks, along the wharves, you hear a thousand words, never yet printed in the repertoire of any lexicon.' What resulted was sometimes as mechanical as the long lists in *A Song for Occupations*, but his resolve for inclusiveness also produced dozens of snap-shot impressions as accurate as

The butcher-boy puts off his killing-clothes, or sharpens his knife
    at the stall in the market,
I loiter enjoying his repartee and his shuffle and break-down.
                              (*Song of Myself*, 12)

Watching men in action called out of him some of his most fluid phrases, which seem to bathe and surround the objects they describe – as this, of the blacksmiths:

The *lithe sheer* of their waists plays even with their massive arms.
                              (*Song of Myself*, 12)

Or this:

The negro holds firmly the reins of his four horses, the block
    swags underneath on its tied-over chain.
                              (*Song of Myself*, 13)

Or a line that is itself a description of the very process by which he enfolds such movement:

In me the caresser of life wherever moving, backward as well as
   forward *sluing*.

(*Song of Myself*, 13)

At times he produced suggestive coinages of his own:

The blab of the pave, tires of carts, sluff of boot-soles, talk of the
   promenaders.

(*Song of Myself*, 8)

Yet he is making various approaches to language even in that one
line. 'Blab' and 'sluff' have risen from his desire to suggest actual
sounds, but 'promenaders', which also sounds well, has clearly been
employed for that reason alone since it does not belong to the talk
of any American folk. 'Pave' instead of 'pavement' is the kind of
bastard word that, to use another, Whitman liked to 'promulge'.
Sometimes it is hard to tell whether such words sprang from intention
or ignorance, particularly in view of the appearance of 'semitic' in
place of 'seminal' ('semitic muscle,' 'semitic milk') in both the 1855
preface and the first printing of *A Woman Waits for Me*. Most frequently his hybrids take the form of the free substitution of one part
of speech for another – sometimes quite effectively ('the soothe of the
waves'), sometimes less so (she that 'birth'd him').

   Although it has been estimated that Whitman had a vocabulary of
more than thirteen thousand words, of which slightly over half were
used by him only once, the number of his authentic coinages is not
very large. Probably the largest group is composed of his agent-
nouns, which is not surprising for a poet who was so occupied with
types and classes of men and women. Unfortunately these also furnish
some of the ugliest-sounding words in his pages, 'originatress',
'revoltress', 'dispensatress', which have hardly been surpassed even
in the age of the realtor and the beautician. He was luckier with an
occasional abstract noun like 'presidentiad', though this is offset by
a needless monstrosity like 'savantism'. The one kind of coinage
where his ear was listening sensitively is in such compounds as 'the
transparent green-shine' of the water around the naked swimmer in
I Sing the Body Electric, or that evoking the apples hanging 'indolent-
ripe' in *Halcyon Days*.

   His belief in the need to speak not merely for Americans but for the workers of all lands seems to have given the impetus for his odd habit of introducing random words from other languages, to the point of talking about 'the ouvrier class'! He took from the Italian chiefly the terms of the opera, also 'viva', 'romanza', and even 'ambulanza'. From the Spanish he was pleased to borrow the orotund way of naming his countrymen 'Americanos', while the occasional circulation of Mexican dollars in the States during the eighteen-forties may have given him his word 'Libertad'. His favorite 'camerado', an archaic English version of the Spanish 'camarada', seems most likely to have come to him from the pages of the Waverley novels, of which he had been an enthusiastic reader in his youth. But the smattering of French which he picked up on his trip to New Orleans, and which constituted the most extensive knowledge that he ever was to have of another tongue, furnished him with the majority of his borrowings. It allowed him to talk of his 'amour' and his 'eleves', of a 'soiree' or an 'accoucheur', of 'trottoirs' and 'feuillage' and 'delicatesse'; to say that his were not 'the songs of an ennuyeed person', or to shout, 'Allons! from all formules! . . . Allons! the road is before us!' Frequently he was speaking no language, as when he proclaimed himself 'no dainty dolce affetuoso'. But he could go much farther than that into a foreign jargon in his desire to 'eclaircise the myths Asiatic' in his Passage to India, or to fulfil 'the rapt promises and luminè of seers'. He could address God, with ecstatic and monumental tastelessness, as 'thou reservoir'.

Many of these are samples of the confused American effort to talk big by using high-sounding terms with only the vaguest notion of their original meaning. The resultant fantastic transformations have enlivened every stage of our history, from the frontiersman's determination to twist his tongue around the syllables of the French settlement at Chemincouvert, Ark., which ended up with the name being turned into Smackover, down to Ring Lardner's dumb nurse who thought people were calling her 'a mormon or something'. In Whitman's case, the fact that he was a reader and so could depend upon letters as well as upon sounds overheard kept him from drifting to such gorgeous lengths. His transformations retain some battered semblance of the original word, which, with the happy pride of the half-educated in the learned term, he then deployed grandly for purposes of his own. Often the attraction for him in the French words ran counter to the identification he usually desired between the word and the thing, since it sprang from intoxication with the mere sound. You can observe the same tendency in some of the jotted lists of his notebooks, 'Cantaloupe. Muskmelon. Cantabile. Cacique City', or in his shaping such a generalized description of the earth as 'O vast rondure swimming in space'. When caught up by the desire to include the whole universe in his embrace, he could be swept far into the intense inane, chanting in *Night on the Prairies* of 'immortality and peace':

How plenteous! how spiritual! how resumé!

The two diverging strains in his use of language were with him to the end, for he never outgrew his tendency to lapse from specific images into undifferentiated and lifeless abstractions, as in the closing phrase of this description of his grandfather: 'jovial, red, stout, with sonorous voice and characteristic physiognomy'. In some of his latest poems, *Sands at Seventy*, he could still be satisfied with the merest rhetoric:

Of ye, O God, Life, Nature, Freedom, Poetry.
                    (*A Carol Closing Sixty-Nine*)

In his fondness for all his *Leaves*, he seems never to have perceived what we can note in the two halves of a single line,

I concentrate toward them that are nigh, I wait on the door slab,
                    (*Song of Myself*, 51)

– the contrast between the clumsy stilted opening and the simple close. The total pattern of his speech is, therefore, difficult to chart, since it is formed both by the improviser's carelessness about words and by the kind of attention to them indicated in his telling Burroughs that he had been 'searching for twenty-five years for the word to express what the twilight note of the robin meant to him'. He also engaged in endless minute revisions of his poems, the purpose of which is often baffling. Although sometimes serving to fuse the syllables into an ampler rhythm, as in the transformation of

Out of the rocked cradle

into one of his most memorable opening lines; they seem almost as likely to add up to nothing more than the dozens of minor substitutions in *Salut au Monde*, which leave it the flat and formless catalogue that it was in the beginning.

In a warm appreciation of Burns in *November Boughs*, Whitman said that 'his brightest hit is his use of the Scotch patois, so full of terms flavored like wild fruits or berries'. Thinking not only of Burns he relished a special charm in 'the very neglect, unfinish, careless nudity', which were not to be found in more polished language and verse. But his suggested comparison between the Scotch poet and himself would bring out at once the important difference that Whitman is not using anything like a folk-speech. Indeed, his phrasing is generally remote from any customary locutions of the sort that he jotted down as notes for one unwritten poem. This was to have been based on a free rendering of local native calls, such as 'Here goes your fine fat oysters – Rock Point oysters – here they go.' When put beside such natural words and cadences, Whitman's usual diction is clearly not that of a countryman but of what he called himself, 'a jour printer'. In its curious amalgamation of homely and simple usage with half-remembered terms he read once somewhere, and with casual inventions of the moment, he often gives the impression of using a language not quite his own. In his determination to strike up for a new world, he deliberately rid himself of foreign models. But, so far as his speech is concerned, this was only very partially possible, and consequently Whitman reveals the peculiarly American combination of a childish freshness with a mechanical and desiccated repetition of book terms that had had significance for the more complex civilization in which they had had their roots and growth. The freshness has come, as it did to Huck Finn, through instinctive rejection of the authority of those terms, in Whitman's reaction against what he called Emerson's cold intellectuality: 'Suppose his books becoming absorbed, the permanent chyle of American general and particular character – what a well-washed and grammatical, but bloodless and helpless race we should turn out!'

Yet the broken chrysalis of the old restrictions still hangs about Whitman. Every page betrays that his language is deeply ingrained with the educational habits of a middle-class people who put a fierce emphasis on the importance of the written word. His speech did not spring primarily from contact with the soil, for though his father was a descendant of Long Island farmers, he was also a citizen of the age of reason, an acquaintance and admirer of Tom Paine. Nor did Whitman himself develop his diction as Thoreau did, by the slow absorption through every pore of the folkways of a single spot of earth. He was attracted by the wider sweep of the city, and though his language is a natural product, it is the natural product of a Brooklyn journalist of the 1840s who had previously been a country schoolteacher and a carpenter's helper, and who had finally felt an irresistible impulse to be a poet.

(517–32)

Lionel Trilling

'Sermon on a Text from Whitman', *Nation*, vol. 160 1945

Democratic Vistas is Walt Whitman's most important single work in prose, yet it has never been familiar to American readers. For this there is some reason. The large pamphlet is the rather awkward amalgamation of two earlier pamphlets; it is often eloquent, but it is all too often marked by that dull explosiveness of syntax which Whitman found appropriate to his prophetic moods in prose; it is full of half-educated words and phrases – we hear of 'the ostent', of 'orbic bards', of 'literatuses', of 'stores of cephalic knowledge', of the 'vertebration of the manly and womanly personalism', jargon bad enough in itself, ridiculous in the man who made so much fuss about literary pretentiousness in others, but forgivable in the genius who was trying, outside the established intellectual order, to see the future and the truth. For all its faults of manner, the little book is great; and in any discussion of the relation of American literature to American life it is a central document.

As its name suggests, *Democratic Vistas* is about the future of democracy. The future of democracy is made to depend, in a sense, on literature. I say 'in a sense' because in point of fact Whitman believes that democracy depends on a certain condition of mind or state of being which is not induced by literature alone, but here he is concerned to urge upon literature its duty of fostering this crucial emotion.

Published in 1871, the pamphlet is in part the expression of Whitman's disappointment after his nearly mystical experience of the Civil War. To Whitman, his nation had been justified by the war. The personal qualities of the young soldiers he had nursed in the Washington hospitals seemed to him to have proved what he called the 'religious' value of democracy. In terms of human quality – and for Whitman this was the only criterion – the American experiment was a success. Yet the years after the war terribly denied that success. Whitman can admire the glow and bustle of national expansion, but he sees that behind the façade there is reason for dejection and despair. 'Society in these states,' he says, 'is cankered, crude, superstitious, rotten.' He sees a lack of all 'moral conscientious fiber'. He sees hypocrisy, superciliousness, a false intellectuality; puny bodies; bad manners; tepid amours – 'the men believe not in the women, nor the women in the men.' The business classes are depraved, the class of civil servants no less so. It is in *Democratic Vistas* that Whitman makes the often-quoted remark about the grandeur of a well-contested American election, but now he feels that politics is no longer spontaneous and representative – 'these savage, wolfish parties alarm me.'

To find a way of national salvation he turns to literature. In part what he wants from literature is what every nationalist critic wants; it is what Goethe in his nationalist moments wanted – a national 'myth', a moral identity for the country, what Whitman himself calls in a hideous but telling phrase, 'an American stock personality'.

But Whitman wants something more. He is in the great romantic tradition, and he shares as fully as possible the large romantic belief in the political mission of the 'literatus'. With affinities to Wordsworth, Shelley, Carlyle, and Arnold, his view of the relation of literature to politics is closest to Schiller's. I do not know whether he had read Schiller's *Letters on Art* – and certainly his statement is far less philosophically elaborate than Schiller's and no doubt the better for that – but like Schiller he conceives of literature as the intermediary between the necessary authority of government and the ideal condition of human freedom.

We must remember that for Whitman authority was no bad thing. He says that democracy may be defined by its free diversity, but he is not so naïve as to think that free diversity can exist without authority. If *Democratic Vistas* begins with ideas derived from John Stuart Mill's

On Liberty, it goes on to speak handsomely of Carlyle's 'Shooting Niagara', that desperate prediction of the anarchy democracy may bring.

The whole pamphlet is a tissue of such contradictions, or, rather, modulations. Whitman is always showing himself as a more complex intelligence than perhaps he wanted to be, or than many of his readers want him to be. We often hear that Whitman's thought is anti-dualistic. In actual fact, he lived in a world of dualisms – body-soul, past-future, mass-individual, liberty-authority, life-death. His characteristic way of thought is to support one term of a dualism, then hasten to protect the other. For him the oppositions, although antagonistic to each other, are not negations of each other. In more senses than one Whitman's view of the world was dialectical: the world as he knew it was the dialogue of the disagreement between the great antagonistic principles. In *Democratic Vistas* what concerns him is the antagonism between authority, the representation of the mass, the average, and freedom or individualism, what he calls 'personalism'. Democracy can exist only if authority can organize diversity; but democracy dies if authority encroaches on personalism. It is here, at this moment of delicate balance, that the call goes out to the poet.

It is not possible in short space to suggest the full richness and complication of *Democratic Vistas* or even to paraphrase all that Whitman says in it about literature. It is important to remark, however, how subtle a view Whitman took of the relation of literature to politics. He believes that literature is more important than congresses or acts of state, for literature affects the depths of a nation's scarcely conscious soul. He thinks that literature must deal with 'the people', yet he does not think that it does its proper work by dealing directly with politics or by exposing social conditions. Indeed, Whitman is very firm against what he calls 'the growing excess and arrogance of realism'. The true poet, he says, works by 'analogies', by 'curious removes, indirections'. In the face of the common belief that Whitman is the ancestor of the social realists, these words suggest that Marianne Moore, much more than Carl Sandburg, is his true descendant.

I said that Whitman made democracy depend on a certain condition of mind or state of being for which literature had a responsibility. 'There is, in sanest hours, a consciousness, a thought that rises, independent, lifted out from all else, calm, like the stars, shining eternal. This is the thought of identity – yours for you, whoever you are, as mine for me. Miracle of miracles, beyond statement, most spiritual of earth's dreams, yet hardest basic fact, and only entrance to all facts.' This, for Whitman, is the emotion which guarantees democracy.

It is worth observing that Whitman talks about personal *identity*, not about personal *value*. The sense of personal value is something very different. It suggests the comparative, the competitive – all the horrors of the struggle for status into which democracy, as we know it, corrupts itself. What Whitman is talking about does not permit comparison – it is the single absolute in the democratic conception.

Elsewhere in the pamphlet Whitman speaks of this sense of identity as the 'centripetal isolation of a human being in himself', and goes on: 'Whatever the name, its acceptance and thorough infusion through the organization of political commonalty now shooting Aurora-like about the world, are of utmost importance, as the principle itself is needed for life's sake. It forms, in a sort, or is to form, the compensating balance wheel of the successful working machinery of aggregate America.'

It lies as he says, 'beyond statement', but he knows what it is, and he knows what it does, and he knows how it can be generated. Literature can generate it. But not literature only. Whitman himself got it from Italian opera, or from crossing Brooklyn Ferry, or from certain aspects of the sea. Mark Twain got it from the Mississippi and from Lake Tahoe, Thoreau from the woods – in the American experience it is commonly given by a certain relation to nature. In the human experience generally it is given by the full awareness and valuation of the biological crises – birth, love, death. Whitman, the poet of vital affirmation, got it perhaps most intensely from contemplating death. He thought that the coming American poets must have a deep consciousness of death. Whitman's very best poems are personal in theme; of these the two most remarkable are about death; and of these two even the great lament for Lincoln, *When Lilacs Last in the Dooryard Bloom'd*, is less fine than *Out of the Cradle Endlessly Rocking*, of which an English critic has said that it is 'the world's supreme song of separation'.

If you pick up Samuel Sillen's recent selection from Whitman – it is called *Walt Whitman, Poet of American Democracy* – you will not find *Out of the Cradle Endlessly Rocking*. Nor can this exclusion be accounted for by lack of space – not when Dr Sillen gives us thirty-five pages of his own ideas about Whitman to 125 pages of the poet himself. You will not find it because Dr Sillen 'aims to present Whitman as a living force in the war against fascist barbarism as well as in the peace which America and the other United Nations seek to achieve through unconditional victory'. And Dr Sillen goes on: 'Only a volume that is politically partisan in this sense could be truly representative of Whitman.' To demonstrate an explicit partisanship Dr Sillen selects much of Whitman's work that is of merely indifferent quality. We conclude that what is 'truly representative' of a poet need not be his best work.

It is in line with Dr Sillen's own political partisanship that he emphasizes the interest of the Russians in Whitman and Whitman's own considerable interest in Russia. This reciprocal interest undoubtedly has its significance; still, a less partisan editor would have kept it in mind that the French and German feeling for Whitman has been as notable as the Russian; or, remembering that Whitman's interest in Russia was shared by other Americans (Henry Adams and Brooks Adams among them), remembering too that Whitman could say in his large loose way, 'The Russians I look upon as overgrown boys and girls', a more critical editor would have used a tone a little less like that of a church father finding in Virgil's Fourth Eclogue the prophecy of Christ. But Dr Sillen wants a Whitman who is not only the poet of American democracy but also the poet of Russian nationalism and internationalism. He wants a Whitman canon that coincides with the ideals of current Russian thought. Whitman on the size of the country, on national growth, national loyalty, devotion to a leader, sexual acceptance, responsibility for oppressed minorities, confidence in a bulking material future, Whitman patting his country on its broad back – this is the Whitman Dr Sillen wants, even though it is not always the poetically best Whitman.

And this Whitman Dr Sillen 'arranges' – but only 125 pages of him in a format that is most prodigal of space: the kind of arrangement Dr Sillen wants requires a minimum of the poet. The arrangement is made 'logically' in order to 'help clarify [Whitman's] basic interests and attitudes'. This language of a sociology major is perhaps odd when used of a poet who was concerned with the arrangement of his own works, although not much concerned with logic. But with such language Dr Sillen cuts Whitman down to size. Thus, if Whitman says, 'Do I contradict myself?|Very well then I contradict myself|(I am large, I contain multitudes),' Dr Sillen, with a proper disgust at inconsistency, bustles to assure us that Whitman doesn't *really* contradict himself – this is Whitman for the peace table, at which, as we know, contradictions will be forbidden – and to comfort us with the thought that 'the apparent contradictions may be united'.

And 'united' they are, just as if they were nations. For example, Dr Sillen wishes Whitman to be as pious as himself in the matter of science and materialism. He quotes: 'I accept Reality and dare not question it,|Materialism first and last imbuing.|Hurrah for positive science! long live exact demonstration!' Perfectly characteristic – but Whitman could also say, 'To the cry, now victorious – the cry of sense, science, flesh, incomes, farms, merchandise, logic, intellectual demonstrations . . . fear not, my brethren, my sisters, to sound out with equally determined voice, that conviction brooding within the recesses of every envisioned soul – illusions, apparitions, figments all!' Dr Sillen is not unaware that Whitman made statements like this second one. Indeed, his awareness constrains him to qualify his own remarks about Whitman's materialism. But he makes his qualifications in this way: 'This is not to suggest that Whitman was a consistent philosophical materialist, for he never did cast off the idealistic elements of his thinking inherited from Emerson and Hegel.'

Never did cast off – as if this aspect of Whitman's thought were a dead skin, as if everything that was characteristic of his mind, including the hurrah for positive science, did not arise from his idealistic metaphysics. Democracy certainly does not depend on philosophical idealism, but Whitman's own democratic impulse did spring from his idealistic philosophy. The 'I' of Whitman – and this explains why it is often hard to identify ourselves with it as we read – is not always a person: it is often the personal image of the idealistic absolute. That is why Whitman contains multitudes – and contradictions. Walt Whitman, democracy, and the absolute are images of each other. They contain everything, even what Dr Sillen with a quaint severity calls 'devotees of a life relieved of social discipline' – a strange word, that 'relieved': is social discipline then so burdensome? – and they contain both the moment when we love science and material things and the moment when we are not satisfied by them. They contain both our impulse of subordination to the interests of the mass of men and our impulse of personal identity, each giving health and value to the other.

One's-self I sing, a simple separate person,
Yet utter the word Democratic, the word En-Masse
                            (*One's-Self I Sing*)

These are the first lines of *Leaves of Grass* and they are the first lines of Dr Sillen's selection. But Dr Sillen's response is all to the second line. En-Masse delights him but not the simple separate person. As a consequence he omits from his selection Whitman's finest expression of identity, the great elegy *Out of the Cradle Endlessly Rocking*.

I am certainly not trying to take Dr Sillen to task simply for omitting a single poem, no matter how fine. Nor am I trying to say that Whitman is not political or has no political relevance now, for I think quite the contrary is true. All over the world people and peoples, where they have not lost their lives, have lost their sense of personal identity to an extent painful beyond imagination. If a poet can possibly help restore it to them, Whitman is that poet. And as peace seems to approach, we, who will have some part of their fates in our hands, might well refresh ourselves on the nature of the hardest basic fact and entrance to all facts. Further, if the Russians now read Whitman avidly, as Dr Sillen says they do, what a good sign it is, not merely flattering that a great ally should read our national poet but reassuring to those people, and they are numerous, who have kept some reserve about the Russian polity on the ground of its insufficiency of 'personalism'. Yes, Whitman is indeed a political poet, and relevant now.

And so I could understand it very well if Dr Sillen, making a selection of Whitman with reference not only to America but also to Russia, had pointed to *Out of the Cradle* and said, 'We in our democracy have had many failures, as no doubt you in yours. But we have had our successes too, and this is one – this poet of democracy who can feel this way about life, with this intensity, this ecstasy of love and loss, affirming in the song of our American mocking-bird our highest feelings about human life.'

Had Dr Sillen done this he would have been truly a political man, as Whitman was. But he is only a 'political' man; he is unable to suppose that the Whitman of contradictions, of deepest simple personal feeling, can have reference either to American or to Russian democracy.

Dr Sillen is committed to a political tradition of culture, which has, indeed, never looked with favor on the emotion that Whitman thought came in sanest moments, the emotion on which, as he believed, democracy depended. And Dr Sillen's tradition of culture has of course had a considerable success, especially lately, when it has become demure and non-agitational, adopting – as in Dr Sillen's introduction – the educational tone of those old professors of ours who knew what they were doing when they put us to sleep so that they could speak to our dreams. The chief reason for the success of Dr Sillen's tradition is that all of us, latently and unconsciously, fear in ourselves the sense of identity, and wish to lose it.

The signs of this fear may be variously found. What seems now to mark our ultimate political hope is a willingness to give up all concern with the internal *quality* of the simple separate person and an unwillingness to believe that the adventurous expressions of art have an intimate relation to the adventure of political freedom. For instance, J. Donald Adams, with an eye to democracy, tells us that books of the future will take a certain reassuring shape, specifications to be provided by what he calls 'the many'. Or the liberal New York *Post* assures its readers that they do right to sneer at James Joyce: he is hard to read and does not advocate social legislation for the people. Or *PM*, for many the palladium of progressive thought, gives but grudging space to written literature, on the theory that the people are not interested in it. I remember the fishy – not hostile but perplexed – stare with which a famous liberal editor received my remark that culture was integral with politics; the gist of his polite reply was that some day we would finish with politics and *then* we would have literature. Of my friends of political good-will it might be said that their tolerant indifference to literature is in proportion to the personal salvation they hope to derive from their feelings of political good-will.

Well, political and social contradictions being now what they are, it is understandable that we should begin to fear even those vital contradictions, incident upon being human, which literature expresses – and why, like Dr Sillen, we should suppose that they must be brushed aside for something we no doubt call a constructive point of view. For none of us quite likes himself these days, and so we are worried when a poet speaks of the sense of identity as being the miracle of miracles and also the hardest basic fact. Yet it is we, who despise ourselves and who fear the very thing that our democratic poet called the product of 'sanest moments' – it is we who feel the responsibility of spreading democracy throughout the world. If there was ever a 'contradiction' to scare us, here indeed is one within ourselves.

In modern times insurgent poets from Wordsworth through Baudelaire through Joyce have dealt in 'contradictions' which they have expressed by paradox, strangeness, and even 'absurdity'. Their purpose has always been ultimately a political one; they wanted to shock us out of the way of seeing forced upon us by the political past and the institutional present. They have appealed beyond the institutional barrier to the sense of identity, knowing it to be spunky, alive, resistant – the basic fact and the hardest, hard enough to be the touchstone of every idea. Whitman was such a poet. I have mentioned Marianne Moore as such another. E. E. Cummings, not now in general esteem with people of high political feeling, is such another. There are many more. If I had the job of instructing anybody in democracy, I would send him first to the generous pages of these poets and say, 'There is the hardest basic political democratic fact.' And then I would point to Dr Sillen's volume – not because it is in itself important and decisive but because it represents much that is – and say, 'And there, as you will now quickly see, is its negation.'

(215–20)

Yvor Winters

from 'The Significance of *The Bridge* by Hart Crane, or What Are We to Think of Professor X?', *In Defense of Reason* 1947

The ideas of Emerson were, as I have said, merely the commonplaces of the Romantic movement; but his language was that of the Calvin-

istic pulpit. He was able to present the anarchic and anti-moral
doctrines of European Romanticism in a language which for two
hundred years had been capable of arousing the most intense and the
most obscure emotions of the American people. He could speak of
matter as if it were God; of the flesh as if it were spirit; of emotion as
if it were Divine Grace; of impulse as if it were conscience; and of
automatism as if it were the mystical experience. And he was addressing an audience which, like himself, had been so conditioned by two
hundred years of Calvinistic discipline, that the doctrines confused
nothing, at the outset, except the mind: Emerson and his contemporaries, in surrendering to what they took for impulse, were
governed by New England habit; they mistook second nature for
nature. They were moral parasites upon a Christian doctrine which
they were endeavoring to destroy. The same may be said of Whitman,
Emerson's most influential disciple, except that Whitman came
closer to putting the doctrine into practice in the matter of literary
form: whereas Emerson, as a poet, imitated the poets of the early
seventeenth century, whose style had been formed in congruence with
the doctrines of Aristotle, Aquinas, and Hooker.

I cannot summarize the opinions of Whitman in this essay as fully
as I have summarized those of Emerson. I must ask my readers to
accept on faith, until they find it convenient to check the matter, the
generally accepted view that the main ideas of Whitman are identical
with those of Emerson. Whitman believed this; Emerson believed it;
and scholarly specialists in both men believe it. I wish to quote a part –
only a small part–of Professor Floyd Stovall's summary of Whitman's
views. Professor Stovall is a reputable scholar. Every detail which he
gives is referred by a footnote to its source in Whitman. I believe that
his summary, purely as a summary, is accurate. He writes:

He saw that creation is a continuous organic growth, not a work
that is begun or finished, and the creative force is the procreative
impulse in nature. *Progress is the infallible consequence* of this creative
force in nature, *and though the universe is perfect at any given
moment, it is growing constantly toward higher orders of perfection.*
If new forms are needed they are produced as surely as if designed
from the beginning. 'When the materials are all prepared and
ready, the architects shall appear.' Every moment is a

consummation developed from endless past consummations and preparing for endless consummations in the future . . .

Nature is not only perfect but also divine. Indeed it is perfect because it is divine. There is no division in nature . . . no separate deity looking down from some detached heaven upon a temporal world that his hand created and may destroy at pleasure. That which is at all is of God . . . *Whatever is is well, and whatever will be will be well* . . . God is in every object, because every object has an eternal soul and passes eventually into spiritual results . . .

The seed of perfection is in each person, but *no matter how far he advances, his desire for further advancement remains insatiable.*

The final purpose of this restlessness of spirit in man and nature is the continuity of life. Nothing is real or valid, not even God, except in relation to this purpose . . . Something, Whitman perceives, drives man forward along the way to perfection, which passes through birth, life, death, and burial; he does not fully understand what it is, but he knows that it is form, union, plan – that it is happiness and eternal life.

Whitman calls it soul, this mysterious something, strangely linked with the procreative impulse, that gives form and continuity to the life of nature and impels man toward happiness and immortality . . .

The ignorance both of philosophy and theology exhibited in such ideas as these is sufficient to strike one with terror. But I must limit myself to only a few comments at the present moment. I wish to call attention especially to the passages which I have italicized: (1) 'Progress is the infallible consequence', or to put it more briefly, progress is infallible; (2) 'though the universe is perfect at any given moment, it is growing constantly toward higher orders of perfection'; (3) 'Whatever is is well, and whatever will be will be well'; and (4) 'No matter how far man advances, his desire for further advancement remains insatiable.'

I wish to insist on this: that it is impossible to speak of higher orders of perfection unless one can define what one means by the highest order and by the lowest order, and this Whitman does not venture to do. Higher and lower, better and worse, have no meaning except in relation to highest and lowest, best and worst. Since Whitman has identified God with the evolving (that is, with the changing) universe, he is unable to locate a concept of best or highest, toward which evolution is moving, for that concept would then be outside of God and would supersede God; it would be, in theological language, God's final cause; and such a concept would be nonsense. Whitman tells us that whatever happens to exist is perfect, but that any change is necessarily toward a 'higher' order of perfection. The practical effect of these notions is merely to deify change: change becomes good of necessity. We have no way of determining where we are going, but we should keep moving at all costs and as fast as possible; we have faith in progress. It seems to me unnecessary to dwell upon the dangers of such a concept.

Hart Crane was not born into the New England of Emerson, nor even into the New York of Whitman; he was born in 1899 in Cleveland, Ohio. The social restraints, the products of generations of religious discipline, which operated to minimize the influence of Romantic philosophy in the personal lives of Emerson and of Whitman, were at most only slightly operative in Crane's career. He was unfortunate in having a somewhat violent emotional constitution: his behavior on the whole would seem to indicate a more or less manic-depressive make-up, although this diagnosis is the post-mortem guess of an amateur, and is based on evidence which is largely hearsay. He was certainly homosexual, however, and he became a chronic and extreme alcoholic. I should judge that he cultivated these weaknesses on principle; in any event, it is well known that he cultivated them assiduously; and as an avowed Whitmanian, he would have been justified by his principles in cultivating all of his impulses. I saw Crane during the Christmas week of 1927, when he was approximately twenty-nine years old; his hair was graying, his skin had the dull red color with reticulated grayish traceries which so often goes with advanced alcoholism, and his ears and knuckles were beginning to look a little like those of a pugilist. About a year later he was deported from France as a result of his starting an exceptionally violent commotion in a bar-room and perhaps as a result of other activities. In 1932 he committed suicide by leaping from a steamer into the Caribbean Sea.

The doctrine of Emerson and Whitman, if really put into practice, should naturally lead to suicide: in the first place, if the impulses are indulged systematically and passionately, they can lead only to madness; in the second place, death, according to the doctrine, is not only a release from suffering but is also and inevitably the way to beatitude. There is no question, according to the doctrine, of moral preparation for salvation; death leads automatically to salvation. During the last year and a half of Crane's life, to judge from the accounts of those who were with him in Mexico, he must have been insane or drunk or both almost without interruption; but before this time he must have contemplated the possibilities of suicide. When his friend Harry Crosby committed suicide in one of the eastern cities, I wrote Crane a note of condolence and asked him to express my sympathy to Mrs Crosby. Crane replied somewhat casually that I need not feel disturbed about the affair, that he was fairly sure Crosby had regarded it as a great adventure.

In the course of my correspondence with Crane, I must somewhere have made a moralizing remark which I have now forgotten but of which Crane disapproved. I remember Crane's answer: he said that he had never in his life done anything of which he had been ashamed, and he said this not in anger, but in simple philosophical seriousness. This would be a sufficiently surprising remark from any son of Adam, but as one thinks of it and of Crane in retrospect, one can understand it, I believe, only in one way, as an assertion of religious faith, neither more nor less.

(587–90)

Randall Jarrell

'Some Lines from Whitman', *Poetry and the Age* 1953

Whitman, Dickinson, and Melville seem to me the best poets of the nineteenth century here in America. Melville's poetry has been grotesquely underestimated, but of course it is only in the last four or five years that it has been much read; in the long run, in spite of the awkwardness and amateurishness of so much of it, it will surely be thought well of. (In the short run it will probably be thought entirely too well of. Melville is a great poet only in the prose of *Moby Dick*.) Dickinson's poetry has been thoroughly read, and well though un-differentiatingly loved – after a few decades or centuries almost everybody will be able to see through Dickinson to her poems. But something odd has happened to the living changing part of Whitman's reputation: nowadays it is people who are not particularly interested in poetry, people who say that they read a poem for what it says, not for how it says it, who admire Whitman most. Whitman is often written about, either approvingly or disapprovingly, as if he were the Thomas Wolfe of nineteenth-century democracy, the hero of a de Mille movie about Walt Whitman. (People even talk about a war in which Walt Whitman and Henry James chose up sides, to begin with, and in which you and I will go on fighting till the day we die.) All this sort of thing, and all the bad poetry that there of course is in Whitman – for any poet has written enough bad poetry to scare away anybody – has helped to scare away from Whitman most 'serious readers of modern poetry'. They do not talk of his poems, as a rule, with any real liking or knowledge. Serious readers, people who are ashamed of not knowing all Hopkins by heart, are not at all ashamed to say, 'I don't really know Whitman very well.' This may harm Whitman in your eyes, they know, but that is a chance that poets have to take. Yet 'their' Hopkins, that good critic and great poet, wrote about Whitman, after seeing five or six of his poems in a newspaper review: 'I may as well say what I should not otherwise have said, that I always knew in my heart Walt Whitman's mind to be more like my own than any other man's living. As he is a very great scoundrel this is not a very pleasant confession.' And Henry James, the leader of 'their' side in that awful imaginary war of which I spoke, once read Whitman to Edith Wharton (much as Mozart used to imitate, on the piano, the organ) with such power and solemnity that both sat shaken and silent; it was after this reading that James expressed his regret at Whitman's 'too extensive acquaintance with the foreign languages'. Almost all the most 'original and advanced' poets and critics and readers of the last part of the nineteenth century thought Whitman as original and advanced as themselves, in manner as well as in matter. Can Whitman really be a sort of Thomas Wolfe or Carl Sandburg or Robinson Jeffers or Henry Miller – or a sort of Balzac of poetry, whose every part is crude but whose whole is somehow great? He is not, nor could he be; a poem, like Pope's spider, 'lives along the line', and all the dead lines in the world will not make one live poem. As Blake says, 'all sublimity is

founded on minute discrimination', and it is in these 'minute particulars' of Blake's that any poem has its primary existence.

To show Whitman for what he is one does not need to praise or
explain or argue, one needs simply to quote. He himself said, 'I and
mine do not convince by arguments, similes, rhymes,|We convince
by our presence.' Even a few of his phrases are enough to show us that
Whitman was no sweeping rhetorician, but a poet of the greatest
and oddest delicacy and originality and sensitivity, so far as words are
concerned. This is, after all, the poet who said, 'Blind loving wrestling
touch, sheath'd hooded sharp-tooth'd touch'; who said, 'Smartly
attired, countenance smiling, form upright, death under the breast-
bones, hell under the skull-bones'; who said, 'Agonies are one of
my changes of garments'; who saw grass as the 'flag of my disposition', saw 'the sharp-peak'd farmhouse, with its scallop'd scum and
slender shoots from the gutters', heard a plane's 'wild ascending lisp',
and saw and heard how at the amputation 'what is removed drops
horribly in a pail'. This is the poet for whom the sea was 'howler and
scooper of storms', reaching out to us with 'crooked inviting
fingers'; who went 'leaping chasms with a pike-pointed staff, clinging to topples of brittle and blue'; who, a runaway slave, saw how
'my gore dribs, thinn'd with the ooze of my skin'; who went 'litho-
graphing Kronos . . . buying drafts of Osiris'; who stared out at the
'little plentiful mannikins skipping around in collars and tail'd coat,|I
am aware who they are, (they are positively not worms or fleas).' For
he is, at his best, beautifully witty: he says gravely, 'I find I incor-
porate gneiss, coals, long-threaded moss, fruits, grain, esculent roots,|
And am stucco'd with quadrupeds and birds all over'; and of these
quadrupeds and birds, 'not one is respectable or unhappy over the
whole earth.' He calls advice: 'Unscrew the locks from the doors!
Unscrew the doors from their jambs!' He publishes the results of
research: 'Having pried through the strata, analys'd to a hair, coun-
sel'd with doctors and calculated close,|I find no sweeter fat than sticks
to my own bones.' Everybody remembers how he told the Muse to
'cross out please those immensely overpaid accounts,|That matter of
Troy and Achilles' wrath, and Aeneas', Odysseus' wanderings', but
his account of the arrival of the 'illustrious emigré' here in the New
World is even better: 'Bluff'd not a bit by drainpipe, gasometer,
artificial fertilizers,|Smiling and pleas'd with palpable intent to stay,|

She's here, install'd amid the kitchenware.' Or he sees, like another Breughel, 'the mechanic's wife with the babe at her nipple interceding for every person born,|Three scythes at harvest whizzing in a row from three lusty angels with shirts bagg'd out at their waists,|The snag-toothed hostler with red hair redeeming sins past and to come' – the passage has enough wit not only (in Johnson's phrase) to keep it sweet, but enough to make it believable. He says:

I project my hat, sit shame-faced, and beg.

Enough! Enough! Enough!
Somehow I have been stunn'd. Stand back!
Give me a little time beyond my cuff'd head, slumbers, dreams, gaping,
I discover myself on the verge of a usual mistake.
                              (*Song of Myself*, 37, 38)

There is in such changes of tone as these the essence of wit. And Whitman is even more far-fetched than he is witty; he can say about Doubters, in the most improbable and explosive of juxtapositions: 'I know every one of you, I know the sea of torment, doubt, despair and unbelief.|How the flukes splash! How they contort rapid as lightning, with splashes and spouts of blood!' Who else would have said about God: 'As the hugging and loving bed-fellow sleeps at my side through the night, and withdraws at the break of day with stealthy tread,|Leaving me baskets cover'd with white towels, swelling the house with their plenty?' – the Psalmist himself, his cup running over, would have looked at Whitman with dazzled eyes. (Whitman was persuaded by friends to hide the fact that it was God he was talking about.) He says, 'Flaunt of the sunshine I need not your bask – lie over!' This unusual employment of verbs is usual enough in participle-loving Whitman, who also asks you to 'look in my face while I snuff the sidle of evening', or tells you, 'I effuse my flesh in eddies, and drift it in lacy jags.' Here are some typical beginnings of poems: 'City of orgies, walks, and joys. . . . Not heaving from my ribb'd breast only. . . . O take my hand Walt Whitman! Such gliding wonders! Such sights and sounds! Such join'd unended links. . . .' He says to the objects of the world, 'You have waited, you always wait, you dumb, beautiful ministers'; sees 'the sun and stars that float

in the open air,| The apple-shaped earth'; says, 'O suns – O grass of
graves – O perpetual transfers and promotions,|If you do not say
anything how can I say anything?' Not many poets have written
better, in queerer and more convincing and more individual language,
about the world's *gliding wonders*: the phrase seems particularly right
for Whitman. He speaks of those 'circling rivers the breath', of the
'savage old mother incessantly crying,|To the boy's soul's questions
sullenly timing, some drown'd secret hissing' – ends a poem, once,
'We have voided all but freedom and our own joy.' How can one
quote enough? If the reader thinks that all this is like Thomas Wolfe
he *is* Thomas Wolfe; nothing else could explain it. Poetry like this is
as far as possible from the work of any ordinary rhetorician, whose
phrases cascade over us like suds of the oldest and most-advertised
detergent.

The interesting thing about Whitman's worst language (for, just
as few poets have ever written better, few poets have ever written
worse) is how unusually absurd, how really ingeniously bad, such
language is. I will quote none of the most famous examples; but even
a line like 'O *culpable! I acknowledge. I exposé!*' is not anything that
you and I could do – only a man with the most extraordinary feel for
language, or none whatsoever, could have cooked up Whitman's
worst messes. For instance: what other man in all the history of this
planet would have said, 'I am a habitan of Vienna'? (One has an
immediate vision of him as a sort of French-Canadian half breed to
whom the Viennese are offering, with trepidation, through the bars of
a zoological garden, little mounds of whipped cream.) And *enclaircise*
– why, it's as bad as *explicate!* We are right to resent his having made
up his own horrors, instead of sticking to the ones that we ourselves
employ. But when Whitman says, 'I dote on myself, there is that lot
of me and all so luscious', we should realize that we are not the only
ones who are amused. And the queerly bad and merely queer and
queerly good will often change into one another without warning:
'Hefts of the moving world, at innocent gambols silently rising, fresh-
ly exuding,|Scooting obliquely high and low' – not good, but
queer! – suddenly becomes, 'Something I cannot see puts up libidinous
prongs,|Seas of bright juice suffuse heaven', and it is sunrise.

But it is not in individual lines and phrases, but in passages of some
length, that Whitman is at his best. In the following quotation

Whitman has something difficult to express, something that there are many formulas, all bad, for expressing; he expresses it with complete success, in language of the most dazzling originality:

The orchestra whirls me wider than Uranus flies,
It wrenches such ardors from me I did not know I possess'd them,
It sails me, I dab with bare feet, they are lick'd by the indolent waves,
I am cut by bitter and angry hail, I lose my breath,
Steep'd amid honey'd morphine, my windpipe throttled in fakes of death,
At length let up again to feel the puzzle of puzzles,
And that we call Being.

(Song of Myself, 26)

One hardly knows what to point at – everything works. But *wrenches* and *did not know I possess'd them*; the incredible *it sails me, I dab with bare feet*; *lick'd by the indolent*; *steep'd amid honey'd morphine*; *my windpipe throttled in fakes of death* – no wonder Crane admired Whitman! This originality, as absolute in its way as that of Berlioz' orchestration, is often at Whitman's command:

I am a dance – play up there! the fit is whirling me fast!
I am the ever-laughing – it is new moon and twilight,
I see the hiding of douceurs, I see nimble ghosts whichever way I look,
Cache and cache again deep in the ground and sea, and where it is neither ground nor sea.
Well do they do their jobs those journeymen divine,
Only from me can they hide nothing, and would not if they could,
I reckon I am their boss and they make me a pet besides,
And surround me and lead me and run ahead when I walk,
To lift their sunning covers to signify me with stretch'd arms, and resume the way;
Onward we move, a gay gang of blackguards! with mirth-shouting music and wild-flapping pennants of joy!

(The Sleepers)

If you did not believe Hopkins' remark about Whitman, that *gay gang of blackguards* ought to shake you. Whitman shares Hopkins' passion for 'dappled' effects, but he slides in and out of them with ambiguous swiftness. And he has at his command a language of the calmest and most prosaic reality, one that seems to do no more than present:

The little one sleeps in its cradle.
I lift the gauze and look a long time, and silently brush away flies
  with my hand.

The youngster and the red-faced girl turn aside up the bushy hill,
I peeringly view them from the top.

The suicide sprawls on the bloody floor of the bedroom.
I witness the corpse with its dabbled hair, I note where the pistol
  has fallen.

                    (*Song of Myself*, 8)

It is like magic: that is, something has been done to us without our knowing how it was done; but if we look at the lines again we see the *gauze, silently, youngster, red-faced, bushy, peeringly, dabbled* – not that this is all we see. 'Present! present!' said James; these are presented, put down side by side to form a little 'view of life', from the cradle to the last bloody floor of the bedroom. Very often the things presented form nothing but a list:

The pure contralto sings in the organ loft,
The carpenter dresses his plank, the tongue of his foreplane
  whistles its wild ascending lisp,
The married and unmarried children ride home to their
  Thanksgiving dinner,
The pilot seizes the king-pin, he heaves down with a strong arm,
The mate stands braced in the whale-boat, lance and harpoon are
  ready,
The duck-shooter walks by silent and cautious stretches,
The deacons are ordain'd with cross'd hands at the altar,
The spinning-girl retreats and advances to the hum of the big
  wheel,
The farmer stops by the bars as he walks on a First-day loafe and
  looks at the oats and rye,
The lunatic is carried at last to the asylum a confirm'd case,

(He will never sleep any more as he did in the cot in his mother's
    bedroom;)
The jour printer with gray head and gaunt jaws works at his case,
He turns his quid of tobacco while his eyes blur with the
    manuscript,
The malform'd limbs are tied to the surgeon's table,
What is removed drops horribly in a pail; . . .

(Song of Myself, 15)

It is only a list – but what a list! And how delicately, in what different
ways – likeness and opposition and continuation and climax and
anticlimax – the transitions are managed, whenever Whitman wants
to manage them. Notice them in the next quotation, another 'mere
list':

The bride unrumples her white dress, the minute-hand of the
    clock moves slowly,
The opium-eater reclines with rigid head and just-open'd lips,
The prostitute draggles her shawl, her bonnet bobs on her tipsy
    and pimpled neck. . . .

(Song of Myself, 15)

The first line is joined to the third by *unrumples* and *draggles, white dress
and shawl*; the second to the third by *rigid head, bobs, tipsy, neck*; the
first to the second by slowly, *'just-open'd*, and the slowing-down of
time in both states. And occasionally one of these lists is metamor-
phosed into something we have no name for; the man who would
call the next quotation a mere list – anybody will feel this – would boil
his babies up for soap:

Ever the hard unsunk ground,
Ever the eaters and drinkers, ever the upward and downward
    sun, ever the air and the ceaseless tides,
Ever myself and my neighbors, refreshing, wicked, real,
Ever the old inexplicable query, ever that thorned thumb, that
    breath of itches and thirsts,
Ever the vexer's hoot! hoot! till we find where the sly one hides
    and bring him forth,
Ever love, ever the sobbing liquid of life,
Ever the bandage under the chin, ever the trestles of death.

(Song of Myself, 42)

Sometimes Whitman will take what would generally be considered an unpromising subject (in this case, a woman peeping at men in bathing naked) and treat it with such tenderness and subtlety and understanding that we are ashamed of ourselves for having thought it unpromising, and murmur that Chekhov himself couldn't have treated it better:

Twenty-eight young men bathe by the shore,
Twenty-eight young men and all so friendly,
Twenty-eight years of womanly life and all so lonesome.

She owns the fine house by the rise of the bank,
She hides handsome and richly drest aft the blinds of the window.
Which of the young men does she like the best?
Ah the homeliest of them is beautiful to her.

Where are you off to, lady? for I see you,
You splash in the water there, yet stay stock still in your room.

Dancing and laughing along the beach came the twenty-ninth
    bather,
The rest did not see her, but she saw them and loved them.

The beards of the young men glisten'd with wet, it ran from their
    long hair,
Little streams pass'd all over their bodies.

An unseen hand also pass'd over their bodies,
It descended tremblingly from their temples and ribs.

The young men float on their backs, their white bellies bulge to
    the sun, they do not ask who seizes fast to them,
They do not know who puffs and declines with pendant and
    bending arch,
They do not think whom they souse with spray.
                                    (*Song of Myself*, 11)

And in the same poem (that *Song of Myself* in which one finds half his best work) the writer can say of a sea-fight:

Stretch'd and still lies the midnight,
Two great hulls motionless on the breast of the darkness,

Our vessel riddled and slowly sinking, preparations to pass to the
   one we have conquer'd,
The captain on the quarter-deck coldly giving his orders through
   a countenance white as a sheet,
Near by the corpse of the child that serv'd in the cabin,
The dead face of an old salt with long white hair and carefully
   curl'd whiskers,
The flames spite of all that can be done flickering aloft and
   below,
The husky voices of the two or three officers yet fit for duty,
Formless stacks of bodies and bodies by themselves, dabs of flesh
   upon the masts and spars,
Cut of cordage, dangle of rigging, slight shock of the soothe of
   waves,
Black and impassive guns, litter of powder-parcels, strong scent,
A few large stars overhead, silent and mournful shining,
Delicate sniffs of sea-breeze, smells of sedgy grass and fields by the
   shore, death-messages given in charge to survivors,
The hiss of the surgeon's knife, the gnawing teeth of his saw,
Wheeze, cluck, swash of falling blood, short wild scream, and
   long, dull, tapering groan,
These so, these irretrievable.

(Song of Myself, 36)

There are faults in this passage, and they *do not matter*: the serious
truth, the complete realization of these last lines make us remember
that few poets have shown more of the tears of things, and the joy
of things, and of the reality beneath either tears of joy. Even Whitman's most general or political statements sometimes are good:
everybody knows his 'When liberty goes out of a place it is not the
first to go, nor the second or third to go,|It waits for all the rest to go,
it is the last'; these sentences about the United States just before the
Civil War may be less familiar:

Are those really Congressmen? are those the great Judges? is that
   the President?
Then I will sleep awhile yet, for I see that these States sleep, for
   reasons;

(With gathering murk, with muttering thunder and lambent shoots
  we all duly awake,
South, North, East, West, inland and seaboard, we will surely
  awake.)
                                              (*To the States*)

How well, with what firmness and dignity and command, Whitman
does such passages! And Whitman's doubts that he has done them or
anything else well – ah, there is nothing he does better:

The best I had done seemed to me blank and suspicious,
My great thoughts as I supposed them, were they not in reality
  meagre?
I am he who knew what it was to be evil,
I too knitted the old knot of contrariety . . .
Saw many I loved in the street or ferry-boat or public assembly,
  yet never told them a word,
Lived the same life with the rest, the same old laughing, gnawing,
  sleeping,
Played the part that still looks back on the actor and actress,
The same old role, the role that is what we make it . . .
                                        (*Crossing Brooklyn Ferry*, 6)

Whitman says once that the 'look of the bay mare shames silliness
out of me'. This is true – sometimes it is true; but more often the
silliness and affection and cant and exaggeration are there shamelessly,
the Old Adam that was in Whitman from the beginning and the
awful new one that he created to keep it company. But as he says,
'I know perfectly well my own egotism,|Know my omnivorous
lines and must not write any less.' He says over and over that there are
in him good and bad, wise and foolish, anything at all and its antonym,
and he is telling the truth; there is in him almost everything in the
world, so that one responds to him, willingly or unwillingly, almost
as one does to the world, that world which makes the hairs of one's
flesh stand up, which seems both evil beyond any rejection and
wonderful beyond any acceptance. We cannot help seeing that there
is something absurd about any judgment we make of its whole – for
there is no 'point of view' at which we can stand to make the judgment, and the moral categories that mean most to us seem no more

to apply to its whole than our spatial or temporal or causal categories seem to apply to its beginning or its end. (But we need no arguments to make our judgments seem absurd – we feel their absurdity without argument.) In some like sense Whitman is a world, a waste with, here and there, systems blazing at random out of the darkness. Only an innocent and rigidly methodical mind will reject it for this dis-organization, particularly since there are in it, here and there, little systems as beautifully and astonishingly organized as the rings and satellites of Saturn:

I understand the large hearts of heroes,
The courage of present times and all times,
How the skipper saw the crowded and rudderless wreck of the
    steam-ship, and Death chasing it up and down the storm,
How he knuckled tight and gave not back an inch, and was
    faithful of days and faithful of nights,
And chalked in large letters on a board, Be of good cheer, we will
    not desert you;
How he follow'd with them and tack'd with them three days and
    would not give it up,
How he saved the drifting company at last,
How the lank loose-gown'd women looked when boated from
    the side of their prepared graves,
How the silent old-faced infants and the lifted sick, and the sharp-
    lipp'd unshaved men;
All this I swallow, it tastes good, I like it well, it becomes mine,
I am the man, I suffered, I was there.
                                          (*Song of Myself*, 33)

In the last lines of this quotation Whitman has reached – as great writers always reach – a point at which criticism seems not only unnecessary but absurd; these lines are so good that even admiration feels like insolence, and one is ashamed of anything that one can find to say about them. How anyone can dismiss or accept patronizingly the man who wrote them, I do not understand.

The enormous and apparent advantages of form, of omission and selection, of the highest degree of organization, are accompanied by important disadvantages – and there are far greater works than *Leaves of Grass* to make us realize this. But if we compare Whitman with that very beautiful poet Alfred Tennyson, the most skilful of all Whitman's contemporaries, we are at once aware of how limiting Tennyson's forms have been, of how much Tennyson has had to leave out, even in those discursive poems where he is trying to put everything in. Whitman's poems *represent* his world and himself much more satisfactorily than Tennyson's do his. In the past a few poets have both formed and represented, each in the highest degree; but in modern times what controlling, organizing, selecting poet has created a world with as much in it as Whitman's, a world that so plainly *is* the world? Of all modern poets he has, quantitatively speaking, 'the most comprehensive soul' – and, qualitatively, a most comprehensive and comprehending one, with charities and concessions and qualifications that are rare in any time.

'Do I contradict myself? Very well then I contradict myself,' wrote Whitman, as everybody remembers, and this is not naïve, or something he got from Emerson, or a complacent pose. When you organize one of the contradictory elements out of your work of art, you are getting rid not just of it, but of the contradiction of which it was a part; and it is the contradictions in works of art which make them able to represent to us – as logical and methodical generalizations cannot – our world and our selves, which are also full of contradictions. In Whitman we do not get the controlled, compressed, seemingly concordant contradictions of the great lyric poets, of a poem like, say, Hardy's *During Wind and Rain*; Whitman's contradictions are sometimes announced openly, but are more often scattered at random throughout the poems. For instance: Whitman specializes in ways of saying that there is in some sense (a very Hegelian one, generally) no evil – he says a hundred times that evil is not Real; but he also specializes in making lists of the evil of the world, lists of an unarguable reality. After his minister has recounted 'the rounded catalogue divine complete', Whitman comes home and puts down what has been left out: 'the countless (nineteen-twentieths) low and evil, crude and savage . . . the barren soil, the evil men, the slag and hideous rot.' He ends another such catalogue with the plain unexcusing 'All these – all meanness and agony without end I sitting look out upon,|See, hear, and am silent.' Whitman offered himself to everybody, and said brilliantly and at length what a good thing he was offering:

Sure as the most certain sure, plumb in the uprights, well
   entretied, braced in the beams,
Stout as a horse, affectionate, haughty, electrical,
I and this mystery here we stand.
                         (*Song of Myself*, 3)

Just for oddness, characteristicalness, differentness, what more could
you ask in a letter of recommendation? (Whitman sounds as if he were
recommending a house – haunted, but what foundations!) But after
a few pages he is oddly different:

Apart from the pulling and hauling stands what I am,
Stands amused, complacent, compassionating, idle, unitary,
Looks down, is erect, or bends an arm on an impalpable certain
   rest
Looking with side curved head curious what will come next,
Both in and out of the game and watching and wondering at it.
                         (*Song of Myself*, 4)

Tamburlaine is already beginning to sound like Hamlet: the employer
feels uneasily, 'Why, I might as well hire myself. . . .' And, a few
pages later, Whitman puts down in ordinary-sized type, in the middle
of the page, this warning to any *new person drawn toward me*:

Do you think I am trusty and faithful?
Do you see no further than this façade, this smooth and tolerant
   manner of me?
Do you suppose yourself advancing on real ground toward a real
   heroic man?
Have you no thought O dreamer that it may be all maya, illusion?
                  (*Are You the New Person Drawn
                  Toward Me?*)

Having wonderful dreams, telling wonderful lies, was a temptation
Whitman could never resist; but telling the truth was a temptation he
could never resist, either. When you buy him you know what you
are buying. And only an innocent and solemn and systematic mind
will condemn him for his contradictions: Whitman's catalogues of
evils represent realities, and his denials of their reality represent other
realities, of feeling and intuition and desire. If he is faithless to logic,

to Reality As It Is – whatever that is – he is faithful to the feel of things, to reality as it seems; this is all that a poet has to be faithful to, and philosophers have been known to leave logic and Reality for it.

Whitman is more coordinate and parallel than anybody, is *the* poet of parallel present participles, of twenty verbs joined by a single subject: all this helps to give his work its feeling of raw hypnotic reality, of being that world which also streams over us joined only by *ands*, until we supply the subordinating conjunctions; and since as children we see the *ands* and not the *becauses*, this method helps to give Whitman some of the freshness of childhood. How inexhaustibly interesting the world is in Whitman! Arnold all his life kept wishing that he could see the world 'with a plainness as near, as flashing' as that with which Moses and Rebekah and the Argonauts saw it. He asked with elegiac nostalgia, 'Who can see the green earth any more| As she was by the sources of Time?' – and all the time there was somebody alive who saw it so, as plain and near and flashing, and with a kind of calm, pastoral, Biblical dignity and elegance as well, sometimes. The *thereness* and *suchness* of the world are incarnate in Whitman as they are in few other writers.

They might have put on his tombstone WALT WHITMAN: HE HAD HIS NERVE. He is the rashest, the most inexplicable and unlikely – the most impossible, one wants to say – of poets. He somehow *is* in a class by himself, so that one compares him with other poets about as readily as one compares *Alice* with other books. (Even his free verse has a completely different effect from anybody else's.) Who would think of comparing him with Tennyson or Browning or Arnold or Baudelaire? – it is Homer, or the sagas, or something far away and long ago, that comes to one's mind only to be dismissed; for sometimes Whitman *is* epic, just as *Moby Dick* is, and it surprises us to be able to use truthfully this word that we have misused so many times. Whitman *is* grand, and elevated, and comprehensive, and real with an astonishing reality, and many other things – the critic points at his qualities in despair and wonder, all method failing, and simply calls them by their names. And the range of these qualities is the most extraordinary thing of all. We can surely say about him, 'He was a man, take him for all in all. I shall not look upon his like again' – and wish that people had seen this and not tried to be his like: one

Whitman is miracle enough, and when he comes again it will be the end of the world.

I have said so little about Whitman's faults because they are so plain: baby critics who have barely learned to complain of the lack of ambiguity in *Peter Rabbit* can tell you all that is wrong with *Leaves of Grass*. But a good many of my readers must have felt that it is ridiculous to write an essay about the obvious fact that Whitman is a great poet. It is ridiculous – just as, in 1851, it would have been ridiculous for anyone to write an essay about the obvious fact that Pope was no 'classic of our prose' but a great poet. Critics have to spend half their time reiterating whatever ridiculously obvious things their age or the critics of their age have found it necessary to forget: they say despairingly, at parties, that Wordsworth is a great poet, and *won't* bore you, and tell Mr Leavis that Milton is a great poet whose deposition *hasn't* been accomplished with astonishing ease by a few words from Eliot. . . . There is something essentially ridiculous about critics, anyway: what is good is good without our saying so, and beneath all our majesty we know this.

Let me finish by mentioning another quality of Whitman's – a quality, delightful to me, that I have said nothing of. If some day a tourist notices, among the ruins of New York City, a copy of *Leaves of Grass*, and stops and picks it up and reads some lines in it, she will be able to say to herself: 'How very American! If he and his country had not existed, it would have been impossible to imagine them.'

(101–20)

Charles Feidelson Jr

from *Symbolism in American Literature* 1953

One cannot say as much for Emerson and Whitman, whose faith in symbolic reality quickly disposed of awkward questions. The symbolism which for Hawthorne was no more than a sporadic intuition became for them an explicit metaphysical principle. Hawthorne's conscious philosophy belonged to the eighteenth century; his symbolic imagination to the nineteenth. His critical vocabulary, with its perpetual contrast between 'fiction' and 'reality', 'fancy' and 'fact', 'imagination' and 'actuality', was an eighteenth-century formula applied to a nineteenth-century art, just as his allegorical technique was the product of eighteenth-century reason at work on an antirational sensibility. But empirical fact and rational form had no hold on Emerson and Whitman, whose 'transcendentalism' was specifically opposed to neoclassic doctrine and method. While Hawthorne's figure of Man Seeing largely preserves the static mold of the Lockian theory of perception, Emerson recreates that archetype in the image of the Voyager:

But man thyself, and all things unfix, dispart, and flee. Nothing will stand the eye of a man, – neither lion, nor person, nor planet, nor time, nor condition. Each bullies us for a season; but gaze, and it opens that most solid seeming wall, yields its secret, receives us into its depth and advances our front so much farther into the recesses of being, to some new frontier as yet unvisited by the elder voyagers.

(*Journals, 1909–14,* vol. 2, p. 407)

If man is by nature an explorer, the 'eyes, and ears, and skin' are actively poetic, not merely registers of sense data. The 'symbolical' meaning of rails and barns and dung forks – a significance which we do not 'understand' or 'know' in the accepted fashion – is generated by the advance of the mind into the recesses of being.

'No one will get at my verses,' Whitman declared, 'who insists upon viewing them as a literary performance, or attempt at such performance, or as aiming mainly toward art or aestheticism.' In his conscious literary theory literature is subordinate to sociology, 'the United States themselves are essentially the greatest poem', the poet must 'tally' the American scene, and the function of poetry is the creation of heroic citizens. Yet it is obvious that a larger principle governs both his poetic and his sociological doctrine; no one will get at his verses who insists upon viewing them as a sociological performance. Whitman intimates that the link between his poems and American life is actually a new method exemplified by both:

One main contrast of the ideas behind every page of my verses, compared with establish'd poems, is their different relative attitude towards God, towards the objective universe, and still more (by reflection, confession, assumption, etc.) the quite changed attitude of the ego, the one chanting or talking, towards himself and towards his fellow-humanity. It is certainly time for America, above all, to begin this readjustment in the scope and basic point of view of verse; for everything else has changed.

('A Backward Glance O'er
Travel'd Roads')

The distinctive quality of Whitman's poetry depends on this change of standpoint. In his effort 'to articulate and faithfully express ... [his] own physical, emotional, moral, intellectual, and aesthetic Personality, in the midst of, and tallying, the momentous spirit and facts of its immediate days', his interest is not so much in the Personality or the environment *per se* as in the 'changed attitude of the ego'. The new method is better defined in the poems themselves than in the critical prose. The ego appears in the poems as a traveler and explorer, not as a static observer; its object is 'to know the universe itself as a road, as many roads, as roads for traveling souls'. The shift of image from the contemplative eye of 'establish'd poems' to the voyaging ego of Whitman's poetry records a large-scale theoretical shift from the categories of 'substance' to those of 'process.' Whitman's 'perpetual journey' is not analogous to a sight-seeing trip, though his catalogues might give that impression; the mind and the material world into which it ventures are not ultimately different in kind. Instead, what seems at first a penetration of nature by the mind is actually a process in which the known world comes into being. The 'child who went forth every day, and who now goes, and will always go forth every day', is indistinguishable from the world of his experience: 'The first object he look'd upon, that object he became,|And that object became part of him.' The true voyage is the endless becoming of reality:

Allons! to that which is endless as it was beginningless,
To undergo much, tramp of days, rests of nights,
To merge all in the travel they tend to, and the days and nights
    they tend to,
Again to merge them in the start of superior journeys. . . .
(*Song of the Open Road*, 13)

Here there is no clear distinction among the traveler, the road, and the journey, for the journey is nothing but the progressive unity of the voyager and the lands he enters; perception, which unites the seer and the seen, is identical with the real process of becoming. God, in this context, is a 'seething principle', and human society is a flow of 'shapes ever projecting other shapes'. Whitman's 'readjustment in the scope and basic point of view of verse' is actually a transmutation of all supposed entities into events.

A poem, therefore, instead of referring to a completed act of perception, constitutes the act itself, both in the author and in the reader; instead of describing reality, a poem is a realization. When Whitman writes, 'See, steamers steaming through my poems', he is admonishing both himself and his audience that no distinction can be made between themselves, the steamers, and the words. Indeed, no distinction can be made between the poet and the reader: 'It is you talking just as much as myself, I act as the tongue of you.' His new method was predicated not only on the sense of creative vision – itself a process which renders a world in process – but also, as part and parcel of that consciousness, on the sense of creative speech. The 'I' of Whitman's poems speaks the world that he sees, and sees the world that he speaks, and does this by *becoming* the reality of his vision and of his words, in which the reader also participates. Most of Whitman's poems, more or less explicitly, are 'voyages' in this metaphysical sense. This was Whitman's genre, his 'new theory of literary composition for imaginative works'. Even in the most personal lyrics of *Children of Adam* and *Calamus*, the 'one chanting or talking' is not simply the poet; the chant is neither pure self-expression nor pure description; what is talked about is oddly confused with the talker and the talking; and the audience is potentially both the subject and the writer. *Song of Myself*, though it breathes the personal egotism of Whitman, makes sense as a whole only when the self is taken dramatically and identified with 'the procreant urge of the world'.

Consider the last four sections of *Starting from Paumanok* – the entire poem being the *Song of Myself* in miniature. Here at the end of the poem it appears that to start from Paumanok is to start far back of the speaker's birth in the opening line. The beginnings (of the speaker, of America, and of the world) are 'aboriginal', as typified by the Indian name; the beginnings, indeed, by a leap of thought, become the perpetual genesis of 'a world primal again', announced by the poet's voice. In the following section, with its images of incessant motion, the announcement itself is the genesis of the world; the voice is equated with the becoming of reality. Retrospectively, one sees that the preliminary statement of the poem – 'Solitary, singing in the West, I strike up for a New World' – has ushered in a song which not only is addressed to and descriptive of America but also is the vehicle, at once product and creator, of a metaphysical 'newness'. In the course of the poem the solitary voice of the individual poet has expanded into the presence of an all-inclusive Word – 'a word to clear one's path ahead endlessly'. And the speaker's union with his hearer is imaged in the final section as the love relationship of 'camerados' on the journey. The method of *Starting from Paumanok* does not palliate Whitman's diffuseness and arbitrary choice of material; rather, by depriving him of a static point of view, it is the immediate cause of these defects. Yet the principle behind this poem, the exploitation of Speech as the literary aspect of eternal process, is the source of whatever literary value resides in *Leaves of Grass*.

'This subject of language,' Whitman confided to Horace Traubel, 'interests me – interests me: I never quite get it out of my mind. I sometimes think the *Leaves* is only a language experiment.' *An American Primer*, Whitman's fragmentary lecture on language, reveals a mind that fed upon words: '*Names* are magic. – One word can pour such a flood through the soul.' The sense of language as inherently significant is his meeeting ground with Hawthorne, for whom a 'deep meaning ... streamed forth' from the scarlet letter. In both cases attention is deflected from 'ideas' and 'objects' to a symbolic medium; and in both cases the perception of a meaningful symbol is opposed to another kind of perception, which Hawthorne calls 'analysis'. Hawthorne would like to reduce the meaning to the rational terms of logical construct or empirical fact; he is plainly uncomfortable at the disturbance of his 'sensibilities'. In practice, he not only translates symbolism into allegory but also affects a rational style which ties his language down to the common-sense world. Whitman's awareness of words in themselves is stronger, and he is militantly hostile to reason. He proposes 'new law-forces of spoken and written language – not merely the pedagogue-forms, correct, regular, familiar with precedents, made for matters of outside pro-priety, fine words, thoughts definitely told out.' He is indifferent to dictionary words and textbook grammar, which he associates with a barren formalism and externality. Fully accepting the intuition at which Hawthorne boggled, he takes his departure from a denial of conventional distinctions: 'Strange and hard that paradox true I give,| Objects gross and the unseen soul are one.' Since Whitman regards meaning as an activity of words rather than an external significance attached to them, language, together with the self and the material world, turns out to be a process, the pouring of the flood. 'A perfect user of words uses things', while at the same time he *is* both the words and the things:

Latent, in a great user of words, must actually be all passions, crimes, trades, animals, stars, God, sex, the past, might, space, metals, and the like – because these are the words, and he who is not these, plays with a foreign tongue, turning helplessly to dictionaries and authorities.

(*An American Primer*)

This kind of speech 'seldomer tells a thing than suggests or necessitates it', because to 'tell' something would be to suppose something outside the language. The reader is not given statements but is set in action, 'on the assumption that the process of reading is not a half-sleep, but, in highest sense, an exercise, a gymnast's struggle.' The poem necessarily works 'by curious removes, indirections', rather than direct imitation of nature, since 'the image-making faculty' runs counter to the habit of mind which views the material world as separable from ideas and speech. Whitman's running battle with the rational assumptions of conventional thought reaches its peak in the hyperbolical *Song of the Rolling Earth*, where he identifies all 'audible words' with the marks on the printed page and glorifies, by way of contrast, 'the unspoken meanings of the earth'. In deliberate paradox he asserts that true poems will somehow be made from these inaudible words. The poem expresses the bravado of his conscious attempt to create a wholly symbolic language in the face of intellectual convention. For that is his purpose: the 'tallying' of things and man, to which he often alludes mysteriously, is simply the presence of language in each and the presence of each in language. The 'language experiment' of *Leaves of Grass* – its promise of 'new potentialities of speech' – depends on the symbolic status claimed by the book as a whole and in every part. 'From the eyesight proceeds another eyesight and from the hearing proceeds another hearing and from the voice proceeds another voice eternally curious of the harmony of things with man.'

The patent symbols of Whitman's best poem, *When Lilacs Last in the Dooryard Bloom'd*, are conditioned by the thoroughgoing symbolism of his poetic attitude. As in most elegies, the person mourned is hardly more than the occasion of the work; but this poem, unlike *Lycidas* or *Adonais*, does not transmute the central figure merely by generalizing him out of all recognition. Lincoln is seldom mentioned either as a person or as a type. Instead, the focus of the poem is a presentation of the poet's mind at work in the context of Lincoln's death. If the true subject of *Lycidas* and *Adonais* is not Edward King or John Keats but the Poet, the true subject of Whitman's *Lilacs* is not the Poet but the poetic process. And even this subject is not treated simply by generalizing a particular situation. The act of poetizing and the context in which it takes place have continuity in time and space but no particular existence. Both are 'ever-returning'; the tenses shift; the poet is in different places at once; and at the end this whole phase of creation is moving inexorably forward.

Within this framework the symbols behave like characters in a drama, the plot of which is the achievement of a poetic utterance. The spring, the constant process of rebirth, is threaded by the journey of the coffin, the constant process of death, and in the first section it presents the poet with twin symbols: the perennially blooming lilac and the drooping star. The spring also brings to the poet the 'thought of him I love', in which the duality of life and death is repeated. The thought of the dead merges with the fallen star in Section 2; the thought of love merges with the life of the lilac, from which the poet breaks a sprig in Section 3. Thus the lilac and the star enter the poem not as objects to which the poet assigns a meaning but as elements in the undifferentiated stream of thoughts and things; and the spring, the real process of becoming, which involves the real process of dissolution, is also the genesis of poetic vision. The complete pattern of the poem is established with the advent of the bird in the fourth section. For here, in the song of the thrush, the lilac and star are united (the bird sings 'death's outlet song of life'), and the potentiality of the poet's 'thought' is intimated. The song of the bird and the thought of the poet, which also unites life and death, both lay claim to the third place in the 'trinity' brought by spring; they are, as it were, the actuality and the possibility of poetic utterance, which reconciles opposite appearances.

The drama of the poem will be a movement from possible to actual poetic speech, as represented by the 'tallying' of the songs of the poet and the thrush. Although it is a movement without steps, the whole being implicit in every moment, there is a graduation of emphasis. Ostensibly, the visions of the coffin and the star (Sections 5 through 8) delay the unison of poet and bird, so that full actualization is reserved for the end of the poem. On the other hand, the verse that renders the apparition of the coffin *is* 'death's outlet song of life'. The poetic act of evoking the dark journey is treated as the showering of death with lilac:

Here, coffin that slowly passes,
I give you my sprig of lilac. . . .

Blossoms and branches green to coffins all I bring,
For fresh as the morning, thus would I chant a song for you,
O sane and sacred death.

Even as the poet lingers, he has attained his end. And the star of Section 8, the counterpart of the coffin, functions in much the same way. The episode that occurred 'a month since' – when 'my soul in its trouble dissatisfied sank, as where you sad orb,|Concluded, dropt in the night, and was gone' – was a failure of the poetic spring. The soul was united with the star but not with the lilac. Yet the passage is preceded by the triumphant statement, 'Now I know what you must have meant', and knowledge issues in the ability to render the episode in verse. The perception of meaning gives life to the fact of death; the star meant the death of Lincoln, but the evolution of the meaning is poetry.

The recurrence of the song of the thrush in the following section and in Section 13 is a reminder of the poetic principle which underlies the entire poem. In a sense, the words, 'I hear your notes, I hear your call', apply to all that precedes and all that is to come, for the whole poem, existing in an eternal present, is the 'loud human song' of the poet's 'brother'. But again Whitman delays the consummation. He is 'detained' from his rendezvous with the bird – although he really 'hears' and 'understands' all the time – by the sight of the 'lustrous star' and by the 'mastering odor' of the lilac. Since both the star and the lilac are inherent in the song of the bird, he actually lingers only in order to proceed. While the song rings in the background, the poet puts the questions presupposed by his own poetizing. How can the life of song be one with the fact of death? – 'O how shall I warble myself for the dead one there I loved?' And what will be the content of the song of death? – 'O what shall I hang on the chamber walls . . .|To adorn the burial-house of him I love?' The questions answer themselves. The breath by which the grave becomes part of his chant is the breath of life; within the poem the image of the 'burial-house' will be overlaid with 'pictures of growing spring'. The delay has served only to renew the initial theme: the poet's chant, like the song of the thrush, is itself the genesis of life and therefore contains both life and death.

The final achievement of poetic utterance comes in Section 14, when the poet, looking forth on the rapid motion of life, experiences death. More exactly, he walks between the 'thought' and the 'knowledge' of death, which move beside him like companions. Just as his poem exists between the 'thought' of the dead, which is para-doxically an act of life, and the actual knowledge of the bird's song, which embodies both dying star and living lilac, the poet himself is in motion from the potential to the actual. From this point to the end of the poem, the sense of movement never flags. The poet's flight into the darkness is a fusion with the stream of music from the bird:

And the charm of the carol rapt me,
As I held as if by their hands my comrades in the night,
And the voice of my spirit tallied the song of the bird.

As the motion of the poet is lost in the motion of the song, the latter is identified with the 'dark mother always gliding near', and in the 'floating' carol death itself becomes the movement of waves that 'undulate round the world'. In effect, poet and bird, poem and song, life and death, are now the sheer process of the carol; as in *Out of the Cradle Endlessly Rocking*, reality is the unfolding Word. The presented song merges into the 'long panoramas of visions' in Section 15, and then the inexorable process begins to leave this moment behind:

Passing the visions, passing the night,
Passing, unloosing the hold of my comrades' hands,
Passing the song of the hermit bird and the tallying song
    of my soul. . . .
Passing, I leave thee lilac with heart-shaped leaves, . . .

I cease from my song for thee, . . .
O comrade lustrous with silver face in the night.

But the poetic activity is continuous; the passing-onward is not a
rejection of the old symbols. 'Lilac and star and bird twined with the
chant of . . . [the] soul' also pass onward because they are activities
and not finite things. The conclusion of this poem dramatizes what
Whitman once stated of *Leaves of Grass* as a whole – that the book
exists as 'a passage way to something rather than a thing in itself
concluded'. Taken seriously, in the sense in which there *can* be no
'thing in itself concluded', this notion is not, as Whitman sometimes
pretended, a mere excuse for haphazard technique but the rationale
of a symbolistic method.

Yet *When Lilacs Last in the Dooryard Bloom'd* is a successful poem
only because it does not fully live up to the theory which it both
states and illustrates. The poem really presupposes a static situation,
which Whitman undertakes to treat as though it were dynamic; in
the course of the poem the death of Lincoln, of which we always
remain aware, is translated into Whitman's terms of undifferentiated
flow. His other long poems generally lack this stabilizing factor.
Whatever the nominal subject, it is soon lost in sheer 'process'; all
roads lead into the *Song of Myself*, in which the bare Ego interacts
with a miscellaneous world. The result is Whitman's characteristic
disorder and turgidity. When the subject is endless, any form becomes arbitrary. While the antirational conception of a poem as the
realization of language gives a new freedom and a new dignity to
poetry, it apparently leads to an aimlessness from which the poem can
be rescued only by returning to rational categories. Otherwise, the
best that can be expected from Whitman's poetic principle is the 'long
varied train of an emblem, dabs of music,|Fingers of the organist
skipping staccato over the keys of the great organ'.

And much worse can be expected. In the last section of *Passage to*

India, Whitman's most deliberate statement of the process theory, the tone is frenetic even for him:

Sail forth – steer for the deep waters only,
Reckless O soul, exploring, I with thee, and thou with me,
For we are bound where mariner has not yet dared to go,
And we will risk the ship, ourselves and all.

What begins in Emerson as a mild contravention of reason – a peaceful journey 'to some frontier as yet unvisited by the elder voyagers' – becomes in Whitman a freedom from all 'limits and imaginary lines',

. . . from all formules!
From your formules, O bat-eyed and materialistic priests.
(*Song of the Open Road*, 10)

Thus the looseness of form in Whitman's verse is not merely a technical defect; it is the counterpart of an intellectual anarchism designed to overthrow conventional reality by dissolving all rational order. Moreover, like Hawthorne in the malarial gardens of Rome, Whitman has his *frisson* at this inversion of established values – and without Hawthorne's reservations: 'I know my words are weapons full of danger, full of death,|For I confront peace, security, and all the settled laws, to unsettle them.' Mixed with the obtrusive health of the *Calamus* poems is a daredevil flouting of convention:

The way is suspicious, the result uncertain, perhaps destructive, . . .
The whole past theory of your life and all conformity to the lives
    around you would have to be abandon'd, . . .
Nor will my poems do good only, they will do just as much evil,
    perhaps more. . . .
(*Whoever You are Holding Me Now
in Hand*)

Nowadays we are too much in the habit of blaming 'romanticism' for any irrationality in literature. Certainly the romantic spirit was enamored of a fluid reality, which could not be contained in the old channels, and the romantic often opened the dikes deliberately, just to see what would happen. The Voyager is a romantic figure, the ocean a romantic realm. Yet a distinction is in order. The antirationalism of the romantic voyage is a wilful projection of feeling;

the romantic sea is the image of a world subservient to emotion. But the symbolistic voyage is a process of becoming: Whitman is less concerned with exploration of emotion than with exploration as a mode of existence. Similarly, his poems not only are *about* voyaging but also enact the voyage, so that their content (the image of the metaphysical journey) is primarily a reflection of their literary method, in which the writer and his subject become part of the stream of language. It follows that Whitman's hostility to reason has another, more complicated source than the romantic vision of a world suffused with feeling. Like Emerson, he finds the antonym of reason not in emotion but in the 'symbolical'; like Hawthorne and Melville, he contrasts 'analysis' with 'meaning', 'arithmetic' with 'significance'. For his object is not so much to impose a new form on the world as to adopt a new stance in which the world takes on new shapes. His difficulty is that his method works too well: the shapes proliferate endlessly, and, having deprived himself of an external standpoint, he has no means of controlling them. On the other hand, the occasional violence of his antirationalism is the result of an opposite difficulty: while he would like to be sublimely indifferent to established distinctions, reason fights back as he seeks to transcend it, and he is forced into the position of the iconoclast.

(16–27)

William Carlos Williams

from 'An Essay on *Leaves of Grass*', in M. Hindus (ed.), *Leaves of Grass One Hundred Years After* 1955

Leaves of Grass! It was a good title for a book of poems, especially for a new book of American poems. It was a challenge to the entire concept of the poetic idea, and from a new viewpoint, a rebel viewpoint, an American viewpoint. In a word and at the beginning it enunciated a shocking truth, that the common ground is of itself a poetic source. There had been inklings before this that such was the case in the works of Robert Burns and the poet Wordsworth, but in this instance the very forms of the writing had been altered: it had gone over to the style of the words as they appeared on the page.

Whitman's so-called 'free verse' was an assault on the very citadel of the poem itself; it constituted a direct challenge to all living poets to show cause why they should not do likewise. It is a challenge that still holds good after a century of vigorous life during which it has been practically continuously under fire but never defeated.

From the beginning Whitman realized that the matter was largely technical. It had to be free verse or nothing with him and he seldom varied from that practice – and never for more than the writing of an occasional poem. It was a sharp break, and if he was to go astray he had no one but himself to blame for it. It was a technical matter, true enough, and he would stick it out to the end, but to do any more with it than simply to write the poems was beyond him.

He had seen a great light but forgot almost at once after the first revelation everything but his 'message', the idea which originally set him in motion, the idea on which he had been nurtured, the idea of democracy – and took his eye off the words themselves which should have held him.

The point is purely academic – the man had his hands full with the conduct of his life and couldn't, if they had come up, be bothered with other matters. As a result, he made no further progress as an artist but, in spite of various topical achievements, continued to write with diminishing effectiveness for the remainder of his life.

He didn't know any better. He didn't have the training to construct his verses after a conscious mold which would have given him power over them to turn them this way, then that, at will. He only knew how to give them birth and to release them to go their own way. He was preoccupied with the great ideas of the time, to which he was devoted, but, after all, poems are made out of words not ideas. He never showed any evidence of knowing this and the unresolved forms consequent upon his beginnings remained in the end just as he left them. . . .

The young men who are students of literature today in our universities do not believe in seeking within the literary forms, the lines, the foot, the way in which to expand their efforts to know the universe, as Whitman did, but are content to follow the theologians and Mr Eliot. In that, they are children of the times; they risk nothing, for by risking an expanded freedom you are very likely to come a cropper. What, in the words of Hjalmar Ekdahl in *The Wild Duck*, are you going to invent? . . .

Where have the leads which are *not* aesthetic tended to take us in the present century? By paying attention to detail and our telescopes and microscopes and the reinterpretations of their findings, we realize that man has long since broken from the confinement of the more rigid of his taboos. It is reasonable to suppose that he will in the future, in spite of certain setbacks, continue to follow the same course.

Man finds himself on the earth, whether he likes it or not, with nowhere else to go. What then is to become of him? Obviously we can't stand still or we shall be destroyed. Then if there is no room for us on the outside we shall, in spite of orselves, have to go *in*: into the cell, the atom, the poetic line, for our discoveries. We have to break the old apart to make room for ourselves, whatever may be our tragedy and however we may fear it. By making room within the line itself for his inventions, Whitman revealed himself to be a worthy and courageous man of his age and, to boot, a far-seeing one.

(22–31)

Richard Chase

from *Walt Whitman Reconsidered* 1955

Whitman was one of those writers who, like Mark Twain, Shaw, Dostoevsky, and Yeats, present themselves through their art or their public life in the guise of more than one self. (In his notebook Whitman had written, perhaps as early as 1847, 'I cannot understand the mystery, but I am always conscious of myself as two.' And he provisionally identified the 'two' as 'my soul and I'.) Invoking the Dionysian rites and the Aristophanic comedy, Nietzsche asserted the necessity of the double personality. 'Everything that is profound loves the mask', he wrote; 'the profoundest things have a hatred even of figure and likeness. Should not the *contrary* be the right disguise for the shame of a God to go about in?' Like other modern writers Whitman found it temperamentally pleasurable as well as strategically necessary to interpose a half-ironic image of himself between the world and that profound part of his personality which hated figure and likeness – the unconscious mind with its spontaneous, lawless, poetic impulses. He invented not one but several public personalities –

the worldly, dandified young metropolitan journalist of the early 1840s; the homely, Christlike carpenter and radical of the early 1850s; the full-bearded, sunburned, clean-limbed, vigorously sexed, burly common man of the later fifties and early sixties; the male nurse and good gray poet of the Washington period; the sage of Camden of the late years.

In having contrived so striking a procession of public images (actually all but the young journalist-dandy are aspects of one large public gesture) Whitman is unique among American writers. The masks interest us only because we see that they are not assumed merely to fool the public. There was, to be sure, a certain strain of insincerity in Whitman. He wrote anonymous panegyrics of *Leaves of Grass* and generally puffed his own writings when he got the chance. He allowed early biographies of himself to be published (he even collaborated more or less in their composition) which contained misleading information, such as, that the author of *Leaves of Grass* had, by 1855, traveled throughout the United States and therefore knew at first hand the geographical phenomena the poems celebrate. Yet without wishing to condone dishonesty, one may suggest that modern Americans are far too sensitive about sincerity – except in personal relationships, it is after all one of the minor virtues. Whitman may have gone off the deep end in pursuit of sympathy and comradeship, but at least he does not come bounding up to us with that doglike guilelessness our contemporary culture admires. He wore the mask of the American humorist; he was quirky, ironic, 'indirect', guileful. As he remarked to Edward Carpenter, one of his English admirers, 'There is something in my nature *furtive* like an old hen! ... Sloane Kennedy [another disciple] calls me "artful" – which about hits the mark.'

Whitman was a democratic version of that modern personality adumbrated in the *Rameau's Nephew* of Diderot – the divided, multiple personality, a shifting amalgam of sycophancy and sloth, of mimetic brilliance and Dionysian inspiration, of calculating common sense and philosophic insight, of raffish Bohemianism, of Rousseauistic disorientation and primitivism – a mind neurotic, lonely, unstable, libidinous, envious, indolent, suffused with yeasty eruptions from the unconscious depths, turning uncertainly from self-assertion to self-recrimination and despair, brooding with the same sense of mystery on the most sublime and the most vulgar and sordid aspects of life.

As I say, one is not for long touched or interested by a writer's public poses when these are too preponderantly fake – as in the case of Oscar Wilde. The poses, we feel, must be largely a necessity induced in the writer by his own personality or by the culture he lives in. Certainly they were so induced in Whitman.

Looked at as a matter of public relations, the problem is simple. Whitman was a poet of a very advanced and difficult sort; he was of dubious sex. This gave him two wars to fight with the advancing bourgeois America, and two wars to fight with himself, so much a part was he of this America, so much did he share in its tastes and believe in its moral proscriptions. The culture of his time admired, (much more so than our culture does today) the prophet, the orator, the sententious democratic reformer; and it admired rough plebeian masculinity. It would condone oddity of behaviour (more so than now) so long as the main requirements were met. Whitman met them. When he discovered how strong was the public condemnation of sex in literature, Whitman added to the façade the 'good gray poet' (or gratefully allowed it to be added by his disciple and apologist O'Connor). These poses are, of course, involved extensively in Whitman's poetry, a large portion of Leaves of Grass being little more than a rhetorical proclamation of them. From the point of view of art and under the aspect of eternity the public figure and his democratic program (valuable as these are in themselves) were the massive irrelevance and waste required for the indulgence of the essential Whitman – the young comic god and profound elegist.

Whitman had it somewhat easier than Melville or Mark Twain. Neurotic, riven, and vividly paradoxical as his personality was, many of the conflicting elements were subsumable under his monumental inertia and placidity, which allowed him to live more at rest than they in nineteenth-century America. The battle of Melville and Mark Twain with their times, though not more fundamental than that of Whitman, was more violent and more wearing. One might find a genetic explanation for this in the fact that all three had rather un-stable fathers who 'failed', but that whereas Melville and Mark Twain had mothers who were inclined to be harsh and morally overbearing and for whom they came to have very equivocal feelings, Whitman's mother was what is supposed to be the American male's ideal – she was firm, patient, hard-working, sympathetic and loving, and she lived on in her son.

In effect Whitman was cannier than either Melville or Mark Twain. His battle was more covert, more furtive; his essential genius was buried deep in his massive, slow-moving personality, showed itself on few occasions (not at all until he was thirty-six), masked itself behind a consistent and extensive series of public gestures, and quickly disappeared altogether. Despite the failure of *Leaves of Grass*, Whitman did not suffer the long nervous exacerbations of Melville and Mark Twain. One may note that Van Wyck Brooks was wrong to suggest, in *The Ordeal of Mark Twain*, that when Whitman retired to Camden in 1873, he was retreating like a whipped dog from a hostile and unappreciative America – this is the kind of speculation that invites the philistine reply: 'No, he went because he had a stroke and his brother George lived in Camden.' (I would add, however, that after critics like Bernard De Voto have recaptured nineteenth-century American culture in what plentitude it had, Brooks' biography of Mark Twain seems still *essentially* right, although errant in many particulars. His book remains a classic in the study of the position of our great writers in the nineteenth century.)

Is Whitman, then, an example of what is known as the alienated artist? Certainly, there is much evidence to convince us that he gave people the impression of living outside the usual order of things, related to but different from the world of ordinary men – an impression which encouraged his disciples in later years to regard him as a genuinely new species of man and to approach him with something of that awe which mankind reserves for the shaman, the holy idiot, prophet, or priest. This peculiar estrangement from the world is one of the striking facts about Whitman. One notices that, for reasons among which his bisexuality must figure prominently, he never had any relationships with others which were not strongly susceptible of abstract and ideal meaning; the give and take of ordinary human friendship were unknown to him. His relationships were those of the loving son to the blameless mother, the tender father to the idealized young man (the wounded veteran, the young horsecar driver), the master to his disciples. Especially in his later years people found Whitman cold, secretive, stubbornly impersonal but at the same time paradoxically wistful and appealing.

This alienation, impelling Whitman to resort to symbolic and ideal forms of reattachment, is one of the major sources of his art. And one may think that he was a great poet as long as he could believe in the availability, reality, and endurance of the self that gazed in wonder at the world and as long as he could accept its apartness either by pro-clamations of the power of the self alone or of the identity of the self with all things and all men. Thus in *Song of Myself* (to anticipate for a moment) the world and its people are seen from a position apart: 'they are not the Me myself.' But the separation is nothing to fear, because however illusory the world may be, nothing can alienate the self: 'What is commonest, cheapest, nearest, easiest is Me.' The decline of Whitman the great poet begins when he comes to think that he is alienated not only from the world but from himself and that this alienation can no longer be felt as a challenge to be met by aggressive poetic expression or in contemplative elegiac verse but is felt, rather, as a threat which can be met only by extra-poetic means – by becoming, that is, the hospital visitor, the self-publicist, the good gray poet, the sage and master. The perception of this self-alienation, the sense of 'the real Me' being 'withdrawn far, mocking me', is expressed in the beautiful elegy *As I Ebb'd with the Ocean of Life*.

If the masks he wore and the poems he wrote served Whitman as façades to hide behind, they also served to symbolize and countervail or deny his alienation. As Mark Van Doren says, 'Whitman's best poetry came out of his contradictions, and out of his struggle either to resolve them or to remove them.' Van Doren adds that Whitman was far from the average man he talked of being; indeed, a gulf opens 'between him and us, and leaves him standing strangely on the other side. Across such a space we can contemplate better than we formerly could his predilection for the theme of death.' When the gulf across which Whitman stared at the rest of the world and finally at himself could no longer be symbolically bridged, it became in itself the obsessive object of contemplation.

Sociologically speaking, Whitman's poses were the reflex of his culture. From the point of view of his art, they were the concerted maneuver which allowed him to produce a small body of great poetry. Psychologically speaking, they were the ego ideals which sought to control an unruly unconscious, or to mediate between it and the world. If we turn to the difficult, and doubtless insoluble, problem of explaining how, apparently almost overnignt, Walt Whitman ceased being merely a desultory editor, hack writer and carpenter and became a great poet, we will doubtless conclude that only a line of psychological speculation can avoid sententious irrelevancies. Of course, it will not solve the problem. (There is hardly any literary evidence which allows us to trace a development of either thought or style. The scanty notebooks, going back as early as 1847, are of little interest. The few scattered examples of Whitman's early poetry, extending from imitations of Scott to a broken versification dimly resembling that of *Leaves of Grass*, are of some technical interest. They raise the question – but hardly more – as to how Whitman achieved the language without which he would not have been a poet. In this connexion, however, the reader may find the concluding pages of chapter II of interest.)

The three most frequently recurring explanations of Whitman's transformation from editor-carpenter to poet seem inadmissible. The first is that New Orleans and the octoroon Whitman met there converted the provincial Quakerish youth to life and liberated his creative powers. If we are right in thinking that Whitman was rather virginal than overtly sexual, we cannot give credence to the New Orleans explanation, in so far as this refers to a sexual connexion. And in any case even so slow a personality as Whitman's would probably not require seven years (from 1848–1855) to exhibit the results of so momentous an experience.

A second explanation is that at some time after the New Orleans trip and subsequent adventures probably involving sexual attempts, Whitman had the tragic but purgative and liberating experience of recognizing and accepting the fact that he was homosexual. But here again the objection must be that Whitman's sexuality was so diffuse and sublimated that it could never have generated in him any definitive disposition or crucial recognition and acceptance of such a disposition. Furthermore, the evidence that Whitman had heterosexual relations is almost as substantial as the evidence that he was homosexual – and neither is *very* substantial.

A third explanation is that Whitman had a mystical experience, not necessarily involving sex, which gave him his characteristic vision, that at some crucial moment he was 'illuminated' and perceived the universe in all its totality – 'cosmic consciousness', Dr Richard Bucke,

one of the disciples and an 'alienist', called it. Observers so acute as
Santayana and William James concluded that the essential quality of
Whitman's mind was mysticism, although to the literary critic it
does not seem so. Comparisons have been made between Whitman
and the Oriental mystics: St Paul and Rousseau, struck down by the
apocalyptic influx of light, have been recalled. There may be sometimes a kind of mysticism at work in Whitman's poetry. But it is
hardly ever distinguishable from merely vague thought and diffuse
metaphor – and therefore it seems more gratuitous or honorific than
accurate to refer to it as mysticism. But from a literary point of view
this 'mysticism' is surely not 'characteristic.' And in fact the more one
reviews the evidence and the more one reads the poems, the less likely
does the 'mystical experience' seem and the less relevant to an understanding of such poems as *Song of Myself* does it become, even if it
occurred. As we have noted before, there is no evidence about
Whitman which encourages us to think him capable of any stern,
overwhelming, or intense spiritual experience. Except in his poems,
his mind and emotions were not grasping, imperious and rapid like
those of St Paul or Rousseau, nor capable of the disciplined maso-
chism of the Oriental mystic. Whitman made the right analogy: he
was like the grass, he was a 'slow arriver', his poetic powers emerged
gradually and painfully, and whatever definite redispositions there
were secret and subliminal but of the native soil.

Furthermore, it seems a matter of general principle that poetic
experience, although it may include it, cannot be equated with or
produced by mystic experience, properly so called. Mysticism leads
to the ecstatic contemplation of the naught; it does not of itself
produce poetry, which is a metaphorical construction of the aught.
Poetry is made by the imagination, and, as Santayana insists, the life
of reason depends on our ability to distinguish between the imaginative and the mystic (although he himself failed to do so in his attack
on Whitman). I do not wish to deny the usefulness of the word
'mysticism' in speaking of the general tenor of Whitman's mind,
but only to doubt its relevance to the strictly literary question and to
the question of his emergence as a poet.

A more convincing line of speculation as to how Whitman became
a poet probably has to begin with the theory developed by Jean Catel
in his *Walt Whitman: la naissance du poète* (1929), a much more solid

piece of Freudian analysis than Holloway's. Catel notes the morose, disorganized personality of Walt's father, the anxious instability of the family as it moved from house to house, the unfolding fate of Walt's brothers and sisters which, as we have noted, was to be on the whole a story of sickness, depravity, and insanity – when Alcott visited Whitman in 1856 he found that Walt shared a bed with his twenty-one-year-old brother Eddie, the imbecile and epileptic. One observes the uncertainty of Whitman's life as a young man, after he had emerged from what the poet himself called his 'unhappy' boyhood. From the time Walt began to work in printing shops up until 1855, and thereafter for that matter, his career consisted of a series of advances and retreats, of abortive attempts to hold jobs, to become a writer of editorials, sketches and short stories. One postulates the failure and pain of the young man's sexual experiments, the anxiety consequent upon his gradual realization of his bisexuality and his auto-eroticism – the 'I' in *Song of Myself* has two aspects or voices: the wistful, lonely, hurt, feminine, erotically demanding voice which alternates with that of the bearded, sunburned, masculine, democratic 'rough'. And the poem contains passages, of course, which are frankly auto-erotic.

The emergence of Whitman's genius may be understood as the consequence of his having failed because of neurotic disturbances to make terms with the world. In the early 1850s he found a compensatory way of dealing with a world which threatened to defeat him. If he could not subdue it on its own terms, he would do so by committing himself entirely to that rich fantasy life of which he felt himself increasingly capable. (That Whitman conceived of his own poetic emergence in a way that substantiates the present argument is shown by his remark that 'the *Democratic Review* essays and tales came from the surface of the mind, and had no connexion with what lay below – a great deal of which indeed was below consciousness. At last came the time when the concealed growth had to come to light.') His power of fantasy would allow him to escape into an innocent, regressive, Eden-like realm and it would also allow him symbolically to assault and overwhelm a world of ordinary reality which had proved to be, on its own terms, too much for him. He would utterly escape and defy the world's attempt to establish in his shifting psychic economy a superego – to impose upon him this or that conventional 'identity'.

He would allow his unconscious the freedom it demanded. He would free the ego of all prudential considerations, and make it dance to the tune of the unconscious. He would write a poem full of the sense of release and novelty, redolent with the uncanny unpredictableness of images fresh from the subliminal mind, and the subject of the poem would be the self – that is, the unconscious mind – 'the infinite and omnigenous' self, and it would describe the self as a timeless universal continuum but also as having the capacity to advance and retreat, to merge with and to extricate itself at will from any and all 'identities'. The poem would be full of philosophy and high thought, to be sure, but it would purvey the philosophy in a style determined by the sheer solipsism and incongruity of unconscious thought.

So free and aggressive an assertion of unconscious impulse, like any outburst that flouts the prudent, moralizing part of the mind, might be expected to generate a good deal of guilt. And this will account in part for the rather extensive revisions Whitman made of *Song of Myself* in later editions, carefully excising or rewording sections which spoke too frankly of such matters as adolescent sexual confusions. It will account for his deliberate silence about what he was doing in the period just before 1855, and it gives us a lead toward explaining the whole elaborate evasion which constituted his public pose and which he fostered and condoned in the early biographies. Whitman was by no means always the free spirit he was in *Song of Myself*. Taking him by and large, he was canny and prudential. In an early notebook he had written that to be an American 'is to be illimitably proud, independent, self-possessed, generous, and gentle. It is to accept nothing except what is equally free and eligible to anybody else. It is to be poor rather than rich – but to prefer death sooner than any mean dependence. ... Prudence is part of it, because prudence is the right arm of independence.' Nothing could be more characteristic of Whitman than that last sentence. It reminds one of his amusing exhortation to Traubel in later years: 'Be radical, be radical, be not too damn radical.'

The analysis of Whitman's personality set forth in the last paragraphs cannot, of course, fully account for Whitman the poet. It is impossible to say why, given his psychic difficulties, he became a poet and not (like his brother Jesse) a psychotic case, except that he had 'genius'. On a historical view, however, one notices a happy conjunction of forces, involving Whitman's emerging personality and the assumptions of the culture he lived in, partly as Whitman instinctively understood and shared them, partly as he found them rationalized and given a language in the essays of Emerson.

In order to arrive at the vision of things which we find in *Song of Myself*, the self had to be apprehended as a felt presence as an idea, and as a metaphor or conceit. It had to be identified with the unconscious at least completely enough so that it would take on to itself some of the powers and qualities of the unconscious. But first (the chronology is, of course, for purposes of discussion only) Whitman had to liberate within himself and become aware of his unconscious mind in its poetry-making aspect. That he had done this by 1855 is shown by another poem which appeared in the first edition, *The Sleepers*. As we shall note below, this poem is of interest to the psychological investigator because of its presentation of the dream activity of the mind as the way in which universal equality and unity are achieved, the way in which joy and vitality are released, and, most important, the way in which the poetic imagination is achieved.

Given the unconscious so conceived, what was needed before *Song of Myself* could be written was the idea of the self and some reason for connecting the self with the unconscious. Several things forced the self upon Whitman's attention. He was characteristically, as he said, conscious of himself as 'two' (psychologically perhaps the result of his bisexual nature). The democracy of which Whitman was so natively a part exalted the free, self-sufficient individual, having lost under the impact of Jeffersonian and Jacksonian theories much of whatever sense of traditional, institutional life and the place of the individual therein it had once possessed. The Quaker tendency of the Whitman family enhanced the sense of the inner mystery. Transcendentalist theory made the self a godlike power – omniscient, omnipresent, omnipotent. In 'Self-Reliance' Emerson mythicized the self in a way which could hardly fail to have the most conclusive and electric effect on a mind such as Whitman's.

What is the aboriginal self, on which a universal reliance may be grounded? [Emerson asked.] The inquiry leads us to that source, at once the essence of genius, of virtue, and of life, which we call spontaneity or instinct. We denote this primary wisdom as intuition, whilst all later teachings are tuitions. In that deep force, the last fact behind which analysis cannot go, all things find their common origin.

Taking a psychological view of this characteristic formulation (as the references to 'spontaneity', 'instinct', and the 'deep force' of the mind allow us to do), we understand Emerson to say that an inquiry into the self, both in its individual and its universal aspects, leads us to the unconscious part of the mind. In another sense, Emerson is apparently saying that the self, considered as 'aboriginal', *is* the unconscious, that in its aboriginal aspect, it not only leads us to the unconscious – to the 'last fact behind which analysis cannot go' – it *is* this 'last fact'.

One need not find Emerson's words perfectly clear as psychology or metaphysics to see in them a remarkably suggestive and fertile poetic metaphor. And it must certainly have been as such that the formulation appealed to Whitman. In this basic metaphor Emerson can be said to have made connexions among the self or identity, the unconscious, and the universal, and to have given the whole vision the status of 'wisdom' in just such a manner as would precipitate a similar crystalization in the mind of Whitman. All the elements were in Whitman, the products of his peculiar temperament and of his democratic surroundings. But it was from Emerson that he first sensed how they might be put together.

The release and acceptance of unconscious poetry-making powers is described in *The Sleepers*. As the *Whitman Handbook* avers, it has long been recognized that 'no other composition is so revealing of the methods by which [Whitman] sublimated his life into the universal symbols of poetry.' A detailed reading of the poem would be tedious and probably misleading. But as a way of penetrating the evocative surface of *The Sleepers* the burdensome language of science may prove temporarily useful. *The Sleepers* is a poem about the descent of the as yet unformed and unstable ego into the id, its confrontation there of the dark, human tragedy, its emergence in a new, more stable form. Or in Whitmanesque language, the subject of the poem is the surrender of the self to the 'night', the identification of the self with the 'night' and the subsequent emergence of the self, newly constituted and participant in forms of unity, health, and felicity.

At the beginning, the poet is 'wandering and confused, lost to myself, ill-assorted, contradictory.' But at the end – having dared to descend into the night so that now he can defiantly exclaim, 'Why should I be afraid to trust myself to you?' – the wandering has direction, the self is no longer alienated, abysses are bridged, contradictions resolved.

To follow Whitman while, as he says, 'I become the other dreamers' is to encounter a series of hauntingly beautiful if sometimes elusive emotions and symbols. There is the gratifying sense of surrender and release, impelling the poet to exclaim:

I am a dance – play up there! The fit is whirling me fast!
I am the ever-laughing. . . .
Onward we move, a gay gang of blackguards! with mirth-
    shouting music and wild-flapping pennants of joy!

There are the more somber moments when we behold the dark motives and characters of that family drama which underlies some of the greatest of tragic poems. Insistently present is the encompassing image of the mother, who appears in the guise of the young woman who receives a shadowy lover, as the 'sleepless widow' who looks out on 'the winter midnight' and sees the shrouded coffin of her husband, and as the goddess-like squaw whom, like so many things in this poem, Whitman recalls from childhood experience. The mother plays her central part among the shifting scenes in which we catch a glimpse of the 'beautiful gigantic swimmer swimming naked through the eddies of the sea' until, bruised on the rocks, he is borne 'swiftly and out of sight', [a] 'brave corpse'; in which we stand with the poet on a frozen, wintry beach watching while the corpses of a wrecked ship's passengers are brought ashore; and in which we see George Washington, cold, weeping, and pale, bidding farewell, in his tender, fatherly manner, to his surviving soldiers.

The dark actions of the poem having been played out, the conflicts and guilt feelings having been allayed, the ostensibly ill-assorted personages having been brought into relation, there can follow a pleasurable idyl which celebrates forms of unity. 'The wildest and bloodiest is over, and all is peace.' No longer is the poet 'lost' to himself. Alienation, separation, contradiction – these sources of un-conscious conflict and pain but also of rationality and imagination are not abolished; rather they are envisioned as parts of a larger order. So Whitman seems to mean when he says that 'the diverse shall be no less diverse, but they shall flow and unite – they unite now.' The flow and the unity refer no doubt to Whitman's 'philosophy', his idea of a dialectically emergent, creative, and benign universe. But they also refer to his unique poetic method, the achievement of which *The Sleepers* may be understood to announce and describe. The self has been powerfully reconstituted by its descent into the night and so is ready to perform its vivid feats in *Song of Myself*. But so has the poetic style which a difficult subject demands. Such a complicated and unique style cannot be defined easily, and I wish to do no more at this point than to observe, what other writers have noticed, that a stream-of-consciousness method underlies the structure of Whitman's poetry. He is likely to be at his very best when a cat-and-mouse game is going on between the conscious and the unconscious, when unexpected dreamlike images emerge apparently unheralded and have to be dealt with by an imaginative intelligence which is not often capable of large, executive organizations of meaning but which is triumphantly capable of local forms of order produced by a comic or elegiac sensibility. Of all Whitman's poems *The Sleepers* is nearest to a pure stream-of-consciousness method, with its impressive flow of what seem absolutely inevitable archetypal images. This poem is characteristic of Whitman at his best; for where the self is dancing, penetrating the veil of death, confronting exciting emanations from the unconscious, and rebounding into the midst of life, it is always an interesting protagonist.

The evidence, if such it may be accounted, of *The Sleepers* would seem to suggest anew the improbability that a decisive mystical or sexual experience was what transformed Whitman from a journalist and carpenter into a poet. This poem implies that 'the diverse', could now be made to 'flow and unite' because the poet had reached the point where he could liberate his inner energies by a return to his earliest memories, long suppressed perhaps but now freed and imaginatively symbolized. This inner psychic advance happily coincided with the effect upon Whitman's imagination of certain cultural and literary influences, the most important of which were suggested above. All this is of course a truism, in the sense that it describes the way in which all poets become poets. But the ingenuous critic will pretend

to offer no more, and may rest content with having suggested some of
the particular qualities of his particular truism.

(41-57)

In considering *Crossing Brooklyn Ferry*, one does not have to look
for the perfect representation of its underlying metaphor anywhere
but in the poem itself; surely it is one of the best Whitman wrote.
Thoreau appears to be on solid ground in expressing his preference
for this poem and for *Song of Myself*. In *Song of the Open Road* Whitman had been seeking a less witty, more purely lyric expression of the
exuberance which was one of his strong points and to expand it into
the scope of vision and prophecy. In *Crossing Brooklyn Ferry* he brings
a new lyric austerity and control to his capacity for pathos and musing
reflection.

Everything conspires to the advantage of the poem. The river, the
sea, always called out the best in a poet whose emotions were as
languid, powerful, and recurrent as the tides and whose flowing
depths were modified by an incorrigible gamesomeness; he was like
the profound river, which 'frolicked on' with its 'crested and
scallop-edg'd waves'. The river is the perfect symbol for the 'float
forever held in solution' from which 'identities' are 'struck', just as
the objects visualized in 'mast-hemm'd Manhattan' and in Brooklyn,
as well as the gulls and boats dropping downstream, are perfect
symbols of 'identity.' Nor is the river less adequate as the mighty,
primitive power across whose contrary tides the ferry carries man to
eternity – which, the poem asserts, is the locus of everything that
brings men into harmony or serves as the principle of the continuity
of human feelings in space and through time.

It is usually a good sign when Whitman begins overtly to doubt
himself, since his capacity for meditative self-doubt leads him to
write some of his best poems, notably *Out of the Cradle*, although, to
be sure, self-doubt could also lead him to mere compensatory
rhetoric. In *Crossing Brooklyn Ferry* the musing confession of weakness and uncertainty finds its first full voice, and it becomes a saving
grace in the poem:

It is not upon you alone the dark patches fall,
The dark threw its patches down upon me also;

The best I had done seem'd to me blank and suspicious;
My great thoughts as I supposed them, were they not in reality
   meagre?
Nor is it you alone who know what it is to be evil,
I am he who knew what it was to be evil,
I too knitted the old knot of contrariety,
Blabb'd, blush'd, resented, lied, stole, grudg'd,
Had guile, anger, lust, hot wishes I dared not speak,
Was wayward, vain, greedy, shallow, sly, cowardly, malignant,
The wolf, the snake, the hog, not wanting in me,
The cheating look, the frivolous word, the adulterous wish, not
   wanting,
Refusals, hates, postponements, meanness, laziness, none of these
   wanting.

The technical superiority of *Crossing Brooklyn Ferry* is in the comparative austerity of the diction and the felicity of the images the river,
the tides, the ferry boat, the sunset, the circling gulls, the ships with
their tall masts, the hills on the shore, the flags and pennants. In this
poem Whitman has found the 'objects' he groped for in *Song of the
Open Road*. In alleging that these objects – the 'dumb beautiful
ministers' – mediate between man and eternity, Whitman has made
them mediate between the uncompleted particulars of the poem and
the fixed perfection of poetic form.

Both *Song of the Open Road* and *Crossing Brooklyn Ferry* benefit by
Whitman's peculiar affinity for images of motion, his capacity to
capture the sensation he himself cherished in his rambles about Long
Island, his observation of birds in flight, and of sail boats on the Sound,
his inveterate ferry boat and horse-car riding. *Crossing Brooklyn
Ferry*, allowing him to associate images of motion with the sea and
the river, called for exactly that kind of supple, indolent, flowing
motion which Whitman could supremely render. F. O. Matthiessen
cites Coleridge to the point; Whitman usually fails, Matthiessen
writes 'when his verbal imagery is violently active, and only when it is
more supple succeeds in endowing his poetry, with the sensuousness
that Coleridge held indispensable to insure a "framework of objecti-
vity." Such a framework, in turn, is essential for "that definiteness and
articulation of imagery, and that modification of the images them-

selves, without which poetry becomes flattened into mere didactics of practice, or evaporated into a hazy, unthoughtful day-dreaming.'" As a measure of Whitman's relative success and failure in his more lyric mode – for example, in *Crossing Brooklyn Ferry* and *Song of the Open Road* – this could hardly be improved on.

If any one poem of Whitman's can be more confidently alleged than the others in refutation of Santayana's attack on 'the poetry of barbarism,' it is *Crossing Brooklyn Ferry*. Admitting for a moment the dubious idea that Santayana's attack on Whitman's *philosophy* is a legitimate attack on his *poetry*, one must believe that the assault is indeed formidable. But like other critics Santayana sees only one side of Whitman, the primitive bard who turned to live with the animals, the naïve, indolent, rustic whose style 'reproduces the method of a rich, spontaneous, absolutely lazy fancy.' This was Whitman's way of being a 'barbarian' – that is, 'a man who regards his passions as their own excuse for being; who does not domesticate them either by understanding their cause or by conceiving their ideal goal.' There will always be a sense in which one must attend to Santayana's denunciation of the nineteenth-century romantic naturalists, among whom he places Whitman. It is true that they often do wind up – Hegel, Browning, even Nietzsche – by merely worshipping the brute nature they had apparently been bent on observing from a firmly constituted realm of ideal values. It is true that the life of reason depends on living in some way in the two-story, Platonic-materialist world of Santayana. Yet the life of reason is only up to a point the life of poetry. And judged from the philosophical point of view, such a poem as *Crossing Brooklyn Ferry* seems adequately to provide and perfectly to constitute both nature and the ideal, to create a world in which, as Whitman says, the things of nature 'furnish' their 'parts toward eternity'. But Santayana's essay will always be valuable. It is contemptible only in one sentence – 'Even during the civil war, when he heard the drum-taps so clearly, he could only gaze at the picturesque and terrible aspect of the struggle, and linger among the wounded day after day with a canine devotion; he could not be aroused either to clear thought or to positive action.' A certain elegant callousness is the price of Santayana's admirable philosophy, as naïve philosophy is the price of Whitman's poetry.

(107–110)

Malcolm Cowley

from his Introduction to *Leaves of Grass: The First (1855) Edition*
1959

[*Song of Myself*] is hardly at all concerned with American nationalism, political democracy, contemporary progress, or other social themes that are commonly associated with Whitman's work. The 'incomparable things' that Emerson found in it are philosophical and religious principles. Its subject is a state of illumination induced by two (or three) separate moments of ecstasy. In more or less narrative sequence it describes those moments, their sequels in life, and the doctrines to which they give rise. The doctrines are not expounded by logical steps or supported by arguments; instead they are presented dramatically, that is, as the new convictions of a hero, and they are revealed by successive unfoldings of his states of mind.

The hero as pictured in the frontispiece this hero named 'I' or 'Walt Whitman' in the text – should not be confused with the Whitman of daily life. He is, as I said, a dramatized or idealized figure, and he is put forward as a representative American workingman, but one who prefers to loaf and invite his soul. Thus, he is rough, sunburned, bearded; he cocks his hat as he pleases, indoors or out; but in the text of the first edition he has no local or family background, and he is deprived of strictly individual characteristics, with the exception of curiosity, boastfulness, and an abnormally developed sense of touch. His really distinguishing feature is that he has been granted a vision, as a result of which he has realized the potentialities latent in every American and indeed, he says, in every living person, even 'the brutish koboo, called the ordure of humanity'. This dramatization of the hero makes it possible for the living Whitman to exalt him – as he would not have ventured, at the time, to exalt himself – but also to poke mild fun at the hero for his gab and loitering, for his tall talk or 'omnivorous words', and for sounding his barbaric yawp over the roofs of the world. The religious feeling in *Song of Myself* is counterpoised by a humor that takes the form of slangy and mischievous impudence or drawling Yankee self-ridicule.

There has been a good deal of discussion about the structure of the poem. In spite of revealing analyses made by a few Whitman scholars, notably Carl F. Strauch and James E. Miller Jr, a feeling still seems to prevail that it has no structure properly speaking; that it is inspired but uneven, repetitive, and especially weak in its transitions from one theme to another. I suspect that much of this feeling may be due to Whitman's later changes in the text, including his arbitrary scheme, first introduced in the 1867 edition, of dividing the poem into fifty-two numbered paragraphs or chants. One is tempted to read the chants as if they were separate poems, thus overlooking the unity and flow of the work as a whole. It may also be, however, that most of the scholars have been looking for a geometrical pattern, such as can be found and diagramed in some of the later poems. If there is no such pattern in *Song of Myself*, that is because the poem was written on a different principle, one much closer to the spirit of the Symbolists or even the Surrealists.

The true structure of the poem is not primarily logical but psychological, and is not a geometrical figure but a musical progression. As music *Song of Myself* is not a symphony with contrasting movements, nor is it an operatic work like *Out of the Cradle Endlessly Rocking*, with an overture, arias, recitatives, and a finale. It comes closer to being a rhapsody or tone poem, one that modulates from theme to theme, often changing in key and tempo, falling into reveries and rising toward moments of climax, but always preserving its unity of feeling as it moves onward in a wavelike flow. It is a poem that bears the marks of having been conceived as a whole and written in one prolonged burst of inspiration, but its unity is also the result of conscious art, as can be seen from Whitman's corrections in the early manuscripts. He did not recognize all the bad lines, some of which survive in the printed text, but there is no line in the first edition that seems false to a single prevailing tone. There are passages weaker than others, but none without a place in the general scheme. The repetitions are always musical variations and amplifications. Some of the transitions seem abrupt when the poem is read as if it were an essay, but Whitman was not working in terms of 'therefore' and 'however'. He preferred to let one image suggest another image, which in turn suggests a new statement of mood or doctrine. His themes modulate into one another by pure association, as in a waking dream, with the result that all his transitions seem instinctively right.

In spite of these oneiric elements, the form of the poem is something more than a forward movement in rising and subsiding waves of emotion. There is also a firm narrative structure, one that becomes easier to grasp when we start by dividing the poem into a number of parts or sequences. I think there are nine of these, but the exact number is not important; another critic might say there were seven (as Professor Miller does), or eight or ten. Some of the transitions are gradual, and in such cases it is hard to determine the exact line that ends one sequence and starts another. The essential point is that the parts, however defined, follow one another in irreversible order, like the beginning, middle, and end of any good narrative. My own outline, not necessarily final, would run as follows:

First sequence (chants 1–4): the poet or hero introduced to his audience. Leaning and loafing at his ease, 'observing a spear of summer grass', he presents himself as a man who lives outdoors and worships his own naked body, not the least part of which is vile. He is also in love with his deeper self or soul, but explains that it is not to be confused with his mere personality. His joyful contentment can be shared by you, the listener, 'For every atom belonging to me as good belongs to you.'

Second sequence (chant 5): the ecstasy. This consists in the rapt union of the poet and his soul, and it is described – figuratively, on the present occasion – in terms of sexual union. The poet now has a sense of loving brotherhood with God and with all mankind. His eyes being truly open for the first time, he sees that even the humblest objects contain the infinite universe:

And limitless are leaves stiff or drooping in the fields,
And brown ants in little wells beneath them,
And mossy scabs of the wormfence, and heaped stones, and elder
    and mullein and pokeweed.

Third sequence (chants 6–19): the grass. Chant 6 starts with one of Whitman's brilliant transitions. A child comes with both hands full of those same leaves from the fields. 'What is the grass?' the child asks – and suddenly we are presented with the central image of the poem, that is, the grass as symbolizing the miracle of common things and the divinity (which implies both the equality and the immortality) of ordinary persons. During the remainder of the sequence, the poet observes men and women – and animals too – at their daily occupations.

He is part of this life, he says, and even his thoughts are those of all men in all ages and lands. There are two things to be noted about the sequence, which contains some of Whitman's freshest lyrics. First, the people with a few exceptions (such as the trapper and his bride) are those whom Whitman has known all his life, while the scenes described at length are Manhattan streets and Long Island beaches or countryside. Second, the poet merely roams, watches, and listens, like a sort of Tiresias. The keynote of the sequence – as Professor Strauch was the first to explain – is the two words 'I observe.'

Fourth sequence (chants 20–25): the poet in person. 'Hankering, gross, mystical, nude', he venerates himself as august and immortal, but so, he says, is everyone else. He is the poet of the body and of the soul, of night, earth, and sea, and of vice and feebleness as well as virtue, so that 'many long dumb voices' speak through his lips, including those of slaves, prostitutes, even beetles rolling balls of dung. All life to him is such a miracle of beauty that the sunrise would kill him if he could not find expression for it – 'If I could not now and always send sunrise out of me.' The sequence ends with a dialogue between the poet and his power of speech, during which the poet insists that his deeper self – 'the best I am' – is beyond expression.

Fifth sequence (chants 26–29): ecstasy through the senses. Beginning with chant 26, the poem sets out in a new direction. The poet decides to be completely passive: 'I think I will do nothing for a long time but listen.' What he hears at first are quiet familiar sounds like the gossip of flames on the hearth and the bustle of growing wheat; but the sounds rise quickly to a higher pitch, becoming the matchless voice of a trained soprano, and he is plunged into an ecstasy of hearing, or rather of Being. Then he starts over again, still passively, with the sense of touch, and finds himself rising to the ecstasy of sexual union. This time the union is actual, not figurative, as can be seen from the much longer version of chant 29 preserved in an early notebook.

Sixth sequence (chants 30–38): the power of identification. After his first ecstasy, as presented in chant 5, the poet had acquired a sort of microscopic vision that enabled him to find infinite wonders in the smallest and most familiar things. The second ecstasy (or pair of ecstasies) has an entirely different effect, conferring as it does a sort of vision that is both telescopic and spiritual. The poet sees far into space and time; 'afoot with my vision' he ranges over the continent and goes speeding through the heavens among tailed meteors. His secret is the power of identification. Since everything emanates from the universal soul, and since his own soul is of the same essence, he can identify himself with every object and with every person living or dead, heroic or criminal. Thus, he is massacred with the Texans at Goliad, he fights on the *Bonhomme Richard*, he dies on the cross, and he rises again as 'one of an average unending procession'. Whereas the keynote of the third sequence was 'I observe', here it becomes 'I am' – 'I am a free companion' – 'My voice is the wife's voice, the screech by the rail of the stairs' – 'I am the man. . . . I suffered. . . . I was there.'

Seventh sequence (chants 39–41): the superman. When Indian sages emerge from the state of samadhi or absorption, they often have the feeling of being omnipotent. It is so with the poet, who now feels gifted with superhuman powers. He is the universally beloved Answerer (chant 39), then the Healer, raising men from their death-beds (40), and then the Prophet (41) of a new religion that outbids 'the old cautious hucksters' by announcing that men are divine and will eventually be gods.

Eighth sequence (chants 42–50): the sermon. 'A call in the midst of the crowd' is the poet's voice, 'orotund sweeping and final.' He is about to offer a statement of the doctrines implied by the narrative (but note that his statement comes at the right point psychologically and plays its part in the narrative sequence). As strangers listen, he proclaims that society is full of injustice, but that the reality beneath it is deathless persons (chant 42); that he accepts and practices all religions, but looks beyond them to 'what is untried and afterward' (43); that he and his listeners are the fruit of ages, and the seed of untold ages to be (44); that our final goal is appointed: 'God will be there and wait till we come' (45); that he tramps a perpetual journey and longs for companions, to whom he will reveal a new world by washing the gum from their eyes – but each must then continue the journey alone (46); that he is the teacher of men who work in the open air (47); that he is not curious about God, but sees God every-where, at every moment (48); that we shall all be reborn in different forms ('No doubt I have died myself ten thousand times before'); and that the evil in the world is like moonlight, a mere reflection of the sun (49). The end of the sermon (chant 50) is the hardest passage to interpret in the whole poem. I think, though I cannot be certain, that the poet is harking back to the period after one of his ten thousand deaths, when he slept and slept long before his next awakening. He seems to remember vague shapes, and he beseeches these Outlines, as he calls them, to let him reveal the 'word unsaid'. Then turning back to his audience, 'It is not chaos or death,' he says. 'It is form and union and plan. . . . it is eternal life. . . . it is happiness.'

Ninth sequence (chants 51–52): the poet's farewell. Having finished his sermon, the poet gets ready to depart, that is, to die and wait for another incarnation or 'fold of the future', while still inviting others to follow. At the beginning of the poem he had been leaning and loafing at ease in the summer grass. Now, having rounded the circle, he bequeaths himself to the dirt 'to grow from the grass I love'. I do not see how any careful reader, unless blinded with preconceptions, could overlook the unity of the poem in tone and image and direction.

(xiv–xx)

Leslie Fiedler

from 'Walt Whitman: Portrait of the Artist as a Middle-Aged Hero', *No! in Thunder* 1960

The key poems of Whitman's book were written from sometime just before 1855 to 1860; that is, from the moment the poet approached his thirty-fifth year to the moment he left behind his fortieth. They are, therefore, the expression of what the French call the *crise de quarante*, the crisis of entering middle age, of accepting once and for all what one unredeemably is. Whitman is a Romantic poet in many senses; but he is not, like most Romantics, a poet of adolescence, except as the nostalgia of adolescence in him survives and blends into the disenchantment of middle age. His production before his thirty-fifth year is trivial and conventional, his few poems, inept in form and melancholy in tone, concerned with death and the vanity of ambition. Most of his earliest writing is in prose, chiefly newspaper stories, but also a temperance novel and a handful of shorter fictions centering around fantasies of children beaten, abused and murdered. The almost pathological self-pity projected in such stories, the fear of authority and the desperate identification with the misunderstood child are a clue to all of Whitman's work; but it is not till his youth is over that he is able to make of such symptoms works of art.

The poetry written by Whitman after his fortieth year consists by and large of variations on the themes established between 1855 and 1860. The Civil War and especially the death of Lincoln provided him with what seem new subjects for verse. But even that remarkable threnody *When Lilacs Last in the Dooryard Bloom'd* in the main merely recapitulates the feelings and even the symbols of *Out of the Cradle*. There is, indeed, a disturbing vagueness about the former poem, a sense that its occasion is only nominal, that it mourns someone or something only accidentally represented by Lincoln. The shorter war pieces are least successful when they are concerned with actual combat, most convincing when they deal with Whitman in his role of *The Wound-Dresser*, male nurse and loving consoler of the dying – a role he had already imagined for himself in *Song of Myself*.

> To anyone dying, thither I speed and twist the knob of the door ...
>
> (*Song of Myself*, 39)

> Let the physician and the priest go home ...
> I am he bringing help for the sick as they pant on their
>   backs ...
>
> (*Song of Myself*, 41)

It is as if, after his fortieth year, Whitman could not even live (much less write) anything he had not already set down in the work from which he was unable to disentangle his aging self.

At any rate the crisis of his own middle age remained always more real for Whitman *as a poet* than the great national crises of secession and war, and at the center of that personal crisis is a crushing sense of loneliness, of being unloved. In the years between 1855 and 1860, he apparently came to realize more and more clearly that not only would he never get married (he probably never experienced any deep heterosexual love), but that there would never be for him any stable, continuing relationship either with male or female. This terrible truth his heart had guessed (he tells us in *Out of the Cradle*) even as a child; for him there would be no love not intimately blended with death, no satisfaction for all his yearning this side of the grave.

Only with the creatures of his fancy, with an imagined 'you' (sometimes conceived as a lost lover; sometimes as the perfect 'Camerado', God; sometimes as an indiscriminate Everyman; often as the reader; most often as a second self, 'the real Me') could he enter into an orgasmic unity. His poems are at once a prayer for such a union and that imaginary orgasm itself. No poet engages the reader with so fervid and intimate a clasp; no writer describes the act of reading so erotically.

(Is it night? Are we here together alone?)
It is I you hold and who holds you,
I spring from the pages into your arms . . .
Your breath falls around me like dew, your pulse lulls the
   tympans of my ears,
I feel immerged from head to foot,
Delicious, enough.

                    (*So Long!*)

Song of Myself, though it stands at the center of Whitman's epic attempt and can be read as a heroic poem intended to define the ethos of a nation, is also a love poem: simultaneously a love song, a love affair (the poet's only successful one) and a love child (the only real offspring of his passion, for surely the five illegitimate children of whom he liked to boast were fantasies). But who is the poet's beloved, the Beatrice he could never leave off wooing, the Penelope to whom he could never return? As the hero of his poem is called 'I', so the loved one is called 'you'; and their vague pronominal romance is the thematic center of *Song of Myself*. It is an odd subject for the Great American Poem: the celebration (half-heroic, half-ironic) of the mating between an 'I' whose reality is constantly questioned and an even more elusive 'you'. The latter pronoun in Whitman's verse almost always is followed by the phrase 'whoever you are.' 'You whoever you are' – this must be surely the most compulsively repeated four-word phrase in *Leaves of Grass*, for it embodies a riddle which torments the poet even more than that of the Self: the riddle of the Other.

Is there an Other to whom one can speak: a real beloved, a real audience, a real God? Unless such a 'you' really exists, there is no point, no possibility of converting private 'vision' into public 'song'. It is because Whitman's personal concern on this score coincides with a more general problem that he touches us so deeply. His loneliness becomes a symbol for the alienation of the modern artist and of modern man in a godless universe. He lived, after all, at a moment when some thinkers were declaring the death of God, and wrote at a time when poets grew increasingly unsure of whom they were addressing.

Unlike Homer and Dante, Whitman could not assume a certain class of reader, but had to create his own public even as he had to create his own themes. His prose of being a popular poet, the bard of the common man, fooled neither him nor the common man, and must not deceive the unwary reader. Like most modern poets, he addressed and continues to address a shrinking and uncertain audience.

That is why to write at all required of him an act of faith, faith that a real 'you' existed somewhere; and that faith he desperately sustained. *Song of Myself* begins with the word 'I' but ends with 'you', a 'you' believed in though never possessed.

I stop somewhere waiting for you.

It is, then, a poem of faith, its doubts incidental and repressed. 'My foothold is tenon'd and mortis'd in granite', the poet insists. 'I accept Reality and I dare not question it . . .' 'The Lord will be there and wait till I come . . .'. In other poems, however, this faith falters or is utterly lost. In *The Sleepers*, for instance, the daylight has departed and with it all certainty. The poet begins 'wandering and confused, lost to myself', and ends seeking through his dreams the embrace of a 'you' who is not this time the Great Camerado, but the Great Mother: the darkness out of which his 'I' has emerged and to which it must return.

I will duly pass the day O my mother and duly return to you.

Though *The Sleepers*, like *Song of Myself*, moves from a concern with 'I' toward a commitment to 'you', its tone is altogether different, melancholy and subdued. It provides a transition to the third of the great 'I-you' poems, *As I Ebb'd with the Ocean of Life*, which opens on the line which gives it its title and closes, 'You up there walking or sitting,|Whoever you are, we too lie in drifts at your feet.' The final verses are thoroughly ambiguous, referring at once to

God (whosoever that may be) and 'this phantom looking down', which is to say, the poet's 'real Me', which he imagines eluding him, 'untouch'd, untold, altogether unreach'd,|Withdrawn far, mocking me with mock-congratulatory signs and bows|With peals of distant ironical laughter at every word I have written. . . .' There is no elation this time, no boasting, however, hysterical; the poet begins 'baffl'd, balk'd, bent to the very earth' and ends confessing, 'I have not once had the least idea who or what I am.'

But what happens to the love affair of 'I' and 'you' when the poet cannot even believe in his own 'I', which blurs and dissolves as he contemplates the 'Mystery of Being'? After his initial nausea before the ambiguity of his own existence ('Steep'd amid honey'd morphine, my windpipe throttled in fakes of death'), the poet of many masks and poses finds a kind of amusement in conceiving of all life as a cosmic hoax ('Have you no thought O dreamer that it may all be maya, illusion?'). Indeed, the play of illusion and reality, the teasing search for and the trifling with the 'real Me', 'the real real', 'the real of the real', becomes a major theme of Whitman's poetry, a theme on which the last word is spoken in the poem Whitman himself chose to stand at the end of his book, *Good-Bye My Fancy*.

May-be it is yourself now really ushering me to the true songs,
    (who knows?)
May-be it is you the mortal knob really undoing, turning . . .

The poet of dogmatic assertion has come to rest on the tentative hope of 'may-be'; and the meanings of 'you' (you, lover, whom I fancy – you, poem, which my fancy has created) have grown even more complex.

(61–75)

Roy Harvey Pearce

'Whitman Justified: The Poet in 1860', *Minnesota Review*, vol. 1 1961

Where are we going, Walt Whitman? The doors close in an hour.
Which way does your beard point tonight?
                    (Allen Ginsberg, *A Supermarket in California*)

My title comes from the fourteenth of the *Chants Democratic* in the 1860 *Leaves of Grass*. (This is the poem which finally became *Poets to Come*.) The first two stanzas read:

Poets to come!
Not to-day is to justify me, and Democracy, and what we are for,
But you, a new brood, native, athletic, continental, greater than
  before known,
You must justify me.

Indeed, if it were not for you, what would I be?
What is the little I have done, except to arouse you?

Whitman is, he concludes, 'the bard' of a 'future' for which he writes only 'one or two indicative words'.

The vision is Utopian, of course – and became increasingly so in the 1870s and '80s, when he was calling for, even guaranteeing, a state of things whereby poems would work so as eventually to make for the withering away of poetry. In a preface of 1872 he could claim:

The people, especially the young men and women of America, must begin to learn that Religion, (like Poetry,) is something far, far different from what they supposed. It is, indeed, too important to the power and perpetuity of the New World to be consigned any longer to the churches, old or new, Catholic or Protestant – Saint this, or Saint that. . . . It must be consigned henceforth to Democracy *en masse*, and to Literature. It must enter into the Poems of the Nation. It must make the Nation.

And by 1888 (in 'A Backward Glance O'er Travel'd Roads') he could claim that, contrary to European critical opinion, verse was not a dying technique.

Only a firmer, vastly broader, new area begins to exist – nay, is already formed – to which the poetic genius must emigrate. Whatever may have been the case in years gone by, the true use for the imaginative faculty of modern times is to give ultimate vivification to facts, to science, and to common lives, endowing them with glows and glories and final illustriousness which belongs to every real thing, and to real things only. Without that ultimate vivification – which the poet or other artist alone can give – reality would seem to be incomplete, and science, democracy, and life itself, finally in vain.

These two statements (and they are quite typical) sum up Whitman' growing sense of the power of poetry, and thus of the poet: Religions operating as poetry – and *only* as poetry – can make the nation,, vivify it: or, in the language of a late poem like *Passage to India*, 'eclaircise' it.

'In the prophetic literature of these states', he had written in 1871 (in *Democratic Vistas*), '. . . Nature, true Nature, and the true idea of Nature, long absent, must, above all, become fully restored, enlarged, and must furnish the pervading atmosphere to poems . . .' And later in the same essay: 'The poems of life are great, but there must be poems of the purports of life, not only in itself, but beyond itself.' Life beyond life, poetry beyond poetry: This idea came to count for more and more in Whitman's conception of his vocation, and accordingly, of that of the poets who were to come. The last edition (1892) of *Leaves of Grass* is surely the testament of the sort of 'divine literatus' whom he had earlier prophesied. Indeed, he had not only prophesied himself but made the prophecy come true. But, as he acknowledged, this was not the only form of his testament. For, when he wrote of the last edition, 'I am determined to have the world know what *I* was pleased to do', he yet recognized: 'In the long run the world will do as it pleases with the book.' The question remains: How may we use the book so as to know what we please to do with it? And more: What does the book, in its structure and function, in its growth, teach us about the vocation of poet in the modern world? And more: How may it help the poets who yet are to come discover, and so define, their vocation?

The hard fact – so it seems to me – is that Whitman fails as prophetic poet, precisely because he was such a powerfully *humane* poet. The adjective makes us flinch, perhaps: but only because, like Whitman, we have found the beliefs it implies so difficult to hold to that we have come – if not to seek for the prophetic utterances which will offer us something in their stead, then to discount them as disruptive of the high sense of our private selves on which we ground our hopes for the lives we live. Still, it might be that a close reading of Whitman, the poet of 1860 – for it is he whom I suggest we must recover – will teach us what it might be like once more to hold to them. Be that as it may, the record of Whitman's life would suggest that his own power, his own humanity, was at the end too much for him. In any case, when he tried to write prophetic poetry, he came eventually to sacrifice man – that finite creature, locked in time and history, at once agonized and exalted by his humanity – for what he has encouraged some of his advocates again to call cosmic man – the cosmic man of, say, these lines from *Passage to India*:

Passage, immediate passage! the blood burns in my veins!
Away O soul! hoist instantly the anchor!
Cut the hawsers – haul out – shake every sail!
Have we not stood here like trees in the ground long enough?
Have we not grovel'd here long enough, eating and drinking like
    mere brutes?
Have we not darken'd and dazed ourselves with books long
    enough.

Sail forth   steer for the deep waters only,
Reckless O soul, exploring, I with thee, and thou with me,
For we are bound where mariner has not yet dared to go,
And we will risk the ship, ourselves and all.

O my brave soul!
O farther farther sail!
O daring joy, but safe! are they not all the seas of God?
O farther farther, farther sail!

It is the idea of that 'daring joy, but safe' – everywhere in the poem – which prevents one from assenting to this passage and all that comes before it. The passage of a soul, whether it is everyman's or a saint's, is not 'safe', however 'joyful'. So that Whitman cannot focus the poem on the sort of *human* experience to which one might assent, because one could acknowledge its essential humanity. The figures in the passage proliferate farther and farther out from whatever center in which they have originated, until one wonders if there ever was a center. Probably not, because the experience of the protagonist in this poem is that of cosmic man, who, because he is everywhere, is nowhere; who, because he can be everything, is nothing. *This* Whitman, I believe, is he who mistakes vivification for creation, the ecstasy of cadence for the ecstasy of belief, efficient cause for final cause, poet for prophet. Which is not, I emphasize, the same as conceiving of the poet *as* prophet.

Whitman's genius was such as to render him incapable of the kind of discipline of the imagination which would make for the genuine sort of prophetic poetry we find in, say, Blake and Yeats: of whom we *can* say that they were poets *as* prophets; for whom we can observe that poetry is the vehicle for prophecy, not its tenor. Whitman is at best, at *his* best, *visionary*, and sees beyond his world to what it might be – thus, what, failing to be, it is. Blake and Yeats are at best, at *their* best, *prophetic*, and see through their world to what it really is – thus, what, pretending not to be, it might be. Visionary poetry projects a world which the poet would teach us to learn to acknowledge as our own; it comes to have the uncanniness of the terribly familiar. Prophetic poetry projects a world which the poet would teach us is alien to our own yet central to our seeing it as it really is – a world built upon truths we have hoped in vain to forget. We say of the visionary world that we could have made it – at least in dream – work. We say of the prophetic world that we could not possibly have made it, for it was there already. The ground of visionary poetry is indeed dream – work and magical thought; the ground of prophetic poetry, revelation and mythical thought. Thus the special language of prophetic poetry – one of its most marked formal characteristics – must, by the definition of its purpose, be foreign to us (for it reveals a world, and the strange things in it, hidden from us); yet, by the paradox of prophecy, it is a language native to us (for the things it reveals, being universal – out of the realm of day to day time, space, and conception – put all of us, all of our 'actual' world, under their aegis). We can 'understand' that language because its grammar and syntax are analogous to our own; understanding it, we assent to – and perhaps believe in – the metaphysical system which its structure and vocabulary entail; trying to account for its origin, we agree with the poet that he has been, in some quite literal sense, 'inspired'.

Now, when the mood came over him – as it did increasingly – perhaps Whitman did claim to have been 'inspired' in this literal sense. But even so, his later work fails as prophetic poetry (for that is what it is meant to be) precisely because, like the earlier work, it projects not a world to which the poet stands as witness, but one to which he stands as maker. Yet he asks of the world projected in the later work that, in accordance with the requirements of prophetic poetry, it have the effect of revelation; that its language be at once of and not of our workaday world; that it imply what in *Democratic Vistas* he called a 'New World metaphysics'. Yet the editions of *Leaves of Grass* from 1867 on fail of the centrality and integrity of properly prophetic poetry: fail, I think, because the poet mistakenly assumes that poetry, when it is made to deal with the universe at large, *becomes* prophecy. For all his revisions and manipulations of his text, for all his enlargement of his themes, the later Whitman is but a visionary poet. And, since he asks more of it than it can properly yield, the vision, and consequently the poetry, even the conception of the poet, get increasingly tenuous. A certain strength is there, of course. But it is the strength of an earlier Whitman, who perhaps prophesied, but could not bring about, his own metamorphosis from poet to prophet. His genius was too great to let him forget that, after all, it was *poets* who were to come.

True enough, he wrote, toward the end of 'A Backward Glance O'er Travel'd Roads':

But it is not on *Leaves of Grass* distinctively as *literature*, or a specimen therefor, that I feel to dwell, or advance claims. No one will get at my verses who insists upon viewing them as a literary performance, or attempt at such performance, or as aiming mainly toward art or aestheticism.

One says: How right, how sad, how wasteful! For, ironically enough, Whitman's words characterize the *failure* of the 1892 *Leaves of Grass*. And one turns to the earlier Whitman, I daresay the authentic Whitman, whose verses did aim mainly toward art and aestheticism: toward a definition of the vocation of the poet in that part of the modern world which was the United States.

For me, then, the most important edition of *Leaves of Grass* is the 1860 edition; and its most important poem is *A Word out of the Sea* (which, of course, became *Out of the Cradle Endlessly Rocking* in later editions.) Here Whitman may be best justified: as a poet. The burden of this essay will be to justify Whitman's way with poetry in the 1860 volume; to show how the structure and movement of this volume and of some of the principal poems in it (above all, *A Word out of the Sea*) are such as to furnish a valid and integral way for a poet dedicated to saving poetry for the modern world, thus – as poet, and only as poet – dedicated to saving the modern world for poetry. The Whitman of the 1860 *Leaves of Grass* would be a sage, a seer, a sayer. But he speaks of only what he knows directly and he asks of his speech only that it report fully and honestly and frankly, only that it evoke other speeches, other poems, of its kind. The poems in this volume do justify Whitman's claims for poetry in general – but in terms of what he may in fact give us, not of what he would like, or even need, to give us. The strength of the major poems in the volume is that they somehow resist *our* need for more than they present, and make us rest satisfied – or as satisfied as we ever can be – with what they give. Above all, this is true of *A Word out of the Sea* – as it is less true, and so characteristic of the later Whitman, the poet of *Out of the Cradle Endlessly Rocking*.

The 1855, 1856, and 1860 *Leaves of Grass* make a complete sequence – one in which the poet invents modern poetry, explores its possibility as an instrument for studying the world at large and himself as somehow vitally constitutive of it, and comes finally to define, expound, and exemplify the poet's vocation in the modern world. The sequence, in brief, is from language to argument; and it is controlled at all points by a powerful sense of the ego which is struggling to move from language to argument and which must come to realize the limits of its own humanity, which are the limits of argument. If, as we well know, the poet as envisaged in the 1855 and 1856 *Leaves of Grass* is the counterpart of him of whom Emerson wrote in 'The Poet' (1844), the poet envisaged in the 1860 *Leaves of Grass* is the counterpart of him of whom Emerson wrote in his essay on Goethe in *Representative Men* (1850): Not Shakespeare, not Plato, not Swedenberg would do for the modern world, which yet 'wants its poet-priest, a reconciler . . .' Goethe was one such: 'the writer, or secretary, who is to report the doings of the miraculous spirit of life that everywhere throbs and works. His office is a reception of the facts into the mind, and then a selection of the eminent and characteristic experiences.' Note: just a 'writer' – (what John Holloway in an important book of a few years ago called the *Victorian Sage*: a philosopher of a kind, but one who constructs his argument according to a grammar of assent). Emerson had concluded:

The world is young: the former great men call to us affectionately.
We too must write Bibles, to unite again the heavens and the earthly
world. The secret of genius is to suffer no fiction to exist for us;
to realize all that we know; in the high refinement of modern
life, in arts, in sciences, in books, in men, to exact good faith,
reality and a purpose; and first, last, midst and without end, to
honor every truth by use.

The 1860 *Leaves of Grass*, as one of Whitman's notebook entries indicates, was to be a Bible too: 'The Great Construction of the New
Bible. . . . It ought to be ready in 1859.' It was to offer a 'third religion',
Whitman wrote. And in a way it does; but, for well and for ill, that
religion is a religion of man – man as he is, locked in his humanity
and needing a religion, yet not claiming to have it by virtue of needing it; not hypnotizing himself into declaring that he has it. (For
Whitman a little cadence was a dangerous, if exciting, thing, much
cadence, disastrous.) The Whitman of the 1860 *Leaves of Grass* is,
par excellence, Emerson's 'secretary', reporting 'the doings of the
miraculous spirit of life that everywhere throbs and works.' To
accept a miracle, to live in its presence, even to try to comprehend it –
this is not the same as trying to work one, even claiming to have
worked one. And – as the poets who have come after him have
variously testified in their puzzled, ambiguous relation to him –
Whitman's way with the language of poetry, going against the grain
of mass communications and 'positivism', may well teach us how to
recognize and acknowledge miracles. It cannot teach us how to work
them; or even how to earn them. One can well imagine how hard it
must be for a poet to go so far with language, only to discover that
he can go no farther. Such a discovery constitutes the principal
element of greatness in the 1860 *Leaves of Grass*, perhaps the principal
element of greatness in Whitman's poetry as a whole.
    I have said that in 1855 Whitman 'invented' modern poetry. By
this I mean only that, along with other major poets of the middle of
the century, he participated – but in a strangely isolated way – in the
development of romanticist poetics toward and beyond its symbolist
phase. (*To invent* may mean, among other things, 'to stumble upon'.)
I do not mean to claim too much for the word *symbolist* here; I use
it only generally to indicate that Whitman too came to realize that a

poet's vocation was fatefully tied to the state of the language which constituted his medium. He discovered with Baudelaire – although without Baudelaire's (and incidentally Emerson's) overwhelming sense of the problem of 'correspondences', that, as regards language, 'tout vit, tout agit, tout se correspond'. The medium thus had a 'life' of its own, and so might generate 'life' – the 'life' of poetry. Poetry, on this view, thus became *sui generis*, a unique mode of discourse; and the role of the poet became more and more explicitly to be that of the creator: one who might 'free' language to 'mean' – a creator in a medium, pure and simple. We have in Whitman's early work a version of that conception of poet and poetry with which we are now so familiar: To whom was the poet responsible? Not to whom, the reply ran, but to what? And the answer: to language. And language as such was seen to be the sole, overriding means to establish, or reestablish community. The perhaps inevitable drift – not only in Whitman's work but of that of his contemporaries and of the poets who have come – was toward an idea of poetry as a means of communion, perhaps modern man's sole means of communion, his religion. Professor Abrams (in *The Mirror and the Lamp*) concludes his account of these developments thus:

It was only in the early Victorian period, when all discourse was explicitly or tacitly thrown into the two exhaustive modes of imaginative and rational, expressive and assertive, that religion fell together with poetry in opposition to science, and that religion, as a consequence, was converted into poetry, and poetry into a kind of religion.

Professor Abrams is speaking about developments in England. In the United States, conditions were somewhat simpler and, withal, more extreme. From the beginning, that is to say, Whitman was sure that the imaginative and rational might well be subsumed under a 'higher' category, which was poetry. So that – as I have indicated in my remarks on Whitman and prophetic poetry – for him there was eventually entailed the idea that the New Bible might be just that, a total and inclusive account of cosmic man, of man as one of an infinitude of gods bound up in Nature. It is a nice question whether or not the 'symbolist' dedication to the idea of language-as-communion must *inevitably* lead to a search for a metalinguistic structure of analogies and correspondences and then to an idea of poetry as religion and religion as poetry. And it is a nicer question whether or not 'symbolist' poetics – with its emphasis on medium as against matrix, language *per se* as against language-in-culture – is characterized by a certain weakness in linguistic theory. Whitman's work raises these questions; and a full critique of his work would entail a critique of his theory of poetry, thus of his theory of language, thus of his theory of culture. But this is not the place to speak of critics to come, much less to prophesy them.

In any case, we must grant Whitman his special kind of 'unmediated vision'. But we are not by that token obliged to grant, or claim for him a 'mysticism' – or for that matter, 'an inverted mysticism'; or to declare that, *ecce*, his poetry is at once *'mystical and irreligious'*; or to see in the Whitman of 1855 a good (prematurely) grey guru. (I cite here the recent claims for this Whitman of James Miller, Karl Shapiro, and Malcolm Cowley – who confuse, or conflate, this poet with the one who presided at Camden. And I think of the question, put with such sweet craziness, by Allen Ginsberg, in the line I have used as epigraph.) At its most telling, Whitman's earlier poetry manifests what has been called (by Erich Kahler) an 'existential consciousness', but of a mid-nineteenth-century American sort – its key term, its center of strength and weakness, being not anguish but joy. Or rather, the key term is triumph – as suffering, the poet endures, and rejoices: seeing that it is his vocation as poet to teach men that they can endure. The freedom which ensues is wonderful, not dreadful.

Thus I take the 1855 and 1856 editions of *Leaves of Grass*, which most freshly project this mode of consciousness, as stages on the way to the 1860 edition. In 1855 and 1856 Whitman shows that he has learned to report truthfully what he has seen; in 1860, that he has learned to measure its significance for the poet taken as the 'secretary' – the archetypal man. He strove to go beyond this, but in vain. The movement from the 1855 to the 1856 editions is the movement from the first *Song of Myself* and the first *The Sleepers* (both originally untitled) to the first *Crossing Brooklyn Ferry* (called, in 1856, *Sun-Down Poem*): the poet first learns to discipline himself into regressing deeply into his own pre-conscious; then, with his new-found sense of himself as at once subject and object in his world, he learns to conceive in a new way of the world at large; he is, as though for the first time, 'in' the world. The crucial factor is a restoration of the poet's vital relationship to language. A good, powerfully naïve account of this discovery is that in Whitman's prose *American Primer*, written in the 1850s, but not published until after his death:

What do you think words are? Do you think words are positive and original things in themselves? No: Words are not original and arbitrary in themselves. – Words are a result – they are the progeny of what has been or is in vogue. – If iron architecture comes in vogue, as it seems to be coming, words are wanted to stand for all about iron architecture, for all the work it causes, for the different branches of work and of the workman. . . .

A perfect user of words uses things – they exude in power and beauty from him – miracles in his hands – miracles from his mouth. . . .

A perfect writer would make words sing, dance, do the male and female act, bear children, weep, bleed, rage, stab, steal, fire cannon, steer ships, sack cities, charge with cavalry or infantry, or do anything, that man or woman or the natural powers can do.
[Note the insistence on 'natural' – not 'supernatural' powers.]

Likely there are other words wanted. – Of words wanted, the matter is summed up in this: When the time comes for them to represent any thing or state of things, the words will surely follow. The lack of any words, I say again, is as historical as the existence of words. As for me, I feel a hundred realities, clearly determined in me, that words are not yet formed to represent. . . .

These sentiments generally, and some of these phrasings particularly, got into Whitman's prose meditations. More important, from the beginning they inform the poems. They derive much from Emerson's *The Poet*, of course; but they are not tied to even Emerson's modestly transcendental balloon. The power which Whitman discovers is the power of language, fueled by the imagination, to break through the categories of time, space, and matter and to 'vivify' (a word, as I have said, he used late in his life – so close to Pound's 'Make it new') the persons, places, and things of his world, and so make them available to his readers. In the process – since the readers would, as it were, be using words for the first time – he would make them available to themselves; as poets in spite of themselves.

It is as regards this last claim – that the reader is a poet in spite of himself – that the 1860 *Leaves of Grass* is all-important. For there Whitman most clearly saw that the poet's power to break through the limiting categories of day-to-day existence is just that: a poet's power, obtaining only in so far as the poem obtains, and limited as the poem is limited. In 1860, that is to say, Whitman saw that his Bible was to be a poet's Bible, and had to be built around a conception of the poet's life: his origins, experience, and end; his relation with the persons, places, and things of his world. The 1855 and 1856 *Leaves of Grass* volumes are but *collections* of poems – their organization as rushed and chaotic as is the sensibility of the writer of the *American Primer. Within* individual poems, there is form, a form which centers on the moment in the poet's life which they project. But the 1860 *Leaves of Grass* is an articulated whole, with an *argument*. The argument is that of the poet's life as it furnishes a beginning, middle, and end to an account of his vocation. The 1860 volume is, for all its imperfections, one of the great works in that romantic mode, the autobiography. Or, let us give the genre to which it belongs a more specific name: archetypal autobiography. The 1860 volume is autobiographical as, say, *Moby Dick* and *Walden* are autobiographical; for its hero is a man in the process of writing a book, of writing himself, of making himself, of discovering that the powers of the self are the stronger for being limited. The hero who can say No! in thunder discovers that he can say Yes! in thunder too – but that the thunderation is his own and no one else's.

Now, to say that the 1860 *Leaves of Grass* is quintessentially autobiographical is to say what has been said before: most notably by Schyberg, Asselineau, and Allen. But I mean to say it somewhat differently than they do. For they see in the volume a sign of a crisis in Whitman's personal life; and this is most likely so. Yet I think it is wrong to read the volume as, in this *literal* sense, personal – that is, 'private'. (The Bowers edition of the surviving manuscript of the 1860 edition clearly shows that Whitman – naturally enough, most often in the *Calamus* poems – wanted to keep the book clear of too insistently and privately personal allusions. He was, I think, not trying to 'conceal' – much less 'mask' – his private personality but to transmute it into an archetypal personality. I think that it is a mistake to look so hard, as some critics do, for the 'private' I.) Thus I should read the volume as not a personal but archetypal autobiography: yet another version of that compulsively brought-forth nineteenth-century poem which dealt with the growth of the poet's mind. (Well instructed by our forebears, we now have a variety of names for the form – all demonstrating how deeply, and from what a variety of non-literary perspectives, we have had to deal with the issues which it raises for us: *rite de passage*, quest for identity, search for community, and the like.) Whitman's problem, the poet's problem, was to show that integral to the poet's vocation was his life cycle; that the poet, having discovered his gifts might now use them to discover the relevance of his life, his *lived* life, his *Erlebnis*, his *career*, to the lives of his fellows. It is the fact that his newly discovered use of poetry is grounded in his sense of a life lived-through: it is this fact that evidences Whitman's ability here, more than in any version of *Leaves of Grass*, to contain his gift and use it, rather than be used by it. Of *this* volume Whitman said: 'I am satisfied with *Leaves of Grass* by far the most of it), as expressing what was intended, namely, to express by sharp-cut self assertion, One's Self and also, or may be still more, to map out, to throw together for American use, a gigantic embryo or skeleton of Personality, – fit for the West, for native models.' Later, of course, he wanted more. But he never had the means beyond those in the 1860 edition to get what he wanted. And that has made all the difference.

The 1860 *Leaves of Grass* opens with *Proto-Leaf* (later, much revised, as *Starting from Paumanok*.) Here Whitman announces his themes and, as he had done before calls for his new religion; but he gives no indication that it is to be a religion of anything else but the poet's universalized vocation. (My misuse of the word *religion* is his. I mean neither to be victimized nor saved by following him here.) It might yet, on this account, be a precursor to a religion, in the more usual (and I think proper) sense, as well as a substitute for it. 'Whoever you are! to you endless announcements', he says. There follows 'Walt Whitman', a somewhat modified version of the 1855 poem which became *Song of Myself*. It is still close to the fluid version of 1855; strangely enough, it is so over-articulated (with some 372 sections) that it does not have the rather massive, and therefore relatively dogmatic, articulation of the final version. In all, it gives us an account of the poet's overwhelming discovery of his native powers. Then in the numbered (but not separately titled) series of poems called *Chants Democratic*, the poet – after an apostrophic salutation to his fellows (it ends 'O poets to come, I depend on you!') – celebrates himself again, but now as he conceives of himself in the act of celebrating his world. The chief among these poems – as usual, much modified later – became *By Blue Ontario's Shore, Song of the Broad-Axe, Song for Occupations, Me Imperturbe, I Was Looking a Long While*, and *I Hear America Singing*. Following upon *Walt Whitman*, the *Chants Democratic* sequence successfully establishes the dialectical tension between the poet and his world – the tension being sustained as one is made to realize again and again that out of the discovery of his power for 'making words do the male and female act' in *Walt Whitman*, has come his power to 'vivify' his world in the *Chants Democratic*.

The transition to *Leaves of Grass*, the next sequence – again the poems are numbered, but not separately titled – is natural and necessary. For the poet now asks what it is to make poems in the language which has been precipitated out of the communal experience of his age. The mood throughout is one of a mixture of hope and doubt, and at the end it reaches a certitude strengthened by a sense of the very limitations which initially gave rise to the doubt. The first poem opens – and I shall presently say more about this – with two lines expressing doubt; later – when the prophetic Whitman couldn't conceive of doubting – the lines were dropped in the poem, which became *As I Ebb'd with the Ocean of Life*. The second poem is a version of an 1855 poem, *Great Are the Myths*; and it was finally rejected by Whitman as being, one guesses, too certain in its rejection of the mythic mode toward which he later found himself aspiring. The third poem, which, combined with the sixth later became *Song of the Answerer* opens up the issue of communication as such. The fourth, a version of an 1856 poem which eventually became *This Compost*, conceives of poetry as a kind of naturalistic resurrection. It moves from 'Something startles me where I thought I was safest' – that is, in the poet's relation to the materials of poetry – to a simple acknowledgment at the end that the earth 'gives such divine materials to men, and accepts such leavings from them at last.' The fifth (later *Song of Prudence*) considers the insight central to the poet's vocation. To the categories of 'time, space, reality', the poet would add that of 'prudence' – which teaches that the 'consummations' of poetry are such as to envisage the necessary relationship of all other 'consummations': The imagination's law of the conservation of energy. The sixth (which, as I have said, later became part of *Song of the Answerer*) develops an aspect of the theme of the fourth and fifth; but now that theme is interpreted as it is bound up in the problem of language: 'The words of poems give you more than poems. They give you to form for yourself poems, religions, politics, war, peace, behavior, histories, essays, romances, and everything else.' At this depth of discovery there is no possibility of any kind of logically continuous catalogue of what words 'give you to form for yourself.' Poetry is a means of exhausting man's powers to know the world, and himself in it, as it is. Beyond this, poems

... prepare for death – yet they are not the finish, but rather the
    onset,
They bring none to his or her terminus, or to be content and full;
Whom they take, they take into space, to behold the birth of stars,
    to learn one of the meanings,
To launch off with absolute faith – to sweep through the ceaseless
    rings, and never to be quiet again.

In the seventh poem (later *Faith Poem*), the poet discovers that he 'needs no assurance'; for he is (as he says in the eighth poem, later *Miracles*) a 'realist' and for him the real (by which he means *realia*) constitute 'miracles.' The poet is led, in the ninth poem (later *There Was a Child Went Forth*), to a recollection of his first discovery of the miraculousness of the real: a discovery he only now understands; this poem, taken in relation to the rest of the sequence, properly anticipates *A Word out of the Sea*. The tenth poem opens, in a passage dropped from the later version, *Myself and Mine*, – but one which is essential as a transition in the sequence:

It is ended – I dally no more,
After today I inure myself to run, leap, swim, wrestle, fight ...

Simply enough: the poet, having accepted his vocation and its constraints, is now free – free *through* it; and he must now teach this freedom to others:

I charge that there be no theory or school founded out of me,
I charge you to leave all free, as I have left all free.

The rest of the sequence, some fourteen more poems, celebrates aspects of the poet's new freedom as it might be the freedom of all men. (I forebear giving their later titles.) It is the freedom to rejoice in the miraculousness of the real, and has its own costs. The greatest is a terrible passivity, as though in order to achieve his freedom, man had to offer himself up as the victim of his own newly vivified sensibility. Being as he is, the poet sees (in 12) 'the vast similitude|which| interlocks all . . .'; yet he must admit (in 15) 'that life cannot exhibit all to me –' and 'that I am to wait for what will be exhibited by death.' He is (in 17) the man who must 'sit and look out upon all the sorrows of the world, and upon all oppression and shame'; and he must 'See, hear,|be|silent', only then to speak. He declares (in 20); '. . . whether I continue beyond this book, to maturity| . . . |Depends . . . upon you| . . . you, contemporary America.' Poem 24, wherein the poet completes his archetypal act, and gives himself over to his readers, reads:

Lift me close to your face till I whisper,
What you are holding is in reality no book, nor part of a book,
It is a man, flushed and full-blooded – it is I – So long!
We must separate – Here! take from my lips this kiss,
Whoever you are, I give it especially to you;
So long – and I hope we shall meet again.

I quote this last poem entire, because I want to make it clear that the lapses into desperate sentimentality – and this poem is a prime example – are intrinsically a part of Whitman's autobiographical mode in the 1860 *Leaves of Grass*, as they are of the mode, or genre, which they represent. It will not do to explain them away by putting them in a larger context, or considering them somehow as masked verses – evidences of Whitman the shape-shifter. (Speaking through a *persona*, the poet perforce hides behind it.) Confronting the agonies and ambiguities of his conception of the poet, Whitman too often fell into bathos or sentimentalism. Yet bathos and sentimentalism, I would suggest, are but unsuccessful means – to be set against evidence of successful means – of solving the archetypal autobiographer's central problem: at once being himself and seeing himself; of bearing witness to his own deeds. If what he is, as he sees it, is too much to bear; if he is incapable of bearing it; if his genius is such as not to have prepared him to bear it – why then, his miraculism will fail him precisely because he cannot stand too much reality.

Bathos and sentimentalism – and also anxious, premonitory yearnings for something beyond mere poetry – inevitably mar the rest of the 1860 *Leaves of Grass*: but not fatally, since they are the by-products of its total argument. At some point, most foxes want to be hedgehogs. Whitman is a poet who must be read at large. And I am claiming that Whitman can be best read at large in the 1860 *Leaves of Grass*. When he can be read in smaller compass – as in *A Word out of the Sea* – it is because in a single poem he manages to recapitulate in little what he was developing at large. I should guess – as I shall presently try to show – that the large poem, the 1860 volume, is a necessary setting for the little poem, *A Word out of the Sea*. That poem (later, I remind my reader, *Out of the Cradle . . .*) is one of Whitman's greatest. And I shall want to show that it is even greater than we think. So I must carry through, however cursorily, my glance o'er the 1860 *Leaves of Grass*. There comes next a series of poems (*A Word out of the Sea* is one of them) in which the poet meditates the sheer givenness of the world his poems reveal: he is even capable of seeing himself as one of the givens. But then he must specify in detail the nature of his kind of givenness: which includes the power to give, to bring the given to a new life. Here – after *Salut au Monde, Poem of Joys, A Word out of the Sea, A Leaf of Faces*, and *Europe,* – there is first the *Enfans d'Adam* sequence, and then, after an interlude of generally celebrative poems, the *Calamus* sequence. I want to say of these two sequences only that they are passionate in a curiously objective fashion; I have suggested that the proper word for their mood and tone is neither personal nor impersonal, but archetypal. In contrast, they furnish analogues – directly libidinal analogues, as it were – for the poet's role, seen now not (as in the earlier sequences) from the point of view of a man telling us how he has discovered his gift, put it to use, and measured the cost of using it properly; but seen rather from the point of view of the reader. The *I* of these poems, I suggest, is meant to include the reader – as at once potential poet and reader of poems. So that the *Enfans d'Adam* sequence tell us how it is – what it means, what it costs – to be a maker of poems and the *Calamus* sequence how it is to be a reader of poems – in the first instance the analogue is procreation; in the second it is community. And if Whitman's own homosexuality led him to write more powerfully in the second vein than in the first, we should be mindful of the fact that, in his times as in ours, it seems to be easier to make poems, good poems, even to publish them, than to get readers for them.

Indeed, Whitman announces in the next-to-last of the *Calamus* sequence that we are to be ready for his most 'baffling' words, which come in the last poem of the sequence, later *Full of Life Now*:

When you read these, I, that was visible, am become invisible;
Now it is you, compact, visible, realizing my poems, seeking me,
Fancying how happy you were, if I could be with you, and
    become your lover;
Be it as if I were with you. Be not too certain but I am with you
    now.

Later Whitman changed *lover* to *comrade* – mistakenly, I think; for, as their function in the 1860 volume shows, the *Calamus* poems were to carry through to completion the poet's conception of his painfully loving relation with his readers.

Having, in the *Enfans d'Adam* and *Calamus* sequences, defined the poetic process itself, as he had earlier defined the poet's discovery of that process, Whitman proceeds variously to celebrate himself and his readers at once under the aegis of the *Enfans d'Adam* and the *Calamus* analogue. (As Lorca said in his *Oda*, '*Éste es el mundo, amigo . . .*') Much of the power of the poems, new and old, derives from their place in the sequences. In *Crossing Brooklyn Ferry* and the series of *Messenger Leaves* there are addresses to all and sundry who inhabit Whitman's world, assurances to them that now he can love them for what they are, because now he knows them for what they are. There is then an address to Manahatta – which returns to the problem of naming, but now with an assurance that the problem has disappeared in the solving: 'I was asking for something specific and perfect for my city, and behold! here is the aboriginal name!' Then there is an address in 'Kosmos' to the simple, separate persons – to each of his readers who is 'constructing the house of himself or herself.' Then there is *Sleep Chasings* (a version of the 1855 *The Sleepers*), now a sublime poem, in which the poet can freely acknowledge that the source of his strength is in the relation of his night- to his daytime life, the unconscious and the conscious:

I will stop only a time with the night, and rise betimes
I will duly pass the day, O my mother, and duly return to you.

And *Sleep Chasings* is the more telling for being followed by *Burial* (originally an 1855 poem which eventually became *To Think of Time*). For in his incessant moving between night and day, the poet manages to make poems and so proves immortal. He makes men immortal in his poems, as he teaches them to make themselves immortal in their acts:

To think that you and I did not see, feel, think nor bear our part!
To think that we are now here, and bear our part!

This poem comes nearly at the end of the 1860 volume. Only an address to his soul – immortal, but in a strictly 'poetic' sense – and *So Long!* follow. In the latter we are reminded once again:

This is no book,
Who touches this book, touches a man,
(Is it night? Are we done?)
It is I you hold, and who holds you,
I spring from the pages into your arms – decease calls me forth.

We are reminded thus, to paraphrase a recent Whitmanian, that in the flesh of art we are immortal: which is a commonplace. We are reminded also that in our age, the role of art, of poetry, is to keep us alive enough to be capable of this kind of immortality: which is not quite a commonplace.

The central terms in the argument of the 1860 *Leaves of Grass*, I suggest run something like this: first, in the poems which lead up to *A Word out of the Sea* – self-discovery, self-love, rebirth, diffusion-of-self, art; and second, in the poems which follow *A Word out of the Sea* – love-of-others, death, rebirth, reintegration-of-self, art, immortality. The sequence is that of an ordinary life, extraordinarily

375 Roy Harvey Pearce

lived through; the claims are strictly humanistic. The child manages somehow to achieve adulthood; the movement is from a poetry of diffusion to a poetry of integration. Immortality is the *result* of art, not its origin, nor its cause. The humanism is painful, because one of its crucial elements (centering on 'death' as a 'clew' in *A Word out of the Sea*) is an acknowledgement of all-too-human limitations and constraints. So long as Whitman lived with that acknowledgement, lived *in* that acknowledgement – even when living with it drove him (as it too often did) toward bathos and sentimentalism –, he managed to be a poet, a 'secretary', a 'sage', a seer, a visionary. His religion was the religion of humanity: the only religion that a work of art can *directly* express, whatever other religion it may confront and acknowledge. *Indirectly*, it can confront religion in the more usual and more proper sense; for it can treat of man in his aspiration for something beyond manhood, even if it cannot claim – since its materials are ineluctably those of manhood – to treat directly of that something-beyond. The burden – someone has called it the burden of incertitude; Keats called it 'negative capability' – is a hard one to bear. Whitman, I am suggesting, bore it most successfully, bore it most successfully for us, in the 1860 *Leaves of Grass*.

Which brings me to the most important of the poems first collected in this volume, *A Word out of the Sea*.[1] It was originally published separately in 1859, as *A Child's Reminiscence*. Thus far, I have tried to suggest the proper context in which the poem should be read: as part of the volume for which it was originally written: as a turning point in the argument of that book. Note that *A Word out of the Sea* comes about mid-way in the book after *Walt Whitman* the *Chants Democratic*, *Leaves of Grass*, *Salut au Monde*, and *Poem of Joys* – that is, after those poems which tell us of the poet's discovery of his powers as poet and of his ability to use those powers so to 'vivify' his world, and himself in it: after his discovery that it is man's special delight and his special agony to be at once the subject and object of his meditations; after his discovery that consciousness inevitably entails self-consciousness and a sense of the strengths and weaknesses of self-

1 The complete text of *A Word out of the Sea* is given in the issue of the *Minnesota Review* in which this essay was originally printed, pp. 273–80, and in a facsimile edition of the 1860 *Leaves of Grass* published by the Cornell University Press, 1961.

consciousness. Moreover, *A Word out of the Sea* comes shortly before the *Enfans d'Adam* and *Calamus* sequences – that is, shortly before those poems which work out the dialectic of the subject-object relationship under the analogue of the sexuality of man as creator of his world and of persons, places, and things as its creatures. I cannot but think that Whitman knew what he was doing when he placed *A Word out of the Sea* thus. For he was obligated, in all his autobiographical honesty, to treat directly of man's fallibilities as well as his powers, to try to discover the binding relationship between fallibilities and powers: to estimate the capacity of man to be himself and the cost he would have to pay. The poems which came before *A Word out of the Sea* have little to do with fallibilities; they develop the central terms of the whole argument only this far: self-discovery, self-love, rebirth, art. Theirs is the polymorph perverse world of the child. In them, death only threatens, does not promise; power is what counts. The turning-point in the poet's life can come only with the 'adult' sense of love and death, the beginning and the end of things: out of which issues art, now a mode of immortality. In *A Word out of the Sea* the 1860 volume has its turning-point. Beyond this poem, we must remember are the *Enfans d'Adam* and *Calamus* sequences, and also *Crossing Brooklyn Ferry* and the *Messenger Leaves* sequence.

The 1860 poem begins harshly: *Out of the rocked cradle.* The past participle, unlike the present participle in the later versions, implies no continuing agent for the rocking; the sea here is too inclusive to be a symbol; it is just a fact of life – life's factuality. Then comes the *mélange* of elements associated with the 'sea'. They are among the realities whose miraculousness the poet is on his way to understanding. Note the third line (omitted in later versions) which clearly establishes the autobiographical tone and makes the boy at once the product of nature at large and a particular nature: 'Out of the boy's mother's womb, from the nipples of her breasts.' All this leads to a clear split in point of view, so that we know that the poet-as-adult is making a poem which will be his means to understanding a childhood experience. Initially we are told of the range of experiences out of which this poem comes: the sea as rocked cradle seems at once literally (to the boy) and metaphorically (to the poet) to 'contain' the song of the bird, the boy's mother, the place, the time, the memory of the brother, and the as yet unnamed 'word stronger and more delicious than any' which marks a limit to the meaning of the whole. This is quite explicitly an introduction. For what follows is given a separate title, *Reminiscence*, as though the poet wanted to make quite plain the division between his sense of himself as child and as adult. Then we are presented with the story of the birds, the loss of the beloved, and the song sung (as only *now* the poet knows it) to objectify this loss, so make it bearable, so assure that it can, in *this* life, be transcended. Always we are aware that the poet-as-adult, the creative center of the poem seeks that 'word stronger and more delicious' which will be his means finally to understand his reminiscences and – in the context of this volume (I emphasize: in the context of *this* volume) – serve to define his vocation as poet: at once powerful and fallible. The points of view of bird, child, and adult are kept separate until the passage which reads:

Bird! (then said the boy's Soul,)
Is it indeed toward your mate you sing? or is it mostly to me?
For I that was a child, my tongue's use sleeping,
Now that I have heard you,
Now in a moment I know what I am for – I awake,
And already a thousand singers – a thousand songs, clearer louder,
    more sorrowful than yours,
A thousand warbling echoes have started to life within me,
Never to die.

The boy, even as a man recalling his boyhood, does not, as in later versions, at first address the bird as 'Demon'. He is at this stage incapable of that 'or' – in the latter reading 'Demon or bird'. Even though his soul speaks, he is to discover – some lines later – his special 'poetic' relation to the bird. Moreover, as 'boy', he holds toward death an attitude half-way between that of the bird – who is merely 'instinctive' and that of the man – who is 'reflective', capable of 'reminiscence'. Yet the points of view begin to be hypnotically merged – *after* the fact. In the boy's 'soul' the poet discovers a child's potentiality for adult knowledge; but he keeps it as a potentiality, and he never assigns it to the bird, who (or which) is an occasion merely. Yet having seen that potentiality as such, he can 'now', in the adult present, work toward its realization, confident that the one will follow necessarily in due course from the other. Now, in the adult present, he can ask for 'the clew', 'The word final, superior to all', the word which 'now' he can 'conquer'. I cannot emphasize too much that it is a '*word*' – that the poet is translating the sea (and all it embodies) as prelinguistic fact into a word, knowledge of which will signify his coming to maturity. 'Out of', in the original title, is meant quite literally to indicate a linguistic transformation. In the record of the growth of his mind, he sees *now* that the word will once and for all precipitate the meaning he has willed himself to create, and in the creating to discover. And it comes as he recalls that time when the sea, manifesting the rhythm of life and death itself,

Delaying not, hurrying not,
Whispered me through the night, and very plainly before
    daybreak,
Lisped to me the low and delicious word DEATH,
And again Death – ever Death, Death, Death.

(Not *Death*, merely repeated four times as in later versions – but *ever*, beyond counting. The prophetic Whitman was bound to drop that *ever*, since for him nothing was beyond counting.)

The merging of the points of view occurs as not only past and present, child and adult, but subject and object (i.e., 'The sea . . . whispered me' – not '*to* me') are fused. The poet now knows the word, because he has contrived a situation in which he can control its use; he has discovered (to recall the language of the *American Primer* notes) another reality, one that words until *now* had not been formed to represent. He has, as only a poet can, *made a* word out of the sea – for the duration of the poem understood '*sea*' as it may be into '*death*' – '*ever death*'. His genius is such as to have enabled us to put those quotation marks around the world – guided by him, to have 'bracketed' this portion of our experience with language; and we discover that as language binds in the poet's time, so it is bound in human time.

If the end of the poem is to understand cosmic process as a continual loss of the beloved through death and a consequent gain of death-in-life and life-in-death – if this is the end of the poem, nonetheless it is gained through a creative act, an assertion of life in the face of death, and a discovery and acknowledgment of the limits of such an assertion. And this act is that of the very person, the poet, whom death would deprive of all that is beloved in life. Moreover, the deprivation is quite literally that and shows the poet moving, in high honesty, from the *Enfans d'Adam* sequence to *Calamus*. In the 1860 volume, *A Word out of the Sea* entails the *Calamus* sequence. (What if Whitman had, in *A Word out of the Sea*, written *comrade* instead of *brother*?)

In any case, at this stage of his career, Whitman would not yield to his longing for such comfort as would scant the facts of life and death. There is, I repeat, that opening *rocked*, not *rocking* cradle; there is the quite naturalistic acknowledgment of the 'boy's mother's womb'. And there is stanza 31 (the stanzas in the 1860 poem are numbered, as the stanzas of the final version are not):

O give me some clew!
O if I am to have so much, let me have more!
O a word! O what is my destination?
O I fear it is henceforth chaos!
O how joys, dreads, convolutions, human shapes, and all shapes,
    spring as from graves around me!
O phantoms! you cover all the land, and all the sea!
O I cannot see in the dimness whether you smile or frown upon
    me;
O vapor, a look, a word! O well-beloved!
O you dear women's and men's phantoms!

In the final version, the equivalent stanza reads only:

O give me the clew (it lurks in the night here somewhere,)
O if I am to have so much, let me have more!

The difference between 'some clew' and 'the clew' marks the difference between a poet for whom questions are real and one for whom questions are rhetorical. The later Whitman was convinced that the lurking clew would find him – and to that degree, whatever else he was, was not a poet. The earlier Whitman, in all humility, feared that what might issue out of this experience was 'phantoms' – a good enough word for aborted poems. And often – but not too often – he was right.

Finally, there is not in *A Word out of the Sea* the falsely (and, in the context of the poem, undeservedly) comforting note of 'Or like some old crone rocking the cradle swathed in sweet garments, bending aside.' Indeed, the sentimentality and bathos of this too-much celebrated line, as I think, is given away by the fact that it is the only simile, the only *like* clause, in the poem. And, in relation to the total effect of the poem, the strategic withdrawal of the *Or* which introduces the line is at least unfortunate, at most disastrous.

I make so much of the kind of disaster, as I think it is, because it became increasingly characteristic of Whitman's way with poetry after the 1860 *Leaves of Grass*. Probably there are poems, written later, which show him at his best; and probably some of his revisions and rejections are for the best. But I more and more doubt it, as I doubt that he had reached his best in 1855 and 1856. I do not mean to take the part of Cassandra; but I think it as inadvisable to take the part of Pollyanna. The facts, as I see them, show that Whitman, for whatever reason, after 1860 moved away from the mode of archetypal autobiography toward that of prophecy. He worked hard to make, as he said, a cathedral out of *Leaves of Grass*. He broke up the beautifully wrought sequence of the 1860 volume; so that, even when he let poems stand unrevised, they appear in contexts which take from them their life-giving mixture of tentativeness and assurance, of aspiration, and render them dogmatic, tendentious, and overweening.

In Lawrence's word, Whitman 'mentalized' his poems. To give a few examples of 'mentalizing' revisions of 1860 poems: The opening of the third *Enfans d'Adam* poem reads in the 1860 text:

O my children! O mates!
O the bodies of you, and of all men and women, engirth me,
    and I engirth them.

In the 1867 version the lines read:

I sing the body electric,
The Armies of those I love engirth me and I engirth them.

Another example: the opening line of the fourteenth poem of the same sequence – reads in the 1860 version: 'I am he that aches with love'; and becomes in 1867: 'I am he that aches with amorous love.' (This is the *amorous* which so infuriated Lawrence.) And another example: the opening lines of the fifteenth poem in the sequence – read in the 1860 version: 'Early in the morning,|Walking . . .'; and became in 1867: 'As Adam early in the morning,|Walking . . .' Small examples surely. But note the unsupported and unsupportable claims of 'body electric', 'armies', 'amorous', and the Old Testament 'Adam'.

A larger – but still characteristic – example is Whitman's revision of the first of the 1860 *Leaves of Grass* sequence, which became *As I Ebb'd with the Ocean of life*. The 1860 poem opens thus:

Elemental drifts!
O I wish I could impress others as you and the waves have just
    been impressing me.

As I ebbed with an ebb of the ocean of life,
As I wended the shores I know.

In the poem as it appears in the 1892 edition of *Leaves of Grass*, the first two lines – expressing doubt, as I have pointed out – are missing; the third has been simplified to 'As I ebb'd with the ocean of life' – so that the poet is no longer conceived as part of an 'ebb'. And the fourth line stands as we have it now. Later in the seventh line of the 1892 version, the poet says that he is 'Held by the electric self out of the pride of which I utter poems'. In the 1860 version he says that he is 'Alone, held by the eternal self of me that threatens to get the better of me, and stifle me'. And so it goes – all passion beyond spending (unless vivified by a kind of cosmic electroshock), all poetry beyond the mere writing, all life beyond the mere living – since the poet's tactic, however unconscious, is to claim to have transcended that which must have been hard to live with: his extraordinary ordinary self and the ordinarily extraordinary death that awaits him. Granting the mood and movement of the later editions of *Leaves of Grass*, it is only proper that Whitman would have rejected the eighth poem in the 1860 *Calamus* sequence – which begins 'Long I thought that knowledge alone would suffice me – O if I could but obtain knowledge!' and ends, as the poet is brought to confront the readers to whom he would offer his poems, 'I am indifferent to my own songs – I will go with him I love . . .'.

One more example: this one not of a revision but of an addition to a sequence originating in the 1860 volume. In the 1871 *Leaves of Grass*, Whitman, now wholly committed to making of his poem a series of prophetic books, placed in the *Calamus* sequence the woolly *Base of All Metaphysics*, the last stanza of which reads:

Having studied the new and antique, the Greek and Germanic
    systems,

Kant having studied and stated, Fichte and Schelling and Hegel,
Stated the lore of Plato, and Socrates greater than Plato,
And greater than Socrates sought and stated, Christ divine having
  studied long.
I see reminiscent to-day those Greek and Germanic systems,
See the philosophies of all, Christian churches and tenets see,
Yet underneath Socrates clearly see, and underneath Christ the
  divine I see,
The dear love of man for his comrade, the attraction of friend to
  friend,
Of the well-married husband and wife, of children and parents,
Of city for city and land for land.

Whitman stuck by this poem until the end, and it went unchanged
into the 1892 edition of *Leaves of Grass*, contributing its bit to the
'mentalizing' of the whole. And it is only too typical of additions to
the book made from 1867 on.

This Whitman begins to take over *Leaves of Grass* in the 1867 edition
and is fully in command by the time of the 1871 edition. It is, un-
happily, he whom he knew best and he with whom our poets have
tried to make their pacts and truces – but, as I think, so that during the
uneasy peace they might come to know another (and, as I have tried
to show, earlier) Whitman: whose way with the poetry they seem to
sense but can never quite get to. The way to that Whitman is not
impassable, although working with the Inclusive Edition of *Leaves of
Grass* (upon whose variant readings I have depended) is tedious. But
there is yet a more direct way: reading the 1860 *Leaves of Grass*.

Meantime we must bring ourselves to say of the Whitman of 1892,
the literatus, that he was driven to claim prophetic powers, not to put
poetry to their service. Nothing could hold this Whitman back, not
even the facts of a poet's life. Indeed, life – his own and life in general
– became less 'factual', less 'real' for him. And – since justification
consists in deriving the necessary from the real, of tracing the necessary back to its roots in the real, of showing that the real is necessary –
he no longer had a need to justify himself. Well: In this our world,
where we too find it increasingly hard to assent to the factually real,
where we have got so far as to call the factually real the 'absurd', we
find it increasingly difficult to hold ourselves back: as do our poets,

acting on our behalf. Thus I daresay we need to recover the Whitman of 1860 – with his heroic sense of grounding the necessary in the real. He gave us permission to. I am suggesting that we *need* the poet of 1860, the poet of *A Word out of the Sea*. I mean to say thereby that our poets need him too. And justifying the need, we must justify him who contrived that his need be archetypal of ours.

(261–94)

Richard Chase

'*Out of the Cradle* as a Romance', in R. W. B. Lewis (ed.), *The Presence of Walt Whitman* 1962

The main theme of *Out of the Cradle*, though it does not exhaust the meanings of the poem, is the origin of the poet's genius. Whitman asks for and receives from the sea a 'clew' or 'word', and we are led to understand that his poetic genius originated in childhood and its first intuition of the alienation and loss which are the lot of all beings and which culminate in death. *Out of the Cradle*, then, is a poem about the origin of poetry and to this extent is similar to Yeats's *Byzantium* and certain books of Wordsworth's *Prelude*. If this is not clear from the poem itself, we have as guideposts the two earlier titles Whitman gave to it: *A Child's Reminiscence* and *A Word out of the Sea*.

Is Whitman right, by the way, in tracing the origin of his poetry as he does? At best he seems to be only half right, for the world of experience posited in *Out of the Cradle* is not that of *Song of Myself*, a greater poem and in many ways more characteristic of the author.

What is not so clear is how much else, if anything, the poem means. Is it, as is often said, an 'organic' poem, affirming a whole view of reality in which life and death or love and death are understood as compensatory parts of the living universal rhythm? Mr Miller, in his chapter on *Out of the Cradle*, thinks that it is this kind of poem and provides us with a good statement of his position. He is speaking about the conclusion of the poem:

The sea waves, 'delaying not, hurrying not', repeat their single word, 'Death, death, death, death, death'. The slow and funeral march of the stress ironically recalls the preceding lines of heavy,

repeated stresses, lines of both joy and sorrow. The sea waves'
line not only recalls but also reconciles or merges the joy with the
sorrow, for the hypnotic effect ('Creeping thence steadily up to
my ears and laving me softly all over') precipitates in the soul of
the protagonist not terror but the ecstasy of mystic insight and
affirmation. Something of the nature of that insight is suggested
parenthetically at the end of the poem. Those sea waves striking
unceasingly and rhythmically against the shore, forming the
spiritually fertile 'liquid rims' are 'like some old crone rocking
the cradle'. The poem ends as it began ('Out of the cradle endlessly rocking'), and the cycle of the experience, like the cycle
of life, is begun again. Life and death are not the beginning and
end, but rather ceaseless continuations. Death is birth into
spiritual life. The sea, as it sends its waves unceasingly to the
seashore, is the 'cradle endlessly rocking', just as the spiritual
world, through the mystic experience of death, provides the
'cradle' for man's spiritual birth.

   There are many things to be said about this passage. One might
start with the language and politely desire of Mr Miller that he
eschew the word 'protagonist' unless the sense of the Greek word is
precisely demanded. A 'protagonist' combats something, but what,
in *Out of the Cradle*, is the 'protagonist' combating? It is actually the
poet who speaks in this poem. Then there is that other word that seems
often to go with 'protagonist' – 'insight', the insight we and the
protagonist get when the protagonist has a confrontation with something. The insight Mr Miller attributes to the protagonist is not really
an insight; it is a highly abstract idea, for which there is no warrant
in the poem. Finally the word 'mystic' – 'the ecstasy of.mystic
insight and affirmation' and 'the mystic experience of death'. I can
conceive of a mystic insight, though I would want to call it an
'intuition,' but an affirmation is necessarily of the will and the mystic
experience requires a suspension of the will. Nor do I think much is
gained by saying that the experience of death in the poem is 'mystic'.
It strikes me as being immediate and poignant; the poem would be
poorer if it were not. In talking about poetry we are often tempted to
use the word 'mystic' in order to beg a question or to talk about
something other than what we ought to be talking about: namely, the

poem. I am not particularly interested in whether or not Whitman may be properly called a 'mystic,' because the question is so largely irrelevant to the poems. As I said in my book on Whitman:

It seems a matter of general principle that poetic experience, although it may include it, cannot be equated with or produced by mystic experience, properly so called. Mysticism leads to the ecstatic contemplation of the naught; it does not of itself produce poetry, which is a metaphorical construction of the aught. Poetry is made by the imagination, and, as Santayana insists, the life of reason depends on our ability to distinguish between the imaginative and the mystic (although he himself failed to do so in his attack on Whitman). I do not wish to deny the usefulness of the word 'mysticism' in speaking of the general tenor of Whitman's mind, but only to doubt its relevance to the strictly literary question and to the question of his emergence as a poet.

My general objection to Mr Miller's formulation occurred to me when he passed confidently by the 'old crone rocking the cradle'. I don't feel comfortable with that 'old crone' despite her 'sweet garments' (shrouds can be 'sweet') and despite her cradle-rocking activities. She gives me the creeps and I can't help feeling that at not too many levels of meaning below the surface that cradle is a coffin. It is certainly true that many of Whitman's poems – including some of his best, such as *Song of Myself* – affirm an organic universe and an immortal and universal rhythm of life, but *Out of the Cradle* is not one of them. The quality of experience conveyed by this poem – the experience out of which poetry is born – involves love without an object; it involves anxiety, alienation, insoluble contradiction, and ultimate despair, a despair not assuaged by the sentimental resignation with which it is embraced.

The illusion of a harmonious universe in which opposites or contradictions are reconciled is sustained only at the very beginning of the poem. There the 'musical shuttle' out of 'the mocking-bird's throat' draws into a unity that which is 'down' and that which is 'up':

Down from the shower'd halo,
Up from the mystic play of shadows twining and twisting as if
    they were alive . . .

And at the beginning of the poem the poet can confidently speak of himself as the 'chanter of pains and joys, uniter of here and hereafter'. The feeling of reconciliation and harmony rises to an early pitch in the aria of the two birds:

Shine! Shine! Shine!
Pour down your warmth, great sun!
While we bask, we two together.

Two together!
Winds blow south, or winds blow north,
Day come white, or night come black,
Home, or rivers and mountains from home,
Singing all time, minding no time,
While we two keep together.

But the illusion of unity and continuity is not sustained, or is sustained only fitfully, after this aria. For now the she-bird has suddenly disappeared, and the he-bird sings his melancholy dirge, pouring out meanings, as Whitman cryptically says, 'which I of all men know'. A reader mindful of Whitman's love of melodrama, of which he encountered aplenty in the Italian operas he was so fond of, will find the first ominous note in this ominous poem in the 'surging of the sea', for this surging is described as 'hoarse', and although we may see nothing necessarily frightening in this at first, the context of the poem forces us to remember that ghosts and other demonic creatures are often said to speak with a hoarse and sepulchral voice. Even the 'white arms out in the breakers tirelessly tossing' which Whitman remembers seeing during the childhood experience he is recapturing or re-creating do not seem on reflection to be so attractive and winsome as they do at first. There is something threatening, something beyond human control, something suggestive of a universe indifferent to human destiny, in that tireless tossing. Or perhaps there is something merely suggestive of death, for the arms of a corpse in the sea might toss tirelessly.

The object of love is now unattainable, though there is still the compulsion to pursue it in panic and madness, a pursuit now seen as an act of nature itself:

O madly the sea pushes upon the land,
With love, with love.

And whereas once the white and the black were held together in a unison,

Day come white, or night come black,

they are now seen in an ultimate opposition:

What is that little black thing I see there in the white?

The song of the he-bird now rises to a pitch of desperate assertion:

Shake out carols!
Solitary here, the night's carols!
Carols of lonesome love! death's carols!
Carols under that lagging, yellow, waning moon!
O under that moon where she droops almost down into the sea!
O reckless despairing carols.

And finally the song recedes into a resigned reminiscence of what used to be: 'We two together no more.'

   Although we now hear 'the aria sinking', 'all else' continues; the stars shine, the winds blow, the notes of the bird echo. But 'all else' does not continue in a compensatory or organic harmony. Instead, the world has fallen apart. There is no object for 'the love in the heart long pent' even though it is 'now loose, now at last tumultuously bursting'. This is a world characterized by loss and alienation, not presided over by a benign Great Mother, as Whitman of all poets might have wished, but haunted and agitated by the 'angry moans' of 'the fierce old mother incessantly moaning'. Through the fissures of a disjoined world there enter the demonic powers always drawn upon by the imagination of melodrama. Does the boy, the poet-to-be, receive comforting and joyous answers to his questions about his destiny? Far from it:

The undertone, the savage old mother incessantly crying,
To the boy's soul's questions sullenly timing, some drown'd
   secret hissing,
To the outsetting bard.

   At this point the bird is addressed as 'demon or bird', and I think we are safe in taking 'demon' in both of its usual meanings: the poetic genius and a sinister emanation from some unknown realm. The latter meaning is confirmed by the imagery that occurs a bit later, where the bird is called a messenger, as if from some infernal place:

The messenger there arous'd, the fire, the sweet hell within,
The unknown want, the destiny of me.

Perhaps it is also sustained by the later phrase 'my dusky demon and brother'. As I have already suggested, neither the fivefold invocation to death, the dusky demon, nor the old crone at the end of *Out of the Cradle* suggests a world stabilized in a compensatory order of life and death. If we have read the poem clearly we do not leave it confident that we live in a world of pain assuaged, contradictions reconciled, and disruptive powers placated, or that poetry originates in such a world. Despite its sentimentality, Whitman's poem is more clairvoyant and more extreme in its perception of disorder and dread than its critics have seen, although these same critics would readily discern the same qualities in the works of other American romancers, such as Cooper, Poe, Hawthorne, and Melville.

Let me recall at this point the fascination Whitman felt for Poe and his writings. As he tells us in *Specimen Days*, he thinks that Poe's verses 'by final judgment, probably belong among the electric lights of imaginative literature, brilliant and dazzling, but with no heat.' Nevertheless, he says, there is 'an indescribable magnetism' about these poems with their 'incorrigible propensity toward nocturnal themes' and their 'demoniac undertone behind every page'. And Whitman tells us that he had gradually lost his early distaste for Poe's writings. He then recounts a dream he had had about Poe:

I saw a vessel on the sea, at midnight, in a storm . . . flying uncontrolled with torn sails and broken spars through the wild sleet and winds and waves of the night. On the deck was a slender, slight, beautiful figure, a dim man apparently enjoying all the terror, the murk, and the dislocation of which he was the centre and the victim.

That makes a good description of the author of *Out of the Cradle* – a dim man apparently enjoying all the terror, the murk, and the dislocation of which he was the center and the victim.

But, it might be asked, is not my account of *Out of the Cradle* at odds with the obvious feelings the poet means to leave us with? These feelings involve sadness, to be sure, but they seem to culminate, if not in happiness, then in resignation in the face of loss and unrequited love. And death itself, it might be argued, is not felt to be terrible; indeed it is embraced with a kind of tender eroticism, not to mention gustatory delight – 'the low and delicious word death'. It seems to me that the language of the poem sustains these feelings of resignation and benignity so well that it is all too easy to take them as the sum and substance of the poem. As D. H. Lawrence admonishes us, we must look below the surface of these American authors. When we look below the surface of *Out of the Cradle* we seem to see the dark workings-out of a human drama being played on a stage set by a dramatist with a dubious moral to propose, namely that we should accept death and that this acceptance may be the origin of such creations as Whitman's poetry. This would be excellent morality if the sense of it were: 'Let us accept death as a fact, and let this fact thereby enhance our Life.' But Whitman does not say anything like this. He is titillated by death and he forms a sentimental attachment to it. The idyl of the two birds ends near the beginning of the poem, but the idyllic tone, modulated into a somber key, strangely continues. And in fact what the poet does is nothing less than endow the ominous drama of the savage old mother, the lagging moon, and the dusky demon with the emotional quality of an idyl; he thus successfully muffles and suffuses but cannot banish what is going on under the surface. The melodious words and the bland universe of experience make one level of the poem, but the submerged, disrupted, and ultimately nihilistic impulses remain active.

We do not have to be professional psychoanalysts in order to make the plausible conjecture that the reason for the disjunction between the manifest and the latent content of Whitman's poem is to be found in the poet's own emotional life. The generally accepted view of Whitman is that he was more or less bisexual, that he tended toward the homosexual, that he was perhaps not very active sexually at all, and that love, for him, was either fraternal or maternal – he was unable to endow a father image with emotional power or to convey, except in very abstract terms, the nature of heterosexual love. In *Out of the Cradle* the neurotic Whitman has it all his own way. There is no image of paternity: 'fish-shaped' Paumanok is not identified with the father here, although it is in *As I Ebb'd with the Ocean of Life*. The marriage of sexual equals is symbolically exorcised in the loss of the she-bird by the he-bird. The he-bird is not felt as a father, but as 'my dusky demon and brother'. In this world bereft of the father-principle, the mother is all-encompassing, like the sea. But what is the price the poet has to pay for his denial and extinction of the father? Well, of course, it is anxiety and ambivalence, involving both love and dread, toward the mother. Thus, it is not surprising that while the poet is enjoying with such swooning pleasure the rocking of the cradle, the mother supplying the motive power should be an 'old crone' who 'bends aside' and whispers hoarsely.

On the surface, in other words, the embracing of death is presented as pleasurable and as the beginning of creative acts. Beneath the surface it is recognized as an act of neurotic regression which generates powerful and sinister impulses that threaten the destruction of personality. This is why I speak of the 'melodramatic' quality of *Out of the Cradle*, apart from its obvious use of some of the trappings of this mode of art. Whitman's distinctive emotional nature is to be found in the conflicts of the unresolved Oedipus complex we all of us more or less live with (and it is here rather than in the sentimental invocation to death that we discover the real origins of Whitman's poetry – in so far as we discover them at all). Melodrama, like some forms of comedy – farce, for example – is precisely a drama of unresolved conflicts or contradictions.

The poem called *Tears* is a kind of footnote to the more lachrymose sections of *Out of the Cradle*. This short lyric starts out as a rather impressive piece but at the end, where we read about 'the unloosen'd ocean|Of tears! tears! tears!' it is hard not to be reminded of Alice in Wonderland, swimming in the ocean she has made with her weeping. Nevertheless the ambiguity or doubleness of *Out of the Cradle* is well represented, and in a more literal way, in *Tears*. Here the poet imagines himself to be 'sedate and decorous by day, with calm countenance and regulated pace'. But at night he is a ghost with a 'muffled head' weeping desperately on the beach:

O who is that ghost? that form in the dark, with tears?
What shapeless lump is that, bent, crouch'd there on the sand?
Streaming tears, sobbing tears, throes, choked with wild cries;
O storm, embodied, rising, careering with swift steps along the beach?
O wild and dismal night storm, with wind . . .

There is nothing here about an 'outsetting bard'. There is only an undifferentiated horror and in a gothicized setting an almost total extinction of personality.

If I am right in assigning to *Out of the Cradle* such terms as romance, idyl, and melodrama, it cannot, as I have noted before, be also a tragic poem. It would be surprising indeed if a work of personal confession whose main emotions culminate, as we must see, in a sentimental nihilism should be also a tragic work. The poem does not work its way through its own inner contradictions, its *agon*, and then proceed, as does tragedy, to issue in a higher synthesis or harmony. The embracing of death is not accompanied by a purgated emotion, because the emotion is not won; it is, we cannot help feeling, merely held in reserve so that at the proper time the poet can fall back on it. It is an emotion all too easily come by, in other words a sentimental, though not a shallow, emotion. *Song of Myself* can hardly be called a tragedy either, but that poem strikes me as having more of the essential nature of tragic art than does *Out of the Cradle* – at least, *Song of Myself* has, in the correct sense of the word, a protagonist. *Out of the Cradle* is a much more unified work of art than Melville's *Pierre* (to venture a distant comparison); but it seems to me to be related to *Song of Myself* roughly as *Pierre* – also a work that begins in idyl and ends in melodrama – is related to *Moby Dick*. After the great aggressive act of creating a superb work of art there follows, for aesthetic, moral, or psychological reasons we cannot quite define, the rather desperate act of neurotic self-exposure. The poet who in *Song of Myself* glorified in the amplitude of a many-faceted personality has come in the *Sea-Drift* poems to doubt the very possibility of personality. He has been led, for whatever reason, to wonder whether the glorious autonomous self has not now become (in the memorable words of Frederik Schyberg) 'only a chance bit of wreckage thrown up on the shore of existence.'

The characteristic form of American fiction which I call in a special sense 'romance' is one which defines itself by its substitution of two-dimensional figures, often allegorized, for the rounded characters who appear in the more ample form of the novel. It defines itself, that is, by a reduction of personality. For this reason, among the others I have pointed out, romance is a suitable form for *Out of the Cradle Endlessly Rocking*.

(59–71)

Roger Asselineau

'Style – From Mysticism to Art', *The Evolution of Walt Whitman* 1962

Emerson one day confided to a friend that *Leaves of Grass* reminded him at one time of the *Bhagavad Gita* and the *New York Herald*. Its style is indeed most incongruous. Lyrical flights are to be found side by side with prosaic banalities, mystical effusions with the most familiar expressions from the spoken language. Sometimes Whitman transcribes an everyday scene with extreme simplicity and the greatest transparence:

The little one sleeps in its cradle,
I lift the gauze and look a long time, and silently brush
    away flies with my hand.

(*Song of Myself*, 8)

Sometimes he heaps up abstract words interminably with an enthusiasm which the reader does not always share:

Great is Liberty! great is Equality! . . .
Great is Youth – equally great is Old Age . . .
Great is Wealth – great is Poverty – great is Expression – great
    is Silence . . .

(*Great Are the Myths*)

Even more, the same verse sometimes brings these two clashing elements together:

I concentrate toward them that are nigh, I wait on the
    door-slab.

(*Song of Myself*, 51)

Too often one passes without transition from the loose, woolly, pretentious language of the journalist who pads his text with big words to the rapid and precise evocation of a concrete detail. It even happens that his best passages are spoiled by the brusque intrusion of a learned word in a very simple context:

The field-sprouts of Fourth-month and Fifth-month became
    part of him.

Winter-grain sprouts and those of the light-yellow corn and
     the *esculent roots* of the garden . . .[1]

(*There Was a Child Went Forth*)

The same jarring note is sometimes produced by the unexpected use
of a slang term:

The spotted hawk swoops by and accuses me, he complains of
     my *gab* and my loitering.[1]

(*Song of Myself*, 52)

Thus, most often, the different stylistic elements, instead of being
used separately and kept free from all admixture, enter into complex
combinations. The concrete passages, in particular, are not always the
realistic and perfectly objective little pictures of the sort which we
have quoted above. Habitually, the mind of the poet diffuses its own
divinity over the void of the external world; grass is not that inert
substance which a child carries to him in his fist, but 'the flag of [his]
disposition, out of hopeful green stuff woven.' His sensibility and, all
the more, his sensuality, often modify the image of things which he
gives to us:

Smile O voluptuous cool-breath'd earth!
Earth of slumbering and liquid trees . . .
Earth of the vitreous pour of the full moon just tinged
     with blue . . .

(*Song of Myself*, 21)

Matter then is dissolved; trees become liquid and contours fluid (these
two adjectives 'liquid' and 'fluid' recur frequently in his verse). One
is witness to a mysterious transmutation of the real in which his
imagination also intervenes. For Whitman is not content with what
he has before his eyes; he wants to evoke, to imply, as it were, all the
rest of the world, the infinity of space, and the 'amplitude of time'.
He soon abandons the stallion whose beauty and dash so much impressed him:

I but use you a moment and then I resign you stallion . . . and do
     not need your paces, and outgallop them,
And myself as I stand or sit pass faster than you.

(1855, 'I celebrate myself', p. 35)

[1] Asselineau's italics. [Ed.]

Hence cosmic visions of this sort:

My ties and ballasts leave me, I travel ... I sail ... my elbows
    rest in sea-gaps,
I skirt sierras ... my palms cover continents ...
I fly the flight of a fluid and swallowing soul,
My course runs below the soundings of plummets ...
                                    (1855, 'I celebrate myself', p. 35;
                                    Song of Myself, 33)

He is transformed into a comet and travels round the universe with
the speed of light:

I depart as air, I shake my white locks at the runaway sun,
I effuse my flesh in eddies, and drift it in lacy jags.
                                    (*Song of Myself*, 52)

This dissolution of himself and this fluidity of the world permit the
boldest and most unexpected images:

My foothold is tenon'd and mortis'd in granite ...
                                    (*Song of Myself*, 20)

... a leaf of grass is no less than the journey-work of the stars ...
... [I] am stucco'd with quadrupeds and birds all over
                                    (*Song of Myself*, 31)

... the sobbing liquid of life ...
                                    (*Song of Myself*, 42)

The complexity and the discords of his style are not due solely to his
lack of education and to his habits as a journalist, they derive also
from the duality of his point of view on the world. Sometimes he
places himself on the plane of the senses and describes the visible in
simple and direct terms. Sometimes, as a mystic, he transcends
physical appearances and tries to suggest the invisible. As he himself
says:

I help myself to material and immaterial ...
                                    (*Song of Myself*, 33)

Thus is explained the co-existence in his work of descriptive passages
and of somewhat obscure lines where he tried to express the inexpres-

sible and translate those mysterious hieroglyphics which in his eyes all material objects were. The problem of the inexpressible haunted him.

There is something that comes to one now and perpetually,
It is not what is printed, preach'd, discussed, it eludes discussion
   and print . . .
It is for you whoever you are, it is no farther from you than your
   hearing and sight are from you,
It is hinted by nearest, commonest, readiest, it is ever provoked
   by them . . .
                    (*A Song for Occupations*, 2)

I do not know it – it is without name – it is a word unsaid,
It is not in any dictionary, utterance, symbol.
                    (*Song for Myself*, 50)

How can one resolve this insoluble problem? A frontal attack is impossible. One can only approach it indirectly. And that is precisely what Whitman does. As early as 1855 he understood that in order to evoke 'transcendent' reality he had to be 'indirect and not direct or descriptive or epic' (what Paul Claudel calls 'la divine loi de l'expression détournée'):

I swear [he said the following year] I see what is better than to
   tell the best,
It is always to leave the best untold.
                  (1856, *Poem of the Sayer of the
                  Words of the Earth*, p. 329; *A Song
                  of the Rolling Earth*, 3)

And, in 1860, defining the 'laws for creation', he formulated this precept:

There shall be no subject too pronounced – all works shall
   illustrate the divine law of indirections.
                  (1860, *Chants Democratic*, No. 13;
                  Laws for Creations)

So, instead of saying, he must suggest – not by means of the music of his verse, as the symbolists tried to do later, for it never for a moment occurred to him – but by means of images since 'the unseen is proved by the seen.' This may lead to a certain obscurity, but a poem must be a beginning rather than an end and it belongs to the reader to take up the poet's suggestions and to finish it. In short, Whitman defined here beforehand the fundamental principles of symbolism; and he was still more explicit in *Specimen Days*: 'The play of imagination with the sensuous objects of Nature for symbols, and Faith . . . make up the curious chess-game of a poem . . .'. These ideas were not altogether new; they had already broken through in the subjective theories of the romantics and the transcendentalists, but no one had yet applied them with as much audacity as Whitman and no poet before him had dared to express his *joie de vivre* by means of an image as 'indirect' as this:

As God comes a loving bed-fellow and sleeps at my side all night
    and close on the peep of the day,
And leaves for me baskets covered with white towels, swelling
    the house with their plenty.

(*Song of Myself*, 3)

We have here, it is true, an extreme case where the oneiric character of the evocation and the gratuitousness of the associations almost announce surrealism. Whitman, in general, was reluctant to go in that direction. Comparing himself to Blake about 1868–70 in an essay which he never had occasion to publish, he wrote:

Blake's visions grow to be the rule, displace the normal
condition, fill the field, spurn this visible, objective life, and seat
the subjective spirit on an absolute throne, wilful and
uncontrolled. But Whitman, though he occasionally prances off
. . . always holds the mastery over himself, and even in his most
intoxicated lunges or pirouettes, never once loses control, or even
equilibrium.

('Faint Clews', p. 53)

The passing from the objective to the subjective plane is thus deliberate and conscious with him, and conscious, too, is his care never to lose contact with objective reality. One is reminded of Wordsworth's skylark which, unlike Shelley's, never forgets in the midst of her wild flight that she has left her nest on the earth; much as Whitman launched his 'yawp' over the rooftops of the world, his feet remained firmly planted on the ground.

The most felicitous passages of *Leaves of Grass* are thus those in which Whitman has succeeded in fusing the diverse elements of his style, those in which he suggests rather than describes and soars rather than trudges through interminable objective catalogues, those, too, in which he takes flight but does not get lost in the clouds. His expression is effective whenever he manages to interweave abstractions and familiar terms as in:

I believe in those wing'd purposes . . .

(*Song of Myself*, 13)

Or in:

Agonies are one of my changes of garments.

(*Song of Myself*, 33)

These unexpected combinations give a new vigor to his style. But he fails every time he lets one of these elements prevail over the others, notably when he falls into didacticism and preaches in abstract terms his democratic gospel or his personal religion:

There can be any number of supremes – one does not
    countervail another any more than one eyesight countervails
    another, or one life countervails another.

All is eligible to all . . .

(*By Blue Ontario's Shore*, 3)

'How plenteous! how spiritual! how résumé!' he went so far as to say in 1860.

Such are the characteristics of Whitman's style in the first two editions of *Leaves of Grass*; but we might have drawn our examples from later editions as well, for until the end his qualities and his faults remained the same. *Grand is the Seen* written at the end of his career is the exact counterpart of *Great are the Myths* published in 1853. Is that to say that he made no progress in the interval? Not at all. The patient labor of revising his work which he undertook from 1856 to 1881 was not in vain and reveals an increasingly finer artistic sense. Matthiessen claims that these corrections are disconcerting and cannot always be justified, but we do not share his opinion on this point. If some of them appear useless, most of them serve a purpose and can be vindicated.

First of all, as we have pointed out, Whitman in growing old understood that it had been maladroit and tasteless to shock his readers by introducing crude details in contexts where one would not expect to find them. So, without really renouncing the poems which had a sexual inspiration, he gradually eliminated from the others such verses as:

Have you sucked the nipples of the breasts of the mother of many
   children!

> (1856, *A Poem of Many in One*,[1]
> p. 192)

and:

And have an unseen something to be in contact with them also.
   (*The Sleepers*)

The first of these lines was suppressed in 1860, that is to say, the very year, he added *Calamus* and *Children of Adam* to *Leaves of Grass*.

He very soon also tried to avoid the monotony of certain repetitions and in particular the coordinating conjunctions which he had over-used in the first edition. Numerous are the *and*'s and the *or*'s which disappeared in 1856. Later he got rid of the O's, realizing that that was a little too facile a method for a lyric take-off. As early as 1867 he suppressed 'Apostroph', where they swarmed and eliminated many others in 1881, for instance, in *Out of the Cradle Endlessly Rocking*, where one critic in 1860 had counted thirty-five O's. It had taken Whitman twenty years to come round to his view. Generally speaking, he attempted to remove all the repetitions which had no expressive value and whose monotony weighted his verse, particularly all the useless *I*'s which came after coordinating conjunctions, as well as the numerous I *swear*'s which in fact added nothing. He also cut out a number of awkward lines such as 'A breed whose testimony is behaviour.'

If you would be better than all that has ever been before, come
   listen to me and I will tell you,

---

1 Later called *By Blue Ontario's Shore*. [Ed.]

in 1867 became:

If you would be freer than all that has been before come listen to
  me.

(By Blue Ontario's Shore)

He also suppressed a number of colloquial phrases the incongruity
of which in certain passages he now perceived. Thus it was that in
1867 he no longer retained 'plenty of them' at the end of the following
line:

If you remember your foolish and outlaw'd deeds, do you think I
  cannot remember my own foolish and outlaw'd deeds?

(A Song for Occupations)

'You mean devil' similarly disappeared from *Myself and Mine*. The
Prince of Wales who had been democratically hailed as 'sweet boy'
in 1860, became 'young prince' in 1881. In *The Centenarian's Story*
he avoided the colloquial usage of 'good' as an adverb, and in 1871
he eliminated from *Crossing Brooklyn Ferry* 'Dully for you!' and
'Blab, blush, lie, steal,' which were undoubtedly very expressive, but
which he now considered too slangy. In 1881 he redoubled his
severity with himself and suppressed not only these youthful lines
from *Song of Myself*:

That life is a suck and a sell, and nothing remains in the end but
  threadbare crape and tears.
Washes and razors for foofoos – for me freckles and a bristling
  beard.

He suppressed also the playful lines which he had composed in 1871
to amuse his audience at the American Institute Exhibition:

She comes! this famous Female [the Muse] – as was indeed to be
  expected;
(For who, so ever youthful, 'cute and handsome would wish to
  stay in mansions such as those . . .
With all the fun that's going – and all the best society?)

(Song of the Exposition)

But all his corrections did not have such a negative character. He
profited from this minute labor of revision to render his text more

expressive and to choose his words with more care. In particular he rid himself of a number of catch-all adjectives like 'wondrous' or 'mystic', either suppressing them completely, or replacing them by less vague and more appropriate epithets. Thus, 'the mystic midnight' became 'the vacant midnight' and 'my insolent poems' was changed in 1881 into 'my arrogant poems', which is certainly more appropriate. In *To Think o' Time*, speaking in the name of the dead, he had at first written:

> To think of all these wonders of city and country and . . . we
>   taking small interest in them . . .

but 'small' was exaggerated and he replaced it later with 'no'. He had in the same way rather imprudently qualified the trot of the horses of a hearse as 'rapid'; after 1860 he contented himself with 'steady'.

Sometimes he introduced color adjectives to enhance the descriptive passages. For example, he added the entire line:

> Scarlet and blue and snowy white,

to *Cavalry Crossing a Ford*, and appended the complementary indication 'yellow-flower'd' to the rather uninteresting mention of a cottonwood in a Southern landscape. Almost everywhere dull and banal expressions gave place to more expressive words. Whereas in 1867 he merely 'sang' on the shores of Lake Ontario, in 1881 he 'thrill'd'. 'The English pluck' of John Paul Jones's adversaries later became 'the surly English pluck', which is indeed a very apt phrase.

Certain lines were thus completely transformed, like:

> Alone, held by the eternal self of me that threatens to get the
>   better of me, and stifle me,

which was, in 1881, changed to:

> Held by this electric self out of the pride of which I utter
>   poems . . .
>
> (*As I Ebb'd with the Ocean of Life*,)

The poetic charge of the second version is singularly higher; it is magnetized as it were, by the introduction of the adjective 'electric'.

'I hear American mouthsongs' was flat and awkward; it became 'I hear America singing' in 1867 and the line now really sings.

He also added some images here and there, for example, the line 'Thou but the apples, long, long, long, a-growing' to *Thou Mother with Thy Equal Brood*, and realizing the evocative power of the historical present he substituted it for the preterite in some stories like that of the seafight between the *Bonhomme Richard* and an English frigate. All these corrections liberated the latent energy of many passages.

But he turned his attention more particularly to titles and first lines and it was there that he obtained the most spectacular results. In 1856 all his titles were of a depressing monotony and an annoying clumsiness: *Poem of Walt Whitman, an American*, *Poem of The Daily Work of the Workmen and the Workwomen of These States*, *Poem of the Heart of the Son of Manhattan Island*, *Poem of the Last Explanation of Prudence*, *Poem of the Propositions of Nakedness*, and in 1860 they were not much better since most of the poems were simply numbered. In 1867, however, he did his best to find picturesque titles. Thus, *Proto-Leaf*, a barbarous expression, was replaced by *Starting from Paumanok* which is concrete and dynamic, and the former *Poem of Walt Whitman, an American* became in 1881, after many metamorphoses, *Song of Myself*, a title which admirably sums up its central theme. The *Poem of the Body* which originally began with:

The bodies of men and women engirth me and I engirth them ...

started in 1867 with:

I sing the body electric ...

which is singularly more promising. It was during that year that he found the title of *One Hour of Madness and Joy*, of *Trickle-Drops*, of *On the Beach at Night Alone*. But it was only later and after much searching that he arrived at *As I Ebb'd with the Ocean of Life*, *By Blue Ontario's Shore*, *Aboard at a Ship's Helm*, *Out of the Cradle Endlessly Rocking*, *A Song of the Rolling Earth*, and so on.

He also rounded off certain lines whose ends seemed too abrupt – especially, it appears, while preparing the 1881 edition. Thus,

You shall sit in the middle well-poised thousands of years,

became:

You shall sit in the middle well-pois'd thousands and thousands of
    years ...

(A Broadway Pageant, 3)

In the poem entitled I was Looking a Long While the last line:

All for the average man of to-day,

which lacked force and vividness, was changed to:

All for the modern – all for the average man of today,

which is at once more rhythmical and more vehement. Whitman,
moreover, took pains not only with his titles and with the ends of
lines but also with the ends of his poems. In particular, he added to
A Farm Picture a last line which has a most happy effect and enlarges
to infinity what was originally a rather banal vignette. And, what was
an even more characteristic correction, he introduced into his longer
poems, like Song of Myself, either at the beginning or at the end of the
different sections, lines destined to serve, according to the individual
instance, as an introduction or a conclusion, in order to prepare the
transitions and reinforce the cohesiveness of the whole. In other
words, he became increasingly mindful of form.

    But at the same time, in proportion as his inspiration lost its force,
he tended to be more and more content with very short poems for
which no problem of composition existed. He had already used this
formula as early as 1856 in Drum-Taps, where he had included a
number of short descriptive poems like A Farm Picture, Cavalry
Crossing a Ford, By the Bivouac's Fitful Flame, The Torch, The Ship, and
The Runner, or very brief philosophical poems like A Child's Amaze.
From 1881 on, he wrote only poems of this sort, but, refusing to
admit the decline of his inspiration, he claimed that in so doing he
was deliberately limiting himself in order to conform to a principle
posed by Poe, namely 'that (at any rate for our occasions, our day)
there can be no such thing as a long poem. The same thought', he
added, 'had been haunting my mind before, but Poe's argument,
though short, work'd the sum and proved it to me.' He merely
omitted to say that, to Poe's mind, the short poem adapted to the
capabilities of the modern reader might reach a length of about a

hundred lines, as in the case of *The Raven*, and this was rather far from the few lines with which the author of *November Boughs* now contented himself.

Whitman thus attached more and more importance to form as his poetic material became thinner. Whereas in the preface to the 1855 edition of *Leaves of Grass* he affected a sovereign scorn for polish and ornaments, and made everything depend on the power of inspiration, ten years later, he rejoiced that *Drum-Taps* was 'certainly more perfect as a work of art, being adjusted in all its proportions, and its passion having the indispensable merit that . . . the true artist can see it is . . . under control.' And it is probably during this period that he gave himself this advice:

In future *Leaves of Grass*. *Be more severe* with the final revision of the poem, nothing will do, not one word or sentence, that is not *perfectly clear* – with positive purpose – harmony with the name, nature, drift of the poem. Also *no ornaments*, especially *no ornamental adjectives*, unless they have come molten hot, and imperiously prove themselves. No *ornamental similes at all* – *not one: perfect transparent clearness* sanity and health are wanted – that is the *divine style* – O if it can be attained –

It is obvious that he was then very far from the superb assurance he had shown in 1855 and this text proves that all his later revisions were perfectly conscious. As early as 1860 he had begun to understand his error:

Now I reverse what I said, and affirm that all depends on the
    aesthetic or intellectual,
And that criticism is great – and that refinement is greatest of
    all . . .

(1860, Says)

Unfortunately it was too late. He could still revise his early poems, but he could not recast them, and, in spite of the progress he achieved, his art remained fundamentally the same. So, at the end of his life, he himself realized the inferiority of his work from the point of view of form. Casting a backward glance over the roads he had traveled he readily acknowledged in 1888 that as far as descriptive talent, dramatic situations, and especially verbal melody and all the conventional techniques of poetry were concerned, *Leaves of Grass* was eclipsed by many masterpieces of the past. And beating his breast three years later he added: 'I have probably not been enough afraid of careless touches, from the first . . . nor of parrot-like repetitions – nor platitudes and the commonplace.'

Thus the mystic who, in 1855, had wished to communicate the revelation which he had received and announce to the world a new gospel by slow degrees became an artist more and more conscious of his imperfections, but, to a large extent, incapable of remedying them. How could he have done so? In spite of his growing respect for art, all discipline seemed to him a useless constraint and any convention a dangerous artifice which risked raising a barrier between his thought and the reader. To art he opposed what he called simplicity, that is to say, strict adherence to nature. As a mystic, he was thus able to write: 'In these *Leaves* everything is literally photographed. Nothing is poetized, no divergence, not a step, not an inch, nothing for beauty's sake, no euphemism, no rhyme. And, in the same year, as an artist, he on the contrary affirmed the necessity of a transposition: 'No useless attempt to repeat the material creation, by daguerreotyping the exact likeness by mortal mental means.' This contradiction gives the measure of his predicament. In fact, of course, he had to transpose, but he was not any less convinced that he had remained completely faithful to nature. When in 1879 he traveled in the Rocky Mountains he thought that he saw in their chaotic mass the symbol of his own poems. 'I have found the law of my own poems,' he explained at the sight of 'this plenitude of material, complete absence of art.' To art, for him a synonym for artifice, he thus preferred Nature, 'the only complete, actual poem', with its disorder, its immensity, its indescribably secret life.

To this instinctive preference his belief in the unlimited power of inspiration was obscurely related, as well as his faith in the efficacy of the slow germination which precedes the birth of a poem:

The rhyme and uniformity of perfect poems show the free growth of metrical laws and bud from them as unerringly and loosely as lilacs or roses on a bush, and take shapes as compact as the shapes of chestnuts and oranges and melons and pears and shed the perfume impalpable to form.

(1855, Preface to *Leaves of Grass*)

In other words, thought and inspiration determine expression, so
that what counts in the last analysis is thought and not form, which is
only its reflection. Whatever its apparent disorder may be, the poem,
simply because it grew and matured in the soul of the poet, has the
same profound unity and the same beauty as Nature, which was
created by God, the supreme poet. The theory was not new. We
recognize here the principle of organic unity which Coleridge had
borrowed from Schlegel and had discussed many times in his critical
writings, in particular in the *Biographia Literaria* where Whitman may
have discovered it. This doctrine suited him perfectly since it authorized him to reject every rule of composition and prosody.

If it permits one to break free from rules, the theory of organic
unity, however, does not exempt the poet from work. It requires
much groping to release what is gestating within him. The impression of ease or 'abandon', as he said, which Whitman's work gives,
was, in fact, the result of careful planning. His simplicity is labored,
and that is why he approved the famous line of Ben Jonson. 'A good
poet's made as well as born.' The first version of *Leaves of Grass*, far
from having been written at one sitting, evolved slowly from a considerable number of drafts of the kind which Emory Holloway has
published and which represent the work of several years. The short
poems of his old age required as much trouble. There exist at the
Library of Congress ten different drafts of *Supplement Hours*.

An examination of the papers left by Whitman permits a recon-
struction of his method. Contrary to poets like Valéry, for whom the
starting-point is a rhythm or a musical motif, Whitman seems always
to have taken off from a word or an idea expressed in prose. His
manuscripts show it. This initial material was later elaborated and
expressed rhythmically. That is what happened for instance to this
list of words which R. M. Bucke published in *Notes and Fragments*:
'Perfect Sanity – Divine Instinct – Breadth of Vision – Healthy
Rudeness of Body. Withdrawnness. Gayety, Sun-tan and air-sweetness.' Out of this material Whitman later made two lines of the poem
which eventually became *Song of the Answerer*:

Divine instinct, breadth of vision, the law of reason, health,
    rudeness of body, withdrawnness,
Gayety, sun-tan, air-sweetness, such are some of the words of poems.

The germ of *Night on the Prairies* which has been found in his papers also appears in the form of a brief sketch in prose entitled 'Idea of a poem'. And on another rough draft one can read this revealing injunction: 'Make this more rhythmic.' Sometimes the first line provoked a rich germination within him and in that case, as the ideas appeared, he noted them down on the first scraps of paper he could find: old envelopes, the backs of proof-sheets, all of which gradually accumulated and soon formed a bundle which he pinned together so as not to lose them. Then he would sort his scraps, add, cut out, change the order of the various fragments, re-arrange them endlessly. And, when he felt that the process of germination was complete, he placed his pieces of paper end to end and recopied them, or pasted them on large sheets, as he did for *Eidólons*, the definitive manuscript of which may be seen at the Boston Public Library. Thus, his method was essentially agglutinative. His poems were composed like mosaics and, as in mosaics, a number of lines or passages are interchangeable. Whitman himself, in the course of the successive editions, did not hesitate to change the order of certain paragraphs. This method of composition explains the looseness and desultoriness of so many of his poems, but it enabled him to gather all the insights that a poetic idea gave birth to in his mind and to respect the slow organic growth of his work. So he used it all his life. It was his way of reconciling his mysticism with his art, of preserving the spontaneity of his inspiration while imposing upon it a certain form.

This loose method was thus one of the constants of Whitman's art. For him the spirit always took precedence over the letter. He said one day to Horace Traubel: 'I have never given any study merely to expression.' He was right, but he might well have added: 'I have thought increasingly of form.'

(II, 207–24)

Gay Wilson Allen

'Walt Whitman: The Search for a "Democratic" Structure', *Walt Whitman Handbook* 1962 (first published 1946)

In so far as the expanding ego psychology results in an enumerative style, the cataloging of a representative and symbolical succession of images, conveying the sensation of pantheistic unity and endless becoming, it is itself a literary technique. But though this psychology may be called the background or basic method of Whitman's poetic technique, the catalog itself was not chronologically the first stylistic device which he adopted. It emerged only after he had found a verse structure appropriate for expressing his cosmic inspiration and democratic sentiment. Nowhere in the universe does he recognize caste or subordination. Everything is equally perfect and equally divine. He admits no supremes, or rather insists that 'There can be any number of supremes.'[1]

The expression of such doctrines demands a form in which units are co-ordinate, distinctions eliminated, all flowing together in a synonymous or 'democratic' structure. He needed a grammatical and rhetorical structure which would be cumulative in effect rather than logical or progressive.

Possibly, as many critics have believed, he found such a structure in the primitive rhythms of the King James Bible, though some of the resemblances may be accidental. The structure of Hebraic poetry, even in English translation, is almost lacking in subordination. The original language of the Old Testament was extremely deficient in connectives as the numerous 'ands' of the King James translation bear witness.[2] It was a language for direct assertion and the expression of emotion rather than abstract thought or intellectual subtleties. Tied to such a language, the Hebraic poet developed a rhythm of thought, repeating and balancing ideas and sentences (or independent clauses) instead of syllables or accents. He may have had other prosodic conventions also, no longer understood or easily discernible; but at least in the English

1 *By Blue Ontario's Shore*, 3.
2 See A. S. Cook, 'The "Authorized Version" and Its Influence', *Cambridge History of English Literature*, G. P. Putnam's Sons, 1910, vol. 4, pp. 29–58.

translation this rhythm of thought or parellelism characterizes Biblical versification.[1]

That Walt Whitman fully understood the nature of these Biblical rhythms is doubtful, and certainly his own language did not tie him down to such a verse system. Despite the fact that he was thoroughly familiar with the Bible and was undoubtedly influenced by the scriptures in many ways, it may, therefore, have been a coincidence that in searching for a medium to express his pantheism he naturally (we might almost say atavistically) stumbled upon parallelism as his basic structure. Furthermore, parallelism is found in primitive poetry other than the Biblical; in fact, seems to be typically primitive,[2] and it is perhaps not surprising that in the attempt to get rid of conventional techniques Whitman should have rediscovered a primitive one.

But whatever the sources of Whitman's verse techniques, the style of the King James Version is generally agreed to provide convenient analogies for the prosodic analysis of *Leaves of Grass*.[3]

'The principles which governed Hebrew verse', says Gardiner, 'can be recovered only in part, but fortunately the one principle which really affects the form of the English has been clearly made out, the principle of parallel structure: in the Hebrew poetry the line was the unit, and the second line balanced the first, completing or supplementing its meaning.[4]

Even the scholars of the Middle ages were aware of the parallelism of Biblical verse (*Verdoppelten Ausdruck* or 'double expression',[5] they

1 See S. R. Driver, *Introduction to the Literature of the Old Testament*, Scribner's Sons, 1910, pp. 361ff. Also E. Kautzsch, *Die Poesie und die poetischen Bücher des Alten Testaments*, Tübingen und Leipzig, 1902, p. 2. Bishop Lowth first pointed out the metrical principles of parallelism in the Bible in *De sacra poesi Hebraeorum praelectiones academiae Oxoni habitae*, 1753 – see Driver, op. cit., p. 362. In the main the Lowth system is the basis for R. G. Moulton's arrangement of Biblical poetry in his *Modern Reader's Bible*, Macmillan, 1922. See also note 3 below.

2 E.g., in American Indian rhythms – cf. Mary Austin's *The American Rhythm*, Harcourt Brace, 1913.

3 Observed by many critics and biographers, but first elaborated by Gay Wilson Allen, 'Biblical Analogies for Walt Whitman's Prosody', *Revue Anglo-Américaine*, vol. 10, pp. 490–507 (August, 1933) – basis for same author's chapter on Whitman in *American Prosody*, American Book Co., 1935, pp. 217–43.

4 J. H. Gardiner, *The Bible as English Literature*, Scribner's Sons, 1906, p. 107.

5 Kautzsch, op. cit., p. 2.

409 Gay Wilson Allen

called it) but it was first fully explained by Bishop Lowth in a Latin speech given at Oxford in 1753. Since his scheme demonstrates the single line as the unit, let us examine it.

1. *Synonymous* parallelism: This is the most frequent kind of thought rhythm in Biblical poetry. 'The second line enforces the thought of the first by repeating, and, as it were, *echoing* it in a varied form, producing an effect at once grateful to the ear and satisfying to the mind.'[1]

How shall I curse, whom God hath not cursed?
And how shall I defy, whom the Lord hath not defied?
(*Numbers* xxiii, 8)

The second line, however, does not have to be identical in thought with the first. It may be merely similar or parallel to it.

Sun, stand thou still upon Gibeon;
And thou, Moon, upon the valley of Aijalon.
(*Joshua* x, 12)

2. *Antithetic* parallelism: The second line denies or contrasts with the first:

A wise son maketh a glad father,
But a foolish son is the heaviness of his mother.
(*Proverbs* x, 1)

For the Lord knoweth the way of the righteous;
But the way of the wicked shall perish.
(*Psalms* i, 6)

3. *Synthetic* or *constructive* parallelism: Here the second line (sometimes several consecutive lines) supplements or completes the first. (Although all Biblical poetry tends more toward the 'end-stopped' than the 'run-on' line, it will be noticed that synthetic parallelism does often have a certain degree of *enjambement*.)

Better is a dinner of herbs where love is,
Than a stalled ox and hatred therewith,
(*Proverbs* xv, 17)

1 Driver, op. cit., p. 340.

410 Gay Wilson Allen

Answer not a fool according to his folly,
Lest thou also be like unto him.

(Proverbs xxvi, 4)

As a bird that wandereth from her nest,
So is a man that wandereth from his place.

(Proverbs xxvii, 8)

'A comparison, a reason, a consequence, a motive, often constitutes one of the lines in a synthetic parallelism.'[1]

4. To Lowth's three kinds of parallelism Driver adds a fourth which for convenience we may include here. It is called *climactic* parallelism – or sometimes 'ascending rhythm'. 'Here the first line is itself incomplete, and the second line takes up words from it and completes them.'[2]

Give unto the Lord, O ye sons of the mighty,
Give unto the Lord *glory and strength*.

(Psalms xxix, 1)

The voice of the Lord shaketh the wilderness;
The Lord shaketh the wilderness *of Kadesh*.

(Psalms xxix, 8)

Till thy people pass over, O Lord,
Till the people pass over *which thou hast purchased*.

(Exodus xv, 16)

It will be noticed in these examples that parallelism is sometimes a repetition of grammatical constructions and often of words, but the main principle is the balancing of thoughts alongside or against each other. And this produces not only a rhythmical thought-pattern, but also, and consequently, a speech rhythm which we will consider later. This brief summary presents only the most elementary aspects of Biblical rhythm, but it is sufficient to establish the fact that in parallelism, or in the 'rhythm of thought', *the single line must by necessity be the stylistic unit*. Before taking up other aspects of parallelism let us see if this fundamental principle is found in Whitman's poetry.

Many critics have recognized parallelism as a rhythmical principle in *Leaves of Grass*. Perry even suggested that *The Lily and the Bee*,

1 Driver, op. cit., p. 340.   2 ibid.

by Samuel Warren, published in England in 1851 and promptly re-printed in America by Harpers, may have given Whitman the model for his versification,[1] though Carpenter has pointed out that Whitman's new style had already been formed by 1851.[2] Perry's conjecture is important, however, because parallelism is unquestion-ably the stylistic principle of *The Lily and the Bee*, and in making the conjecture he is rightly calling attention to this principle of Whitman's style.

But if parallelism is the foundation of the rhythmical styles of *Leaves of Grass*, then, as we have already seen in the summary of the Lowth system, the verse must be the unit. Any reader can observe that this is true in *Leaves of Grass*, and many critics have pointed it out. De Selincourt says:

The constitution of a line in *Leaves of Grass* is such that, taken in its context, the poetic idea to be conveyed by the words is only a perfectly derived from them when they are related to the line as unit; and the equivalence of the lines is their equivalent appeal to our attention as contributors to the developing expression of the poetic idea of the whole.[3]

And Ross adds, more concretely:

Whitman's verse – with the exception that it is not metered – is farther removed from prose than is traditional verse itself, for the reason that the traditional verse, is, like prose, composed in sentences, whereas Whitman's verse is composed in lines . . . A run-on line is rare in Whitman – so rare that it may be considered a 'slip'. The law of his structure is that *the unit of sense is the measure of the line*. The lines, in sense, are end-stopped. Whitman employed everywhere a system of punctuation to indicate his structure. Look down any page of *Leaves of Grass*, and you will find almost every line ending in a comma; you will find a period at the end of a group of lines or a whole poem. Syntactically, there may be many sentences in the groups of the whole poem, there may be two or three sentences in one line. But Whitman

1 Bliss Perry, *Walt Whitman*, Houghton Mifflin, 1906, p. 92.
2 George Rice Carpenter, *Walt Whitman*, Macmillan, 1924, p. 42.
3 Basil De Selincourt, *Walt Whitman: A Critical Study*, Martin Secker, 1914, pp. 103–4.

was composing by lines, not by sentences, and he punctuated accordingly.[1]

Whitman's Parallelism

It was only after a decade or more of experimentation that Whitman definitely adopted parallelism as his basic verse structure. In a poem of 1850, *Blood-Money*,[2] he was already fumbling for this technique, but here he was paraphrasing both the thought and the prose rhythm of the New Testament (*Matthew* 26–27):

Of the olden time, when it came to pass
That the beautiful god, Jesus, should finish his work on earth,
Then went Judas, and sold the divine youth,
And took pay for his body.

The run-on lines show how far the poet still is from the characteristic style of *Leaves of Grass*. He is experimenting with phrasal or clausal units; not yet 'thought rhythm'. But his arrangement of the verse is a step in that direction.

In *Europe*, another poem of 1850, we also see the new form slowly evolving. It begins with long lines that at first glance look like the typical verse of the later poems, but on closer observation we see that they are not.

Suddenly, out of the stale and drowsy lair, the lair of slaves,
Like lightning it le'pt forth ... half startled at itself,
Its feet upon the ashes and the rags. .... Its hands tight to the throat
   of kings.

The disregard for grammatical structure suggests the poet's mature style – the antecedent of *it* is merely implied and the predicate is entirely lacking, – but the lines are only vaguely synonymous.

We see the next stage of this evolving style in the 1855 Preface, which, significantly, is arranged as prose, but the thought-units are

1 E. C. Ross, 'Whitman's Verse', *Modern Language Notes*, vol. 45, pp. 363–4 (June, 1930). Autrey Nell Wiley demonstrates this view in 'Reiterative Devices in *Leaves of Grass*', *American Literature*, vol. 1, pp. 161–70 (May 1929). She says: 'In more than 10,500 lines in *Leaves of Grass*, there are, by my count, only twenty run-on lines', p. 161.
2 Whitman himself misdated this poem 1843. It was published in *The Tribune*, Supplement, 22 March 1850, and the occasion of the satire was Webster's speech on 7 March 1850, regarding the Fugitive Slave Law.

often separated by three periods, indicating that the author is striving for a rhythmical effect which conventional prose punctuation cannot achieve.

He sees eternity less like a play with a prologue and a denouement ... he sees eternity in men and women ... he does not see men and women as dreams or dots. Faith is the antiseptic of the soul ... it pervades the common people and preserves them ... they never give up believing and expecting and trusting.

The greatest poet forms the consistence of what is to be from what has been and is. He drags the dead out of their coffins and stands them again on their feet ... he says to the past, Rise and walk before me that I may realize you. He learns the lesson ... he places himself where the future becomes present. The greatest poet does not only dazzle his rays over character and scenes and passions ... he finally ascends and finishes all ... he exhibits the pinnacles that no man can tell what they are for or what is beyond. ... He glows a moment on the extremest verge. He is most wonderful in his last half-hidden smile or frown ...[1]

Notice that the parallelism asserts without qualifications. The poet is chanting convictions about which there is to be no argument, no discussion. He develops or elaborates the theme by enumeration, eliminating so far as possible transitional and connective words. The form is rhapsodic, the tone that of inspired utterance.

In this Preface the third person is used, but the rhetorical form is that of the expanding ego, as clearly revealed in this catalog:

On him rise solid growths that offset the growths of pine and cedar and hemlock and liveoak and locust and chestnut and cypress and hickory and limetree and cottonwood and tuliptree and cactus and wildvine and tamarind and persimmon ... and tangles as tangled as any canebrake or swamp ... and forests coated with transparent ice and icicles hanging from the boughs and crackling in the wind ... and sides and peaks of mountains ...[2]

1 Emory Holloway (ed.), *Inclusive Edition of Leaves of Grass*, Doubleday, Doran & Co., 1931, pp. 492–5.
2 ibid., p. 490.

The 'ands' are evidently an attempt to convey the effect of endless
continuity in an eternal present – the cosmic unity which the poet
incarnates as he sweeps over the continent. Here in this rhapsodic
Preface, both in the ideas and the manner in which they are expressed,
we see the kind of literary form and style which Whitman has adopted
as analogous to his 'purports and facts'.

And in ten of the twelve poems of the 1855 edition of *Leaves of
Grass* parallelism is the structural device, chiefly the *synonymous*
variety, though the others are found also, especially the *cumulative*
and *climactic*. As a matter of fact, it is often difficult to separate these
three, for as Whitman asserts or repeats the same idea in different
ways – like a musician playing variations on a theme – he tends to
build up to an emotional, if not logical, climax. The opening lines of
Song of Myself are obviously cumulative in effect:

I celebrate myself, [and sing myself],[1]
And what I assume you shall assume,
For every atom belonging to me as good belongs to you.

The following lines are synonymous in thought, though there is a
cumulation and building up of the emotion:

I loafe and invite my soul,
I lean and loafe at my ease . . . observing a spear of summer grass.

No doubt much of this effect is due to the pronounced caesura –
which we will consider later.)

In this poem, as in the following ones, the parallelism has three
functions. First of all it provides the basic structure for the lines. Each
line makes an independent statement, either a complete or an elliptical
sentence. In the second place, this repetition of thought (with variations) produces a loose rhythmical chanting or rhapsodic style. And,
finally, the parallelism binds the lines together, forming a unit something like a stanza in conventional versification.

This grass is very dark to be from the white heads of old mothers,
Darker than the colorless beards of old men,
Dark to come from under the faint red roofs of mouths.

Bracketed words represent additions to the 1855 edition.

O I perceive after all so many uttering tongues!
And I perceive they do not come from the roofs of mouths for
    nothing.
I wish I could translate the hints about the dead young men and
    women,
And the hints about old men and mothers, and the offspring taken
    soon out of their laps.

What do you think has become of the young and old men?
And what do you think has become of the women and children?

They are alive and well somewhere;
The smallest sprout shows there is really no death,
And if ever there was it led forward life, and does not wait at the
    end to arrest it,

And ceased the moment life appeared.
All goes onward and outward . . . and nothing collapses,
And to die is different from what any one supposed, and luckier.

                              (*Song of Myself*, 6)

Here Whitman's characteristic structure and rhythm is completely
developed and he handles it with ease and assurance. But that he does
not yet completely trust it is perhaps indicated by the occasional use of
a semicolon (as in next to last stanza or strophe above) and four periods
to emphasize a caesura. In his later verse (including revisions of this
poem) he depended upon commas in both places.

In the above extract from *Song of Myself* the similarity of the parallelism to that of Biblical poetry is probably closer than in more
typical passages of Whitman's longer poems, for the couplet, triplet,
and quatrain are found more often in the Bible than in *Leaves of Grass*;
and the Bible does not have either long passages of synonymous
parallelism or extended catalogs. The Biblical poets were not, like
Whitman, attempting to inventory the universe in order to symbolize
its fluxional unity. They found unity in their monotheism, not (or
seldom) in a pantheism. But when Whitman's poetic vision sweeps
over the occupations of the land, as in section 15 of *Song of Myself*, he
enumerates dozens of examples in more or less synonymous paral-
lelistic form. And he repeats the performance in section 33 in a kind
of omnipresent world-panorama of scenes, activities, and pictures of
life, in a strophe (or sentence) of 82 lines.

Another poem in the first edition, later known as *There Was a Child Went Forth*, further amplifies both the psychology of the poet's identification of his consciousness with all forms of being and his expression of it through enumeration and parallelism:

There was a child went forth every day,
And the first object he looked upon and received with wonder or
  pity or love or dread, that object he became,
And that object became part of him for the day or a certain part
  of the day ... or for many years or stretching cycles of years.

Then comes the list – early lilacs, grass, morning glories, March-born lambs, persons, streets, oceans, etc. – a veritable photomontage. The catalog and parallelism techniques arise from the same psychological impulse and achieve the same general effects of poetic identification.

The catalog, however, is most typical of the 1855–6 poems, when Whitman's cosmic inspiration found its most spontaneous and unrestrained expression. But even here we find a number of strophes arranged or organized as 'envelopes' of parallelism, a device which the poet found especially useful in the shorter and more orderly poems of *Calamus*, *Drum-Taps*, and the old-age lyrics. It is essentially a stanzaic form, something like the quatrain of the Italian sonnet. The first line advances a thought or image, succeeding lines amplify or illustrate it by synonymous parallelism, and the final line completes the whole by reiterating the original line or concluding the thought. For example, in section 21 of *Song of Myself*:

Smile O voluptuous coolbreathed earth!
Earth of the slumbering and liquid trees!
Earth of departed sunset! Earth of the mountains misty-topt!
Earth of the vitreous pour of the full moon just tinged with blue!
Earth of shine and dark mottling the tide of the river!
Earth of the limpid gray clouds brighter and clearer for my sake!
Far-swooping elbowed earth! Rich apple-blossomed earth!
Smile, for your lover comes!

Far more common, however, is the incomplete envelope, the conclusion being omitted, as in the 1860 *Song at Sunset*:

Good in all,
In the satisfaction and aplomb of animals

In the annual return of the seasons,
In the hilarity of youth
In the strength and flush of manhood,
In the grandeur and exquisiteness of old age,
In the superb vistas of death.

But of course an 'incomplete envelope' is not an envelope at all. Without a conclusion it is not a container. And it is characteristic of Whitman, especially in 1855-6, that he more often preferred not to finish his comparisons, analogies, representative examples of reality, but let them trail off into infinity. In his later poems, however, the envelope often provides a structure and unity for the whole composition, as in *Joy, Shipmate, Joy!*:

Joy, shipmate, joy!
(Pleas'd to my soul at death I cry)
Our life is closed, our life begins,
The long, long anchorage we leave,
The ship is clear at last, she leaps!
She swiftly courses from the shore,
Joy, shipmate, joy!

Other Reiterative Devices

In the above discussion parallelism was referred to as both a *structure* and a *rhythm* in Whitman's verse technique. Since rhythm means orderly or schematic repetition, a poem can have several kinds of rhythms, sometimes so coordinated in the total effect that it is difficult to isolate and evaluate the separate function of each. Thus Whitman's parallelism can give esthetic pleasure as a recognizable pattern of thought, which is to say that it is the basis of the structure of the composition. This does not necessarily result in a repetition or rhythm of sounds, cadences, music, etc. But since thoughts are expressed by means of spoken sounds (or symbols that represent spoken sounds), it is possible for the *thought rhythm* to produce, or to be accompanied by, *phonic rhythm*. The latter need not be a rhythm of accents or stressed syllables (though it often is in *Leaves of Grass* as will be demonstrated later). Rime, or repetition of similar sounds according to a definite pattern, is another kind of phonic rhythm, and may serve several purposes, such as pleasing the ear (which has been conditioned to anticipate certain sounds at regular intervals) or grouping the lines and thereby (in many subtle ways) emphasizing the thought.

Whitmans' parallelism, or thought rhythm, is so often accompanied and reinforced by parallel wording and sounds that the two techniques are often almost identical. An easy way to collect examples of his 'thought rhythm' is to glance down the left-hand margin and notice the lines beginning with the same word, and usually the same grammatical construction: 'I will ... I will ... I will...' or 'Where ... Where ... Where ...' or When ... When ... When', etc.[1]

These repetitions of words or phrases are often found in modern conventional meters. Tennyson, for example,[2] repeats consecutively the same word or phrase throughout many passages; and the refrain and repetend in Poe's versification is the same device in a somewhat different manner. In conventional meters these reiterations may even set up a rhythm of their own, either syncopating or completely distorting the regular metrical pattern. But there is this very important difference between reiteration in rime and meter and reiteration in *Leaves of Grass:* in the former the poem has a set pattern of accent (iambic, trochaic, anapaestic, etc.), whereas in Whitman's verse the pattern of sounds and musical effects is entirely dependent upon the thought and structure of the separate lines.

In every emotionally and intellectually pleasing poem in *Leaves of Grass* these reiterations do set up a recognizable pattern of sounds.[3] Since the line is not bound by a specific number of syllables, or terminated by conventional rime, the sound patterns may seem to the untrained reader entirely free and lawless. It was part of Whitman's 'organic' style to make his rhythms freer than those of classical and conventional versification, but they are no freer than those of the best musical compositions of opera and symphony. They can, of course, be too free to recognize, in which case Whitman failed as a poet – and like almost all major poets, he has many failures to his name. But in the best poems of *Leaves of Grass* – such as *Out of the Cradle Endlessly Rocking, When Lilacs Last in the Dooryard Bloom'd,* or *Passage to India,*

1 Cf. *Song of Myself,* 33, or *Salut au Monde!*

2 Cf. Emile Lauvriere, *Repetition and Parallelism in Tennyson,* Oxford University Press, 1901.

3 Here again Emerson's theory preceded Whitman's practice. In the section on 'Melody, Rhyme, and Form' in his essay on *Poetry and Imagination* Emerson wrote: 'Another form of rhyme is iterations of phrases ...'

– the combined thought and sound patterns are as definite and organized as in *Lycidas* or *Samson Agonistes*.

Several names have been given Whitman's reiterative devices in addition to the ones used here (phonic reiteration, etc.) Miss Autrey Nell Wiley, who has made the most thorough study of this subject, uses the rhetorical terms *epanaphora* and *epanalepsis*.[1] The nineteenth-century Italian scholar, Jannaccone,[2] calls these reiterations *rima psichica iniziale e terminale* (initial and terminal psychic rime) and *rima psichica media e terminale*. 'Psychic rime'[3] is a suggestive term, but it probably overemphasizes the analogy with conventional rime – though it is important to notice the initial, medial, and terminal positions of Whitman's reiterations. The initial is most common, as in the 'Cradle' poem:

Out of the cradle endlessly rocking,
Out of the mocking bird's throat, the musical shuttle,
Out of the Ninth-month midnight.

Although this reiteration might be regarded as 'psychic rime', its most significant function is the setting up of a cadence to dominate the whole line, as the 'Give me' reiteration does in *Give Me the Splendid Silent Sun*, or the 'What', 'I hear', 'I see', etc. in *Salut au Monde!* though scarcely any poem in *Leaves of Grass* is without the combined use of parallelism and reiteration. Often a short poem is a single 'envelope' of parallelism with initial reiteration, as in *I Sit and Look Out*:

I sit and look out upon all the sorrows of the world, and upon all
    oppression and shame,
I hear secret convulsive sobs from young men at anguish with
    themselves, remorseful after deeds done,
I see in low life the mother misused by her children, dying,
    neglected, gaunt, desperate,
I see the wife misused by her husband, I see the treacherous seducer
    of young women,

1 See note 1, p. 412.
2 P. Jannaccone, *La poesia di Walt Whitman e l'evoluzione delle forme ritmiche*, Torino, 1898, pp. 64ff.
3 Cf. note 3, p. 418.

I mark the ranklings of jealousy and unrequited love attempted to
　　be hid, I see these sights on the earth,
I see the workings of battle, pestilence, tyranny, I see martyrs and
　　prisoners,
I observe a famine at sea, I observe the sailors casting lots who
　　shall be kill'd to preserve the lives of the rest,
I observe the slights and degradations cast by arrogant persons upon
　　laborers, the poor, and upon negroes, and the like;
All these – all the meanness and agony without end I sitting look
　　out upon,
See, hear, and am silent.

Initial reiteration, as in the above passage, occurs oftener in *Leaves
of Grass* than either medial or final. Miss Wiley has estimated that 41
per cent of the more than 10,500 lines in the *Leaves* contains epanalepsis
or initial reiteration.[1] But words and phrases are frequently repeated
in other positions. *When Lilacs Last in the Dooryard Bloom'd* contains
an effective example of a word from the first line repeated and interwoven throughout succeeding lines:

Over the breast of the spring, the land, *amid* cities,
Amid lanes and through old woods, where lately the violets peep'd
　　from the ground, spotting the gray debris,
Amid the grass in the fields each side of the lanes, *passing* the
　　endless grass,
Passing the yellow-spear'd wheat, every grain from its shroud in the
　　dark-brown fields uprisen,
Passing the apple-tree blows of white and pink in the orchards,
Carrying a corpse to where it shall rest in the grave,
Night and day journeys a coffin.

Here the reiterations have little to do with cadences but aid greatly in
the effect of ceaseless motion – and even of *enjambement*, so rare in
Leaves of Grass – as the body of the assassinated president is carried
'night and day' from Washington to the plains of Illinois.

　　Final reiteration is found, though Whitman used it sparingly, perhaps because it too closely resembles refrains and repetends in conventional versification, and also because he had little use for the kind of

1 Wiley, op. cit., pp. 161–2.

melody and singing lyricism which these devices produce. When he does use final reiteration it is more for rhetorical emphasis than music, as in section 24 of *Song of Myself*:

Root of wash'd sweet-flag! timorous pond-snipe! nest of guarded
  duplicate eggs! *it shall be you!*
Mix'd tussled hay of head, beard, brawn, *it shall be you!*
Trickling sap of maple, fibre of manly wheat, *it shall be you!*
Sun so generous *it shall be you!*

and so on throughout sixteen lines.

Sometimes Whitman uses reiteration through the entire line, as in *By Blue Ontario's Shore*:

I will know if I am to be less than they,
I will see if I am not as majestic as they,
I will see if I am not as subtle and real as they,
I will see if I am to be less generous than they, . . .

C. Alphonso Smith in his study of repetitions in English and American poetry (he does not mention Whitman, however) has defined the difference between reiterations in prose and poetry:

In prose, a word or group of words is repeated for emphasis; whereas in verse, repetition is chiefly employed not for emphasis (compare the use of the refrain), but for melody of rhythm, for continuousness or sonorousness of effect, for unity of impression, for banding lines or stanzas, and for the more indefinable though not less important purposes of suggestiveness.[1]

Of course Smith is thinking of conventional versification, but continuousness of effect, unity of impression, joining of lines and stanzas, and suggestiveness all apply to Whitman's use of reiteration.

Although Whitman's reiteration is not musical in the sense that Poe's is (*i.e.*, for melody and harmony), it is musical in a larger sense. Many critics have developed the analogy of music in Whitman's technique, but De Selincourt's comments are especially pertinent here. 'The progress of Whitman's verse', he says, 'has much in common with that of musical composition. For we are carrying the sense of

1 C. Alphonso Smith, *Repetition and Parallelism in English Verse*, New York, 1894, p. 9.

past effects along with us more closely and depending more intimately upon them than is possible in normal verse.'[1] And he observes that:

... repetition, which the artist in language scrupulously avoids, is the foundation and substance of musical expression. Now Whitman ... uses words and phrases more as if they were notes of music than any other writer ... it was to him part of the virtue and essence of life that its forms and processes were endlessly reduplicated; and poetry, which was delight in life, must somehow, he thought, mirror this elemental abundance.[2]

Of course Whitman's repetition concerns not only words and phrases (Jannaccone's 'psychic rime') but thought patterns as well. In fact, his favorite method of organizing a long poem like *The Sleepers, Proud Music of the Storm, Mystic Trumpeter,* or even *Song of the Red-Wood Tree* is, as remarked elsewhere, symphonic. He likes to advance a theme, develop it by enumeration and representative symbols, advance other themes and develop them in similar manners, then repeat, summarize, and emphasize. Thus Whitman's repetition of thought, of words, of cadences, – playing variations on each out of exuberance and unrestrained joy both in the thought and form –, all combine to give him the satisfaction and conviction that he has 'expressed' himself, not logically or even coherently, but by suggestion and by sharing his own emotions with the reader. This is true even though the background of nearly every poem in *Leaves of Grass* is 'Ideas' rather than simple lyric emotion; but Whitman develops these ideas like a poet-musician, not like a philosopher or a polemical writer.

Another kind of reiteration which Whitman uses both for the thought and the musical effect is what Jannaccone calls 'grammatical' and 'logical rime'[3] – though *grammatical rhythm* might be a more convenient and appropriate term. Instead of repeating the same identical word or phrase, he repeats a part of speech or grammatical construction at certain places in the line. This has nearly the same effect on the rhythm and cadence as the reiteration of the same word

1 De Selincourt, op. cit., p. 104.
2 ibid., p. 108.
3 Jannaccone, op. cit., pp. 67ff.

or phrase, especially when 'grammatical rime' is initial. For example, parallel verbs:

Flow on, river! *flow* with the flood-tide, and *ebb* with the ebb-
    tide!
Frolic on, crested and scallop-edg'd waves!
Gorgeous clouds of the sunset *drench* with your splendor me or
    the men and women generations after me!
Cross from shore to shore, countless crowds of passengers!
Stand up, tall masts of Mannahatta,
                                    (*Crossing Brooklyn Ferry*)

The following Jannaccone calls 'logical rime':[1]

Long and long has the *grass* been *growing*,
Long and long has the *rain* been *falling*,
Long has the *globe* been rolling *round*,
                            (*Song of the Exposition*, 1)

Not only are *growing*, *falling*, and *rolling* grammatically parallel, but they are also the natural (and logical) things for the *grass*, the *rain*, and the *globe* to be doing.

Sometimes Whitman reiterates cognates:

The *song* is to the *singer*, and comes back most to him,
The *teaching* is to the *teacher*, and comes back most to him,
The *murder* is to the *murderer*, and comes back most to him, etc.
                        (*A Song of the Rolling Earth*, 2)

In all these examples the various kinds of reiterations produce also a pattern of accents which can be scanned like conventional verse.

Long and long has the grass been growing, ...

Parallelism gives these lines a *thought* rhythm, but this is reinforced by the phonic recurrences, giving additional rhythm which depends upon *sounds* for its effect. Of course these examples are unusually regular (or simple), whereas the same principles in other passages give a much greater variety and complexity of phonic stress. But the combined reiterations always (at least when successful) produce a composite

1 ibid., p. 73.

musical pattern – a pattern more plastic than any to be found in conventional versification, but one which the ear can be trained to appreciate no less than patterns of rime and meter.

(387–409)

Martin Green

from 'Twain and Whitman', *Re-appraisals* 1963

Different as they are, we feel, if we read [Twain and Whitman] honestly, that both are equally non-literary. This feeling takes the form, when we read Whitman, of anguished protests – 'You're making a fool of yourself – look what you're saying – this is exactly what you can't *do* in a poem'. In Twain's case, until we dismiss our literary expectations, it takes the form of a resentful impatience, 'Don't be so funny – don't be so charming – what did you really feel?'

Non-literary here refers of course to the major meanings of literary. Obviously Twain was one of the world's great artists in the minor meanings. Nobody ever used words more skilfully; he defined and achieved his purposes beautifully. But in the use of language to aesthetic effects, the most important surely involve the definition of truths of personal experience – personal here implying a self-responsible adult personality, whose reactions and discriminations are in some measure moral self-commitments, whose self-expression seeks the response of other such personalities. It is in this sense that Twain is not concerned with personal truth, and that therefore literary criteria do not apply themselves to his work. They do apply themselves to Whitman – because he so loudly offers to discuss personal truth – but they are hideously offended by what they find there. He is non-literary in the minor meanings of the word, too.

In Whitman's case the point is fairly easily made. The 'I' of *Song of Myself* is first of all Walt Whitman, later all Americans, later the Unconscious or World Spirit; and though there is some humorous interplay of differentness between those selves, there is also a more remarkable indeterminate sliding from one into another. The self-responsible personality disappears. The crucial distinction, between what the poet felt, and what he might have felt if he had been some-body else, is fatally blurred; and this blurring extends to his tone as well as to his vision. He is not speaking *to* any more than *as* a person. The social situation he sets up with his readers is always tending to become that of a speaker before a huge shapeless crowd, highly excitable and responsive and uncritical, each of whom he has to merge with himself, and with each other. There are no satisfactory persons in Whitman's poetic world, neither the 'I' nor the 'You', and consequently there is no satisfaction in it for the reader.

Despite Whitman's official reputation many literary people will grant this argument fairly easily. The difficulty is to make the opposite point, that Whitman remains an important writer.

This is not just because of the fragments of successful poetry that are scattered through *Leaves of Grass*. Richard Chase has put the case for them very ably in *Walt Whitman Reconsidered*; one would add only that Whitman is also, from time to time, a very poignant poet of sexual provocation.

Ever the old inexplicable query, ever that thorn'd thumb, that
    breath of itches and thirsts,
Ever the vexer's hoot, hoot, till we find where the sly one hides
    and bring him forth,
Ever love, ever the sobbing liquid of life,
Ever the bandage under the chin, ever the trestle of death.
                              (*Song of Myself*, 42)

And in another piece, after a reference to the 'guile, anger, lust, hot wishes I dared not speak', he continues,

Was called by my nighest name by clear loud voices of young
    men, as they saw me approaching or passing,
Felt their arms on my neck as I stood, or the negligent leaning of
    their flesh against me as I sat,
Saw many I loved in the street or ferry-boat or public assembly,
    yet never told them a word,
Lived the same life with the rest, the same laughing, gnawing,
    sleeping,
Play'd the part that still looks back on the actor or actress,

The same old role, the role that is what we make it, as great as
  we like,
Or as small as we like, or both great and small.
                        (*Crossing Brooklyn Ferry*, 6)

There are such moments, but they are always succeeded, or inter-
fused, with something so much the opposite that it remains an essentially painful experience to read *Leaves of Grass* with one's literary
sensibility aroused. ('I dote on myself, there is that lot of me and all so
luscious' may serve as a sufficient reminder of all that is referred to.)
Whitman is not only non-literary, he is anti-literary. He offers to
discuss personal experience, and then forces on us everything but that
– catalogues of objects, political exhortations, ideas of sexuality, day-
dreams, grotesque posturings. Even his catalogues are of things he had
read about, not seen and heard himself. In a word, he does not tell us
the truth. Quite often, he tells lies; he says he has felt and seen things
which he has not. Again and again, he makes a fool of himself; having
invited us into his mind, with our keenest expectations aroused, he
appears before us in a tatty series of road company spangles, cutting
capers he's never properly practised. And all the time he asks his
readers to cease to be persons (people who respect their own emotions,
who commit themselves in a reaction only when that further extends
and defines their personality in new and risky areas of experience)
and to become partisans, members of a crowd, merging with each
other in a stock response. In reading Whitman, therefore, despite
moments of pleasure, a reader has to force himself, to go against his
nature as reader.

In *not* reading Whitman, however, an intelligent man also makes an
unnatural sacrifice. Not for the fragments of successful poetry, but for
the outline of a significant literary venture that everywhere comes
through when you read sympathetically. Whitman confronted the
ideas of his time, some of its crucial experience, its poetic theory, its
language, and strove to make something large out of them. He failed
atrociously in nine-tenths of his particular effects, but his general
intention, coming dimly through, engages our interest. One can
understand why he was a source for better poets, and very different
ones, coming after him. But we can only respond to that intention,
act on that interest, if we switch off the spotlight of critical awareness

– the crucial component in any literary discipline – and work in the penumbra of a general humanism; a general interest in intellectual history, aesthetic theory and so on. It is because it is so hard for literary critics to do this, and because Whitman must, as time goes by, become more and more their property, that he is generally neglected today. With rare exceptions like Mr Chase, he has been abandoned to the obscurity of an official reputation; and so long as literary study retains its rigour, this is perhaps the kindest fate that can befall him, unjust though it is. The solution to the problem of 'American' literature has in his case been oblivion.

(125–9)

Denis Donoghue

'Walt Whitman', *Connoisseurs of Chaos* 1965

'Connoisseur of Chaos' is an elegant dialogue by Wallace Stevens that holds aboriginal experience at the safe distance of contemplation. The first voice says that the law of inherent opposites, of essential unity, is 'as pleasant as port'. The contrast of life and death is 'pretty', presumably because it is suavely contained in the essential unity. 'The squirming facts exceed the squamous mind', yes, but nevertheless 'relation' appears and expands, and as April comes to summer, it seems good. The second voice speaks with distaste of an order too fixed, too 'Plantagenet', and conjures a pensive man, a man of saving grace, the grace of imagination:

The pensive man . . . He sees that eagle float
For which the intricate Alps are a single nest.[1]

If the pensive man is the 'man-hero' of Stevens' 'Notes toward a Supreme Fiction', we are at the center of Stevens' world, his *fluent mundo*. There is no better place from which to view the athletic *mundo* of Walt Whitman, because Stevens gives us all the terms we need, and his fluency shows us how much sweat and spirit Whitman had to expend before an American poet could deploy those terms with such control, such elegance. I have in mind such terms as chaos, order,

1 *Collected Poems of Wallace Stevens*, Faber and Faber, 1955, p. 215.

the great disorder which is itself an order, 'relation', 'the pensive man'. Whitman wielded all these, or their rugged equivalents, and he had to press them into being before Stevens could put them on show, like Yeats' circus animals. Whitman's version of Stevens' pensive man, for instance, is the 'equable man' invoked in the preface to the first edition of *Leaves of Grass* and again in *By Blue Ontario's Shore*, and in both cases identified with 'the poet', a generic figure, master of the intricate Alps. And if we need Whitman's tone of voice to shape the meaning of the phrase, we have it: 'Now there shall be a man cohered out of tumult and chaos.' The man thus cohered is not Whitman himself or any particular man, not even Lincoln, but a man still in vision, in prophecy. Whitman sees him whenever he looks into the middle distance or enters a brown study. Once, for Edward Dowden's benefit, he described the 'spine or verteber principle' of *Leaves of Grass* as 'a model or ideal (for the service of the New World and to be gradually absorbed in it) of a complete healthy, heroic, practical modern Man.'[1] Indeed, the best way to read *Leaves of Grass* is to consider it Whitman's notes toward a supreme fiction; the supreme fiction that in Whitman and Stevens is Man.

I have no wish to force upon Whitman and Stevens a congruity foreign to their tempers. Indeed, Whitman's shadow falls more directly upon the poems of Ezra Pound and William Carlos Williams than upon Stevens' philosophical discriminations. So we will not push the association too far. But even the differences between the two poets are vivid. Stevens' poems press toward a moment of stillness in which perception is acute and all the harmonies sing. I think of this as Stevens' answer to that quite different stillness in T. S. Eliot's poems in which the poet, like a celebrant priest, hands over his individuality to the ritual of the sacrifice, and the result is a calm of self, all stillness, all repose. Whitman is not interested in such 'moments', either Eliot's or Stevens', nor is he interested in the spectacular moments of Hart Crane or Marius the Epicurean. He demands that the continuities shall flow all the time, not merely at Key West but wherever a man happens to be. The peaks of feeling do not satisfy him; he wants the whole landscape, nothing less. Hence the defining 'figure' of Whitman's mind is the equals sign – equals, not plus or minus. Where

1 Walt Whitman, *Correspondence*, vol. 2, *1868–75*, ed. Edwin Haviland Miller, New York University Press, 1961, p. 154. Letter of 18 January 1872.

the New England Fathers set up a covenant with God, based on severance and inequality, Whitman set up a covenant with nature, governed by the energy that makes all things equal. If he found two things traditionally considered enemies, he would declare their identity, or at least make them friends in a larger community. Ideally, A is A and B is B, and in the flow of energy A equals B.

This explains why Whitman was never troubled by the problem that confronted every major Romantic poet – the nature of the self. He does not hunt and trail and worry the problem, as Coleridge does, or Keats, Byron, Wordsworth, even Emerson. He would never have written a poem like Coleridge's *Frost at Midnight*, never have tried to write Wordsworth's *Prelude*, because Wordsworth and Coleridge in those poems are vexed by question marks, plus and minus signs, and Whitman's act of faith has erased these as impertinent. For him life is – in Yeats' phrase – 'the fire that makes all simple'; simple because equal. He would speak of 'the old knot of contrarieties', but he was always sure he could open it. (At least until the Civil War; later he would tell a different story.)

Hence he begins by saying, Let x equal the self. Then x equals A plus B plus C plus D plus E, and so on, where each letter stands for a new experience contained and possessed, and the self is the sum of its possessions. This is the law of Whitman's lists. If you say that the self – x – is the sum of its possessions, A, B, C, D, and so on, then the more you add to the right-hand side of the equation, the more you enrich the left, and you do this without bothering about the 'nature' of the x. You assume, as most Romantic poets did, that the self is not at any moment fixed, complete, or predetermined, and then you are free to develop or enlarge it at any time by adding to its experience. This is one of the differences between Whitman and Joyce, two writers who wanted to 'put everything in'. Joyce wanted to put everything in so that he could exhibit the power of a mind in control of whatever it contained. Whitman wanted to put everything in so that he could declare the essential unity of a world rampant with multiplicity. He gives the principle, the law of his equation, in *Our Old Feuillage*:

O lands! all so dear to me – what you are, (whatever it is,) I
    putting it at random in these songs, become a part of that,
    whatever it is,

Southward there, I screaming, with wings slow flapping, with the
   myriads of gulls wintering along the coasts of Florida . . .

He can put it in at random – or seems to do so – because once in, it
will take its proper place. And in this equation it doesn't matter,
mathematically, whether you put M before or after N; the equation
persists. The great advantage of the equation is that while it is at any
moment true and valid, you can add further items to the right-hand
side without disrupting it; the x, the self, is 'growing' at the same
rate.

   Whitman was thrilled and sometimes dazzled by the felicities of his
equation. He never lost faith in it; and if he questioned it, notably in
As I Ebb'd with the Ocean of Life, the question merely testifies to the
power of the sea as a symbol of 'merging' and obliteration, one of the
perennial temptations of American literature. In one of the recurrent
'moments' of American literature the imagination confronts reality
in the guise of a poet gazing at the sea. The imperious singer in
Stevens' *The Idea of Order at Key West* walks by the sea and partly
invents it with her song. But whether she invents it or discovers it,
she will master it, because she stands and walks and sings for Wallace
Stevens, not another poet. Whitman is more representative of
American experience when the sea throws down a challenge to his
self hood that he is not sure he can survive, and in one of his rare and
extreme moments he says:

O baffled, balk'd, bent to the very earth,
Oppress'd with myself that I have dared to open my mouth,
Aware now that amid all that blab whose echoes recoil upon me I
   have not once had the least idea who or what I am,
But that before all my arrogant poems the real Me stands yet
   untouch'd, untold, altogether unreach'd . . .
                                        (*As I Ebb'd With the Ocean of Life*, 2)

The sea is Stevens' reality, and Whitman's too, and for once in this
extreme moment Whitman fears that the sea has obliterated all the
dense particulars of reality on which his equation depends – and then
there is nothing but the void. In *Sea-Drift* he will be his own man again
but only when he has settled and populated the sea with ships and sea
captains and swimmers and a child and her father walking on the

beach at night, feeling the 'vast similitude' that 'interlocks all'. The equation is, in the nick of time, verified.

But it is verified. In the essay 'Experience' Emerson says that one of the consequences of the Fall of Man is that the Me is utterly separated from the Not-Me. But Whitman disposes of the problem briskly by declaring that the Me is simply the sum of the Not-Me it contains. And he implies, of course, that it is the part of prudence as well as faith to make that sum as large as possible. One should keep adding to the self as Whitman kept adding to *Leaves of Grass*, thereby gaining the best of all possible worlds, being and becoming. Any experience genuinely assimilated adds to what Whitman calls 'the Me myself'. Hence he will say, 'The press of my foot to the earth springs a hundred affections', and again, 'Is this then a touch? . . . quivering me to a new identity . . .' The equation would also allow for the incorporation of any and every kind of experience. There would be no problem, for instance, in the rivalry of poet and scientist, one of the issues warily touched in Wordsworth's great *Preface*. Whitman can bring science into the equation simply by calling it, as he does in the preface of 1872, 'a new sunrise'. He can therefore avoid the slough of self-pity that we call 'romantic irony'. And he can evade one of the perennial problems, that of appearance and reality, simply by declaring their identity. He would never have said, as Stevens did, 'Let be be finale of seem.' Whitman wants the whole opera, not just the finale, so he declares that what seems is, here and now, and is good. Freed from metaphysical embarrassments, Whitman could devote himself to his equations, collecting experiences as the dominant culture of his day collected material possessions, and – in a sense – for 'similar' reasons: because the verification of the self depended upon an exhibited affluence, perhaps even upon conspicuous waste. T. S. Eliot has spent many years persuading us that our possessions are vulgar, ephemeral. Hence we attend to him as we listen to our consciences, and no more frequently. Whitman spent most of his life sponsoring an affluent society, with this admonition, that our possessions should include sympathies, accords, pleasures, marriages, pains, passions, the sun and the stars as well as gadgets. But judged simply as an esthetic – though how simple is that? – Whitman's creed was uncannily faithful to the dominant metaphors of his place and time. He did not repudiate the metaphors; he thought they were excellent and would serve every occasion, if only you worked them hard enough, put everything in, material and spiritual.

Because his equations were designed to include everything, like and unlike, city and country, they could also include evil. It was William James, I think, who brought into critical currency the notion that Whitman lacked a sense of evil. In a lecture of 1895 he spoke of 'our dear old Walt Whitman's works' as the handbook of that 'temperamental optimism' that is 'incapable of believing that anything seriously evil can exist.'[1] What James started Yeats continued, in a famous passage in *A Vision*. But it will not do. No one will ask Whitman to speak like Saint Augustine, Kierkegaard, or that accomplished neo-Augustinian of our own day, Graham Greene. But it is wilful to argue that Whitman was blind to evil or that he felt it sluggishly. Some of the most haunting passages in *Song of Myself* are apprehensions of sickness and pain, 'the silent old-faced infants and the lifted sick'. It is not that Whitman was insensitive to the pain of others, but – I concede only this – that he was a little too ready to assimilate this pain to the genial law of his own equation. In *Song of Myself*, after a long passage invoking pain and suffering, he says:

All this I swallow, it tastes good, I like it well, it becomes mine, I am the man, I suffer'd, I was there.

Even if we read this as a hymn to the sympathetic imagination, or, alternatively, in the Nietzschean sense that life is somehow justified by the courage its endurance requires, still we jib at its fluency. It is one thing to suffer, and it is another thing to sympathize with the suffering of others, and these experiences are not identical, no matter what Whitman's equations say. In an earlier part of *Song of Myself* he says:

The pleasures of heaven are with me and the pains of hell are with me,
The first I graft and increase upon myself, the latter I translate into a new tongue.

It is the ease with which he translates the pain of others that constitutes the failure of response. This is why, reading the poems, we are so relieved and assuaged to come upon the poem *I Sit and Look Out* in

1 William James, *The Will To Believe*, Dover Publications, n.d., pp. 32ff.

the collection *By the Roadside*, where Whitman says, towards the end of a vision of pain:

I observe a famine at sea, I observe the sailors casting lots who
    shall be kill'd to preserve the lives of the rest,
I observe the slights and degradations cast by arrogant persons
    upon laborers, the poor, and upon negroes, and the like;
All these – all the meanness and agony without end I sitting look
    out upon,
See, hear, and am silent.[1]

If Whitman's equations can include evil, they should have no difficulty with death. Sometimes he euphemistically translates death to read 'immortality', as in the last lines of *To Think of Time*, which read in the first version:

I swear I think there is nothing but immortality!
That the exquisite scheme is for it, and the nebulous float is for
    it, and the cohering is for it,
And all preparation is for it . . . and identity is for it . . . and life
    and death are for it.[2]

And generally Whitman assumes that death merely inaugurates a new cycle of life and is therefore not a thing to fear or bewail. There were moments in which, like many nineteenth-century poets and dramatists, he was more than half in love with easeful death. Several passages, even in *Sea-Drift*, sound like program notes to Wagner's *Tristan*, the motif being 'the low and delicious word Death', whispers of heavenly death. But for the most part death and evil are contained in the expanding self, the x, and therefore 'justified'.

Given the primary equation by which the self is identified with the sum of its contents, Whitman goes on to declare other equations, especially where the old orthodoxies luxuriated in antagonism – soul and body, for instance, which in Whitman's animal faith are distinct

1 Whitman, *Complete Poetry and Selected Prose*, ed. James E. Miller Jr, Houghton Mifflin, 1959, p. 197. All verse quotations, unless otherwise specified, are from this edition.
2 See the first edition, reprinted with an introduction by Malcolm Cowley, Viking Press, 1959, p. 104. Later Whitman changed 'death' to 'materials'. See *Complete Poetry and Selected Prose*, p. 308.

but without difference. He would eliminate the distinction with an equation, thus earning D. H. Lawrence's celebrated praise. Throughout *Leaves of Grass* this equation persists, and Whitman returns to assert it several times in 'A Backward Glance'. 'Behold, the body includes and is the meaning, the main concern, and includes and is the soul', he says in *Starting from Paumanok*, and again, in effect, in *Children of Adam* and *Song of Myself*. A later poet, W. B. Yeats, in at least one of his moods would present the fullness of being as 'a perfectly proportioned human body' in splendid animation, and he would point to certain passages in Dante for theory and to 'certain beautiful women' for proof. The same hope would send Yeats into the theater and toward certain spectacularly theatrical poems, poems all gesture and nonchalance. Yeats would bring his thought to drama, to crisis. But Whitman was not content with a few fine crises. The electrical body would have to certify the soul at all times, and he would 'sing' it to encourage it to do so. Where Dante had behind him the doctrine and incitement of the Incarnation, the word made flesh, Whitman had only the prompting of his own animal faith. But for him it was, of course, enough. This is why, discussing Yeats, we constantly need terms drawn from the theater; but these are useless in reading Whitman. In Whitman – both in our reading and his writing – the relevant terms are those that define the entire range of experience centered on the body. Above all, Whitman needs terms that evade the importunities of an arrogant and jealous consciousness, because he is honor-bound to dissolve the old dichotomies of soul and body, mind and matter, consciousness and experience. In short, he needs all those words that are themselves equals signs, terms that denote the intersection of subject and object, the Me and the Not-Me. In a long list the central term is 'contact.'

From the first page of the first edition of *Leaves of Grass* this word reverberates through the poems and prose. 'I am mad for it to be in contact with me', he says of the atmosphere, and in *A Song for Occupations*, 'I pass so poorly with paper and types … I must pass with the contact of bodies and souls.' *Children of Adam* is virtually a tone poem on contact. And even when the key terms are more general, they are acceptable to Whitman only if they can prove their origin in bodily experience; many are phrenological terms. He chooses words like *inhale, adhere, respiration, adhesiveness, meeting, inspiration, acceptation, realization, give, receive, press, swallow.* In *The Mechanical Operation of the Spirit* Swift's irony challenges us to deny that our terms for the 'higher' exertions are drawn directly from the 'lower' bodily and mechanical facts, the 'high' being therefore merely a sublimation of the 'low'. Whitman is not interested in such irony; he has no wish to entrench himself in a fort from which he can deflate our pretensions. He convinces by praise, by celebration, by allowing himself to be fully known. And this is a kinetic, muscular process. In *Resolution and Independence* Wordsworth trusts in his own wise passiveness to register the meaning of the old man's life. He takes it in as he takes in the landscape in which the old man figures; he assumes that such meanings come 'naturally' and quietly to the suitably qualified observer. But when Whitman in the third stanza of *I Sing the Body Electric* confronts an old man and enters the meaning of his existence, we can almost foretell that the last grace of the encounter will be a touching, a contact, not just a 'seeing':

When he went with his five sons and many grandsons to hunt or
    fish, you would pick him out as the most beautiful and vigorous
    of the gang,
You would wish long and long to be with him . . . you would
    wish to sit by him in the boat, that you and he might touch
    each other.

Emerson would worry because objects can touch each other only at one point. Whitman did not worry. One point was enough; you had only to ensure that there would be, always, one. In reading Samuel Beckett, if you derive any comfort from the impingement of subject and object, you will be advised that the incorrigible mobility of the subject makes the entire experience a humiliation. In Whitman the general rule is that subject and object are verifiable, trustworthy, sufficiently stable to merit local habitations and names and to justify the pleasure we take in their contact. And because this contact is to be felt now and will persist indefinitely as the sweet law of our lives, Whitman's favorite tense is the continuous present.

A life of such continuous intimacy, a life of contact, is Whitman's ideal human image. It will blur the distinction between man and God, thus setting up yet another equation, the largest in intention. Whitman effects this equation in *A Song of Joys* and celebrates it in *Song at Sunset*:

To be this incredible God I am!
To have gone forth among other Gods, these men and women
  I love!

This divinity flows and sanctifies, by contact, everything it sees, hears, touches, tastes, or smells; it is Whitman's version of the laying on of hands. Stevens will say, 'God and the human imagination are one', and he will offer as proof the extreme reaches of his own perception. But this is not Whitman's faith. Stevens is convinced that man is God to the degree of his vision, his perception, his visual imagination. Whitman is convinced that man is God to the latitude of his contact. In Whitman's heaven we communicate by touch. In *Song of the Redwood-Tree* the new earth and the new heaven are one, an earthly paradise of contact, silent because it is itself the ultimate poem that renders all lesser poems redundant. Kenneth Burke says that man craves images of 'perfection', is 'rotten with perfection'. Whitman claimed, in the world of experience, everything, simply – like mountaineers possessing themselves of Everest – because it was there. If it existed, Whitman had to touch it; if it was possible, it was for that very reason a necessity, a compulsion. And because the limits of the possible and the actual must coincide, and this requires extreme pressure of invocation, he must command the High Style, almost the Sublime.

The sources of this compulsion – much more than a 'vision' of life – are not at all clear. Whitman found a few of the signposts he needed in Emerson, and he pursued them far beyond the point at which Emerson elected to rest. He picked up a certain spirit of the age from the German idealists by way of Coleridge and the transcendentalists. A few echoes of Oriental lore reached him from Thoreau. From Hegel he took the consolation of historical approval. His debts to Carlyle and the American poets he favored are another story, and hardly an exciting one. But in fact his own native temper, I think, dictated most of his lines. What we loosely call his optimism, what we loosely call his romanticism, were matters of temper rather than theory or conviction. But it is worth while to relate optimism and romanticism quite specifically in Whitman, bearing in mind that A. O. Lovejoy has connected these motives in one of his famous *Essays in the History of Ideas*. It is all the more necessary to rehearse this motif, now that optimism has become almost an insulting term in criticism and we are admonished to dedicate ourselves to the proposition that good poems – especially good American poems – are written only on the dark side of the moon.

In linking romanticism and optimism Lovejoy argues that what distinguishes romanticism is a renewed delight in the plenitude, the mystery, the variety, of the created universe. And he traces this feeling back to the old notion that God allows evil to exist and flourish rather than have a missing link in the marvelously diverse chain of being. Anything rather than a lack. This joy in the plenitude of the universe is the difference between Reynolds and Blake. And in *Song of Myself* it sets Whitman praising 'manifold objects, no two alike, and every one good', praising 'my own diversity'. This joy resounds through *Leaves of Grass*, and it persists even in the rueful prose of *Democratic Vistas*. Indeed, even if Whitman had loved 'these States' for no other reason, it would have been enough that they exhibited 'always the free range and diversity'.

Hence one of his fundamental equations is the identification of value with being, not with progress or perfectibility, though he praised Darwin. *Song of the Open Road* is not a myth of perfectibility. Value resides, the poem implies, in the spirit of the journey, not in promissory notes redeemable at the end of the road. In *To Think of Time* he says:

It is not to diffuse you that you were born of your mother and
    father, it is to identify you,
It is not that you should be undecided, but that you should be
    decided,
Something long preparing and formless is arriv'd and form'd in
    you,
You are henceforth secure, whatever comes or goes.

He means secure in being, in identity. In *Democratic Vistas* he says: 'The quality of BEING, in the object's self, according to its own central idea and purpose, and of growing therefrom and thereto – not criticism by other standards, and adjustments thereto – is the lesson of Nature'. This virtually summarizes the aggressive remarks that Blake wrote in the margin of Reynolds' *Discourses*, though the inflection is unmistakably Whitman's. Indeed, it is also the point of contact between Whitman and Hopkins. When Hopkins wrote 'The Leaden Echo and the Golden Echo' and registered kinship between his own mind and Whitman's, what he recognized was joy in the multiplicity of created being, joy that his friend Bridges could not feel in such measure. In the essay 'Compensation' Emerson spoke of Being as 'the vast affirmative, excluding negation, self-balanced, and swallowing up all relations, parts and times, within itself.' This is close enough to Whitman for most purposes. But the best text, for our present purpose, to set beside *Leaves of Grass*, is that passage in *Specimen Days* in which Whitman speaks again of the tie between the Me and the Not-Me. Offering this as 'the most profound theme that can occupy the mind of man', Whitman rehearses the several positions of Kant and Schelling and votes resoundingly for Hegel. The whole earth, with all its differences and contrarieties, he says, embodies 'the endless process of Creative thought, which, amid numberless apparent failures and contradictions, is held together by central and never-broken unity – not contradictions or failures at all, but radiations of one consistent and eternal purpose'.[1] In fact, the great purpose is the greatest of all equations.

Whitman will doubt this in certain rare and extreme moments, notably in the beautiful poem in *Calamus* called *Of the Terrible Doubt of Appearances*, where the only answer to the doubt of being and identity is the present satisfaction of companionship, love. But for the most part Whitman's poems move upon a very simple epistemology, a realist faith. The 'base of all metaphysics', he finds in the poem of that name, is:

The dear love of man for his comrade, the attraction of friend
    to friend,
Of the well-married husband and wife, of children and parents,
Of city for city and land for land.

So philosophic idealism and its doubts will touch him, but will never really endanger the security of being and identity. In *Democratic Vistas* he says:

1 Whitman, *Prose Works, 1892, vol. 1, Specimen Days*, ed. Floyd Stovall, New York Univ. Press, 1963, p. 259.

There is, in sanest hours, a consciousness, a thought that rises, independent, lifted out from all else, calm, like the stars, shining eternal. This is the thought of identity – yours for you, whoever you are, as mine for me. Miracle of miracles, beyond statement, most spiritual and vaguest of earth's dreams, yet hardest basic fact, and only entrance to all facts.

This is the spirit of Whitman's poetry, the temper of his greatest things. We seldom think of him as a poet of plot, act, and event. We think of him as a loud voice, a prophet, and often wish in weariness that he would cultivate the piano. But in fact his greatest poems are written in devotion to being, identity, time, event, and action. He is the guardian of being, and he is content to let essence take care of itself, or, better still, to let it reside silently and confidently in being. When Stevens says 'the imperfect is our paradise', he is Whitman's pupil, his ephebe, as again when he says 'the gods of China are always Chinese'. Stevens would often try to disengage essence from being, to have spirit in some 'essential' purity, but his greatest poems lay aside this metaphysical chemistry. And so too with Whitman. When he pours all his trust and joy into 'contact', the actual, the finite, the verifiably human, the harmonies rise with wonderful grace and tact. I have in mind, among many, the twenty-eight men bathing, the beautifully tender 'Out of the Rolling Ocean the Crowd', 'We Two, How Long We Were Fool'd', the marriage of the trapper and the red girl – this has often been impugned, but it can stand any amount of critical strain – the runaway slave, the 'old-time sea-fight', the wounded whale in *A Song of Joys*. These represent the strongest elements in Whitman and are not at all dependent upon his lungs, his *ortissimo*. They are contact poems written by a poet in easy possession of his powers, touching an object a human action, and touching it not at all to destroy it but to acknowledge it; there is no bravado.

These things were possible because Whitman acknowledged a reality good enough – rich enough, vivid enough – to celebrate. To develop or explode into being is to verify a primal energy; and to celebrate that energy is to share in it, to possess it. This is again the romantic joy in plenitude, in being. The Romantic poet solves the problem of the self by celebrating energy as a value in itself, a primal, non-ethical value, a principle of being upon which a genuine ethic depends – as in Whitman. Because the religious motive – to take this example for the moment – is clearly an energy, poets were loath to reject it. And even when they refused religious belief and turned away from the theologies, they translated the motive into secular terms. This is the secularization of spirituality whose guardian angel is Hegel.[1] Those who condescend to Whitman as an apostle of the good heart have not attended to the sturdiness of his images. In 'A Backward Glance' he says: 'The profoundest service that poems or any other writings can do for their reader is ... to fill him with vigorous and clean manliness, religiousness, and give him good heart as a radical possession and habit.' It is easy to sneer at these terms if we take them individually and with a certain glib sophistication. But when we take them all together, each one supporting the others, we can still sneer, but our vulgarity is clear, even to ourselves. Again, in *Specimen Days* Whitman says, in the same spirit, that the really human purpose is 'to bring people back from their persistent strayings and sickly abstractions, to the costless average, divine, original concrete'. And the necessary principle of energy is to be found – where else? – in nature.

Indeed, one of the notable things in Whitman is his attempt to draw a little of the old meaning of the word 'nature' into the new romantic ethos of plenitude. Sometimes he speaks of nature, admittedly, when he has in mind only daffodils and the great outdoors, but more often – as in *Song of Myself* – nature means 'the perfect fitness and equanimity of things', and it will certainly include what he calls, in the original preface, 'the eternal tendencies of all toward happiness'. Nature is the principle of energy allowing that a thing shall be itself. After this the thing can be implicated in hundreds of relationships; and these in turn will depend for their vitality upon the original blessing of identity. Nature is, to use Yeats' terms on another occasion, 'self-creating, self-delighting', and as Whitman says in *Myself and Mine*:

Let others finish specimens, I never finish specimens,
I start them by exhaustless laws as Nature does, fresh and modern
    continually.

1 See Lionel Trilling, 'On the Modern Element in Modern Literature'; in Stanley Burnshaw (ed.), *Varieties of Literary Experience*, Peter Owen, 1963, pp. 407–33.

In short, nature is the principle that exhibits itself in being, delights in plenitude, and reconciles difference. It is the new decorum.

Hence the proper attitude, the secular equivalent of religious piety, is Emerson's 'nonchalance'. When the principle of energy is diffused through all things and courses through an individual man, the proof is ease, grace, tact. In *One Hour to Madness and Joy* Whitman invokes it: 'To find a new unthought of nonchalance with the best of Nature'. This nonchalance will, of course – like Stevens' Supreme Fiction – give pleasure; and it is part of Whitman's morality to disengage the pleasure principle from an antecedent scruple. In his world the principle of pleasure is verified by the energy that animates it, and it is therefore, in the easiest of his translations, 'good'. When Yeats thought of nonchalance and praised it – as he often did – he took the word from Castiglione's *sprezzatura* and borrowed its air of high breeding, aristocratic hauteur, a handsome spread of civility and splendor. But just as Whitman celebrates the average and calls it divine, so also he commandeers a traditional aristocratic term and hands it over to his new democratic man. And one of the promises he makes on these ceremonial occasions is that the democratic man of nonchalance will be released from the current obsession with time and transience. It is the part of faith and prudence to accept the flow of time, to set aside the 'quest for permanence'. If Saturday is succeeded by Sunday, this is the natural course and order of things and not at all an instance of what Samuel Beckett, glossing Proust, will call 'the poisonous ingenuity of Time in the science of affliction'. Stevens is again the poet who has most vividly acknowledged the natural course of things, and he has done something to liberate us from our bondage to Grecian urns and the idiom of bangs and whimpers. In this he stands with Whitman, and, if anything, more firmly, because the Whitman of the later poems sometimes slipped back into the feeling that, alas, death's the end of all. But both poets find, even in the shadow of time and death, that unities are still possible. Each poet goes his own way, singing unities of self in quite different terms. But they share the basic feeling. Whitman's nonchalant hero will not always satisfy Stevens, even when the hero walks among his peers with superb presence in *Song of the Answerer*, and finds gratifying harmonics in *Song of the Rolling Earth*. It isn't characteristic of Stevens to celebrate the glamorous resources of ordinary people – their nonchalance – as he did, for once, in the poem *Ordinary Women*.

We are concerned with the nature of Whitman's poetry in its most characteristic phases, in the years before the war. After the war, as students of Whitman agree, there is a notable change. Whitman's 'bumps' would persist, his cast of mind would remain substantially what it had always been, he would make the same demands upon himself and others. But most of the demands would be frustrated and the great equations would not, finally, work out. It was too late to change, and there were no kindly spirits to bring him, as they would bring Yeats, new metaphors, new analogies. Postwar America disappointed Whitman precisely because it failed to live up to the demands of the old metaphors – demands of tact and grace. He would still try to 'humanize' the new world with the old familial metaphors; he would try to hold the new fact close to the old value. And he would resist as long as possible the feeling that the new world of 'things' was hostile to the freedom of man. A naturalistic philosophy was already audible that would seal man's faith, his obliteration beneath the mountains of alien things. But Whitman would resist. He would insist and then hope and finally pray that products are not hostile to their producers, nature is not hostile to man's purposes. But it was to be a rear-guard action, as *Song of the Exposition* makes clear, and more and more the rueful note would win out, the old equations now subverted by the new mathematics. And when fact split apart from value, when relation was impossible, then of course the grammar of contact was impossible too. It was the only grammar Whitman knew, the only grammar certified by the human body. Once this failed, a genuine culture was impossible, a culture, that is, based on the 'daily toils' of all the people, the nature of human sympathies, the axioms of the body. If man is cut adrift from nature, the next step is the separation of man from man – no contact. Some poets can bear this; a few thrive on it; and some, like Emily Dickinson, have their own resources of metaphor that allow them to proceed. But the destitution of Whitman's later poetry arises from the gap between the old metaphors and the new facts; and Whitman could fill the gap only with petulance, the tone of the broken sage.

(But in a sense, when this happened, his crucial work was already done. So we can go back.)

To get the beauty of Whitman's poetry hot, one should quote it in long, rolling stretches. No poet was ever less revealed in the single word, the crystallizing phrase, the reverberating epithet. The unit in Whitman's verse is indeed the phrase, a loose-limbed structure of four or five words easily held together and moving along because the cadence is the limit of the speaker's breath. This is part of what William Carlos Williams learned from Whitman – the natural cadence, the flow of breath as a structure good enough for most purposes and better for humanity than the counting of syllables. For both poets the ideal is what Williams called 'a redeeming language', a language to bridge the gap between subject and object, thereby certifying both and praising bridges. And, again, in both poets the function of language is to verify an intricate network of relationships, contacts, between person and person, person and place, person and thing. Williams once praised a poem by Marianne Moore as an anthology of transit, presumably because the words wasted no time sitting down to admire themselves but got on with the job of transmission. The same applies to many of his own poems and to most of Whitman's. No wonder Whitman loved bridges, ferries, and wrote some of his finest poetry in *Crossing Brooklyn Ferry* – a passage like this, for instance:

I too many and many a time cross'd the river of old,
Watched the Twelfth-month sea-gulls, saw them high in the air
   floating with motionless wings, oscillating their bodies,
Saw how the glistening yellow lit up parts of their bodies and
   left the rest in strong shadow,
Saw the slow-wheeling circles and the gradual edging toward the
   south,
Saw the reflection of the summer sky in the water,
Had my eyes dazzled by the shimmering track of beams,
Look'd at the fine centrifugal spokes of light round the shape of
   my head in the sunlit water,
Look'd on the haze on the hills southward and south-westward,
Look'd on the vapor as it flew in fleeces tinged with violet . . .

If we take this as poetry of description or invocation, it is obviously flat. We have only to compare Whitman's sea gulls with Hopkins' windhover to see that Whitman doesn't even begin to compete in that line. Where Hopkins loads every vein with ore, Whitman waits for another day. But this is superficial, and the real difference escapes. Hopkins, from the whole range of being and multiplicity, seizes upon one moment, one action, and forces it to disclose all the meaning there is. His methods are pressure, force, concentration; he is a specialist in applied pressure. But Whitman is a general practitioner; for him each existent is a zone of consanguinity, a place where people gather for 'natural' worship. Hence in his esthetic it is more important that the poet annex his objects by terms of contact than that he should bear down hard upon any one of them. In *Crossing Brooklyn Ferry* Whitman is not describing the scene with the aid of sea gulls, vapors, ships, and summer skies. He addresses a future man and claims fellowship with him by showing that he too – Walt Whitman – was an eligible participant in the same scene. And his proof is the network of sympathetic relationships that he establishes between all his objects. What he calls, in *I Sing the Body Electric*, 'the flush of the known universe' is nearly as much his theme as it is Hopkins'. But Hopkins drills for it at a few likely spots and writes his poems when the juice spurts out and sometimes, in desolation and bitterness, when it doesn't. Whitman does not drill. He is an electrician and he believes that electricity is everywhere and can be carried along in wires and lines. Every human recognition, every contact, adds to the great network. And because this is an eminently human activity, he will speak of it in human and natural terms. He will say 'many and many a time' instead of 'often', because the first is traditional to the story-teller before printed books and the isolated reader. He will make each line a breath length, because this is the natural division of speech. He will begin each line, especially in the definitive version, with the word of contact – *watch'd, saw, look'd* – until all the relationships are ensured, winding out the wires. This is the great electrical circuit, not the chain, of being.

Hence the energy released in Whitman's poetry is invariably directed to extend the lines of contact. And once contact is effected he tends to leave his objects alone. He has no interest in fidgeting with metaphors to amplify the objects; each is what it is. We often think of him as an incorrigibly adjectival poet, forgetting that he wrote hundreds of lines that are as lean as words can be when we want them to be lean. A line like 'The flags of all nations, the falling of them at sunset' does not claim, by itself, to be 'interesting'. It refuses the attention of the anthologist and directs him to move along to more spectacular places. It does not even parade its modesty. It is one part of the network, no more, no less. 'The falling of them at sunset' is a little more idiosyncratic than 'their falling', which would be the bare notation, but even this is a modest claim. What we attend to in this line is the grace, the civility, of the two phrases, laid side by side to record an event that is significant because the whole network, the vast similitude, is significant, and not otherwise. This is why, reading Whitman, we have to attend to his Grand Style, yes, his Sublime; but we have also to attend to that marvelously pure middle style and the civility that enabled him to write a poem like *There Was a Child Went Forth*. The qualities of the middle style are too often taken for granted, as if we could all possess them if only we could manage a free weekend. But we have to attend to them all over again if we are to give Whitman his due. Indeed, one of Whitman's greatest contributions to modern poetry – and therefore to modern life – is the grace that enabled him to write this:

There was a child went forth every day,
And the first object he looked upon and received with wonder
  or pity or love or dread, that object he became . . .

I might push the argument a little further. If Whitman did not exist, American poets in search of the Grand Style would not need to invent him; they could find what they want in Whittier and Bryant. But without Whitman's verse and Emerson's prose, I cannot see how Williams would have written *To Daphne and Virginia* or Frost *An Old Man's Winter Night*, each with his high grace in the middle style.

In fact, the question to ask about Whitman is not, How did he manage it? Rather, Why, since he has so much, does he not have everything? Why are so many of his poems tainted with the meretricious, the provincial? Why does he trail away and in later years peter out in muscle-bound verse and prose, in gawkiness and excess? Why does he lose what Williams called 'measure'? Why, to be specific, are the first three editions of *Leaves of Grass* so much more controlled, more finely adjudged than the others? Why are so many of his poems, as he said of Dr Schliemann's letters, 'interesting but fishy'?

I have already suggested part of the answer: the failure of the old metaphors to cope with the new facts. And there is also, of course, the risk entailed in his devotion to his own equations, the risk of facility. We are unhappy with Emerson when he soars too easily above the facts of the case, and we praise Thoreau for a scruple foreign to his master. The difficulty in Whitman's equations is that once the equals sign is inserted, the transaction is finished, and can only be succeeded by another in the same form. Yeats said, in a celebrated formulation, that from the quarrel with others we make only rhetoric, from the quarrel with ourselves, poetry. Perhaps the trouble is that Whitman's equations virtually eliminated the quarrel with himself. To write poetry at all, Whitman had to trust himself; doubts, hesitations, scruples would have killed the poems even before they were properly born. And to write his own particular kind of poem, Whitman needed to trust himself in all weathers – totally. This meant not only that he was temperamentally disinclined to quarrel with himself but that his imagination was deployed at large, along a broad range, rather than in minute adjustments and measures. He would never have written poems like Yeats' *Dialogue of Self and Soul* or *Vacillation*, because the first is all conflict and the second is all hovering, and to vacillate or to hover is to break the electrical circuit, in Whitman's world an act of gross disloyalty. He is one of the great praisers, and this is one of his most admirable qualities, but it made it practically impossible for him to test his own insights. Once he had them, they became his very own, and like a father he loved all his children equally.

A few sentences from André Gide will show another kind of temper, radically different from Whitman's, will show what it means to be born with a critical scruple, like a birthmark. In his *Journal* for January 3, 1892, Gide wrote:

And every moment, at every word I write, at each gesture I make, I am terrified at the thought that this is one more ineradicable feature of my physiognomy becoming fixed: a hesitant, impersonal physiognomy, an amorphous physiognomy, since I have not been capable of choosing and tracing its contours confidently.[1]

1 *The Journals of André Gide*, trans. Justin O'Brien, Knopf, 1955, vol. 1, p. 18.

This would never have distressed Whitman. Both Whitman and Gide thought of each experience as an addition to the self, but while this delighted Whitman, it terrified Gide. Whitman was content to live and work with the given; he did not demand the privilege of creating himself, literally, out of nothing. In these matters he who hesitates is not lost, he is a special kind of writer, and very often his scruple will save him and he will be stronger as a result. Whitman never hesitated: his animal faith in himself was an everlasting yes. The world was all before him, and he walked through it, a new Adam.

But when we read Whitman with our own scruples – such as they are – we often feel that a more scrupulous poet would have made more of what was there. For one thing, he is the poet of the new day, the present tense and a declared future, but he scants the verifiable past, and the loss to his own poetry is grievous, because the past is one of the great critics of our actions. There is a poem by Stevens called *The Prejudice against the Past* implying that to children every object is what it is, now, this moment, seen as if on a clear day with no memories, whereas the 'aquiline pedants' treat each object as if it were the relic of the heart or the mind. This is a strong image, and we do well to attend to it. It reminds us that there is a childlike element in Whitman's vision, as if all his poems were written on a clear day with no memories. But the loss is grievous. I often wish that Whitman had written a book called *In the American Grain*, because it would then have come at the right time, and later poets could have used it without waiting for William Carlos Williams to write it. It would have come appropriately in its time, from Whitman, a fine garnering of acts and sufferances and values in the United States – the available past. Because Whitman did not write it, we have the impression that America in 1855 had only a brief and insignificant past; and this is an error to which Henry James gave classic status. Fenimore Cooper knew that America had a past, and he helped to define it in his sturdier social novels. But he was not satisfied and he longed to give America a mythology, a heroic anthropology, as well. Indeed, Hawthorne was the only major American writer who attended to an American past on the understanding that it was palpably there and that it could be invoked for present lucidity. And, later, Edith Wharton would write *The Custom of the Country* on much the same understanding.

Whitman, in *Starting from Paumanok*, claimed that he 'conn'd old times', and he protested his respect for the ancients, but he sent them away, though with blessings on their heads. Even in *Democratic Vistas*, courtesy to the past was as much as he could manage. If we would believe De Tocqueville, this is implicit in democracy itself. 'Democracy', he says, 'shuts the past against the poet, opens the future before him.' It may be so, but this is not our concern. When Whitman says, in *Pioneers! O Pioneers!*, 'All the past we leave behind', the gesture is framed by his own temper, for which we do not need to posit national compulsions. The significant acts performed in America in the centuries before 1850 were matters of little moment to Whitman because he could not demonstrate his possession of them. He could demonstrate his possession of the present, by celebration, by praising its plenitude, and he could assert his fellowship with the future. But it is frustrating to see him, in *Song of the Exposition*, roaming with weary elegance through the history and mythology of England, France, Germany, and Egypt at a time when the verifiable meaning of his own country was still waiting to be inspected. He did about as much – or as little – homework on his fated subject as a later poet, Hart Crane, a man of similarly grand intention.

But it would be quite wrong to imply that because Whitman wrote his equations from an American present and an equally American future he is merely an American 'problem', a case study in something-or-other. Whitman is at the center of American literature – at least as relevant as Poe and Mark Twain, more relevant than Emerson – but his significance extends far beyond the United States, because it is moral significance. If it is not that, it is nothing. I am not speaking of his overt influence on European writers, though that influence has been great and is likely to be greater. I have in mind a certain moral bearing, an attitude to life that is defined in Whitman with strange resonance. One can find it elsewhere; its range is broad. I am thinking of his work as an endorsement of certain parts of life that are now, alas, in some disrepute among the elite, what he called the commonplace, the average, that great middle range of experience that is now so maliciously despised. Modern literature has disdained this experience on the grounds that it is a middle-class property and therefore contemptible. The loss to the literature is very great. This is the point at which Whitman impinges upon a failure of response that is no more American than European or Asiatic. We should invite his poems to offer the kind of critique that Thomas Mann's Tonio sent to Lisabeta in that great letter in which he said:

As I write, the sea whispers to me and I close my eyes. I am looking into a world unborn and formless, that needs to be ordered and shaped; I see into a whirl of shadows of human figures who beckon to me to weave spells to redeem them: tragic and laughable figures and some that are both together – and to these I am drawn. But my deepest and secretest love belongs to the blond and blue-eyed, the fair and living, the happy, lovely and commonplace.[1]

I think the achievement of Whitman's greatest poems resides here: that they restore the dignity of the commonplace.

There is very little evidence that contemporary poets are taking Whitman's poems in this way – though it is the only way, I should argue, in which the poems will bear any severe strain. In contemporary American poetry Leaves of Grass is put to work for many masters, but often it is the wrong work. Some poets, like Louis Simpson, bring the book into their poems partly out of reverence and partly in the hope that it will lift some of their own burdens. But it won't. Allen Ginsberg brings Whitman into his poems for a dozen modish reasons, and he seems to think that by dropping Whitman's name often enough he will make everything clear. In A Supermarket in California Ginsberg has done everything that is required of a poet except the one essential thing – to write his poem. And then there are the poets who use Whitman to imply that all you need to be a great poet is homosexual experience and a copy of I and Thou.

Indeed, very few poets seem to me to use Leaves of Grass for a genuine purpose. Robert Duncan is exceptional. The Opening of the Field sets itself the high object of completing the work that Leaves of Grass started. At one point Duncan says:

It is across great scars of wrong
I reach toward the song of kindred men
and strike again the naked string
old Whitman sang from.[2]

1 Death in Venice; Tristan; Tonio Kröger, trans. H. T. Lowe-Porter, Penguin Books, 1955, pp. 189–90.
2 Robert Duncan, The Opening of the Field, Grove Press, 1960, p. 64.

Duncan's 'optimism' ('Flickers of unlikely heat|at the edge of our belief bud forth'), his joy in plenitude ('A bush puts forth roses upon roses|to illustrate the afternoon|abundances of white, scarlet, yellow –| the beautiful profusion takes me'), his image of man as moral agent ('salmon not in the well where the|hazelnut falls|but at the falls battling, inarticulate,|blindly making it'), even his neo-Elizabethan songs, and especially his idiom of Contact ('There is no touch that is not each|to each|reciprocal' and 'Transient beauty of youth|that into immortality goes direct,|forsaking us? Aye, but bedded in touch,| ever-remembered Lord of Sensualities'): these modes of feeling are certified by Whitman. Part of Duncan's care is to take possession of them without injuring them or, worse still, domesticating them, and to proceed from that possession.

So I return to Whitman's equations. The scale of their achievement (which is not to be confused with the length of a shopping-list) is inseparable from the energy and goodwill with which he insisted that all was not yet lost. There were still values to be found in place and time. The proper study of mankind was still man, the world, relationships, places, things, in their temporal being. Reading him again today we are struck by the fact that the equations had to be declared: they came when he called them, but only then and with some reluctance. And we are apt to feel that much of Whitman's sound was invoked to calm his own fury. But we should not push this too far. He committed himself to his equations and to the validity of human life. This was his vote, his voice, to 'redeem the time'.

(23–51)

R. W. B. Lewis

from 'Always Going Out and Coming In', *Trials of the Word* 1965

Whitman, as we have heard his mother saying, was always, 'going out and coming in'. She meant quite literally that her son would go out of the house in the morning, often to travel on the ferry to Manhattan and to absorb the spectacle of life, and would come back into the household to eat and sleep, perhaps to write. But she unwittingly gave a nice maternal formula to the larger, recurring pattern in Whitman's career – the foray into the world and the retreat back into himself and into a creative communion with his genius. The poetry he came in to write – through the 1856 edition just examined – reflected that pattern in content and rhythm, and in a way to celebrate the commanding power of the outward and forward movement. The early poetry bore witness as well, to be sure, of the darker mode of withdrawal, the descent into the abysses of doubt, self-distrust, and the death-consciousness; but it was invariably overcome in a burst of visionary renewal. The poetry of 1855 and 1856 is the poetry of day, of flood tide.

The 1860 *Leaves of Grass*, however, gives voice to genuine desolation. In it, betimes, the self appears as shrunken, indeed as fragmented; the psyche as dying; the creative vigor as dissipated. The most striking of the new poems belong to the poetry not of day but of death. A suggestive and immediate verbal sign of the new atmosphere may be found in the difference of title between so characteristic a poem of 1855 as *There Was a Child Went Forth* and perhaps the key 1860 poem, *As I Ebb'd with the Ocean of Life*. Yet the case must be put delicately and by appeal to paradox. For, in a sense, the new death poetry represents in fact Whitman's most remarkable triumph over his strongest feelings of personal and artistic defeat. There has been a scholarly debate over the precise degree of melancholy in the 1860 edition, one scholar emphasizing the note of dejection and another the occasional note of cheerfulness; but that debate is really beside the point. What we have is poetry that expresses the sense of loss so sharply and vividly that substantive loss is converted into artistic gain.

During the almost four years since June 1856, Whitman had once again gone out and come back in; but this time the withdrawal was compelled by suffering and self-distrust. Whitman's foray into the open world, beginning in the fall of 1856, took the form, first of a brief new interest in the political scene and, second, of a return to journalism, as editor-in-chief of the Brooklyn *Daily Times* from May 1857 until June 1859. In the morning, he busied himself writing editorials and articles for the newspaper; in the afternoon, he traveled into New York, to saunter along lower Broadway and to sit watchful and silent near or amid the literati who gathered in Pfaff's popular Swiss restaurant in the same neighbourhood. In the evening, he continued to write – prolifically: seventy poems, more or less, in the first year after the 1856 edition and probably a few more in the months immediately following. Then there occurred a hiatus: a blank in our knowledge of Whitman's life, and apparently a blank in his creative activity. We cannot say just when the hiatus began – sometime in 1858, one judges. It ended, anyhow, at some time before the publication in the December 1859 issue of the New York *Saturday Press* of a poem called *A Child's Reminiscence*, its familiar title being *Out of the Cradle Endlessly Rocking*.

On the political side, Whitman's disenchantment was even swifter than usual. The choices offered the American public in the election of 1856 – Buchanan, Frémont, and Fillmore – seemed to him false, debased, and meaningless; and he called – in an unpublished pamphlet – for a president who might play the part of 'Redeemer'. His disappointment with the actual, in short, led as before to an appeal for some 'greater than Socrates' to arise in America; and, also as before, Whitman soon turned from the political figure to the *poet*, in fact to himself, to perform the sacred function, asserting in his journal that *Leaves of Grass* was to be 'the New Bible'. (Not until 1866 would the two aspirations fuse in a poem – *When Lilacs Last in the Dooryard Bloom'd* – that found a new idiom of almost biblical sonority to celebrate death in the person of a Redeemer President, Abraham Lincoln.) Meanwhile, however, Whitman's private and inner life was causing him far more grief and dismay than the public life he had been observing.

A chief cause for Whitman's season of despair, according to most Whitman biographers, was a homosexual love affair during the silent months: an affair that undoubtedly took place, that was the source at once of profound joy and profound guilt, and that, when it ended, left Whitman with a desolating sense of loss. Such poems as *A Hand-Mirror* and *Hours Continuing Long, Sore and Heavy-Hearted* testify with painful clarity both to the guilt and to the subsequent misery of loneliness. At the same time, poems such as *As I Ebb'd with the Ocean of Life* and *So Long!* strike a different and perhaps deeper note of loss: a note, that is, of poetic decline, of the loss not so much of a human loved one but of creative energy – accompanied by a loss of confidence in everything that energy had previously brought into being. There had been a hint of this in *Crossing Brooklyn Ferry* in 1856 – 'The best I had done seem'd to me blank and suspicious' – but there self-doubt had been washed away in a flood of assurance. Now it had become central and almost resistant to hope. It may be that the fear of artistic sterility was caused by the moral guilt; but it seems no less likely that the artistic apprehension was itself at the root of the despair variously echoed in 1860. If so, the apprehension was probably due to a certain climacteric in Whitman's psychic career – what is called *la crise de quarantaine*, the psychological crisis some men pass through when they reach the age of forty. Whitman was forty in May 1859; and it was in the month after his birthday that he wrote two aggressive and, one cannot but feel, disturbed articles for the Brooklyn *Daily Times* – on prostitution and the right to unmarried sexual love – that resulted in his dismissal from the paper. Characteristically dismissed, Whitman characteristically withdrew. But no doubt the safest guess is that a conjunction of these factors – *la quarantaine*, the temporary but fearful exhaustion of talent after so long a period of fertility, the unhappy love affair – begot the new poems that gave 'death and night' their prominence in the 1860 edition.

The edition of 1860 contained 154 poems: which is to say that 122 had been composed since 1856 and of these, as has been said, seventy by the summer of 1857. Most of the other fifty, it can be hazarded, were written late in 1859 and in the first six months of 1860. It can also be hazarded that among these latter fifty poems were nearly all the best of the new ones – those grouped under the title *Calamus*, the name Whitman gave to his poetry of masculine love. These include *Scented Herbage, Hours Continuing, Whoever You Are, City of Orgies, A Glimpse, I Saw in Louisiana, Out of the Cradle, As I Ebb'd* (published in the April 1860 issue of the *Atlantic Monthly* as *Bardic Symbols*), and *So Long*!

A Hand-Mirror records a feeling of self-loathing almost unequaled in English or American poetry. And it is representative of the entire volume in its emphatic reversal of an earlier work and an earlier course of feeling. In *This Compost*, in 1856, Whitman was seized with a wonder verging on terror at the capacity of nature and of man to produce the beautiful out of the foul or shameful; here, in 1860, he is smitten with the dreadful conviction of having, in his own being, produced the foul and the shameful out of the potentially beautiful. *Hours Continuing Long, Sore and Heavy-Hearted* is a statement of pain so severe, so unmitigated, that Whitman deleted the poem from all subsequent editions of *Leaves of Grass*. These poems of pain are uncommonly painful to read; and yet, in the other major new poems of 1860, we find Whitman executing what might be called the grand Romantic strategy) – the strategy of converting private devastation into artistic achievement; of composing poetry of high distinction out of a feeling of personal, spiritual, and almost metaphysical extinction. Keats's *Ode on a Grecian Urn* offers an example of the same, at one chronological extreme; as, at another, does Hart Crane's *The Broken Tower*.

That strategy is, indeed, what the 1860 edition may be said to be about; for more than the other versions of *Leaves of Grass*, that of 1860 has a sort of plot buried in it. The plot – in a very reduced summary – consists in the discovery that 'death' is the source and beginning of 'poetry'; with 'death' here understood to involve several kinds and sensations of loss, of suffering, of disempowering guilt, of psychic fragmentation; and 'poetry' as the awakening of the power to catch and to order reality in language. What had so fundamentally changed since 1855 and 1856 was Whitman's concept of reality. In 1855, as we have seen, the thought of death led to a flat denial of it: 'I swear I think there is nothing but immortality.' But in *Scented Herbage* of 1860 he arrives at an opposite conclusion: 'For now', as he says, 'it is convey'd to me that you [death] are . . . the real reality.' If Whitman's poetic faculty had formerly been quickened by his sense of the absolute life, it now finds its inspiration in the adventure of death. In *So Long!* Whitman confesses to the death of his talent: 'It appears to me that I am dying. . . . My songs cease, I abandon them.' Yet in *Scented Herbage* poetry is identified as the very herbage and flower of death, as Baudelaire had a few years earlier identified poetry as the flower of evil; his new poems, for Whitman, are 'growing up above me above death'. By 1860 Whitman had reached the perception of Wallace Stevens – in *Sunday Morning* (1923) – that 'death is the mother of beauty'.

Stevens' phrase might serve as motto for the 1860 edition; as it might also serve for another of the several titles for the poem that was first called *A Child's Reminiscence*, then *A Word out of the Sea*, and finally (in 1871) *Out of the Cradle Endlessly Rocking*. Whatever else occurs in this in every sense brilliant poem, there unmistakably occurs the discovery of poetic power, the magical power of the word, through the experience – here presented as vicarious – of the departure and loss, perhaps the death, of the loved one. It is one of the most handsomely *made* of Whitman's poems; the craft is relaxed, firm, and sure. Only an artist in virtuoso control of his technical resources would attempt a poem with such effortless alternation of narrative (or recitatif) and impassioned aria, such dazzling metrical shifts, such hypnotic exactitude of language, not to mention a narrative 'point of view' of almost Jamesian complexity: the man of forty recalling the child of, say, twelve observing the calamitous love affair of two other beings, and the same man of forty projecting, one assumes, his own recent and adult bereavement into the experience of an empathic child. Whitman, by 1860, was very impressively the poet in that word's original meaning of 'maker', in addition to being still the poet as inspired singer; and *Out of the Cradle Endlessly Rocking* – for all its supple play of shadows and glancing light – will bear the utmost weight of analysis. But it has perhaps been sufficiently probed elsewhere, and I will instead take a longer look at *As I Ebb'd with the Ocean of Life*.

We will not be far wrong, and in any case it will illuminate the pattern of Whitman's career, if we take this poem as an almost systematic inversion of the 1855 poem *There Was a Child Went Forth*, as well as an inversion of a key moment – Sections 4 and 5 – in the 1855 *Song of Myself*. As against that younger Whitman of morning and of spring, of the early lilacs and the red morning-glories, here is the Whitman of the decline of the day and of the year – a poet now found 'musing late in the autumn day' (the phrase should be read slowly, as thought the chief words were, in the older fashion, divided by dots). All the sprouts and blossoms and fruit of *There Was a Child Went Forth* are here replaced, in the poetically stunning second stanza by:

Chaff, straw, splinters of wood, weeds, and the sea-gluten,
Scum, scales from shining rocks, leaves of salt-lettuce, left by the tide;

to which are added, later, 'A few sands and dead leaves', 'a trail of drift and debris', and finally:

. . loose windows, little corpses,
Froth, snowy white, and bubbles,
(See, from my dead lips the ooze exuding at last . . .)

The poem's rhythm, instead of pulsating outward in constantly larger spirals (though it seems to try to do that occasionally), tends to fall back on itself, to fall away, almost to disintegrate; no poem of Whitman's shows a more cunning fusion of technique and content. It is here, quite properly, the falling rather than the rising rhythm that catches the ear. As against:

There was a child went forth,

we now hear:

Where the fierce old mother endlessly cries for her castaways

– a dying fall that conveys the shrinking away, the psychological slide toward death, the slope into oblivion that the poem is otherwise concerned with.

The major turn in the action appears in the grammatical shift from the past tense of Section 1 ('As I ebb'd', etc.) to the present tense of Section 2 ('As I wend', etc.). It is a shift from the known to the un-known, a shift indeed not so much from one moment of time to another as from the temporal to the timeless, and a shift not so much accomplished as desired. For what produces in the poet his feeling of near-death is just his conviction that neither he nor his poetry has ever known or ever touched upon the true and timeless realm of reality. The essential reality from which he now feels he has forever been cut off is rendered as 'the real Me'. To get the full force of the despondent confession of failure, one should place the lines about 'the real me' next to those in Sections 4 and 5 in *Song of Myself* where Whitman had exultantly recalled the exact opposite. There he had celebrated a perfect union between the actual Me and the real Me: between the here-and-now Whitman and that timeless being, that Over-Soul or genius that he addressed as the Me myself. *That*, I suggest, was Whitman's real love affair; that was the union that was consummated in 1855 and that ended – so Whitman temporarily felt – in disunion three or four years later; 'the real Me' was the loved one that departed. And now, divorced and disjoined from the real Me, the actual Me threatens to come apart, to collapse into a trail of drift and debris, with ooze exuding from dead lips. (So, by analogy, a Puritan might have felt when cut off, through sin, from the God that created him.)

Still, as Richard Chase has insisted, this poem is saved from any suggestion of whimpering self-pity by the astonishing and courageous tone of self-mockery – in the image of the real Me ridiculing the collapsing Me:

... before all my arrogant poems the real Me stands yet
  untouched, untold, altogether unreach'd,
Withdrawn far, mocking me with mock-congratulatory signs and
  bows,
With peals of distant ironical laughter at every word I have
  written,
Pointing in silence to these songs, and then to the sand beneath.

It is an image of immeasurable effect. And it is, so to speak, a triumph over its own content. Anyone who could construct an image of the higher power – the one he aspires toward – standing far off and mocking him with little satiric bows and gestures, comparing and consigning his verses to the sandy debris under his feet: such a person has already conquered his sense of sterility, mastered his fear of spiritual and artistic death, rediscovered his genius, and returned to the fullest poetic authority. Within the poem, Whitman identifies the land as his father and the fierce old sea as his mother; he sees himself as alienated no less from them than from the real Me, and he prays to both symbolic parents for a rejuvenation of his poetic force, a resumption of 'the secret of the murmuring I envy'. But the prayer is already answered in the very language in which it is uttered; Whitman never murmured more beautifully; and this is why, at the depth of his ebbing, Whitman can say, parenthetically, that the flow will return.

(21–8)

Louis Simpson

Walt Whitman at Bear Mountain from *Selected Poems* 1965

> . . . life which does not give the preference to any other life, of
> any previous period, which therefore prefers its own
> existence . . .
>
> Ortega y Gasset

Neither on horseback nor seated,
But like himself, squarely on two feet,
The poet of death and lilacs
Loafs by the footpath. Even the bronze looks alive
Where it is folded like cloth. And he seems friendly.

'Where is the Mississippi panorama
And the girl who played the piano?
Where are you, Walt?
The Open Road goes to the used-car lot.

'Where is the nation you promised?
These houses built of wood sustain
Colossal snows,
And the light above the street is sick to death.

'As for the people – see how they neglect you!
Only a poet pauses to read the inscription.'

'I am here', he answered.
'It seems you have found me out.
Yet, did I not warn you that it was Myself
I advertised? Were my words not sufficiently plain?

I gave no prescriptions,
And those who have taken my moods for prophecies
Mistake the matter.'
Then, vastly amused – 'Why do you reproach me?
I freely confess I am wholly disreputable.
Yet I am happy, because you have found me out.'

A crocodile in wrinkled metal loafing . . .

Then all the realtors,
Pickpockets, salesmen, and the actors performing
Official scenarios,
Turned a deaf ear, for they had contracted
American dreams.

But the man who keeps a store on a lonely road,
And the housewife who knows she's dumb,
And the earth, are relieved.

All that grave weight of America
Cancelled! Like Greece and Rome.
The future in ruins!
The castles, the prisons, the cathedrals
Unbuilding, and roses

Blossoming from the stones that are not there . . .
The clouds are lifting from the high Sierras,
The Bay mists clearing.
And the angel in the gate, the flowering plum,
Dances like Italy, imagining red.

Acknowledgements

For permission to use copyright material acknowledgement is made to the following:

For the article by George Santayana from *Harvard Monthly*, to Daniel C. Cory; for the extract from George Santayana, *Interpretation of Poetry and Religion*, to Charles Scribner's Sons and Harper & Row Ltd; for the extract from G. K. Chesterton, *Lunacy and Letters*, to Miss D. Collins and Sheed & Ward Ltd; for the extract from Ezra Pound, *American Literature*, to the author; for the extract from Basil de Selincourt, *Walt Whitman: A Critical Study*, to Martin Secker & Warburg Ltd; for the extract from D. H. Lawrence's Introduction to *New Poems*, to Laurence Pollinger Ltd, the estate of the late Mrs Frieda Lawrence and the Viking Press Inc.; for the extract from D. H. Lawrence, *Studies in Classic American Literature*, to Laurence Pollinger Ltd, the estate of the late Mrs Frieda Lawrence and the Viking Press Inc; for the atricle from T. S. Eliot, to the *New Statesman* and the estate of the late T. S. Eliot; for the article from Amy Lowell in the *Yale Review*, to Houghton Mifflin Inc; for the extract from Constance Rourke, *American Humor*, to Harcourt, Brace & World Inc. and Alice D. Fore; for the extract from Frederick Schyberg, *Walt Whitman*, to Columbia University Press; for the extract from D. Mirsky's article in *Walt Whitman Abroad*, ed. Gay Wilson Allen, to Syracuse University Press; for the extract from Newton Arvin, *Walt Whitman*, to the Macmillan Company of New York; for the extract from F. O. Matthiessen, *American Renaissance*, to Oxford University Press Inc.; for the extract from Lionel Trilling, to the *Nation* and the author; for the extract from Yvor Winters, *In Defense of Reason*, to Rourtledge & Kegan Paul Ltd and the Swallow Press Inc.; for the extract from Randall Jarrell, *Poetry and the Age*, to Alfred A. Knopf, Inc.; for the extract from Charles Fiedelson Jr, *Symbolism and American Literature*, to University of Chicago Press; for the extract from William Carlos Williams's article in *Leaves of Grass One Hundred Years After*, ed. M. Hindus, to MacGibbon & Kee Ltd; for the extract from Richard Chase, *Walt Whitman Reconsidered*, to the estate of the late Richard Chase; for the extract from Malcolm Cowley's Introduction to *Leaves of Grass: The First Edition*, to the Viking Press Inc. and Martin Secker & Warburg Ltd; for the extract from Leslie Fiedler, *No! in Thunder*, to Curtis Brown Ltd, the author and the Beacon Press; for the extract from Roy Harvey Pearce's article, to the Editors of the *Minnesota Review*; for the extract from Richard Chase, *The Presence of Walt Whitman*, to Columbia University Press and the estate of the late Richard Chase; for the extract from Roger Asselineau, *The Evolution of Walt Whitman*, to Harvard University Press; for the extract from Gay Wilson Allen, *Walt Whitman Handbook*, to Hendricks House Inc.; for the extract from Martin Green, *Re-appraisals*, to Hugh Evelyn Ltd; for the extract from Denis Donoghue, *Connoisseurs of Chaos*, to Macmillan Company of New York and Faber & Faber Ltd; for the extract from R. W. B. Lewis, *Trials of the Word*, to Harcourt, Brace & World Inc.; for the poem by Louis Simpson from *Selected Poems*, to Oxford University Press.

Select Bibliography

Editions

Gay Wilson Allen and Sculley Bradley (general editors), *The Collected Writings of Walt Whitman*, New York University Press.
Published so far:
Harold Blodgett and Sculley Bradley (eds.), *Leaves of Grass: Reader's Edition*, 1964; paperback edition, Norton, 1968. (This is a definitive edition of the 1891–2 text.)
Thomas L. Brasher (ed.), *Early Poems and the Fiction*, 1963.
Edwin Haviland Miller (ed.), *The Correspondence of Walt Whitman*, vol. 1, *1842–1867*, 1961; vol. 2, *1868–1875*, 1961; vol. 3, *1876–1885*, 1964.
Floyd Stovall (ed.), *Prose Works 1892*, vol. 1, *Specimen Days*, 1963; vol. 2, *Collect and Other Prose*, 1964.
In preparation:
Harold Blodgett and Sculley Bradley (eds.), *Leaves of Grass: A Variorum Edition*.
R. M. Bucke, T. B. Harned and H. L. Traubel (eds.), *Complete Writings of Walt Whitman*, 10 vols., Putnams, 1902.
C. J. Furness (ed.), *Walt Whitman's Workshop*, Harvard University Press, 1928, reprinted 1964.
Emory Holloway (ed.), *Uncollected Prose and Poetry of Walt Whitman*, 2 vols., Doubleday, 1921; Heinemann, 1922.
Emory Holloway (ed.), *Walt Whitman: Complete Poetry and Selected Prose and Letters*, The Nonesuch Press, 1938, 1967.

Bibliography

Evie Allison Allen, 'A Check List of Whitman Publications: 1945–60', in Gay Wilson Allen, *Walt Whitman as Man, Poet and Legend*, Southern Illinois Press, 1961, pp. 177–244.
Willard Thorp, 'Walt Whitman', in Floyd Stovall (ed.), *Eight American Authors*, Norton, 1963, pp. 271–318, 445–51.

Biography

Gay Wilson Allen, *The Solitary Singer*, Macmillan Co., 1955; reprinted by Grove Press.

Selected Criticism

Gay Wilson Allen, *Walt Whitman Abroad*, Syracuse University Press, 1955.
Gay Wilson Allen, *Walt Whitman Handbook*, Hendricks, 1946; reprinted 1962.
Newton Arvin, *Walt Whitman*, Macmillan Co., 1938.

Roger Asselineau, *The Evolution of Walt Whitman*, Havard University Press, Oxford University Press, vol. 1, 1960, vol. 2, 1962. A translation of *L'évolution de Walt Whitman après la première édition des 'Feuilles d'Herbe'*, 1954.

Harold Blodgett, *Walt Whitman in England*, Oxford University Press, 1934; Cornell University Press.

John Burroughs, *Whitman*, Houghton Mifflin, 1896; second edition A. P. Watt & Sons, 1902.

Edward Carpenter, *Days with Walt Whitman*, Macmillan Co., 1906; George Allen, 1907.

Jean Catel, *Walt Whitman: La naissance du poète*, Rieder, 1929.

Richard Chase, *Walt Whitman Reconsidered*, Gollancz, Sloan, 1955.

Stanley Coffman Jr, 'Form and Meaning in Whitman's *Passage to India*', *P.M.L.A.*, vol. 70, 1955, pp. 337–49.

Basil de Selincourt, *Walt Whitman: A Critical Study*, Secker, 1914; M. Kennerly.

Charles Fiedelson, *Symbolism in American Literature*, University of Chicago, 1953.

Milton Hindus (ed.) *'Leaves of Grass' One Hundred Years After*, Stanford University Press, 1955.

Emory Holloway, *Whitman*, Knopf, 1926.

Hugh Kenner, 'Walt Whitmans's Multitudes', in *Gnomon: Essays in Contemporary Literature*, McDowell, Obolensky, 1958.

D. H. Lawrence, 'Whitman', in *Studies in Classic American Literature*, Secker, 1924; reprinted by Doubleday, 1955.

R. W. B. Lewis (ed.), *The Presence of Walt Whitman*, Columbia University Press, 1962.

Leo Marx, 'The Vernacular Tradition in American Literature', in J. Kwiat and M. Turpie (eds.), *Studies in American Culture*, University of Minnesota Press, 1960, pp. 190–22.

F. O. Matthiessen, *American Renaissance*, Oxford University Press Inc., 1941.

Henry Miller, 'Letter to Pierre Lesdain', in *The Books in My Life*, Peter Owen, 1952, pp. 221–54; reprinted New Directions, 1957.

James E. Miller, *A Critical Guide to Leaves of Grass*, University of Chicago Press, 1957.

Roy Harvey Pearce, *The Continuity of American Poetry*, Princeton University Press, 1961.

Roy Harvey Pearce (ed.), *Whitman*, Prentice-Hall, 1962.

Bliss Perry, *Whitman*, Houghton Mifflin, 1906.

Frederik Schyberg, *Walt Whitman*, Gyldendalski Boghandel, 1933, translation Columbia University Press, 1951.

J. A. Symonds, *Whitman*, J. C. Nimmo, 1893; reprinted by Blom, 1967.

Horace Traubel, *In Re Walt Whitman*, D. McKay, 1893.

Horace Traubel, *Conversations with Walt Whitman in Camden*, vols. 1 and 2, D. Appleton, 1908; vol. 3, M. Kinnerley, 1914; vol. 4, University of Pennsylvania Press, 1953; vol. 5, Southern Illinois University Press, 1964.

Stephen C. Whicher, 'Whitman's Awakening to Death', in R. W. B. Lewis, (ed.), *The Presence of Walt Whitman*, Columbia University Press, 1962.

Index

Extracts included in this anthology are indicated by bold page references.

Penguin Critical Anthologies

Published simultaneously with Walt Whitman

Andrew Marvell Edited by John Carey

Part One **Contemporaneous Criticism, Neglect and Revival**

Introduction. John Milton, Samuel Parker, William Lisle Bowles, Mark Pattison, Hartley Coleridge, Edgar Allan Poe, Edward FitzGerald, Goldwin Smith, Alfred Lord Tennyson, Alice Meynell, T. S. Eliot.

Part Two **Modern Views**

Introduction. The Setting: Christopher Hill, F. W. Bateson, Patrick Cruttwell, J. B. Leishman, Susan Shrapnel. *General Estimates:* William Empson, Joseph H. Summers, Robert Ellrodt, J. B. Broadbent, S. L. Goldberg, Yvor Winters. *An Horation Ode:* Cleanth Brooks, Douglas Bush. *To his Coy Mistress:* John Crowe Ransom, J. V. Cunningham, Barbara Herrnstein Smith, René Wellek and Austin Warren, Harold E. Toliver, R. S. Crane. *The Garden:* William Empson, John McChesney, Don A. Keister, Frank Kermode, Pierre Legouis. *The Nymph Complaining for the Death of Her Fawn:* E. S. LeComte, Karina Williamson. *Upon Appleton House:* Maren-Sofie Røstvig, Robin Grove, Harold E. Toliver, Kitty Scoular. *The Gallery:* Winifred Nowottny. *Mourning:* Winifred Nowottny. *The Satires:* George De F. Lord.

John Carey is a Fellow of St John's College and Lecturer in English at the University of Oxford. He has edited Milton's poems (with Alastair Fowler, 1968) and James Hogg's *Confessions of a Justified Sinner* (1969), and has published a critical book on Milton (1969).

Geoffrey Chaucer Edited by J. A. Burrow

Part One Contemporaneous Criticism

Introduction. Geoffrey Chaucer, Eustache, Deschamps, Thomas Usk, John Gower.

Part Two The Developing Debate

Introduction. Thomas Hoccleve, John Lydgate, William Caxton, William Dunbar, John Skelton, Gavin Douglas, Sir Brian Tuke, Gabriel Harvey, George Puttenham, Sir Philip Sidney, Edmund Spenser, Sir Francis Beaumont, Thomas Speght, Richard Brathwait, Alexander Pope, Edward Phillips, Joseph Addison, John Dryden, Elizabeth Cooper, Samuel Johnson, Joseph Warton, Richard Hurd, Thomas Warton, William Blake, George Crabbe, William Hazlitt, S. T. Coleridge, Francis Jeffrey, Walter Savage Landor, Leigh Hunt, John Ruskin, James Russell Lowell, Walter Bagehot, Matthew Arnold, A. C. Swinburne, T. R. Lounsbury, W. P. Ker.

Part Three Modern Views

Introduction. G. L. Kittredge, Virginia Woolf, J. M. Manly, Walter Raleigh, G. K. Chesterton, A. E. Housman, John Livingston Lowes, Ezra Pound, C. S. Lewis, Nevill Coghill, William Empson, Kemp Malone, John Speirs, Raymond Preston, W. K. Wimsatt, J. A. W. Bennett, Charles Muscatine, Erich Auerbach, Paull F. Baum, E. T. Donaldson, Rosemary Woolf, Bertrand H. Bronson, J. V. Cunningham, R. E. Kaske, John Stevens, R. Neuse, Wolfgang Clemen, A. C. Spearing, F. W. Bateson, P. G. Ruggiers, Gervase Matthew.

J. A. Burrow is a Fellow of Jesus College and Lecturer in English at the University of Oxford.

John Webster Edited by G. K. and S. K. Hunter

Part One Contemporaneous Criticism

Introduction. John Webster, Henry Fitzjeffrey, Orazio Busino, Thomas Middleton, William Rowley, John Ford, Abraham Wright, Samuel Sheppard, Samuel Pepys, Lewis Theobald, Philip Frowde.

Part Two The Developing Debate

Introduction. Charles Lamb, George Darley, R. H. Horne, Charles Kingsley, George Daniel, A. C. Swinburne, John Addington Symonds, William Archer, William Poel, Rupert Brooke, T. S. Eliot.

Part Three Modern Views

Introduction. T. S. Eliot, W. A. Edwards, U. Ellis-Fermor, James Smith, M. C. Bradbrook, Edmund Wilson, David Cecil, Ian Jack, Gabriele Baldini, Travis Bogard, Hereward T. Price, Inga-Stina Ekeblad, R. W. Dent, J. R. Brown, G. K. Hunter, Harold Jenkins, James L. Calderwood, Clifford Leech, Elizabeth Brennan, William Empson, A. W. Allison.

This volume on Webster is the first survey and anthology of Webster criticism to be published, and the account of stage and other adaptations draws on new material.

G. K. Hunter is Professor of English at the University of Warwick; Mrs S. K. Hunter is Lecturer in English at Coventry College of Education.

Edmund Spenser Edited by Paul J. Alpers

Part One Contemporaneous Criticism
Introduction. E. K., Edmund Spenser, Gabriel Harvey, Sir Philip Sidney, William Webbe, Sir Walter Raleigh, Joseph Hall, Everard Guilpin, Edmund Bolton, Robert Salter, Henry Reynolds, Ben Jonson, Sir Kenelm Digby, John Milton, Sir William Davenant.

Part Two Neoclassical and Romantic Criticism
Introduction. Thomas Rymer, John Dryden, Joseph Addison, Alexander Pope, Matthew Prior, John Hughes, Joseph Spence, Samuel Johnson, Thomas Warton, Joseph Warton, Richard Hurd, S. T. Coleridge, William Wordsworth, William Hazlitt, John Keats, Charles Lamb, Sir Walter Scott, John Ruskin, James Russell Lowell, Edward Dowden, Walter Raleigh, W. B. Yeats.

Part Three Modern Views
Introduction. William Empson, C. S. Lewis, D. A. Traversi, G. Wilson Knight, Hallet Smith, C. S. Lewis, Yvor Winters, Alastair Fowler, Harry Berger Jr, Frank Kermode, Northrop Frye, Rosemond Tuve, Martha Craig, Paul J. Alpers, Roger Sale.

Paul J. Alpers, the editor of this comprehensive anthology of Spenser criticism, has also edited *Elizabethan Poetry: Modern Essays in Criticism* (1967) and is the author of *The Poetry of 'The Faerie Queene'* (1967). He is Associate Professor of English in the University of California at Berkeley.